Gorgias/*Gorgias*
The Sicilian Orator and the Platonic Dialogue

ALSO FROM PARNASSOS PRESS

Philosopher Kings and Tragic Heroes
Edited by Heather L. Reid and Davide Tanasi, 2016

Politics and Performance in Western Greece
Edited by Heather L. Reid, Davide Tanasi, and Susi Kimbell, 2017

The Many Faces of Mimēsis
Edited by Heather L. Reid and Jeremy C. DeLong, 2018

Plato at Syracuse
with a new translation of the *Seventh Letter* by Jonah Radding
Edited by Heather L. Reid and Mark Ralkowski, 2019

Looking at Beauty: to Kalon in Western Greece
Edited by Heather L. Reid and Tony Leyh, 2019

Olympic Philosophy:
The Ideas and Ideals behind the Ancient and Modern Olympic Games
by Heather L. Reid, 2020

Conflict and Competition: Agōn in Western Greece
Edited by Heather L. Reid, John Serrati, and Tim Sorg, 2020

Athletics, Gymnastics, and Agōn in Plato
Edited by Heather Reid, Mark Ralkowski and Coleen P. Zoller, 2020

Pindar in Sicily
Edited by Heather L. Reid and Virginia Lewis, 2021

The Poetry in Philosophy: Essays in Honor of Christos Evangeliou
Edited by Phillip Mitsis and Heather L. Reid, 2021

Philodorema*: Essays in Honor of Phillip Mitsis*
Edited by David Konstan and David Sider, 2022

Aretē *in Plato and Aristotle*
Edited by Ryan M. Brown and Jay R. Elliott, 2022

Ageless Aretē
Edited by Heather L. Reid and John Serrati, 2022

Gorgias/*Gorgias*
The Sicilian Orator and the Platonic Dialogue

with new translations of the
Helen, *Palamedes*, and *On Not Being*

edited by
S. Montgomery Ewegen
and Coleen P. Zoller

Parnassos Press
2022

First Printing: 2022
ISBN: 978-1-942495-543 (hardcover)
ISBN: 978-1-942495-536 (paperback)
ISBN: 978-1-942495-550 (ebook)

Parnassos Press
Fonte Aretusa Organization
Siracusa, Sicily and Dakota Dunes SD

www.fontearetusa.org

Cover illustration: bronze statuette of a philosopher on a lamp stand, 1st century BCE from Ostia Antica, Italy. Metropolitan Museum of Art Accession Number:10.231.1. Open access image

Epigraphs

The power of speech over the disposition of the soul is of the same order as the disposition of drugs over the nature of the body. For just as different drugs extract different humors from the body, some putting a stop to disease, others to life, so too do some speeches instill in their listeners pity, others delight, others fear, and others daring, and still others drug and bewitch the soul with an evil persuasion.

τὸν αὐτὸν δὲ λόγον ἔχει ἥ τε τοῦ λόγου δύναμις πρὸς τὴν τῆς ψυχῆς τάξιν ἥ τε τῶν φαρμάκων τάξις πρὸς τὴν τῶν σωμάτων φύσιν. ὥσπερ γὰρ τῶν φαρμάκων ἄλλους ἄλλα χυμοὺς ἐκ τοῦ σώματος ἐξάγει, καὶ τὰ μὲν νόσου τὰ δὲ βίου παύει, οὕτω καὶ τῶν λόγων οἱ μὲν ἐλύπησαν, οἱ δὲ ἔτερψαν, οἱ δὲ ἐφόβησαν, οἱ δὲ εἰς θάρσος κατέστησαν τοὺς ἀκούοντας, οἱ δὲ πειθοῖ τινι κακῇ τὴν ψυχὴν ἐφαρμάκευσαν καὶ ἐξεγοήτευσαν.

Gorgias, *Encomium of Helen*, 14

And what sort of person am I? One who would gladly be refuted if I should say something not true, and one who would gladly refute if someone else should say something not true, being no less gladly refuted than refuting. You see, I think it is a greater good to be refuted, by as much as it is a greater good for oneself to be released from the greatest evil than to release another.

ἐγὼ δὲ τίνων εἰμί; τῶν ἡδέως μὲν ἂν ἐλεγχθέντων, εἴ τι μὴ ἀληθὲς λέγω, ἡδέως δ᾽ ἂν ἐλεγξάντων, εἴ τίς τι μὴ ἀληθὲς λέγοι, οὐκ ἀηδέστερον μέντ᾽ ἂν ἐλεγχθέντων ἢ ἐλεγξάντων· μεῖζον γὰρ αὐτὸ ἀγαθὸν ἡγοῦμαι, ὅσῳπερ μεῖζον ἀγαθόν ἐστιν αὐτὸν ἀπαλλαγῆναι κακοῦ τοῦ μεγίστου ἢ ἄλλον ἀπαλλάξαι.

Plato, *Gorgias* 458a-b

Acknowledgments

The editors are grateful to all the participants in the Gorgias/*Gorgias* conference held at the Exedra Mediterranean Center of Siracusa in November 2021, and to those who contributed papers and translated texts specifically for this book.

Table of Contents

Epigraphs v
Acknowledgments vi

S. Montgomery Ewegen and Coleen P. Zoller
Introduction 1

Gorgias's Works in Greek with Translation

Jurgen R. Gatt
Introduction to the Translations 11

The Encomium of Helen 17
Defense of Palamedes 27
On Nature, Or On Not Being 45

Essays

Livio Rossetti
Provocative Ideas in the Writings of Gorgias 55

François Renaud
Defining Poetry, Defending Prose:
Gorgias's *Encomium of Helen* §9 and Its Reception 73

R.J. Barnes
Gorgias on Speech and the Soul 87

Mauro Serra
The Violence of *Logos*:
A Political Reading of Gorgias's *Helen* 107

Stamatia Dova
Aggressive Contrafactuals in Gorgias's *Palamedes* 131

Erminia Di Iulio
Gorgias's Account(s) of "Seeing" in the *Palamedes* 155

Enrico Piergiacomi
Gorgias's Laughter, or: Laughing Against Philosophy? 173

Edward Schiappa
Plato or Gorgias?:
Considering the Origins of the word *Rhētorikē* in the *Gorgias* 195

Yosef Z. Liebersohn
Gorgias in Plato's *Gorgias, Hē Kaloumenē Rhētorikē,*
and the Birth of Rhetoric 213

Robert Metcalf
Dunamis in *Agōn*:
Gorgias of Leontinoi and Plato's *Gorgias* 235

Sonja Tanner
Child's Play: The Power of Comedy
in Gorgias of Leontinoi and Plato's *Gorgias* 253

S. Montgomery Ewegen
The Comedy of Power in Plato's *Gorgias* 271

Coleen P. Zoller
Taking Our Medicine:
Justice and Reconciliation in Plato's *Gorgias* 289

S. Montgomery Ewegen and Coleen P. Zoller

Introduction

In Plato's *Republic*, Socrates describes a certain quarrel—ancient already at his time—between philosophy and poetry (607b). This quarrel, as the rest of the *Republic* makes clear, has everything to do with the nature of *truth* and the positions of philosophy and poetry with respect to it. According to Socrates, because poetry remains unreflectively bound to its mimetic form, it is unable to access the truth of things and should not be taken seriously by lovers of wisdom (608a). It is on these grounds that he suggests that poetry ought to be excluded from any well-governed city, at least until a compelling defense of its enduring value and benefit has been made (607d). Whether one reads Plato here as seriously endorsing such exclusion, or as offering an ironical condemnation of the very sort of mimetic poetry that largely constitutes the *Republic* itself, these denigrating passages are responsible for extending the quarrel between philosophy and poetry through the Classical period and, in many ways, up to the present day.

Be that as it may, there is another quarrel, no less concerned with truth, to be found within Plato's dialogues: namely, the quarrel between philosophy and sophistry. As a term, "sophistry" came to be associated with various largely itinerant public intellectuals who traveled from city to city demonstrating their intellectual abilities and offering to impart such abilities to others (for a fee). Plato assesses and critiques the rhetorical methods characteristic of sophistry in various dialogues, but nowhere as forcefully or elaborately as he does within the *Gorgias*. As the third longest of Plato's dialogues, the *Gorgias* stages Socrates's most sustained engagement with sophistry, its perceived epistemological shortcomings, and its political dangers. The titular character, whether fairly or not, seems to have been for Plato nearly synonymous with those dangers, as his various mentions of him throughout the dialogues make clear.

Gorgias was born around 485 BCE in Leontinoi, Sicily, and is widely considered to be the most prominent and important of the sophists, if not, indeed, the progenitor of the entire practice. Like many other sophists, Gorgias was itinerant, traveling through various cities performing his rhetorical abilities and charging those interested in instruction. He traveled to Athens on a diplomatic mission in 427 BCE—just about the time that Plato was born—where he earned both the ire of philosophers and the obols of young men keen on learning the powerful art of *logos* that Gorgias professed. That Plato took Gorgias's effect on Athens and its intellectual and political milieu seriously is evident from the fact that he not only wrote a dialogue in which Gorgias is a principal player, but also mentions him in as many as seven other dialogues. Along with Protagoras and the unnamed stranger in the *Sophist* and *Statesman*, Gorgias is representative for Plato of rhetoric and sophistry and all the ways in which they stray from—or even threaten—the philosophical attainment of truth, thereby imperiling the well-being of the *polis*.

Although some of Gorgias's work survives—such as the *Defense of Palamedes* and the *Encomium of Helen*, of which the present volume includes new translations—none of it is as expansive or as widely studied as Plato's *Gorgias*. For this and other reasons, Gorgias's own work has been largely overshadowed by Plato's depiction of him. Based largely on this depiction, there has been a scholarly tendency to treat rhetoric as opposed to, or even antithetical to, philosophy: indeed, the very word "rhetoric," for the modern ear, tends to carry a pejorative sense, serving as a functional synonym for "sophistical."

However, as the contributions to this collection make clear, there is much that is philosophical about Gorgias's work, just as there is much that is rhetorical about Socrates's manner of proceeding in the *Gorgias* (and, indeed, in many other of Plato's dialogues). The careful analyses offered within this volume show that there is great nuance to Plato's treatment of Gorgias's rhetorical abilities, and that Gorgias himself can be understood as a subtle and sophisticated (in the positive sense) philosopher worthy of Plato's focused attention. In short, the essays in this collection show that the relationship between Plato and Gorgias—and, more generally, the relationship between philosophy and rhetoric—is much more complicated, and potentially more mutually beneficial, than a simple "quarrel." In light of such complexity, the crucial questions become: Are philosophy and rhetoric fundamentally at odds with one another? Or, are rhetoric and philosophy complimentary—a suggestion perhaps already made by Socrates within the *Gorgias* when he develops what he calls "true rhetoric"? Finally, what is the true nature of the relationship between Gorgias's own work and Plato's depiction of it?

It was in an effort to further explore these and other questions that a conference was convened in Siracusa, Sicily, in November of 2021. Over a period of ten days—five of which were online, and five of which were in-person—twenty-five presentations were given that focused on a variety of topics pertaining to the historical Gorgias, Plato's depiction of him, and the relationship between the two. Of those twenty-five presentations, thirteen papers, representative of the many and varied ideas that were discussed at the conference, were chosen for inclusion in the present volume. Additionally, new translations with facing Greek of Gorgias's two major surviving works, and of an ancient summary of his *On Not Being*, are included, with a short introduction by Jurgen Gatt.

In the volume's opening essay, Livio Rossetti offers a critical survey of the sequential epochs of scholarly engagement with Gorgias, arguing that the movement from a "prehistoric" engagement to a "historical" one occurred after the 1980s, when scholars began to readily acknowledge the enduring philosophical value of Gorgias's creative ideas. Such ideas are to be found, for example, in the *Encomium of Helen*, which shows itself to be a slightly disguised treatise on the vices of the will, and in *On Not Being*, which, Rossetti argues, includes a substantial criticism of Parmenides's conception of non-being. Rossetti's overall claim is that Gorgias's extant writings reach a truly uncommon level of excellence and are full of substantive moments, even if at every turn their author strove to remain behind the scenes.

Next, François Renaud's essay examines Gorgias's definition of artistic prose within the larger question of the historical transition from poetry to prose. In the *Encomium of Helen*, Gorgias characterizes all poetry as speech with meter, and implicitly argues that the emotional power of rhetorical speech on the soul is equal to that of poetic speech. According to Renaud, Gorgias's defense of prose implies a rivalry with poetry, insofar as the transfer of poetry's means to oratory deliberately blurs the boundaries between poetry and prose, thereby leading to poetry's demotion; moreover, his definition of poetry proves novel in that it differs from the traditional understanding of the art as being purely formal and exclusionary of truth claims and morality. Renaud then shows that, following Gorgias, Isocrates argues that meter is the essential and distinctive trait of poetry, and further insists that it is an intrinsic feature of it. Renaud concludes by examining Strabo's account of the transition from poetry to prose, which defends the superiority of poetry as the mother-tongue of humanity.

In his contribution, R.J. Barnes shows how Gorgias's two divergent theories of communication (found in *On Not Being* and the *Encomium of Helen*) can be seen to complement, rather than contradict, one another (as has often been alleged). Barnes draws attention to an important passage towards the end of Sextus Empiricus's version of *On Not Being* where Gorgias suggests that human communication could function similarly to sense perception, if and only if humans had something of a sixth sense to carry this out. Barnes shows how this passage anticipates the imaginative description of *logos* in the *Encomium of Helen* where Gorgias presents speech as an object that can be apprehended by the human faculties of opinion (*doxa*) and the soul much in the same way as visible objects are apprehended by sight (*opsis*) and the soul.

Mauro Serra's essay, in turn, contends that Gorgias's *Encomium of Helen* revolves around a controversial claim regarding the violence of *logos*. According to Gorgias, persuasion (*peithō*), rather than differing from violence (*bia*) as was classically thought, constitutes a different manifestation of it. Despite numerous attempts made by modern scholars, this claim has not found a completely adequate explanation. Moreover, although much insistence has been given on the didactic nature of the *Encomium*, it has, as Serra shows, generally been limited to considering the text as one of the first manuals in which rhetoric was established as a discipline. Serra argues that the lesson of the *Encomium* is much broader than this and is, in fact, a *political* lesson, at the heart of which we find the recognition of conflict as an unavoidable core of discursive practice. As Serra shows, from Gorgias's perspective violence does not coincide with an unavoidable yet deliberately deceptive and instrumental use of language, but is to some extent intrinsic to the discursive practice itself. In this way, the lesson that Gorgias delivers to his students goes far beyond the obvious self-promotion of his own competence and contains a timely invitation to provide themselves with adequate skills to enter the political arena.

Stamatia Dova's contribution examines the significance of contrary-to-fact conditional sentences in the construction of the argument from implausibility in Gorgias's *Defense of Palamedes*. As she argues, conditional sentences within Palamedes's *Apología* function as syntactical features and rhetorical devices guiding the argument towards a logical conclusion. According to Dova, Gorgias reinvents Palamedes's defense speech as a rhetorical exercise of remarkable vividity (*enárgeia*), contextualizing it within the framework of the hero's wrongful conviction in myth. Central to this myth is Palamedes's pre-Trojan war *élenchos* of Odysseus's attempt at draft evasion, in retaliation for which Odysseus framed Palamedes for treason. By employing a series of powerful hypotheses, Gorgias's Palamedes aims to prove that he was both unwilling and unable to commit treason. Furthermore, he attacks the case for the prosecution by means of past and present contrafactuals suggesting that Odysseus may be acting out of envy, subterfuge, or wickedness. Dova further argues that Palamedes enables Gorgias to explore the limits of forensic oratory, including its ability to discover the truth, prove guilt or innocence, and serve justice. By illustrating the role of contrary-to-fact conditions in Palamedes's refutation of Odysseus's accusations, this essay also sheds new light on the multiplicity of discourses operating in the sophistic reception of Palamedes's myth.

Erminia Di Iulio's essay also addresses Gorgias's *Defense of Palamedes*, focusing on its account of "seeing" in particular. The underlying argument is that the text's emphasis on "seeing" and "sight" is, on the one hand, the sign of a continuity with the past's traditional account of knowledge and truth and, on the other hand, the sign of a continuity with the present and the future (i.e., forensic oratory). Di Iulio takes what she calls a "lexicological" approach, in that she focuses her analysis on the occurrences and meaning of terms linked to sight within the text in order to demonstrate the link between seeing and knowing in ancient thought.

In his essay, Enrico Piergiacomi focuses on Gorgias's fragment B12 in which the rhetorical value of antilogy (i.e., using humorous discourse against serious discourse, and vice versa) is underscored. Arguing that the historical Gorgias employs this strategy in his *On Not Being,* Piergiacomi suggests that he intentionally presented a ridiculous and laughable thesis—namely, that nothing exists—in order to analyze the sort of Eleatic ontology visible, for example, in the work of Parmenides. In this way, Piergiacomi concludes, comedic antilogy serves as a kind of philosophical rhetoric by means of which a philosophical position can be critiqued and undermined.

Edward Schiappa's essay revisits arguments he has made previously that Plato, and not Gorgias, is the most likely suspect for the origin of the word *rhētorikē*. As Schiappa shows, Plato had a well-documented practice of coining terms similar to *rhētorikē* in the process of his philosophical world-building and had both the motive and the opportunity to introduce the term in *Gorgias*. Furthermore, Schiappa contends that the popularization of the word *rhētorikē* by Plato and Aristotle led to important changes in theorizing and teaching what we now call the art of rhetoric.

Continuing with the study of ancient rhetoric and its sources, Yosef Z. Liebersohn's essay offers new insight into the nature of the conversation between Socrates and Gorgias, suggesting a novel approach to the debate over the origins of rhetoric. Focusing on the appearance of the word *rhētorikē* in the *Gorgias*, Liebersohn argues for a correlation between the status of rhetoric in the dramatic time depicted in the *Gorgias* and the way in which the term *rhētorikē* appears in the conversation. The essay suggests that Gorgias and his fellow teachers of rhetoric considered themselves to be engaged in politics, and the term *rhētorikē* did not yet denote for them a fully independent field. It was, however, their own teaching of the subject that led *rhētorikē* to become a new art. It is Socrates's anachronistic task in Plato's *Gorgias* to attempt to draw his interlocutors' attention to this process and to point to the dangers endemic to it.

In his essay, Robert Metcalf undertakes an attempt to better understand the relation between the historical Gorgias and Plato's depiction of him, and specifically how Plato appropriated the focal concepts of *dunamis* (power) and *doxa* (opinion) from Gorgias. He accomplishes this by focusing on philosophical agonism. Agonism in Gorgias's thought is thematized most directly in the *Encomium of Helen*, where Gorgias addresses the *phainomenal* character of *logos*. In Plato's *Gorgias*, in turn, Socrates presents a distinctively philosophical form of *agōn* (contest) involving the refutation of one's opponent, as well as discursive contestation of the *dēmos* as a whole—as distinct from the shameful rhetorical *agōn* practiced by Gorgias and his associates. Metcalf shows how a close examination of Plato's *Gorgias* reveals that Socrates's *elenchos* therein employs precisely the slipperiness and insecurity of *doxa* analyzed in Gorgias's *Encomium of Helen*. Accordingly, the kind of *doxa* at issue in Gorgias's writings as well as Plato's *Gorgias* is the multi-faceted and dramatically interesting sense of *doxa* involving one's reputational standing (i.e., one's appearing-to-oneself and appearing-to-others in public settings). It is this complexity of *doxa* that allows for both philosophical agonism and the comedic significance of rhetorical contests.

In her contribution, Sonja Tanner underscores the important role that comedy and laughter played for both the historical Gorgias and for Plato. According to Tanner, for Gorgias laughter is a weapon for counteracting the seriousness of a dialogical opponent (as analyzed in Piergiacomi's essay), whereas for Plato laughter is a means of critical—and above-all, *philosophical*—self-reflection. Tanner argues that Plato presents Socrates within the *Gorgias* in a laughable way—namely, as the late-learner (*gerontodidaskalos*), a tried-and-true comedic trope visible in other works such as Aristophanes's *Clouds* and Plato's *Euthydemus*. She further argues that by doing so Plato shows Socrates to be engaging in the cultivation of self-knowledge while also provoking the reader into reflecting on her own knowledge vis-à-vis the topics under consideration.

In the penultimate essay, and keeping with the theme of comedy, S. Montgomery Ewegen argues that the *Gorgias* presents itself as a thoroughly comedic text, focusing on the three interrelated and comedic themes of food, irony, and animals. Ewegen contends, however, that such comedy is by no means frivolous, but is rather the register in which Plato carries out his critique of the view of political power held by the sophists and rhetoricians. According to such a view, political power consists in the ability to persuade others by means of speech, effectively submitting others to one's will: it is, in short, the ability to act freely and without consequence. Ewegen demonstrates that by submitting such a view of power to comic ridicule, Plato offers an utterly distinct view: namely, one in which power is shown to consist in *submissiveness* to the philosophical *logos*, a kind of *receptivity* to the truth of things.

In the volume's final essay, Coleen P. Zoller explores the medical analogy for justice in Plato's *Gorgias*. She argues that injustice-doers who "take their medicine" are those who heal because they hold themselves accountable for having done injustice. Asking to be held accountable facilitates both the potential for *self-reconciliation* and *reconciliation with others,* whereas not submitting to justice appears to inhibit the possibility of both. Zoller argues that, while admiration of mercy or forgiveness is not an *explicit* element in Plato's moral philosophy, his sense of justice as psychic medicine is essential to the process of fostering reconciliation both within one's own soul and with others harmed by one's injustice. Rather than a traditional Greek concept of forgiveness, Plato initiates a sketch of what could make a doer of injustice earn the mercy or forgiveness that may be offered. The essay concludes with an analysis of passages from the *Laws* that are relevant to making sense of the medical analogy for justice in Plato's *Gorgias.*

Taken together, the essays in this volume serve as a reminder of the enduring legacy of both Plato's and Gorgias's works and as an attempt to open new possibilities regarding the relationship between them. It aims to capture something of the inquisitive spirit that animated the conference in which versions of these papers originally appeared and to contribute to a better understanding of the complex and fruitful relationship between the work of two of antiquity's most important and provocative thinkers.

Gorgias of Leontinoi

Encomium of Helen
Defense of Palamedes
On Not Being

Jurgen R. Gatt[1]

Introduction to the Translations

Gorgias was born in the Ionian *polis* of Leontinoi, on the island of Sicily, sometime between the first and the second Persian War (c. 485).[2] Little is known of his early life, though he is thought to have been tutored by Empedocles—he is also said to have seen him perform magic[3]—and Gorgias clearly knew Parmenides's poem well when he wrote his *On Not Being*, (perhaps) sometime in the 440s.[4] Gorgias also knew Tisias of Syracuse, an important figure in early rhetoric, and is reported to have travelled with him on an embassy to Athens in 427 B.C.E.[5] The impression he left on the Athenian Assembly was deep, but no less deep was his effect on the Athenian intelligentsia, with Gorgias's influence being found in the works of Antiphon, Thucydides, and Isocrates, and in the fragments of Agathon. Yet, countless other orations must have been recited in his style, and in Thessaly—where Gorgias would eventually settle—oratory became synonymous with his name.[6] His reception,

---

[1] Jurgen R. Gatt is Visiting Lecturer in Classics at the University of Malta and a Lecturer in Systems of Knowledge at G.F. Abela Junior College. His main research interests include the epistemology of testimony in the ancient world, ancient witnesses, Herodotus, and Hippocrates.

[2] For a more detailed biography, see W.K.C. Guthrie, *The Sophists* (Cambridge: University Press, 1971), 269-280; and S. Dimos, *Gorgias: An Edition of the Extant Texts and Fragments with Commentary and Introduction* (PhD thesis: Glasgow, 2001), 9-16.

[3] Diogenes Laertius 8.58–59. Here, I hazard a rationalizing interpretation of this *testimonium*. If such a statement goes back to Gorgias himself–undoubtedly, a very tall order–and if we accept that Empedocles was at least interested in rhetoric (cf. Diogenes Laertius 8.57), then Gorgias is simply stating that he heard his master speaking well, since Gorgias is known to have claimed *logos* to be magical.

[4] Diogenes Laertius 8.58-59.

[5] Pausanias 6.17.8–9. On this embassy, see Diodorus Siculus 12.53.2–5. It was a fateful year for rhetoric in Athens: the infamous Mytilenean debate and Gorgias's embassy must have happened months, or even weeks, apart.

[6] Philostratus, *Ep*. 73, p. 257.2–7 (Kayser).

however, was not always positive. In Argos, it was hostile, and his calls for panhellenism in his Olympian orations fell on deaf ears.[7] In Athens too, Gorgias was derided by Aristophanes and criticized by Isocrates, Plato, and Aristotle. He spent most of his long life as an itinerant teacher of rhetoric, moving from *polis* to *polis,* perhaps aware that his style might grow wearisome through over-exposure. Students flocked to him, undeterred by his steep fees,[8] and in sufficient numbers to earn him a minor fortune. Like Tisias, he is credited with writing a technical treatise on rhetoric, though it is more likely that his instruction was based on stock-arguments and set-piece orations, such as those translated below. After his death, perhaps at the court of the Thessalian tyrant Jason who came to power in 380 B.C.E, his nephew commissioned a statue in his honor at Olympia—where he was undoubtedly a celebrity—and had it inscribed with an epitaph, still preserved. Part of it reads:

No mortal man has ever discovered a finer craft
At exercising the soul in contests of virtue than Gorgias
Whose statue is even dedicated in the sacred ground of Apollo
Not as an illustration of his wealth, but of the piety of his ways.[9]

Though crediting him with the "discovery" of any *technē* is probably hyperbole befitting an epitaph, Gorgias was surely one of the central intellectual figures of the late 5th-century BCE, and an important early master of rhetoric. More importantly, Gorgias occupied a pivotal role in the struggle between poetry and prose, a struggle in which philosophy and rhetoric were often allies. His style, then, can best be described as prose-poetry and is characterized primarily by its assonance, its balanced clauses, and its use of antithesis.[10] When the clauses are short, as in the very beginning of *Helen,* Gorgias's Greek almost turns into song. Commenting on his style, Dionysus of

---

[7] Plutarch *Conjug*. 43 144 B–C.

[8] By Kerferd's calculations and if his source is correct (Diodorus Siculus 12.53.2), then a lecture-series by Gorgias would have cost over 4 kilograms of silver. Kerferd, *Sophistic Movement*, 27-28.

[9] P.A. Hansen, *Carmina Epigraphica Graeca, 2 vols*. (1983–9), CEG 830.

[10] One of the best reviews on Gorgias's style is B. Smith, "Gorgias: A Study of Oratorical Style," *Quarterly Journal of Speech*, 7 (1921): 335-59.

Halicarnassus astutely observed that his motivation was to distinguish oratory from ordinary speech.[11] We may also add that his poetic prose was meant to rival and even threaten the authorial persona of the poet. As he himself states in *Helen*, his speech was meant to bring about pleasure (*terpsis*), as is the case with poetry. Moreover, in likening all speech to verse, and in defining poetry as a mere species of *logos*, Gorgias further erodes the distinction between poet and rhetor. In so doing, he claims for himself, and for rhetoric and prose more broadly, the ancient authority of poetry. And in his promise to add "*logismos*" to his speech—a term favored by the prosaic Hippocratics—Gorgias promises even to outstrip them. It is on the basis of such authority that his *Encomium of Helen* flatly contradicts not only Homer, but all poets, including Stesichorus and Euripides, by claiming that Helen was innocent even if she had gone to Troy.

Gorgias's most profound contribution to philosophy, however, is to be found in his epistemology and in his radical critique of Parmenides's philosophical project. His *On Not Being*—which only exists as two late and long paraphrases—has been read plausibly as a critique of Parmenides's *logic*, an elaborate *reductio ad absurdum* of the Goddess' "much-contested test" (πολύδηριν ἔλεγχον) for truthful utterance. Accepting *ex hypothesi* the Parmenidean analysis of being, and playfully emulating Eleatic deductive logic, Gorgias "proves" that nothing exists, nothing can be known, and nothing demonstrated. The arguments advanced—especially in the second and third parts—are often unconvincing, though it is probable that Gorgias did adhere to some version of these paradoxical conclusions. Thus, we find that the two epideictic-cum-apologetic speeches, his *Defense of Palamedes* and *Encomium of Helen*, though written some twenty years later,[12] largely agree with the negative assessments of *On Not Being*. In the *Helen*, Gorgias explicitly claims that "knowing" in a strong sense (he chooses the Muse-like knowledge of the past, present, and future, as a paradigm) does not exist, and humans often

[11] Dionysius of Halicarnassus, *Imit.* Frag. 5 Aujac.

[12] E. Schiappa, "Gorgias's Helen revisited" *Quarterly Journal of Speech*, 81 (1995), 311 gives 415 to 393 as the range of dates for *Helen*.

must resort to "opinion" as their advisor. Even vision, which Gorgias analyzes in the fourth part of the *Helen*, is not the epistemological resource it is in Homer, but a source of terror and of emotional turmoil. Palamedes, on the other hand, openly questions the possibility of demonstration by means of speech, admitting that it is a "difficult" thing. Indeed, his fate—his inability to prove his innocence despite his knowledge of it—is itself a powerful testament to this impossibility, as Odysseus's mythical victory testifies to the power of persuasive lies. Surely, these claims agree "unanimously and univocally" with Gorgias's *On Not Being*.

With knowledge and demonstration out of the way, Gorgias turns to *logos* as the last refuge for human cognition. Yet, *logos,* which, like vision, exerts its power on the soul directly, operates by means of deception. And deception, in turn, like the *pharmakon,* is a loaded and ambivalent term. Thus, although Gorgias admits that evil persuasion, such as that commandeered by Paris, exists, we also learn that deception can be the handmaiden of wisdom. In a fragment from an unknown work, Gorgias argues that those deceived by tragedy prove themselves to be wiser than those who remain undeceived and bound to the material "reality" of the stage.[13] Similarly, it is through deception that astronomers make that which is invisible visible to the eyes of opinion, thereby convincing their audiences, while a philosopher's conviction in their opinion proves no match to the needs of the *logos*. It is by deceiving, then, that *logos* asserts its mighty power over the human soul, and this because humans do not know, but only opine. Though one might utter the truth, it is a but an adornment to *logos,* desirable, perhaps, but not strictly necessary for speech to assert its power. Indeed, uttering the truth is not even preferable, not only because it is a dangerous ally, as Palamedes declares, but also because "telling those who know what they know [...] does not bring any pleasure" (*Helen* §5). It is ruined, in other words, by demonstration as defined in *On Not Being*. Plato is essentially correct, then, in saying that Gorgias preferred to speak about the probable than about what is true.[14]

---

[13] Plutarch, *Gloria Ath.* 5 348 C.

[14] Plato, *Phaedrus* 267a.

We might, however, take issue both with the Platonic interpretation of this "preference," and of its importance in the history of thought. First of all, we must note that *eikos* does not mean verisimilitude in an abstract metaphysical or even epistemological sense. Rather, when used by orators, it was always applied to a concrete case and related to argumentation. And Gorgias was clearly a pioneering master of this type of argument. Both the *Encomium of Helen* and the *Defense of Palamedes*, and especially the latter, deploy what must have been cutting-edge logical tools. which, alongside Antiphon's *Tetralogies,* were likely at the very forefront of these important, and influential, late 5th-century BCE developments. Moreover, in denying the possibility of demonstrating at the same time as claiming to persuade by means of probability, Gorgias lays down the foundation for the distinction between rigorous proof and mere circumstantial evidence. Lastly, in his "disregard" of truth, we need not see only a Gorgianic version of Protagorean relativism, as some have argued,[15] but also a final expression of the tragic vision of human knowledge already found in Homer, who claimed that "men know nothing."[16] Like Homer, Gorgias believed that some truths—perhaps all truths—were beyond mortals to know. But unlike the poet, the rhetor could not resort to the Muse. Gorgias had to rely entirely on *logos.*

---

[15] E.g., J. de Romilly and J. Lloyd (trans.), *The Great Sophists in Periclean Athens* (Oxford: Clarendon Press, 1992), 97.

[16] Homer, *Iliad* 2.486.

ΕΛΕΝΗΣ ΕΓΚΩΜΙΟΝ*

[1] κόσμος πόλει μὲν εὐανδρία, σώματι δὲ κάλλος, ψυχῇ δὲ σοφία, πράγματι δὲ ἀρετή, λόγῳ δὲ ἀλήθεια· τὰ δὲ ἐναντία τούτων ἀκοσμία. ἄνδρα δὲ καὶ γυναῖκα καὶ λόγον καὶ ἔργον καὶ πόλιν καὶ πρᾶγμα χρὴ τὸ μὲν ἄξιον ἐπαίνου ἐπαίνῳ τιμᾶν, τῷ δὲ ἀναξίῳ μῶμον ἐπιθεῖναι· ἴση γὰρ ἁμαρτία καὶ ἀμαθία μέμφεσθαί τε τὰ ἐπαινετὰ καὶ ἐπαινεῖν τὰ μωμητά.

[2] τοῦ δ' αὐτοῦ ἀνδρὸς λέξαι τε τὸ δέον ὀρθῶς καὶ ἐλέγξαι τοὺς μεμφομένους Ἑλένην, γυναῖκα περὶ ἧς ὁμόφωνος καὶ ὁμόψυ-χος γέγονεν ἥ τε τῶν ποιητῶν ἀκουσάντων πίστις ἥ τε τοῦ ὀνόματος φήμη, ὃ τῶν συμφορῶν μνήμη γέγονεν. ἐγὼ δὲ βούλομαι λογισμόν τινα τῷ λόγῳ δοὺς τὴν μὲν κακῶς ἀκού-ουσαν παῦσαι τῆς αἰτίας, τοὺς δὲ μεμφομένους ψευδομένους ἐπιδεῖξαι καὶ δεῖξαι τἀληθὲς καὶ παῦσαι τῆς ἀμαθίας.

[3] ὅτι μὲν οὖν φύσει καὶ γένει τὰ πρῶτα τῶν πρώτων ἀνδρῶν καὶ γυναικῶν ἡ γυνὴ περὶ ἧς ὅδε ὁ λόγος, οὐκ ἄδηλον οὐδὲ ὀλίγοις. δῆλον γὰρ ὡς μητρὸς μὲν Λήδας, πατρὸς δὲ τοῦ μὲν γενομένου θεοῦ, τοῦ δὲ λεγομένου θνητοῦ, Τυνδάρεω καὶ Διός, ὧν ὁ μὲν διὰ τὸ εἶναι ἔδοξεν, ὁ δὲ διὰ τὸ φάναι ἠλέγχθη, καὶ ἦν ὁ μὲν ἀνδρῶν κράτιστος ὁ δὲ πάντων τύραννος.

[4] ἐκ τοιούτων δὲ γενομένη ἔσχε τὸ ἰσόθεον κάλλος, ὃ λαβοῦσα καὶ οὐ λαθοῦσα ἔσχε· πλείστας δὲ πλείστοις ἐπιθυμίας ἔρωτος ἐνειργάσατο, ἑνὶ δὲ σώματι πολλὰ σώματα συνήγαγεν ἀνδρῶν ἐπὶ μεγάλοις μεγάλα φρονούντων, ὧν οἱ μὲν πλούτου μεγέθη, οἱ δὲ εὐγενείας παλαιᾶς εὐδοξίαν, οἱ δὲ ἀλκῆς οἰκείας εὐεξίαν, οἱ δὲ σοφίας ἐπικτήτου δύναμιν ἔσχον· καὶ ἧκον ἅπαντες ὑπ' ἔρωτός τε φιλονίκου φιλοτιμίας τε ἀνικήτου.

[5] ὅστις μὲν οὖν καὶ δι' ὅτι καὶ ὅπως ἀπέπλησε τὸν ἔρωτα τὴν Ἑλένην λαβών, οὐ λέξω· τὸ γὰρ τοῖς εἰδόσιν ἃ ἴσασι λέγειν πίστιν μὲν ἔχει, τέρψιν δὲ οὐ φέρει.

---

* The Greek text follows that of the Loeb edition: *Early Greek Philosophy, Volume VIII: Sophists, Part 1,* edited and translated by André Laks and Glenn W. Most (Cambridge, MA: Harvard University Press, 2016), with slight modifications.

The Encomium of Helen*

1. Good order, for a city, is the courage of its men; for a body, beauty; for a soul, wisdom; for an action, virtue; for a speech, truth; while the opposite of these is disorder. And in the case of a man and woman, word and deed, city and act, one must honor them with praise if they are worthy, and ascribe blame if they are unworthy. For it is equally erroneous and ignorant to blame the praiseworthy and to praise the blameworthy.

2. It is the same man's task to say correctly what should be said and to refute those who blame Helen, a woman about whom the belief of those who have listened to poets, as well as the sound of her name—which recalls disaster—have become univocal and unanimous. Yet, by adding a certain reasoning to my speech, I want to save the slandered woman from the accusation, to show that those who blame her are lying, to reveal the truth, and to put a stop to ignorance.

3. That the subject of the speech is a woman who, by nature and birth, is preeminent among men and women, is not unclear even to a few. For her mother was clearly Leda, and though her real father was a god, Zeus, it was said to be a man, Tyndareus. The one was suspected to be by being so, the other was proven to be by say-so. And the one was the best of men, the other the overlord of all things.

4. Born of such parents, she acquired a beauty equal to the gods, which she seized upon and did not hide, stirring in several men several desires for love. With one body, she drew together many bodies of men who were thinking of great deeds and their great rewards. Of these, some possessed an abundance of wealth, others a fame of ancient lineage, others a vigor of innate strength, and others the power of acquired wisdom. All of them came, moved by love, a desire for victory, and an unconquerable desire for honor.

5. Who fulfilled his love by taking Helen, for what reasons, and how, I will not say, for though telling those who know what they know carries conviction, it does not bring any pleasure.

---

* Translation by Jurgen R. Gatt

τὸν χρόνον δὲ τῷ λόγῳ τὸν τότε νῦν ὑπερβὰς ἐπὶ τὴν ἀρχὴν τοῦ μέλλοντος λόγου προβήσομαι, καὶ προθήσομαι τὰς αἰτίας, δι᾽ ἃς εἰκὸς ἦν γενέσθαι τὸν τῆς Ἑλένης εἰς τὴν Τροίαν στόλον.

[6] ἢ γὰρ Τύχης βουλήμασι καὶ θεῶν βουλεύμασι καὶ Ἀνάγκης ψηφίσμασιν ἔπραξεν ἃ ἔπραξεν, ἢ βίᾳ ἁρπασθεῖσα, ἢ λόγοις πεισθεῖσα, ἢ ἔρωτος ἡττηθεῖσα>. εἰ μὲν οὖν διὰ τὸ πρῶτον, ἄξιος αἰτιᾶσθαι ὁ αἰτιώμενος· θεοῦ γὰρ προθυμίαν ἀνθρωπίνῃ προμηθίᾳ ἀδύνατον κωλύειν. πέφυκε γὰρ οὐ τὸ κρεῖσσον ὑπὸ τοῦ ἥσσονος κωλύεσθαι, ἀλλὰ τὸ ἧσσον ὑπὸ τοῦ κρείσσονος ἄρχεσθαι καὶ ἄγεσθαι, καὶ τὸ μὲν κρεῖσσον ἡγεῖσθαι, τὸ δὲ ἧσσον ἕπεσθαι. θεὸς δ᾽ ἀνθρώπου κρεῖσσον καὶ βίᾳ καὶ σοφίᾳ καὶ τοῖς ἄλλοις. εἰ οὖν τῇ Τύχῃ καὶ τῷ θεῷ τὴν αἰτίαν ἀναθετέον, καὶ τὴν Ἑλένην τῆς δυσκλείας ἀπολυτέον.

[7] εἰ δὲ βίᾳ ἡρπάσθη καὶ ἀνόμως ἐβιάσθη καὶ ἀδίκως ὑβρίσθη, δῆλον ὅτι ὁ <μὲν> ἁρπάσας ὡς ὑβρίσας ἠδίκησεν, ἡ δὲ ἁρπασθεῖσα ὡς ὑβρισθεῖσα ἐδυστύχησεν. ἄξιος οὖν ὁ μὲν ἐπιχειρήσας βάρβαρος βάρβαρον ἐπιχείρημα καὶ λόγῳ καὶ νόμῳ καὶ ἔργῳ λόγῳ μὲν αἰτίας, νόμῳ δὲ ἀτιμίας, ἔργῳ δὲ ζημίας τυχεῖν· ἡ δὲ βιασθεῖσα καὶ τῆς πατρίδος στερηθεῖσα καὶ τῶν φίλων ὀρφανισθεῖσα πῶς οὐκ ἂν εἰκότως ἐλεηθείη μᾶλλον ἢ κακολογηθείη; ὁ μὲν γὰρ ἔδρασε δεινά, ἡ δὲ ἔπαθε· δίκαιον οὖν τὴν μὲν οἰκτίρειν, τὸν δὲ μισῆσαι.

[8] εἰ δὲ λόγος ὁ πείσας καὶ τὴν ψυχὴν ἀπατήσας, οὐδὲ πρὸς τοῦτο χαλεπὸν ἀπολογήσασθαι καὶ τὴν αἰτίαν ἀπολύσασθαι ὧδε· λόγος δυνάστης μέγας ἐστίν, ὃς σμικροτάτῳ σώματι καὶ ἀφανεστάτῳ θειότατα ἔργα ἀποτελεῖ· δύναται γὰρ καὶ φόβον παῦσαι καὶ λύπην ἀφελεῖν καὶ χαρὰν ἐνεργάσασθαι καὶ ἔλεον ἐπαυξῆσαι. ταῦτα δὲ ὡς οὕτως ἔχει δείξω·

[9] δεῖ δὲ καὶ δόξῃ δεῖξαι τοῖς ἀκούουσι·. τὴν ποίησιν ἅπασαν καὶ νομίζω καὶ ὀνομάζω λόγον ἔχοντα μέτρον· ἧς τοὺς ἀκούοντας εἰσῆλθε καὶ φρίκη περίφοβος καὶ ἔλεος πολύδακρυς καὶ πόθος φιλοπενθής,

So, skipping now over these past times in my speech, I shall move on to the beginning of the next speech, and set forth the causes on account of which Helen's journey to Troy became likely (*eikos*).

6. For she did what she did by the resolutions of Chance, the resolve of the Gods, and the decrees of Necessity, or being abducted by force, or persuaded by words, or else seized by love. If, then, it was on account of the first, it is the guilty who deserves to be found guilty, since it is impossible for human plans to thwart a divine desire. For it is not natural for the stronger to be thwarted by the weaker, but for the weaker to be ruled and moved by the stronger, and for the stronger to lead, and the weaker to follow. And a god is stronger than a human in force, in wisdom, and in other things. Thus, if it is necessary to blame Chance and a divinity, then it is also necessary to acquit Helen of her infamy.

7. And if she was captured by force, unlawfully violated, and unjustly defiled, it is clear that it was the abductor, as the defiler, who acted unjustly, while she who was abducted and defiled suffered a misfortune. Thus, it is he who acted, the barbarian who committed a barbaric act in speech, in law, and in deed, who deserves to meet with censure in speech, disenfranchisement under the law, and punishment in deed. And she who was violated, deprived of her fatherland, swept away from her allies, is it not more reasonable for her to be pitied rather than slandered? He committed terrible deeds, while she suffered them. Thus, it is just to sympathize with her, and to hate him.

8. But if it was speech who persuaded and deceived the mind, it is not difficult to defend oneself against this charge, and to refute this accusation, like so. Speech is a mighty ruler, one which can accomplish the most divine deeds by means of the smallest and most invisible body. For it can put an end to fear, assuage grief, stir happiness and augment delight. I shall demonstrate that this is so.

9. Indeed, it is also necessary to demonstrate it to my hearers by means of opinion. I consider and define all poetry as "speech having meter." And on those who hear it advance shuddering fear, tear-drenched pity, and grief-stricken yearning,

ἐπ' ἀλλοτρίων τε πραγμάτων καὶ σωμάτων εὐτυχίαις καὶ δυσπραγίαις ἴδιόν τι πάθημα διὰ τῶν λόγων ἔπαθεν ἡ ψυχή.

φέρε δὴ πρὸς ἄλλον ἀπ' ἄλλου μεταστῶ λόγον.

[10] αἱ γὰρ ἔνθεοι διὰ λόγων ἐπῳδαὶ ἐπαγωγοὶ ἡδονῆς, ἀπαγωγοὶ λύπης γίνονται· συγγινομένη γὰρ τῇ δόξῃ τῆς ψυχῆς ἡ δύναμις τῆς ἐπῳδῆς ἔθελξε καὶ ἔπεισε καὶ μετέστησεν αὐτὴν γοητείᾳ. γοητείας δὲ καὶ μαγείας δισσαὶ τέχναι εὕρηνται, αἵ εἰσι ψυχῆς ἁμαρτήματα καὶ δόξης ἀπατήματα.

[11] ὅσοι δὲ ὅσους περὶ ὅσων καὶ ἔπεισαν καὶ πείθουσι δὲ ψευδῆ λόγον πλάσαντες. εἰ μὲν γὰρ πάντες περὶ πάντων εἶχον τῶν <τε> παροιχομένων μνήμην τῶν τε παρόντων <ἔννοιαν> τῶν τε μελλόντων πρόνοιαν, οὐκ ἂν ὁμοίως ὅμοιος ἦν ὁ λόγος, ᾗ τὰ νῦν γε οὔτε μνησθῆναι τὸ παροιχόμενον οὔτε σκέψασθαι τὸ παρὸν οὔτε μαντεύσασθαι τὸ μέλλον εὐπόρως ἔχει· ὥστε περὶ τῶν πλείστων οἱ πλεῖστοι τὴν δόξαν σύμβουλον τῇ ψυχῇ παρέχονται. ἡ δὲ δόξα σφαλερὰ καὶ ἀβέβαιος οὖσα σφαλεραῖς καὶ ἀβεβαίοις εὐτυχίαις περιβάλλει τοὺς αὐτῇ χρωμένους.

[12] τίς οὖν αἰτία κωλύει καὶ τὴν Ἑλένην [ὕμνος ἦλθεν] οὐ νέαν οὖσαν, ὁμοίως ἂν ὥσπερ εἰ [βιατήριον] βίᾳ ἡρπάσθη;* [τὸ γὰρ τῆς πειθοῦς ἐξῆν ὁ δὲ νοῦς καίτοι εἰ ἀνάγκη ὁ εἰδὼς ἕξει μὲν οὖν, τὴν δὲ δύναμιν τὴν αὐτὴν ἔχει.] λόγος γὰρ ὁ τὴν ψυχὴν πείσας, ἣν ἔπεισεν, ἠνάγκασε καὶ πείθεσθαι τοῖς λεγομένοις καὶ συναινέσαι τοῖς ποιουμένοις. ὁ μὲν οὖν πείσας ὡς ἀναγκάσας ἀδικεῖ, ἡ δὲ πεισθεῖσα ὡς ἀναγκασθεῖσα τῷ λόγῳ μάτην ἀκούει κακῶς.

---

* The bracketed parts of the sentence are reconstructions. I assume that ἦλθεν stands for an infinitive like ἐλθεῖν after κωλύει, while the nominative ὕμνος is a corrupted dative of instrument. I take βιατήριον to be a corrupted form of the genitive of βιάτωρ *vel sim* (which is otherwise unattested).

and on behalf of the failures and successes of other people's deeds and bodies, one's own soul suffers a peculiar effect on account of words.

Come now, let me move from one type of speech to another.

10. It is through speech that inspired songs become the begetters of pleasure and a release from grief. The power of the song, mixing with the belief of the soul, bewitches, persuades, and transmutes it with witchcraft. And the two crafts of witchcraft and sorcery have been found out for what they are: errors of the soul and the deceptions of opinion.

11. How many have deceived and continue to deceive how many others, and on how many matters, by fabricating false speeches! For if everyone had the memory of all things past, had awareness of all present things, and foreknowledge of all things to come, then speech would in no way be the same. But as things stand, remembering the past, examining the present, and prophesying the future are no easy matter, so that most rely on opinion as their soul's advisor for most things. But opinion is a slippery and unreliable thing, and slippery and unreliable are the fortunes of those who use it.

12. Thus what cause is there to prevent Helen [from leaving under the influence of song], even though she was not young, just as if she were captured by the force [of a forceful agent]? [For that which pertains to persuasion was possible, and the mind, if necessity, he who knows will possess, it possesses the same power.]* For if speech, the persuader of the soul, persuades, it necessitates obedience to things said, and makes one an accomplice to things done. Thus, it is the persuader, as the agent of necessity, who has committed injustice, and she who was persuaded by speech, and thus compelled, is being reproached in vain.

* The meaning of the broken sentence is impossible to recover with confidence. I have given a literal translation of the shards which remain.

[13] ὅτι δ' ἡ πειθὼ προσιοῦσα τῷ λόγῳ καὶ τὴν ψυχὴν ἐτυπώσατο ὅπως ἐβούλετο, χρὴ μαθεῖν πρῶτον μὲν τοὺς τῶν μετεωρολόγων λόγους, οἵτινες δόξαν ἀντὶ δόξης τὴν μὲν ἀφελόμενοι τὴν δ' ἐνεργασάμενοι τὰ ἄπιστα καὶ ἄδηλα φαίνεσθαι τοῖς τῆς δόξης ὄμμασιν ἐποίησαν· δεύτερον δὲ τοὺς ἀναγκαίους διὰ λόγων ἀγῶνας, ἐν οἷς εἷς λόγος πολὺν ὄχλον ἔτερψε καὶ ἔπεισε τέχνῃ γραφείς, οὐκ ἀληθείᾳ λεχθείς· τρίτον δὲ φιλοσόφων λόγων ἁμίλλας, ἐν αἷς δείκνυται καὶ γνώμης τάχος ὡς εὐμετάβολον ποιοῦν τὴν τῆς δόξης πίστιν.

[14] τὸν αὐτὸν δὲ λόγον ἔχει ἥ τε τοῦ λόγου δύναμις πρὸς τὴν τῆς ψυχῆς τάξιν ἥ τε τῶν φαρμάκων τάξις πρὸς τὴν τῶν σωμάτων φύσιν. ὥσπερ γὰρ τῶν φαρμάκων ἄλλους ἄλλα χυμοὺς ἐκ τοῦ σώματος ἐξάγει, καὶ τὰ μὲν νόσου τὰ δὲ βίου παύει, οὕτω καὶ τῶν λόγων οἱ μὲν ἐλύπησαν, οἱ δὲ ἔτερψαν, οἱ δὲ ἐφόβησαν, οἱ δὲ εἰς θάρσος κατέστησαν τοὺς ἀκούοντας, οἱ δὲ πειθοῖ τινι κακῇ τὴν ψυχὴν ἐφαρμάκευσαν καὶ ἐξεγοήτευσαν.

[15] καὶ ὅτι μέν, εἰ λόγῳ ἐπείσθη, οὐκ ἠδίκησεν ἀλλ' ἠτύχησεν, εἴρηται·τὴν δὲ τετάρτην αἰτίαν τῷ τετάρτῳ λόγῳ διέξειμι. εἰ γὰρ ἔρως ἦν ὁ ταῦτα πάντα πράξας, οὐ χαλεπῶς διαφεύξεται τὴν τῆς λεγομένης γεγονέναι ἁμαρτίας αἰτίαν. ἃ γὰρ ὁρῶμεν, ἔχει φύσιν οὐχ ἣν ἡμεῖς θέλομεν, ἀλλ' ἣν ἕκαστον ἔτυχε· διὰ δὲ τῆς ὄψεως ἡ ψυχὴ κἀν τοῖς τρόποις τυποῦται.

[16] αὐτίκα γὰρ ὅταν πολέμια σώματα πολέμιον ἐπὶ πολεμίοις ὁπλίσῃ κόσμον χαλκοῦ καὶ σιδήρου, τοῦ μὲν ἀλεξητήριον τοῦ δὲ προβλήματα, εἰ θεάσηται ἡ ὄψις, ἐταράχθη καὶ ἐτάραξε τὴν ψυχήν, ὥστε πολλάκις κινδύνου τοῦ μέλλοντος <ὡς> ὄντος φεύγουσιν ἐκπλαγέντες. ἰσχυρὰ γὰρ ἡ ἀλήθεια τοῦ νόου διὰ τὸν φόβον εἰσῳκίσθη τὸν ἀπὸ τῆς ὄψεως, ἥτις ἐλθοῦσα ἐποίησεν ἀμελῆσαι καὶ τοῦ καλοῦ τοῦ διὰ τὸν νόμον κρινομένου καὶ τοῦ ἀγαθοῦ τοῦ διὰ τὴν δίκην γινομένου.

13. [To learn] that persuasion, when it is added to speech, molds itself onto the mind however it wishes, one must first note the speeches of the astronomers. These go about demolishing one opinion and stirring up another in its place, making that which is incredible and invisible reveal itself to the eyes of opinion. Secondly, [one must mark] those battles of speeches imposed by legal necessity, in which one speech delights the plentiful crowd and persuades, written with craft and uttered with no truth. Thirdly, [one must note] the battles of the speeches of philosophers, in which it is revealed how easily agility of wit renders malleable the conviction of their beliefs.

14. The power of speech over the disposition of the soul is of the same order as the disposition of drugs over the nature of the body. For just as different drugs extract different humors from the body, some putting a stop to disease, others to life, so too do some speeches instill in their listeners pity, others delight, others fear, and others daring, and still others drug and bewitch the soul with an evil persuasion.

15. It has also been claimed that if she was persuaded by speech, then she did not act unjustly but was subject to a misfortune. I shall now proceed with the fourth cause in the fourth part of my speech. For if love was the agent behind all these things, then she easily escapes from the accusation of the error that is said to have occurred. For the things which we see do not have the nature we want, but that which each happens to have. And on account of vision, the soul is molded even down to its ways.

16. For example, whenever hostile bodies are seen, decked out with hostile intent, a hostile and goodly order of bronze and iron, the one for defense, the other for offence, then one's vision is immediately troubled and troubles the mind. In such a way, people often flee, driven beside themselves by dangers which are yet to come as though they were present. For a pressing truth is established for the mind on account of fear which comes through sight. And it, advancing, makes one careless of what is fine, as judged in accordance to law, and of the good which is brought about by justice.

[17] ἤδη δέ τινες ἰδόντες φοβερὰ καὶ τοῦ παρόντος ἐν τῷ παρόντι χρόνῳ φρονήματος ἐξέστησαν· οὕτως ἀπέσβεσε καὶ ἐξήλασεν ὁ φόβος τὸ νόημα. πολλοὶ δὲ ματαίοις πόνοις καὶ δειναῖς νόσοις καὶ δυσιάτοις μανίαις περιέπεσον· οὕτως εἰκόνας τῶν ὁρωμένων πραγμάτων ἡ ὄψις ἐνέγραψεν ἐν τῷ φρονήματι. καὶ τὰ μὲν δειματοῦντα πολλὰ μὲν παραλείπεται, ὅμοια δ' ἐστὶ τὰ παραλειπόμενα οἷάπερ <τὰ> λεγομενα.

[18] ἀλλὰ μὴν οἱ γραφεῖς ὅταν ἐκ πολλῶν χρωμάτων καὶ σωμάτων ἓν σῶμα καὶ σχῆμα τελείως ἀπεργάσωνται, τέρπουσι τὴν ὄψιν· ἡ δὲ τῶν ἀνδριάντων ποίησις καὶ ἡ τῶν ἀγαλμάτων ἐργασία νόσον ἡδεῖαν παρέσχετο τοῖς ὄμμασιν. οὕτω τὰ μὲν λυπεῖν τὰ δὲ ποθεῖν πέφυκε τὴν ὄψιν. πολλὰ δὲ πολλοῖς πολλῶν ἔρωτα καὶ πόθον ἐνεργάζεται πραγμάτων καὶ σωμάτων.

[19] εἰ οὖν τῷ τοῦ Ἀλεξάνδρου σώματι τὸ τῆς Ἑλένης ὄμμα ἡσθὲν προθυμίαν καὶ ἅμιλλαν ἔρωτος τῇ ψυχῇ παρέδωκε, τί θαυμαστόν; ὃς εἰ μὲν θεὸς <ὢν ἔχει> θεῶν θείαν δύναμιν, πῶς ἂν ὁ ἥσσων εἴη τοῦτον ἀπώσασθαι καὶ ἀμύνασθαι δυνατός; εἰ δ' ἐστὶν ἀνθρώπινον νόσημα καὶ ψυχῆς ἀγνόημα, οὐχ ὡς ἁμάρτημα μεμπτέον ἀλλ' ὡς ἀτύχημα νομιστέον· ἦλθε γάρ, ὡς ἦλθε, Τύχης ἀγρεύμασιν, οὐ γνώμης βουλεύμασιν, καὶ ἔρωτος ἀνάγκαις, οὐ τέχνης παρασκευαῖς.

[20] πῶς οὖν χρὴ δίκαιον ἡγήσασθαι τὸν τῆς Ἑλένης μῶμον, ἥτις εἴτ' ἐρασθεῖσα εἴτε λόγῳ πεισθεῖσα εἴτε βίᾳ ἁρπασθεῖσα εἴτε ὑπὸ θείας ἀνάγκης ἀναγκασθεῖσα ἔπραξεν ἃ ἔπραξε, πάντως διαφεύγει τὴν αἰτίαν;

[21] ἀφεῖλον τῷ λόγῳ δύσκλειαν γυναικός, ἐνέμεινα τῷ νόμῳ ὃν ἐθέμην ἐν ἀρχῇ τοῦ λόγου· ἐπειράθην καταλῦσαι μώμου ἀδικίαν καὶ δόξης ἀμαθίαν, ἐβουλήθην γράψαι τὸν λόγον Ἑλένης μὲν ἐγκώμιον, ἐμὸν δὲ παίγνιον.

17. There are those who, on seeing frightful things, immediately lose their presence of mind in the moment. In such a way can fear extinguish and unhinge thought. And many have fallen to futile hardships, terrible diseases, incurable insanity; for in such a way does sight inscribe into the mind the likenesses of things that have been seen. Many terrifying things have been left out, but those left out are much the same as those mentioned.

18. Next, painters delight the sight whenever they create one complete body and shape out of many colors and bodies. The creation of portraits and the making of statues also provide a delightful illness to the eyes. It is natural, then, that some things distress the eyes and others stir yearning. For several things produce in several people a love and a yearning for several deeds and bodies.

19. And so, if Helen's eyes were pleased by Alexander's body and impressed the desire and turbulence of love on her soul, what is there to wonder about? For if it is a god and in possession of the divine power of gods, then how would the lesser being be able to resist and protect itself? But if it is a human disease and a delusion of the soul, it must not be censured as a mistake, but must be considered a misfortune. For when it comes, it comes because of the bonds of Chance, not the counsels of the mind, and with the necessities of love, not the preparations of craft.

20. How, then, can one consider blaming Helen to be just when she did what she did after falling in love, having been persuaded by speech, captured by force, or compelled by divine will, when in all cases, she is innocent of the accusation?

21. I have, with my speech, released the woman from her infamy and I have kept to the theme which I announced in the beginning of my speech. I have tried to loosen the injustice of blame and ignorance of opinion. I desired to write this speech, an encomium of Helen, and for myself, a trifle.

ΥΠΕΡ ΠΑΛΑΜΗΔΟΥΣ ΑΠΟΛΟΓΙΑ*

[1] Ἡ μὲν κατηγορία καὶ [ἡ ἀπολογία] κρίσις οὐ περὶ θανάτου [γίγνεται]·† θάνατον μὲν γὰρ ἡ φύσις φανερᾷ τῇ ψήφῳ πάντων κατεψηφίσατο τῶν θνητῶν, ᾗπερ ἡμέρᾳ τις ἐγένετο· περὶ δὲ τῆς ἀτιμίας καὶ τῆς τιμῆς ὁ κίνδυνός ἐστι, πότερά με χρὴ . . . δικαίως ἀποθανεῖν, ἢ μετ' ὀνειδῶν μεγίστων καὶ τῆς αἰσχίστης αἰτίας βιαίως ἀποθανεῖν.

[2] δισσῶν δὲ τούτων ὄντων τοῦ μὲν ὑμεῖς ὅλου κρατεῖτε, τοῦ δ' ἐγώ, τῆς μὲν δίκης ἐγώ, τῆς δὲ βίας ὑμεῖς. ἀποκτεῖναι μὲν γάρ με δυνήσεσθε βουλόμενοι ῥᾳδίως· κρατεῖτε γὰρ καὶ τούτων, ὧν οὐδὲν ἐγὼ τυγχάνω κρατῶν.

[3] Εἰ μὲν οὖν ὁ κατήγορος Ὀδυσσεὺς ἢ σαφῶς ἐπιστάμενος προδιδόντα με τὴν Ἑλλάδα τοῖς βαρβάροις ἢ δοξάζων οὕτω ταῦτ' ἔχειν ἐποιεῖτο τὴν κατηγορίαν δι εὔνοιαν τῆς Ἑλλάδος, ἄριστος ἂν ἦν [ὁ] ἀνήρ· πῶς γὰρ οὐχ ὅ γε σῴζων πατρίδα, τοκέας, τὴν πᾶσαν Ἑλλάδα, ἔτι δὲ πρὸς τούτοις τὸν ἀδικοῦντα τιμωρούμενος; εἰ δὲ φθόνῳ καὶ κακοτεχνίᾳ καὶ πανουργίᾳ συνέθηκε ταύτην τὴν αἰτίαν, ὥσπερ δι' ἐκεῖνα κράτιστος ἂν ἦν ἀνήρ, οὕτω διὰ ταῦτα κάκιστος ἀνήρ.

[4] Περὶ τούτων δὲ λέγων πόθεν ἄρξωμαι; τί δὲ πρῶτον εἴπω; ποῖ δὲ τῆς ἀπολογίας τράπωμαι; αἰτία γὰρ ἀνεπίδεικτος ἔκπληξιν ἐμφανῆ ἐμποιεῖ, διὰ δὲ τὴν ἔκπληξιν ἀπορεῖν ἀνάγκη τῷ λόγῳ, ἂν μή τι παρ αὐτῆς τῆς ἀληθείας καὶ τῆς παρούσης ἀνάγκης μάθω, διδασκάλων ἐπικινδυνοτέρων ἢ πορι μωτέρων τυχών.

[5] ὅτι μὲν οὖν οὐ σαφῶς <εἰδὼς> ὁ κατήγορος κατηγορεῖ μου, σαφῶς οἶδα· σύνοιδα γὰρ ἐμαυτῷ σαφῶς οὐδὲν τοιοῦτον πεποιηκώς· οὐδὲ οἶδ' ὅπως ἂν εἰδείη τις ὂν τὸ μὴ γενόμενον

---

* The Greek text follows that of the Loeb edition: *Early Greek Philosophy, Volume VIII: Sophists, Part 1*, edited and translated by André Laks and Glenn W. Most (Cambridge, MA: Harvard University Press, 2016), with slight modifications.

† We added γίγνεται following Aldina; the manuscript has γίγνεσθαι here, which is deleted in the Loeb edition.

Defense of Palamedes*

1. This accusation and [defense] are not a judgment about death. For nature has condemned all mortals to death by open vote from the very day they come to existence. No, what is at stake for me is honor and dishonor— whether to die justly, or to die violently and most shamefully under the most disgraceful charge.

2. The possible outcomes being two, you hold one completely in your hands, and I the other: I, justice; you, violence, since if you wish, you will be able to kill me easily, for you also hold powers that I do not have at all.

3. If, therefore, my accuser, Odysseus, were making his accusation out of goodwill for Greece, either knowing clearly that I betrayed Greece to the barbarians or supposing that I did, then he would be an excellent man. For how could one who rescues his homeland, his parents, and the whole of Greece, while on top of all this punishing the aggressor, not be? If, however, he invented this charge out of envy, fraud, and conniving, just as the previous reasons would make him the greatest man, similarly, these would make him the basest man.

4. But where should I begin speaking about these things? What should I say first? Which way should I turn in my defense? For a charge without proof is clearly startling, and due to this shock I will necessarily be at a loss in my argument, unless I learn something from the truth itself and my present necessity, having come upon teachers more productive of danger than solutions.

5. That my accuser accuses me without clear knowledge, I know clearly. For I am clearly aware within myself that I have done no such thing. And I have no idea how one could know the existence of that which has not occurred.

---

* This translation was drafted by George Alexander Gazis, then revised by a group that included R.J. Barnes, Stamatia Dova, Jurgen Gatt, Phillip Mitsis, and Heather Reid. We have endeavored to use consistent translations for important terms and to keep the order of the translation as close to the Greek as clarity would allow.

εἰ δὲ οἰόμενος οὕτω ταῦτα ἔχειν ἐποιεῖτο τὴν κατηγορίαν, οὐκ ἀληθῆ λέγειν διὰ δισσῶν ὑμῖν ἐπιδείξω τρόπων· οὔτε γὰρ βουληθεὶς ἐδυνάμην ἂν οὔτε δυνάμενος ἐβουλήθην ἔργοις ἐπιχειρεῖν τοιούτοις.

[6] ἐπὶ τοῦτον δὲ τὸν λόγον εἶμι πρῶτον, ὡς ἀδύνατός εἰμι τοῦτο πράττειν. ἔδει γάρ τινα πρῶτον ἀρχὴν γενέσθαι τῆς προδοσίας, ἡ δὲ ἀρχὴ λόγος ἂν εἴη· πρὸ γὰρ τῶν μελλόντων ἔργων ἀνάγκη λόγους γίνεσθαι πρότερον. λόγοι δὲ πῶς ἂν γένοιντο μὴ συνουσίας τινὸς γενομένης; συνουσία δὲ τίνα τρόπον γένοιτ᾽ ἂν μήτ᾽ ἐκείνου πρὸς ἐμὲ πέμψαντος μήτε παρ᾽ ἐμοῦ πρὸς ἐκεῖνον ἐλθόντος; οὐδὲ γαρ αγγελία διὰ γραμματείων ἀφῖκται ἄνευ τοῦ φέροντος.

[7] ἀλλὰ δὴ τοῦτο τῷ λόγῳ δυνατὸν γενέσθαι. καὶ δὴ τοίνυν σύνειμι καὶ σύνεστι κἀκεῖνος ἐμοὶ κἀκείνῳ ἐγώ—τίνα τρόπον; τίνι τίς ὤν; Ἕλλην βαρβάρῳ. πῶς ἀκούων καὶ λέγων; πότερα μόνος μόνῳ; ἀλλ᾽ ἀγνοήσομεν τοὺς ἀλλήλων λόγους. ἀλλὰ μεθ᾽ ἑρμηνέως; τρίτος ἄρα μάρτυς γίνεται τῶν κρύπτεσθαι δεομένων.

[8] ἀλλὰ δὴ καὶ τοῦτο γενέσθω, καίπερ οὐ γενόμενον. ἔδει δὲ μετὰ τούτους πίστιν δοῦναι καὶ δέξασθαι. τίς οὖν ἂν ἦν ἡ πίστις; πότερον ὅρκος; τίς οὖν ἐμοὶ τῷ προδότῃ πιστεύειν ἔμελλεν; ἀλλ᾽ ὅμηροι; τίνες; οἷον ἐγὼ τὸν ἀδελφὸν ἔδωκ᾽ ἄν (οὐ γὰρ εἶχον ἄλλον), ὁ δὲ βάρβαρος τῶν υἱέων τινά· πιστότατα γὰρ ἂν ἦν οὕτως ἐμοί τε παρ᾽ ἐκείνου ἐκείνῳ τε παρ᾽ ἐμοῦ. ταῦτα δὲ γινόμενα πᾶσιν ὑμῖν ἂν ἦν φανερά.

[9] φήσει τις ὡς χρήμασι τὴν πίστιν ἐποιούμεθα, ἐκεῖνος μὲν διδούς, ἐγὼ δὲ λαμβάνων. πότερον οὖν ὀλίγοις; ἀλλ᾽ οὐκ εἰκὸς ἀντὶ μεγάλων ὑπουργημάτων ὀλίγα χρήματα λαμβάνειν. ἀλλὰ πολλοῖς; τίς οὖν ἦν ἡ κομιδή; πῶς δ᾽ ἂν ἐκόμισεν; ἢ πολλοί; πολλῶν γὰρ κομιζόντων πολλοὶ ἂν ἦσαν μάρτυρες τῆς ἐπιβουλῆς, ἑνὸς δὲ κομίζοντος οὐκ ἂν πολύ τι τὸ φερόμενον ἦν.

If, then, the prosecutor mounted his accusation supposing that things occurred this way, I will show you in two different ways that he is not speaking the truth. For neither if I wanted to, could I undertake such actions, nor if I could, would I want to.

6. And I will turn to this argument first, namely that I am not able to do such things. For it is necessary that there was a beginning of the treason and that beginning would be speech, since for plans to be carried out, discussions must first take place. But how would it be possible for these discussions to take place without contact? And how would it be possible for contact to be made without him reaching out to me, or me responding to him? For not even a message written on a tablet could have arrived without someone bringing it.

7. But let us say that this could in fact be done by means of speech, and therefore he met with me and I with him. In what way? Being who and meeting whom? A Greek with a barbarian. Listening to and speaking to each other in what way? How? One to one? But if that was the case, we would not understand each other! Perhaps with an interpreter present? But then a third witness would need to be there for those things that must remain hidden!

8. But let us say that even this in fact happened though it did not. After all these [sc. the negotiations] it would be necessary to give and receive assurances. But what would be the assurance? An oath? Who would trust me, a traitor? Perhaps hostages? Which? I could only offer my brother as a hostage, for I did not have anyone else, and the barbarian one of his sons, for such an arrangement would guarantee the greatest assurance from me to him and him to me. But if such things had happened it would have been evident to all of you.

9. One will claim that we made a deal using money: he giving and me receiving. What amount, then? A small one? But it is not reasonable for great services to receive small compensation! But perhaps a large one? What would be its mode of transportation? And how would it be transported? By many? But if they were many then the witnesses of the plot would be many as well; if, on the other hand, it was only one, what he brought could not have been much.

[10] πότερα δὲ ἐκόμισαν ἡμέρας ἢ νυκτός; ἀλλὰ πολλαὶ καὶ πυκναὶ φυλακαί, δι' ὧν οὐκ ἔστι λαθεῖν. ἀλλ' ἡμέρας; ἀλλά γε τὸ φῶς πολεμεῖ τοῖς τοιούτοις. εἶεν. ἐγὼ δ' ἐξελθὼν ἐδεξάμην, ἢ ἐκεῖνος ὁ φέρων εἰσῆλθεν; ἀμφότερα γὰρ ἄπορα. λαβὼν δὲ δὴ πῶς ἂν ἔκρυψα καὶ τοὺς ἔνδον καὶ τοὺς ἔξω; ποῦ δ' ἂν ἔθηκα; πῶς δ' ἂν ἐφύλαξα; χρώμενος δ' ἂν φανερὸς ἐγενόμην, μὴ χρώμενος δὲ τί ἂν ὠφελούμην ἀπ' αὐτῶν;

[11] καὶ δὴ τοίνυν γενέσθω καὶ τὰ μὴ γενόμενα. συνήλθομεν, εἴπομεν, ἠκούσαμεν, χρήματα παρ' αὐτῶν ἔλαβον, ἔλαθον λαβών, ἔκρυψα. ἔδει δήπου πράττειν ὧν ἕνεκα ταῦτα ἐγένετο. τοῦτο τοίνυν ἔτι τῶν εἰρημένων ἀπορώτερον. πράττων μὲν γὰρ αὐτὸς ἔπραττον ἢ μεθ' ἑτέρων· ἀλλ' οὐχ ἑνὸς ἡ πρᾶξις. ἀλλὰ μεθ' ἑτέρων; τίνων; δηλονότι τῶν συνόντων. πότερον ἐλευθέρων ἢ δούλων; ἐλευθέροις μὲν γὰρ ὑμῖν σύνειμι. τίς οὖν ὑμῶν ξύνοιδε; λεγέτω. δούλοις δὲ πῶς οὐκ ἄπιστον; ἑκόντες <τε> γὰρ ἐπ' ἐλευθερίᾳ χειμαζόμενοί τε δι' ἀνάγκην κατηγοροῦσιν.

[12] ἡ δὲ πρᾶξις πῶς ἂν ἐγένετο; δηλονότι τοὺς πολεμίους εἰσαγαγεῖν ἔδει κρείττονας ὑμῶν· ὅπερ ἀδύνατον. πῶς ἂν οὖν εἰσήγαγον; πότερα διὰ πυλῶν; ἀλλ' οὐκ ἐμὸν ταύτας οὔτε κλῄειν οὔτε ἀνοίγειν, ἀλλ' ἡγεμόνες κύριοι τούτων. ἀλλ' ὑπὲρ τειχέων διὰ κλίμακος; οὔκουν. ἅπαντα γὰρ πλήρη φυλακῶν. ἀλλὰ διελὼν τοῦ τείχους; ἅπασιν ἄρα φανερὰ γένοιτο ἄν. ὑπαίθριος γὰρ ὁ βίος στρατόπεδον γάρ ἔστ' ἐν ὅπλοις, ἐν οἷς πάντες πάντας ὁρῶσι καὶ πάντες ὑπὸ πάντων ὁρῶνται. πάντως ἄρα καὶ πάντῃ ταῦτα πράττειν ἀδύνατον ἦν μοι.

[13] σκέψασθε κοινῇ καὶ τόδε. τίνος ἕνεκα προσῆκε βουληθῆναι ταῦτα πράττειν, εἰ μάλιστα πάντων ἐδυνάμην;

10. And, further to that, how did he bring it? During the day or during the night? Well, during the night there are many guards closely posted, past whom it is impossible to sneak. During the day then? But surely the light of day is an enemy to these things! Be that as it may, did I receive the money by going out of the camp, or did the one bringing the money come in? Neither way is feasible! If, in fact, I received the sum, how did I manage to conceal it both from those inside and those outside the camp? Where would I have put it? How would I have kept it safe? If I used it, I would have been revealed to all. If I did not, how would I be benefitting from it?

11. And let us say that the things that did not happen, did. We met, we talked, we understood each other, I received the money from them successfully, evading notice while doing it, and I managed to hide it away. Then, doubtlessly it was necessary to commit the act on account of which all of the above took place. This would be even more impossible than what has already been discussed. How did I do it? By myself or with others? And with whom? Clearly some of those around me. Which ones then, free men or slaves? The free men surrounding me are you. Which of you knew about it, then? Let him speak! If I used slaves instead, how would that not be risky? For they make accusations either willingly, out of desire for freedom, or under duress, through torture.

12. And what about the act, how would it have been committed? For it would clearly have been necessary to bring in enemies stronger than you, which is impossible. How would I bring them in? Perhaps through the gates? But it is not in my authority to close or open them, for there are designated officers for that task. Perhaps over the walls with a ladder? Surely not. All sides are staffed with guards. Perhaps then by breaching the wall? But that would be evident to everyone, since our life is lived in the open, this being an army camp during war, where everyone sees everyone else and everyone is seen by everyone else. Therefore, in every possible way it was impossible for me to do these things at all.

13. Let us examine this together: for the sake of what was it fitting for me to wish to do these things, had I actually been able to do them all?

οὐδεὶς γὰρ βούλεται προῖκα τοὺς μεγίστους κινδύνους κινδυνεύειν οὐδὲ τὴν μεγίστην κακότητα εἶναι κάκιστος. ἀλλ' ἕνεκα τοῦ; (καὶ αὖθις πρὸς τόδ' ἐπάνειμι.) πότερον <τοῦ> τυραννεῖν; ὑμῶν ἢ τῶν βαρβάρων; ἀλλ' ὑμῶν ἀδύνατον τοσούτων καὶ τοιούτων, οἷς ὑπάρχει ἅπαντα μέγιστα, προγόνων ἀρεταί, χρημάτων πλῆθος, ἀριστεῖαι, ἀλκὴ φρονημάτων, βασιλεία πόλεων.

[14] ἀλλὰ τῶν βαρβάρων; ὁ δὲ παραδώσων τίς; ἐγὼ δὲ ποίᾳ δυνάμει παραλήψομαι Ἕλλην βαρβάρους, εἷς ὢν πολλούς; πείσας ἢ βιασάμενος; οὔτε γὰρ ἐκεῖνοι πεισθῆναι βούλοιντ' ἄν, οὔτ' ἐγὼ βιάσασθαι δυναίμην. ἀλλ' ἴσως ἑκόντες ἑκόντι παραδώσουσιν, μισθὸν τῆς προδοσίας ἀντιδιδόντες; ἀλλά γε ταῦτα πολλῆς μωρίας καὶ πιστεῦσαι καὶ δέξασθαι· τίς γὰρ ἂν ἕλοιτο δουλείαν ἀντ' ἐλευθερίας, ἀντὶ τοῦ κρατίστου τὸ κάκιστον;

[15] εἴποι τις ἂν ὅτι πλούτου καὶ χρημάτων ἐρασθεὶς ἐπεχείρησα τούτοις. ἀλλὰ χρήματα μὲν μέτρια κέκτημαι, πολλῶν δὲ οὐθὲν δέομαι· πολλῶν γὰρ δέονται χρημάτων οἱ πολλὰ δαπανῶντες, ἀλλ' οὐχ οἱ κρείττονες τῶν τῆς φύσεως ἡδονῶν, ἀλλ' οἱ δουλεύοντες ταῖς ἡδοναῖς καὶ ζητοῦντες ἀπὸ πλούτου καὶ μεγαλοπρεπείας τὰς τιμὰς κτᾶσθαι. τούτων δὲ ἐμοὶ πρόσεστιν οὐθέν. ὡς δ' ἀληθῆ λέγω, μάρτυρα πιστὸν παρέξομαι τὸν παροιχόμενον βίον· τῷ δὲ μάρτυρι μάρτυρες ὑμεῖς ἦτε· σύνεστε γάρ μοι, διὸ σύνιστε ταῦτα.

[16] καὶ μὴν οὐδ' ἂν τιμῆς ἕνεκα τοιούτοις ἔργοις ἀνὴρ ἐπιχειρήσειε καὶ μέσως φρόνιμος. ἀπ' ἀρετῆς γὰρ ἀλλ' οὐκ ἀπὸ κακότητος αἱ τιμαί· προδότῃ δὲ τῆς Ἑλλάδος ἀνδρὶ πῶς ἂν γένοιτο τιμή; πρὸς δὲ τούτοις οὐδὲ τιμῆς ἐτύγχανον ἐνδεὴς ὤν· ἐτιμώμην γὰρ ἐπὶ τοῖς ἐντιμοτάτοις ὑπὸ τῶν ἐντιμοτάτων, ὑφ' ὑμῶν ἐπὶ σοφίᾳ.

[17] καὶ μὴν οὐδ' ἀσφαλείας οὕνεκά τις ἂν ταῦτα πράξαι. πᾶσι γὰρ ὅ γε προδότης πολέμιος, τῷ νόμῳ, τῇ δίκῃ, τοῖς θεοῖς, τῷ πλήθει τῶν ἀνθρώπων· τὸν μὲν γὰρ νόμον παραβαίνει, τὴν δὲ δίκην καταλύει, τὸ δὲ πλῆθος διαφθείρει, τὸ δὲ θεῖον ἀτιμάζει. τῷ δὲ τοιούτῳ <ὁ> βίος περὶ κινδύνων τῶν μεγίστων οὐκ ἔχει ἀσφάλειαν.

For no one is willing to risk the greatest dangers for nothing, nor to be accountable for the greatest evil. For the sake of what then? And I will return to this point later. Perhaps for the sake of usurping power? Over you or the barbarians? But over you is impossible since you are so many and so strong and possess all the greatest things: the virtues of your ancestors, wealth of resources, excellence in battles, strength of judgment, kingship of cities.

14. Over the barbarians, then? Who would deliver them to me? By means of what power will I, a Greek, take control over barbarians, I being one and they many? Through persuasion or force? For those people would not be willing to be persuaded, nor would I be able to force them. But perhaps they will deliver themselves willingly to one who was willing as a payment for the treason. It is ludicrous both to believe and to say these things: for who would choose slavery over freedom, the worst over the best?

15. Someone could say that I attempted these things because I fell for wealth and money. But I have already acquired enough money and I do not need more; for those who spend a lot need a lot of money, not those who are stronger than natural pleasures, but those who are slaves to such pleasures and seek to acquire honor and prestige through wealth. None of that pertains to me. That I am telling the truth, I will offer my life so far as a trusted witness; and you have been the witnesses of that witness: since you share your lives with me, so you share this knowledge with me.

16. And in fact, for the sake of honor, no man, even moderately prudent, would attempt such things. For honors come from virtue, not from evil. How could a man who is a traitor of Greece have honor? Moreover, I was not in need of any honor, for I was honored for the most honorable things by the most honorable men, by you for wisdom.

17. And in fact, for the sake of security, no one would do these things. For the traitor is surely an enemy to everything—law, justice, the gods, and the majority of people. He transgresses the law, destroys justice, corrupts the majority, and dishonors the gods. Thus, the life of such a person has no security concerning the greatest dangers.

[18] ἀλλὰ δὴ φίλους ὠφελεῖν βουλόμενος ἢ πολεμίους βλάπτειν; καὶ γὰρ τούτων ἕνεκά τις ἂν ἀδικήσειεν. ἐμοὶ δὲ πᾶν τοὐναντίον ἐγίνετο· τοὺς μὲν φίλους κακῶς ἐποίουν, τοὺς δὲ ἐχθροὺς ὠφέλουν. ἀγαθῶν μὲν οὖν κτῆσιν οὐδεμίαν εἶχεν ἡ πρᾶξις· κακῶς δὲ παθεῖν οὐδὲ εἷς ἐπιθυμῶν πανουργεῖ.

[19] τὸ δὲ λοιπόν ἐστιν, εἴ τινα φόβον ἢ πόνον ἢ κίνδυνον φεύγων ἔπραξα. ταῦτα δ' οὐθεὶς ἂν εἰπεῖν ἔχοι τί μοι προσήκειν. δισσῶν γὰρ τούτων ἕνεκα πάντες πάντα πράττουσιν, ἢ κέρδος τι μετιόντες ἢ ζημίαν φεύγοντες· ὅσα δὲ τούτων ἔξω πανουργεῖται, <ὅτι> κακῶς ἐμαυτὸν ἐποίουν ταῦτα πράττων οὐκ ἄδηλον· προδιδοὺς γὰρ τὴν Ἑλλάδα προὐδίδουν ἐμαυτόν, τοκέας, φίλους, ἀξίωμα προγόνων, ἱερὰ πατρῷα, τάφους, πατρίδα τὴν μεγίστην τῆς Ἑλλάδος. ἃ δὲ πᾶσι περὶ παντός ἐστι, ταῦτα ἂν τοῖς ἀδικηθεῖσιν ἐνεχείρισα.

[20] σκέψασθε δὲ καὶ τόδε. πῶς οὐκ ἂν ἀβίωτος ἦν ὁ βίος μοι πράξαντι ταῦτα; ποῖ γὰρ τραπέσθαι με χρῆν; πότερον εἰς τὴν Ἑλλάδα; δίκην δώσοντα τοῖς ἠδικημένοις; τίς δ' ἂν ἀπείχετό μου τῶν κακῶς πεπονθότων; ἀλλὰ μένειν ἐν τοῖς βαρβάροις; παραμελήσαντα πάντων τῶν μεγίστων, ἐστερημένον τῆς καλλίστης τιμῆς, ἐν αἰσχίστῃ δυσκλείᾳ διάγοντα, τοὺς ἐν τῷ παροι-χομένῳ βίῳ πόνους ἐπ' ἀρετῇ πεπονημένους ἀπορρίψαντα; καὶ ταῦτα δι' ἐμαυτόν, ὅπερ αἴσχιστον ἀνδρί, δυστυχεῖν δι' αὑτόν.

[21] οὐ μὴν οὐδὲ παρὰ τοῖς βαρβάροις πιστῶς ἂν διεκείμην· πῶς γάρ, οἵτινες ἀπιστότατον ἔργον συνηπίσταντό μοι πεποιηκότι, τοὺς φίλους τοῖς ἐχθροῖς παραδεδωκότι; βίος δ οὐ βιωτὸς πίστεως ἐστερημένῳ. χρήματα μὲν γὰρ ἀποβαλὼν ἢ τυραννίδος ἐκπεσὼν ἢ τὴν πατρίδα φυγὼν ἀναλάβοι τις ἄν· ὁ δὲ πίστιν ἀποβαλὼν οὐκ ἂν ἔτι κτήσαιτο. ὅτι μὲν οὖν οὔτ' ἂν ἐδυνάμην οὔτ ἂν ἐβουλόμην προδοῦναι τὴν Ἑλλάδα, διὰ τῶν προειρημένων δέδεικται.

18. But perhaps wishing to benefit friends or harm enemies? Since someone might commit injustice also for these reasons. But in my case, it was entirely the opposite—I was harming my friends while benefitting my enemies. Therefore, the deed brought no acquisition of goods, and no one ever conspires out of a desire to suffer.

19. What remains, then, is whether I acted to escape either some fear, toil, or danger. However, no one would be able to say at all that any of these things applies to me. There are two reasons for the sake of which everyone makes every effort to do everything, either to gain some profit, or to avoid some loss. Whatever things are conspired beyond these reasons, that I harmed myself by doing them is not unclear: for by betraying Greece, I betrayed myself, my parents, my friends, the virtue of my ancestors, the gods of my forefathers, their graves, and the greatest fatherland, Greece. Moreover, those things that are above everything for everyone, I would have delivered to those who have suffered injustice.

20. And consider this as well: how would my life not have been unlivable if I had done these things? Where should I have turned? To Greece? Paying the penalty to those who have suffered injustice? Who having suffered evil would keep their hands off me? Would I stay among the barbarians then? Having neglected all the greatest things, having been deprived of the finest honor, passing my time in the most shameful infamy, throwing away the labors I labored over for virtue's sake in my life so far? And all this because of myself—which is the most shameful thing for a man, to fall into misfortune because of himself.

21. But I would not be trusted even among the barbarians. For how could I be, living among those who know what a treacherous act I have committed, having surrendered my friends to their enemies? Life is unlivable if one has lost their trustworthiness. For one would restore a man who has lost his belongings, or has been deposed by tyranny, or has fled his country. But the one who has lost his trustworthiness can never get it back. Therefore, that I could not, nor would I wish to betray Greece, has been proven adequately by what I have said.

[22] βούλομαι δὲ μετὰ ταῦτα πρὸς τὸν κατήγορον διαλεχθῆναι. τίνι ποτὲ πιστεύσας τοιοῦτος ὢν τοιούτου κατηγορεῖς; ἄξιον γὰρ καταμαθεῖν, οἷος ὢν οἷα λέγεις ὡς ἀνάξιος ἀναξίῳ. πότερα γάρ μου κατηγορεῖς εἰδὼς ἀκριβῶς ἢ δοξάζων; εἰ μὲν γὰρ εἰδώς, οἶσθα ἰδὼν ἢ μετέχων ἤ του <μετέχοντος> πυθόμενος. εἰ μὲν οὖν ἰδών, φράσον τούτοις <τὸν τρόπον>, τὸν τόπον, τὸν χρόνον, πότε, ποῦ, πῶς εἶδες· εἰ δὲ μετέχων, ἔνοχος εἶς ταῖς αὐταῖς αἰτίαις· εἰ δέ του μετέχοντος ἀκούσας, ὅστις ἐστίν, αὐτὸς ἐλθέτω, φανήτω, μαρτυρησάτω. πιστότερον γὰρ οὕτως ἔσται τὸ κατηγόρημα μαρτυρηθέν. ἐπεὶ νῦν γε οὐδέτερος ἡμῶν παρέχεται μάρτυρα.

[23] φήσεις ἴσως ἴσον εἶναι τὸ σέ γε τῶν γενομένων, ὡς σὺ φῄς, μὴ παρέχεσθαι μάρτυρας, τῶν δὲ μὴ γενομένων ἐμέ. τὸ δὲ οὐκ ἴσον ἐστί· τὰ μὲν γὰρ ἀγένητά πως ἀδύνατα μαρτυρηθῆναι, περὶ δὲ τῶν γενομένων οὐ μόνον οὐκ ἀδύνατον, ἀλλὰ καὶ ῥᾴδιον, οὐδὲ μόνον ῥᾴδιον, ἀλλὰ σοὶ μὲν οὐκ ἦν οἷόν <τε> μόνον μάρτυρας ἀλλὰ καὶ ψευδομάρτυρας εὑρεῖν, ἐμοὶ δὲ οὐδέτερον εὑρεῖν τούτων δυνατόν.

[24] Ὅτι μὲν οὖν οὐκ οἶσθ' ἃ κατηγορεῖς, φανερόν.* τὸ δὴ λοιπὸν εἰδότα σε δοξάζειν. εἶτα, ὦ πάντων ἀνθρώπων τολμηρότατε, δόξῃ πιστεύσας, ἀπιστοτάτῳ πράγματι, τὴν ἀλήθειαν οὐκ εἰδώς, τολμᾷς ἄνδρα περὶ θανάτου διώκειν; ᾧ τί τοιοῦτον ἔργον εἰργασμένῳ σύνοισθα; ἀλλὰ μὴν τό γε δοξάσαι κοινὸν ἅπασι περὶ πάντων, καὶ οὐδὲν ἐν τούτῳ σὺ τῶν ἄλλων σοφώτερος. ἀλλ' οὔτε τοῖς δοξάζουσι δεῖ πιστεύειν ἀλλὰ τοῖς εἰδόσιν, οὔτε τὴν δόξαν τῆς ἀληθείας πιστοτέραν νομίζειν, ἀλλὰ τἀναντία τὴν ἀλήθειαν τῆς δόξης.

[25] κατηγόρησας δέ μου διὰ τῶν εἰρημένων λόγων δύο τὰ ἐναντιώτατα, σοφίαν καὶ μανίαν, ὥπερ οὐχ οἷόν τε τὸν αὐτὸν ἄνθρωπον ἔχειν. ὅπου μὲν γάρ με φῄς εἶναι τεχνήεντά τε καὶ δεινὸν καὶ πόριμον,

---

* This phrasing is reflected by Socrates's words at the start of Plato's *Apology* (17a): ὅτι μὲν ὑμεῖς, ὦ ἄνδρες Ἀθηναῖοι, πεπόνθατε ὑπὸ τῶν ἐμῶν κατηγόρων, οὐκ οἶδα.

22. I wish, after this, to address the accuser. Whatever were you relying on, being the sort of man you are, to accuse me, being the sort of man I am? For it is worth understanding, being the sort of man you are, what kind of things you are saying as an unworthy man (*anaxios*) to one who does not deserve it (*anaxios*). Do you accuse me knowing accurately or merely supposing? For if you know, then you know either by seeing, or by participating, or by learning from one who participated. If by seeing, tell these men the way, the place, the time; when where, and how you saw. If you participated, then you are guilty of the same charges; if you heard from someone who took part, whoever he is, let him come forward himself, appear, and give witness. For the accusation, supported by a witness, will be more trustworthy. For now, at least, neither of us is providing a witness.

23. You will perhaps claim that it is of equal value for you not to present witnesses for what you claim happened, as it is for me for what did not happen. But it is not of equal value at all: for how is it possible for things that did not happen to be witnessed? For those things that did happen, however, it is not only not impossible but also easy; not only easy, but for you it is possible not only to find witnesses but also perjurers, yet for me it is possible to find neither.

24. Therefore, that you do not know about the things you are accusing me of is clear. What remains, then, is you suppose that you know. And then you, most reckless of all people, trusting in opinion (a most untrustworthy thing) not knowing the truth, dare to prosecute a man seeking the death penalty? What deed of this sort are you aware of him having committed? But in fact, it is common indeed for everyone to form an opinion about everything, and you are no wiser in this than the rest. But it is necessary to trust not those who have opinions, but those who know, and not to consider opinion more trustworthy than truth, but conversely, truth more than opinion.

25. Further, you accused me through the things said so far of two most incompatible things, sound judgment (*sophia*) and madness (*mania*), which one and the same person cannot have. For when you assert that I am skillful, clever, and resourceful,

σοφίαν μου κατηγορεῖς, ὅπου δὲ λέγεις ὡς προὐδίδουν τὴν Ἑλλάδα, μανίαν· μανία γάρ ἐστιν ἔργοις ἐπιχειρεῖν ἀδυνάτοις, ἀσυμφόροις, αἰσχροῖς, ἀφ' ὧν τοὺς μὲν φίλους βλάψει, τοὺς δ' ἐχθροὺς ὠφελήσει, τὸν δὲ αὑτοῦ βίον ἐπονείδιστον καὶ σφαλερὸν καταστήσει. καίτοι πῶς χρὴ ἀνδρὶ τοιούτῳ πιστεύειν, ὅστις τὸν αὐτὸν λόγον λέγων πρὸς τοὺς αὐτοὺς ἄνδρας περὶ τῶν αὐτῶν τὰ ἐναντιώτατα λέγει;

[26] βουλοίμην δ' ἂν παρὰ σοῦ πυθέσθαι, πότερον τοὺς σοφοὺς ἄνδρας νομίζεις ἀνοήτους ἢ φρονίμους. εἰ μὲν γὰρ ἀνοήτους, καινὸς ὁ λόγος, ἀλλ' οὐκ ἀληθής· εἰ δὲ φρονίμους, οὐ δήπου προσήκει τούς γε φρονοῦντας ἐξαμαρτάνειν τὰς μεγίστας ἁμαρτίας καὶ μᾶλλον αἱρεῖσθαι κακὰ πρότερον τῶν ἀγαθῶν. εἰ μὲν οὖν εἰμι σοφός, οὐχ ἥμαρτον· εἰ δ' ἥμαρτον, οὐ σοφός εἰμι. οὐκοῦν δι' ἀμφότερα ἂν εἴης ψευδής.

[27] ἀντικατηγορῆσαι δέ σου πολλὰ καὶ μεγάλα καὶ παλαιὰ καὶ νέα πράσσοντος δυνάμενος οὐ βούλομαι· <βούλομαι> γὰρ οὐ τοῖς σοῖς κακοῖς ἀλλὰ τοῖς ἐμοῖς ἀγαθοῖς ἀποφεύγειν τὴν αἰτίαν ταύτην. πρὸς μὲν οὖν σὲ ταῦτα.

[28] πρὸς δ' ὑμᾶς, ὦ ἄνδρες κριταί, περὶ ἐμοῦ βούλομαι εἰπεῖν ἐπίφθονον μὲν ἀληθὲς δέ, <μὴ> κατηγορημένῳ μὲν οὐκ ἀνεκτά, κατηγορουμένῳ δὲ προσήκοντα. νῦν γὰρ ἐν ὑμῖν εὐθύνας καὶ λόγον ὑπέχω τοῦ παροιχομένου βίου. δέομαι οὖν ὑμῶν, ἂν ὑμᾶς ὑπομνήσω τῶν τι ἐμοὶ πεπραγμένων καλῶν, μηδένα φθονῆσαι τοῖς λεγομένοις, ἀλλ' ἀναγκαῖον ἡγήσασθαι κατη-γορημένον δεινὰ καὶ ψευδῆ καί τι τῶν ἀληθῶν ἀγαθῶν εἰπεῖν ἐν εἰδόσιν ὑμῖν· ὅπερ ἥδιστόν μοι.

[29] πρῶτον μὲν οὖν καὶ δεύτερον καὶ μέγιστον, διὰ παντὸς ἀπ' ἀρχῆς εἰς τέλος ἀναμάρτητος ὁ παροιχόμενος βίος ἐστί μοι, καθαρὸς πάσης αἰτίας· οὐδεὶς γὰρ ἂν οὐδεμίαν αἰτίαν κακό-τητος ἀληθῆ πρὸς ὑμᾶς περὶ ἐμοῦ εἰπεῖν ἔχοι. καὶ γὰρ οὐδ' αὐτὸς ὁ κατήγορος οὐδεμίαν ἀπόδειξιν εἴρηκεν ὧν εἴρηκεν· οὕτως λοιδορίαν οὐκ ἔχουσαν ἔλεγχον ὁ λόγος αὐτῷ δύναται.

you accuse me of sound judgment, but when you say that I betrayed Greece, of madness; for it is madness to attempt deeds that are impossible, disadvantageous, and shameful, through which the person will harm their friends, benefit their enemies, and render their own life reprehensible and perilous. And so how must one believe such a man, who while making the same speech to the same men about the same things, says the most contradictory things?

26. I wish to learn from you whether you consider wise men to be foolish or sensible. For if you consider them foolish that is indeed a novel argument, but not true; if you consider them sensible, then doubtless it is not fitting for sensible people, at least, to commit the greatest errors and choose evils before goods. If, therefore, I am of sound judgment, I did not err. But if I erred, I am not of sound judgment. Therefore, in either case, you would be a liar.

27. Although I am capable of accusing you in turn of many grave things, both old and new, I do not wish to. For I wish to be exonerated of this charge not through your evil deeds, but through my good ones. That, then, is all I have to say regarding you.

28. But to you, men of the jury, I wish to say some things about myself that attract envy, but are true; something unacceptable for one not under accusation, but appropriate for one under accusation. For I am now submitting to you the records and an account (*logos*) of my life so far. Therefore, I ask you, if I remind you of just a few of the noble things that I have done, that no-one become invidious about what I say, but consider it necessary for someone accused of terrible and untrue things to also speak a little of his true and good actions to you who know them; indeed, this gives me the greatest pleasure.

29. First then, also second and most important, my life so far is entirely, from beginning to end, without error, clear of every charge. For no-one would have even one true charge of evildoing to report to you about me. For not even the accuser himself said what he said with any proof at all. Therefore, his speech is tantamount to slander that cannot be refuted.

[30] φήσαιμι δ' ἄν, καὶ φήσας οὐκ ἂν ψευσαίμην οὐδ' ἂν ἐλεγχθείην, οὐ μόνον ἀναμάρτητος ἀλλὰ καὶ μέγας εὐεργέτης ὑμῶν καὶ τῶν Ἑλλήνων καὶ τῶν ἁπάντων ἀνθρώπων, οὐ μόνον τῶν νῦν ὄντων ἀλλὰ καὶ τῶν μελλόντων, εἶναι. τίς γὰρ ἂν ἐποίησε τὸν ἀνθρώπειον βίον πόριμον ἐξ ἀπόρου καὶ κεκοσμημένον ἐξ ἀκόσμου, τάξεις τε πολεμικὰς εὑρὼν μέγιστον εἰς πλεονεκτήματα, νόμους τε γραπτοὺς φύλακας τοῦ δικαίου, γράμματά τε μνήμης ὄργανον, μέτρα τε καὶ σταθμὰ συναλλαγῶν εὐπόρους διαλλαγάς, ἀριθμόν τε χρημάτων φύλακα, πυρσούς τε κρατίστους καὶ ταχίστους ἀγγέλους, πεσσούς* τε σχολῆς ἄλυπον διατριβήν; τίνος οὖν ἕνεκα ταῦθ' ὑμᾶς ὑπέμνησα;

[31] δηλῶν <μὲν> ὅτι τοῖς τοιούτοις τὸν νοῦν προσέχω, σημεῖον δὲ ποιούμενος ὅτι τῶν αἰσχρῶν καὶ τῶν κακῶν ἔργων ἀπέχομαι· τὸ γὰρ ἐκείνοις τὸν νοῦν προσέχοντα τοῖς τοιούτοις προσέχειν ἀδύνατον. ἀξιῶ δέ, εἰ μηδὲν αὐτὸς ὑμᾶς ἀδικῶ, μηδὲ αὐτὸς ὑφ' ὑμῶν ἀδικηθῆναι.

[32] καὶ γὰρ οὐδὲ τῶν ἄλλων ἐπιτηδευμάτων οὕνεκα ἄξιός εἰμι κακῶς πάσχειν, οὔθ' ὑπὸ νεωτέρων οὔθ' ὑπὸ πρεσβυτέρων. τοῖς μὲν γὰρ πρεσβυτέροις ἄλυπός εἰμι, τοῖς δὲ νεωτέροις οὐκ ἀνωφελής, τοῖς εὐτυχοῦσιν οὐ φθονερός, τῶν δυστυχούντων οἰκτίρμων· οὔτε πενίας ὑπερορῶν, οὔτε πλοῦτον ἀρετῆς ἀλλ' ἀρετὴν πλούτου προτιμῶν· οὔτε ἐν βουλαῖς ἄχρηστος οὔτε ἐν μάχαις ἀργός, ποιῶν τὸ τασσόμενον, πειθόμενος τοῖς ἄρχουσιν. ἀλλὰ γὰρ οὐκ ἐμὸν ἐμαυτὸν ἐπαινεῖν· ὁ δὲ παρὼν καιρὸς ἠνάγκασε, καὶ ταῦτα κατηγορημένον, πάντως ἀπολο-γήσασθαι.

[33] λοιπὸν δὲ περὶ ὑμῶν πρὸς ὑμᾶς ἐστί μοι λόγος, ὃν εἰπὼν παύσομαι τῆς ἀπολογίας. οἶκτος μὲν οὖν καὶ λιταὶ καὶ φίλων παραίτησις ἐν ὄχλῳ μὲν οὔσης τῆς κρίσεως χρήσιμα· παρὰ δ' ὑμῖν τοῖς πρώτοις οὖσι τῶν Ἑλλήνων καὶ δοκοῦσιν, οὐ φίλων βοηθείαις οὐδὲ λιταῖς οὐδὲ οἴκτοις δεῖ πείθειν ὑμᾶς, ἀλλὰ τῷ σαφεστάτῳ δικαίῳ, διδάξαντα τἀληθές, οὐκ ἀπατήσαντά με δεῖ διαφυγεῖν τὴν αἰτίαν ταύτην.

---

* On the game of *petteia* repeatedly mentioned in Plato's dialogues, see Philippe G. Guéniot, "Un jeu clef: la petteia," *Revue de Philosophie Ancienne* 18 (2000): 33–64.

30. I would claim—and in making the claim I would not be lying, nor would I be refuted—that not only am I without error, but also a great benefactor to you and the Greeks and all people, not only those now alive but also those yet to be born. For who else would have made human life well-equipped from ill-equipped, orderly from disorderly, by inventing battle formations as the greatest thing for victory, written laws as guardians of justice, writing as an instrument of memory, measures and weights as convenient commercial conversions, arithmetic as guardian of money, torches as the most powerful and swiftest messengers, and checkers as a painless pastime? For what purpose, then, did I remind you of these things?

31. To make clear that I focus my mind on such things, I thereby give proof that I stay away from shameful and evil deeds. For it is impossible for a person while focusing their mind on those [beneficial] things, to focus on such [evil] deeds. And I believe that, if I myself do not treat you unjustly, neither should I myself be treated unjustly by you.

32. And moreover, I do not deserve to be punished on account of my other deeds, neither by the young, nor by the old. For I am harmless to the old, and not without benefit to the young, unenvious of the fortunate, merciful to the unfortunate. Neither do I look down on poverty, nor do I value wealth over virtue, but virtue over wealth. And I am neither useless in counsel nor slow in battle, doing what is ordered, obeying those in command. Now, it is not for me to praise myself; however, the present situation has forced me to defend myself in every possible way, given that I have been accused of these things.

33. What remains, then, is my speech to you about you, which, having spoken, I will conclude my defense. Lamentation and entreaties and appeal to friends are useful when the judgment lies in the hands of a crowd. But with you being the first among the Greeks and considered so, there is no need to persuade you with the help of friends, entreaties, or lamentation, but with the clearest justice; it is necessary for me to escape this charge having demonstrated the truth and not having deceived you.

[34] ὑμᾶς δὲ χρὴ μὴ τοῖς λόγοις μᾶλλον ἢ τοῖς ἔργοις προσέχειν τὸν νοῦν, μηδὲ τὰς αἰτίας τῶν ἐλέγχων προκρίνειν, μηδὲ τὸν ὀλίγον χρόνον τοῦ πολλοῦ σοφώτερον ἡγεῖσθαι κριτήν, μηδὲ τὴν διαβολὴν τῆς πείρας πιστοτέραν νομίζειν. ἅπαντα γὰρ τοῖς ἀγαθοῖς ἀνδράσι μεγάλης εὐλαβείας ἁμαρτάνειν,* τὰ δὲ ἀνήκεστα τῶν ἀκεστῶν ἔτι μᾶλλον· ταῦτα γὰρ προνοήσασι μὲν δυνατά, μετανοήσασι δὲ ἀνίατα. τῶν δὲ τοιούτων ἐστίν, ὅταν ἄνδρες ἄνδρα περὶ θανάτου κρίνωσιν· ὅπερ ἐστὶ νῦν παρ' ὑμῖν.

[35] εἰ μὲν οὖν ἦν διὰ τῶν λόγων τὴν ἀλήθειαν τῶν ἔργων καθαράν τε γενέσθαι τοῖς ἀκούουσι <καὶ> φανεράν, εὔπορος ἂν εἴη κρίσις ἤδη ἀπὸ τῶν εἰρημένων· ἐπειδὴ δὲ οὐχ οὕτως ἔχει, τὸ μὲν σῶμα τοὐμὸν φυλάξατε, τὸν δὲ πλείω χρόνον ἐπιμείνατε, μετὰ δὲ τῆς ἀληθείας τὴν κρίσιν ποιήσατε. ὑμῖν μὲν γὰρ μέγας ὁ κίνδυνος, ἀδίκοις φανεῖσι δόξαν τὴν μὲν καταβαλεῖν, τὴν δὲ κτήσασθαι. τοῖς δὲ ἀγαθοῖς ἀνδράσιν αἱρετώτερος θάνατος δόξης αἰσχρᾶς· ὁ μὲν γὰρ τοῦ βίου τέλος, ἡ δὲ τῷ βίῳ νόσος.

[36] ἐὰν δὲ ἀδίκως ἀποκτείνητέ με, πολλοῖς γενήσεται φανερόν· ἐγώ τε γὰρ ἁγνός, ὑμῶν τε πᾶσιν Ἕλλησι γνώριμος ἡ κακότης καὶ φανερά. καὶ τὴν αἰτίαν φανερὰν ἅπασιν ὑμεῖς ἕξετε τῆς ἀδικίας, οὐχ ὁ κατήγορος· ἐν ὑμῖν γὰρ τὸ τέλος ἐστὶ τῆς δίκης. ἁμαρτία δ' οὐκ ἂν γένοιτο μείζων ταύτης. οὐ γὰρ μόνον εἰς ἐμὲ καὶ τοκέας τοὺς ἐμοὺς ἁμαρτήσεσθε δικάσαντες ἀδίκως, ἀλλ' ὑμῖν αὐτοῖς δεινὸν ἄθεον ἄδικον ἄνομον ἔργον συνεπιστήσεσθε πεποιηκότες, ἀπεκτονότες ἄνδρα σύμμαχον, χρήσιμον ὑμῖν, εὐεργέτην τῆς Ἑλλάδος, Ἕλληνες Ἕλληνα, φανερὰν οὐδεμίαν ἀδικίαν οὐδὲ πιστὴν αἰτίαν ἀποδείξαντες.

[37] εἴρηται τὰ παρ' ἐμοῦ, καὶ παύομαι. τὸ γὰρ ὑπομνῆσαι τὰ διὰ μακρῶν εἰρημένα συντόμως πρὸς μὲν φαύλους δικαστὰς ἔχει λόγον· τοὺς δὲ πρώτους τῶν πρώτων Ἕλληνας Ἑλλήνων οὐκ ἄξιον οὐδ' ἀξιῶσαι μήτε προσέχειν τὸν νοῦν μήτε μεμνῆσθαι τὰ λεχθέντα.

---

* It is intentionally unclear whether he is referring to the error of putting to death an innocent person with or without great religious dread.

34. And you must not focus your mind on speeches but on deeds, not privilege charges over their refutations, not regard a short period of time a wiser judge than a long one, not consider slander more trustworthy than a trial. For in all respects, good men err in great reverence, even more so in the case of irremediable matters than remediable ones; for these are treatable for those who think ahead, but incurable for those who think too late. One such matter is whenever men judge a man on a charge of death; which is the very thing now before you.

35. If, therefore, it were possible for the truth about actions to become clear and evident to an audience by means of speeches, then it would already be easy to pronounce a judgment based on what has been said. But since things do not stand this way, preserve this body of mine, persevere for a greater time, and make your judgment in accordance with the truth. For the danger to you is great, if you appear unjust, to throw away one reputation and gain another. And for good men, death is more choiceworthy than a shameful reputation; for the former is the end of life, whereas the latter is lifelong illness.

36. If, however, you kill me unjustly it will become evident to many. For I am innocent and your wickedness will be well-known and evident to all the Greeks. And you, not the accuser, will be charged with injustice evident to all; for the result of the trial is in your hands. There could be no greater error than this. For in judging me unjustly you err not only against me and my own parents, but you will know within yourselves that you had committed a terrible, godless, unjust, and lawless deed, and killed a man who is an ally, useful to you, a benefactor of Greece, Greeks [killing] a Greek, having demonstrated no evident injustice or even a credible charge.

37. I have said my part and I conclude. For recounting succinctly things said at length makes sense before inferior judges; but it is not worthy to even consider it worthy of the first Greeks among the first Greeks to neither pay attention to nor remember what has been said.

ΠΕΡΙ ΤΟΥ ΜΗ ΟΝΤΟΣ *

[1] οὐκ εἶναί φησιν οὐδέν· εἰ δ᾽ ἔστιν, ἄγνωστον εἶναι· εἰ δὲ καὶ ἔστι καὶ γνωστόν, ἀλλ᾽ οὐ δηλωτὸν ἄλλοις.

[2] καὶ ὅτι μὲν οὐκ ἔστι, συνθεὶς τὰ ἑτέροις εἰρημένα, ὅσοι περὶ τῶν ὄντων λέγοντες τἀναντία, ὡς δοκοῦσιν, ἀποφαίνονται αὑτοῖς, οἱ μὲν ὅτι ἓν καὶ οὐ πολλά, οἱ δὲ αὖ ὅτι πολλὰ καὶ οὐχ ἕν, καὶ οἱ μὲν ὅτι ἀγένητα, οἱ δ᾽ ὡς γενόμενα ἐπιδεικνύντες ταῦτα, συλλογίζεται κατ᾽ ἀμφοτέρων.

[3] ἀνάγκη γάρ, φησίν, εἴ τί ἐστι, μήτε ἓν μήτε πολλὰ εἶναι, μήτε ἀγένητα μήτε γενόμενα· οὐδὲν <οὖν> ἂν εἴη. εἰ γὰρ εἴη τι, τούτων ἂν θάτερα εἴη. <καὶ> ὅτι οὐκ ἔστιν οὔτε ἓν οὔτε πολλά, οὔτε ἀγένητα οὔτε γενόμενα, τὰ μὲν ὡς Μέλισσος, τὰ δὲ ὡς Ζήνων ἐπιχειρεῖ δεικνύειν μετὰ τὴν πρώτην ἴδιον αὐτοῦ ἀπόδειξιν, ἐν ᾗ λέγει ὅτι οὐκ ἔστιν οὔτε εἶναι οὔτε μὴ εἶναι. †

[4] εἰ μὲν γὰρ τὸ μὴ εἶναι ἔστι μὴ εἶναι, οὐδὲν ἂν ἧττον τὸ μὴ ὂν τοῦ ὄντος εἴη. τό τε γὰρ μὴ ὄν ἐστι μὴ ὄν, καὶ τὸ ὂν ὄν, ὥστε οὐδὲν μᾶλλον εἶναι ἢ οὐκ εἶναι τὰ πράγματα.

[5] εἰ δ᾽ ὅμως τὸ μὴ εἶναί ἐστι, τὸ εἶναι, φησίν, οὐκ ἔστι τὸ ἀντικείμενον. εἰ γὰρ τὸ μὴ εἶναί ἐστι, τὸ εἶναι μὴ εἶναι προσήκει.

[6] ὥστε οὐκ ἂν οὕτως, φησίν, οὐδὲν ἂν εἴη, εἰ μὴ ταὐτόν ἐστιν εἶναί τε καὶ μὴ εἶναι. εἰ δὲ ταὐτό, καὶ οὕτως οὐκ ἂν εἴη οὐδέν· τό τε γὰρ μὴ ὂν οὐκ ἔστι καὶ τὸ ὄν, ἐπείπερ γε ταὐτὸ τῷ μὴ ὄντι. οὗτος μὲν οὖν αὐτὸς ὁ λόγος ἐκείνου.

---

* Gorgias's *On Not Being* and/or *On Nature* is preserved in two partial summaries: Sextus Empiricus (*Against the Mathematicians* 7.65-86) and the anonymous treatise *On Melissus, Xenophanes, Gorgias* (Ps.-Arist. *MXG* 5.1-5; 6.9-25), which is translated here. The general shape of the argument is the same in both but the terminology in *MXG* can be more reliably attributed to Gorgias. See R. Gaines, "Knowledge and Discourse in Gorgias' On the Non-Existent or On Nature" *Philosophy and Rhetoric* 30 (1997): 2-3. On the name of the work, see R. Wardy, *The Birth of Rhetoric* (London: Routledge, 1996), 15-16.

† This expression is repeated below without the compound negatives: τό τε γὰρ μὴ οὐκ ἔστι καὶ τὸ ὄν.

On Not Being*

1. [Gorgias] claims that nothing is; and if it is, it is unknowable; and even if it is and is knowable, that it [is] indemonstrable to others.

2. [To argue] that it is not, he puts together what others have claimed, namely those who made opposite statements of that which exist and who contradicted one another [or so it seems] - some [claiming] that what is, is one and not many, others [claiming] that what is, is many and not one; and likewise some [claiming] that it is un-generated, others demonstrating the opposite, that these things have come to be—and he draws together conclusions against both sides.†

3. For it is necessary, he claims, that if something exists, it is neither one nor many, nor un-generated nor having come to be. And so, nothing would be. For if there were to be something, it would be one of these or the other. He tries to show that it is neither one nor many, nor un-generated not having come to be, at times in the manner of Melissus, at times of Zeno. His first demonstration, however, is his own. In it, he says that it is not possible for it to be and not to be.

4. For if, on the one hand, that which is not is that which is not, then that which is not is no less than that which is, since that which is not is that which is not, and that which is is that which is. Therefore, it is not the case that things are more than they are not.

5. And similarly if, on the other hand, that which is not is, then that which is, being its opposite, is not. For if that which is not is, then it is fitting for that which is not to be.

6. So in this way, he says, nothing would be, unless that which is and that which is not are identical. But if they are identical, then nonetheless nothing would be. For it is not possible that something is and also is not, for the very reason that [that which is] is the same as that which is not. This, then, is his own argument.

---

* Translation by Jurgen R. Gatt

† The Greek tolerates both "against both sides" and "from both sides." This sentence's use of compound verbs might tend to favor the latter. The next sentence, however, which focuses on Gorgias's refutations, favors the former.

[9]* μετὰ δὲ τοῦτον τὸν λόγον φησίν· εἰ δὲ ἔστιν, ἤτοι ἀγένητον ἢ γενόμενον εἶναι. καὶ εἰ μὲν ἀγένητον, ἄπειρον αὐτὸ τοῖς τοῦ Μελίσσου ἀξιώμασι λαμβάνει· τὸ δ᾽ ἄπειρον οὐκ ἂν εἶναί ποτε. οὔτε γὰρ ἐν αὑτῷ οὔτ᾽ ἂν ἐν ἄλλῳ εἶναι· δύο γὰρ ἂν οὕτως ἢ πλείω εἶναι, τό τε ἐνὸν καὶ τὸ ἐν ᾧ, μηδαμοῦ δὲ ὂν οὐδὲν εἶναι κατὰ τὸν τοῦ Ζήνωνος λόγον περὶ τῆς χώρας.

[10] ἀγένητον μὲν οὖν διὰ ταῦτ᾽ οὐκ εἶναι, οὐ μὴν οὐδὲ γενόμενον. γενέσθαι γοῦν οὐδὲν ἂν οὔτ᾽ ἐξ ὄντος οὔτ᾽ ἐκ μὴ ὄντος. εἰ γὰρ τὸ ὂν μεταπέσοι, οὐκ ἂν ἔτ᾽ εἶναι τὸ ὄν, ὥσπερ γ᾽ εἰ καὶ τὸ μὴ ὂν γένοιτο, οὐκ ἂν ἔτι εἴη μὴ ὄν.

[11] οὐδὲ μὴν οὐδ᾽ ἐξ ὄντος ἂν γενέσθαι. εἰ μὲν γὰρ μή ἐστι τὸ μὴ ὄν, οὐδὲν ἂν ἐκ μηδενὸς ἂν γενέσθαι· εἰ δ᾽ ἔστι τὸ μὴ ὄν, δι᾽ ἅπερ οὐδ᾽ ἐκ τοῦ ὄντος, διὰ ταῦτα οὐδ᾽ ἐκ τοῦ μὴ ὄντος γενέσθαι.

[12] εἰ οὖν ἀνάγκη μέν, εἴπερ ἔστι τι, ἤτοι ἀγένητον ἢ γενόμενον εἶναι, ταῦτα δὲ <ἀδύνατα>, ἀδύνατόν τι καὶ εἶναι.

[13] ἔτι εἴπερ ἔστιν, ἓν ἢ πλείω, φησίν, ἐστίν· εἰ δὲ μήτε ἓν μήτε πολλά, οὐδὲν ἂν εἴη. καὶ ἓν μὲν . . . . καὶ ὅτι ἀσώματον ἂν εἴη τὸ . . . . εν κ . . . . ε ἔχον μέν γε . . . . τῷ τοῦ Ζήνωνος λόγῳ. ἑνὸς δὲ ὄντος οὐδ᾽ ἂν . . . . εἶναι οὐδὲ μη . . . . μήτε πολλὰ . . . . εἰ δὲ μήτε . . . . μήτε πολλά ἐστιν, οὐδὲν ἔστιν.

[14] οὐδ᾽ ἂν κινηθῆναί φησιν οὐδέν· εἰ γὰρ κινηθείη, οὐκ ἂν ἔτι εἴη ὡσαύτως ἔχον, ἀλλὰ τὸ μὲν οὐκ ἂν εἴη, τὸ δ᾽ οὐκ ὂν γεγονὸς εἴη.

---

* Sections 7-8 have been eliminated because they consist of commentary on Gorgias's text rather than a summary of it.

9. After this argument he says this: if it exists, then it is either un-generated or it has come into being. And if, on the one hand, it is un-generated, he accepts that it is boundless by way of Melissus's axioms. Yet that which is boundless would, in no way, be. For it would be neither in itself nor in another. For in this way there would be at least two things, that which is and that in which it is. And nothing can be nowhere, according to Zeno's argument about place.

10. For this reason, then, it cannot be un-generated, but neither can it have come to be. Indeed, nothing at all can come to be, neither from that which is, nor from that which is not. For if that which is undergoes change, it would no longer be that which is, just as if that which is not were to come to be, then it would no longer be that which is not.

11. Nor indeed does it come to be from that which is.* For if that which is not is not, then nothing would come to be from nothing. If, on the other hand, that which is not is, then it would not come to be from that which is not for the same reason that it would not come to be from that which is.

12. And so if it is necessary that, assuming that something exists, it is either un-generated or it has come into being then, these things being impossible, it is also impossible for something to be.

13. Again if it is, he says that it is either one or many. And if it is neither one nor many, then that which is would be nothing. And on the one hand, if it is one [...]. And that which [...] would be bodiless [...] holding indeed [...] by Zeno's argument. And if it that which is is one, it would not [...] to be and not [...] nor many [...] unless [...] nor [is that which is] many, so nothing is.

14. Nor would anything whatsoever be moved. For if it is moved, then it would no longer hold in the same way, but something would not be and something else which is not would come into being.

* The argument that follows, which goes against the possibility that that which is is generated from that which is not, implies that a negative is missing here.

[15] ἔτι δὲ εἰ κινεῖται καὶ εἰ μεταφέρεται οὐ συνεχὲς ὄν, διῄρηται, <ᾗ δὲ διῄρηται> τὸ ὄν, οὐκ ἔστιν ταύτῃ· ὥστ' εἰ πάντῃ κινεῖται, πάντῃ διῄρηται.

[16] εἰ δ' οὕτως, πάντῃ οὐκ ἔστιν. ἐκλιπὲς γὰρ ταύτῃ, φησίν, ᾗ διῄρηται, τοῦ ὄντος, ἀντὶ τοῦ κενοῦ τὸ διῃρῆσθαι λέγων, καθάπερ ἐν τοῖς Λευκίππου καλουμένοις λόγοις γέγραπται.

[17] εἰ μὲν οὖν οὐδέν τὰς ἀποδείξεις λέγειν, ἅπαντα <ἄγνωστα>.[*] δεῖν γὰρ τὰ φρονούμενα εἶναι, καὶ τὸ μὴ ὄν, εἴπερ μή ἐστι, μηδὲ φρονεῖσθαι.

[18] εἰ δ' οὕτως, οὐδὲν ἂν εἶναι ψεῦδός φησιν, οὐδ' εἰ ἐν τῷ πελάγει φαίη ἁμιλλᾶσθαι ἅρματα. πάντα γὰρ ἂν ταῦτα εἴη.

[19] καὶ γὰρ τὰ ὁρώμενα καὶ ἀκουόμενα διὰ τοῦτό ἐστιν, ὅτι φρονεῖται ἕκαστα αὐτῶν· εἰ δὲ μὴ διὰ τοῦτο, ἀλλ' ὥσπερ οὐδὲν μᾶλλον ἃ ὁρῶμεν ἔστιν, οὕτω μᾶλλον ἃ ὁρῶμεν ἢ <ἃ> διανοούμεθα.

[20] καὶ γὰρ ὥσπερ ἐκεῖ πολλοὶ ἂν ταῦτα ἴδοιεν, καὶ ἐνταῦθα πολλοὶ ἂν ταῦτα διανοηθεῖεν. τὸ οὖν μᾶλλον δὴ τοιάδ' ἐστί, ποῖα δὲ τἀληθῆ, ἄδηλον.[†] ὥστε καὶ εἰ ἔστιν, ἡμῖν γε ἄγνωστα εἶναι τὰ πράγματα.

---

[*] This sentence is irretrievably corrupt.

[†] Another corrupt sentence.

15. Again, on the other hand, if it is moved and if carried from place to place, not being continuous, it is divided. And in that place that it is divided, it is not. Thus, if it moves everywhere, it is everywhere divided.

16. And if this is so, then in all places it is not. For, he says, at that point at which it is divided there it is lacking from that which is—he uses "to be divided" instead of "the void," as it is called in the arguments which are called "of Leucippus."

17. Thus, if on the one hand the arguments state that nothing [...] they are all unknown. For he says that it is necessary that things which are thought are, and that which is not, if indeed it is not, cannot be thought.

18. If this is so, then he says that nothing whatsoever is false, not even if one were to speak of chariots racing on the sea. For all such things would be.

19. For both that which is seen and that which is heard are for the same reason, namely that each is thought. And if not for this reason, then just as nothing exists more than that which we see, just so we see [nothing] more than that which we think.*

20. For even just as we severally would see these things there, [just so] we severally would also think these things here.† And so, with regards to that which is more, such are [the facts]; what sort are true, however, is unclear. Thus even if it exists, then things are indeed unknowable to us.

* This sentence is corrupt. The above translation assumes that οὐδὲν is carried over from the other sentence and that the relative pronoun ἅ is misplaced. The amended clause reads "οὕτως (οὐδὲν) μᾶλλον ὁρῶμεν ἢ ἃ διανοούμεθα."

† The manuscript gives ἴδοιεν and διανοηθεῖημεν as verbs, one of which must be amended. It is difficult to make sense of the pairing ἐκεῖ... ἐνταῦθα.... Gorgias may be referring to external visual objects (ἐκεῖ) and internal cognitive objects (ἐνταῦθα).

[21] εἰ δὲ καὶ γνωστά, πῶς ἄν τις, φησί, δηλώσειεν ἄλλῳ; ὃ γὰρ εἶδε, πῶς ἄν τις, φησί, τοῦτο εἴποι λόγῳ; ἢ πῶς ἂν ἐκεῖνο δῆλον ἀκούσαντι γίγνοιτο, μὴ ἰδόντι; ὥσπερ γὰρ οὐδὲ ἡ ὄψις τοὺς φθόγγους γιγνώσκει, οὕτως οὐδὲ ἡ ἀκοὴ τὰ χρώματα ἀκούει, ἀλλὰ φθόγγους· καὶ λέγει ὁ λέγων, ἀλλ' οὐ χρῶμα οὐδὲ πρᾶγμα.

[22] ὃ οὖν τις μὴ ἐννοεῖ, πῶς αἰτεῖ παρ' ἄλλου λόγῳ ἢ σημείῳ τινὶ ἑτέρου πράγματος ἐννοήσει, ἀλλ' ἢ ἐὰν μὲν χρῶμα ἰδών, ἐὰν δὲ <ψόφον ἀκο>ύσας; ἀρχὴν γὰρ οὐ <ψόφον> λέγει <ὁ λέ>γων οὐδὲ χρῶμα, ἀλλὰ λόγον, ὥστ' οὐδὲ διανοεῖσθαι χρῶμα ἔστιν, ἀλλ' ὁρᾶν, οὐδὲ ψόφον, ἀλλ' ἀκούειν.

[23] εἰ δὲ καὶ ἐνδέχεται, γιγνώσκει τε καὶ ἃ ἂν γιγνώσκῃ λέγει, ἀλλὰ πῶς ὁ ἀκούων τὸ αὐτὸ ἐννοήσει; οὐ γὰρ οἷόν τε τὸ αὐτὸ ἅμα ἐν πλείοσι καὶ χωρὶς οὖσιν εἶναι· δύο γὰρ ἂν εἴη τὸ ἕν.

[24] εἰ δὲ καὶ εἴη, φησίν, ἐν πλείοσι καὶ ταὐτόν, οὐδὲν κωλύει μὴ ὅμοιον φαίνεσθαι αὐτοῖς, μὴ πάντῃ ὁμοίοις ἐκείνοις οὖσιν καὶ ἐν τῷ αὐτῷ· εἰ γὰρ ἐν τῷ αὐτῷ εἴη, εἷς ἂν[3] ἀλλ' οὐ δύο εἶεν.

[25] φαίνεται δὲ οὐδ' αὐτὸς αὑτῷ ὅμοια αἰσθανόμενος ἐν τῷ αὐτῷ χρόνῳ, ἀλλ' ἕτερα τῇ ἀκοῇ καὶ τῇ ὄψει, καὶ νῦν τε καὶ πάλαι διαφόρως. ὥστε σχολῇ ἄλλῳ πᾶν <ἂν> ταὐτὸ αἴσθοιτό τις.

[26] οὕτως οὖν <εἰ> ἔστι τι γνωστόν, οὐδεὶς ἂν αὐτὸ ἑτέρῳ δηλώσειεν, διά τε τὸ μὴ εἶναι τὰ πράγματα λόγους, καὶ ὅτι οὐδ' ἕτερος ἑτέρῳ ταὐτὸν ἐννοεῖ.

21. And if they are known, how would one, he says, demonstrate them to another? For how can one speak in words that which one sees? Or how would this become clear to one listening, if they have not seen? For just as sight does not recognize sound, so does hearing not hear color, but sound. And the one who speaks does not utter colour, nor things.

22. Thus, how could anyone who has not conceived something, ask for it from another person in speech? And [how could anyone] conceive it by means of some word or symbol, when the thing itself is something different? [How could they] except by seeing, if a color, or by hearing, if a noise. For to begin with, he who speaks does not utter noises or colors, but words. Thus, there is no conceiving of color except by seeing, nor of any sound, except by hearing.

23. And even if it is possible, and the person knows and speaks whatever he would know, how could he who hears conceive the very same thing? For it is not possible for the same thing, at the same time, to be in different [places] which are separate. For that which is would be two.

24. And even if the very same thing were to be in many places, nonetheless nothing prevents it from appearing differently to them, if they themselves are not exactly alike and in the same place; for if it were in the same place, it would be one and not two.

25. But it is clear that a person does not perceive the same things as themselves at the same time but by hearing differently than by sight, and also different now than at a previous time. Thus, one would hardly perceive anything identically to someone else.

26. Just so, then, if there were something which is known, none would show it to another, on account of the fact that things are not words, and because none can conceive the same thing as another.

Essays

Livio Rossetti[1]

Provocative Ideas in the Writings of Gorgias[2]

The Crucial Eighties of the 20th Century

Let me begin by mentioning a book, *The Sophistic Movement*, by the late George Kerferd.[3] Kerferd, who was considered the highest authority in the world on the Sophists at the time, dared to acknowledge, with commendable intellectual honesty, that "the interpretation of what Gorgias is saying is difficult, and we are certainly not yet even in sight of an agreed understanding of its overall significance, let alone its detailed arguments."[4] His admission is impressive since it acknowledged that in 1981 Gorgias's ideas were still a riddle to the scholarly community—and a riddle left aside. But Kerferd's book appeared just after *Si Parménide* by Barbara Cassin,[5] and just before the enlightening *Gorgia ontologo e metafisico* by Giuseppe Mazzara,[6] the valuable booklet on the *Helen* by Douglas MacDowell,[7] as well as several important journal articles. What is more, an international conference devoted to the ancient Sophists took place in Athens in 1982; another devoted entirely to *Gorgia e la*

---

[1] Livio Rossetti served as professor of ancient Greek philosophy at the University of Perugia in Italy until 2009. He founded the *International Plato Society* in 1989 and the *Eleatica* conferences on Prescoratic philosophy in 2004. Among his many books and articles on ancient Greek philosophy, the most recent is *Thales the Measurer* (Routledge 2022) while the provisional title of his next book is *Rethinking the Presocratics*.

[2] I am heavily indebted to Heather Reid and Shane Ewegen for the fine-tuning of these pages. Let me also remember how much I enjoyed participating in the conference at Exedra Mediterranean Center in Siracusa, thanks to Heather Reid, Susi Kimbell, and Sergio Cilea.

[3] George B. Kerferd, *The Sophistic Movement* (Cambridge: Cambridge University Press, 1981).

[4] Kerferd, *Sophistic Movement*, 93.

[5] Barbara Cassin, *Si Parménide. Le traité anonyme "De Melisso Xenophane Gorgia"* (Lille: Presses Universitaires de Lille, 1980).

[6] Giuseppe Mazzara, *Gorgia ontologo e metafisico* (Palermo: ILA Palma, 1982).

[7] Douglas Maurice MacDowell, *Gorgias: Encomium of Helen* (Bristol: Classical Press, 1982).

Sofistica took place in Catania and Lentini (ancient *Leontinoi*) in 1983; and a third, entitled *Qu'est-ce que la sophistique?*, took place in Cérisy, France in 1984.

Three books, three international conferences (while no previous conference on these topics is known to have taken place), and some substantial articles (by Giovanni Casertano and John Poulakos, among others)[8] proved able to profoundly affect the understanding of Gorgias's writings, caused an impressive acceleration of research, and opened the avenue to a comprehensive rethinking of his work, which has recently taken some important further steps. In light of all of this, scholarship prior to 1980 may be seen as "prehistory" to the serious effort to say who Gorgias was, and to evaluate the merit of his ideas, whatever his official profession.

As for the "prehistoric" Gorgias, let me begin by reporting that philologists of the 19th century claimed several times that his *Helen* and *Palamedes* were inauthentic or, at least, of dubious authenticity. Specialists in ancient Greek philosophy were (and often remain) under the influence of Plato, and therefore harbored tenacious prejudices (and a basic distrust) when looking at the Sophists—though Hegel made a crucial step in the opposite direction by arguing that Socrates (and Plato and Aristotle) were inconceivable without the "antithesis" provided by their predecessors. Toward the end of the 19th century, George Grote did his best to take the Sophists seriously, but fundamental change occurred only when Hermann Diels entered the Sophists into his masterwork, *Die Fragmente der Vorsokratiker*, the first edition of which appeared in 1903. Since then, and because of this work, it became almost impossible to exclude the Sophists from the history of philosophy.

Consequently, during the 20th century an increasing number of scholars made a serious effort to rehabilitate the Sophists (Gorgias

---

8 Giovanni Casertano, "L'amour entre logos et pathos. Quelques considérations sur l'Hélène de Gorgias," in *Positions de la Sophistique*, ed. B. Cassin (Paris: Vrin, 1986), 211-20; John Poulakos, "Gorgias's *Encomium of Helen* and the Defence of Rhetoric," *Rhetorica* 1 (1983): 1-16. Stefania Giombini, *Gorgia epidittico* (Passignano sul Trasimeno: Aguaplano, 2012), ch. 1, gives a detailed survey of the scholarly research on Gorgias.

included) "against" Plato's view, while Renzo Vitali made a very promising attempt with *Gorgia Retorica e filosofia*[9] to explain how rhetoric and philosophy interacted in Gorgias's writings. Vitali was able to single out two different evocations of the principle of non-contradiction, one in the *Palamedes* and another in *On Not-Being*. Nevertheless, in his monumental *History of Greek Philosophy*, W.K.C. Guthrie still assumed that Gorgias was essentially a rhetorician and ascribed to him a "Protagorean relativism."[10] In 1983, Poulakos still claimed that Gorgias's *Helen* was meant to be a solemn encomium of rhetoric; and in 1986 Gualtiero Calboli continued to see in Gorgias's writings only rhetorical *figurae*.[11] On the other hand, Kerferd and Mazzara concentrated their attention on Gorgias the philosopher, leaving aside his role as master of communication, as if they were dealing with a two-faced Gorgias in which each face was entitled to ignore the other.[12] Once a sort of "gentle revolution" had started,[13] however, a number of new ideas began to be launched, and it is now clear that the forty years since then have not passed in vain.

---

[9] Renzo Vitali, *Gorgia. Retorica e filosofia* (Urbino: Argalia, 1971).

[10] W.K.C. Guthrie, *A History of Greek Philosophy, Volume 3: The Fifth Century Enlightenment* (Cambridge: Cambridge University Press, 1971).

[11] Poulakos, "Gorgias's *Encomium*;" G. Calboli, "Nota di aggiornamento," in *La prosa d'arte antica dal VI secolo a.C. all'età della Rinascenza*, ed. E. Norden (Roma: Salerno, 1986, 969-1183).

[12] Giuseppe Mazzara, "Unità metodologica e concettuale nel *Peri tou me ontos* e nelle opere epidittiche *Elena* e *Palamede*," *Siculorum Gymnasium* 38 (1985): 171-205 is considerably more comprehensive than his 1982 book *Gorgia ontologo e metafisico*. In general, the dichotomy "philosophers or rhetoricians" has affected scholarly interpreters from Plato's time, all the way through the 20th century, with very few of them considering orators to be (often bad) philosophers. In my experience, only Vitali and Mazzara have considered both sides of this distinction with the necessary care.

[13] It is worth noting that no spectacular event (e.g., the discovery of a new papyrus, or previously unknown source) caused this substantial change in perspective. It seems rather as if it was only a matter of mental concentration and identifying and employing appropriate categories.

New Ideas on the *Palamedes*

Let me begin with the *Palamedes*. A new sort of beginning occurred with the paper read by Anthony Long at the Athenian conference in 1982.[14] Crucial further steps occurred with a paper by Alonso Tordesillas[15] and a master's dissertation on the *Palamedes* by Francesca Francesconi.[16] Tordesillas concentrated on Palamedes's double claim that "I would not have been able to betray the Greeks even if I had the intention to do so" (§6) and that "I could not have wanted to betray them even if I had had the opportunity to do so" (§13). With the unexpected help of notions borrowed from electrotechnics, Tordesillas labelled the first set of reasons as "a parallel connection," and the second as "a serial connection."[17] In this way, the arrangement of what would need to have happened (pre-conditions, opportunities, hindrances, behaviors) in order to yield the supposed betrayal, and the subjective conditions deemed strictly necessary in order to want to mount it, becomes much more understandable, and the force of the argument becomes apparent.

Indeed, according to his first claim, Gorgias's Palamedes considers one-by-one a number of indispensable conditions and argues that none of them could occur (nor in fact did occur). Then, as his second claim, he surveys the subjective conditions related to his position as a Greek *basileus* to conclude that none occurred. In this way, he first turns off the light from each bulb, and then the entire set, to show that no betrayal could have occurred. Based on these premises, Palamedes can conclude that Odysseus's accusation bears the mark of incompetence (i.e., he failed to consider all that has been

---

[14] Anthony Long, "Methods of Argument in Gorgias's *Palamedes*," in *The Sophistic Movement*, ed. K. Boudouris (Athens: IAGP, 1984), 233-41.

[15] Alonso Tordesillas, "Palamèdes contre toutes raisons," in *La naissance de la raison en Grèce*, ed. J.-F. Mattéi (Paris: Presses Universitaires de France, 1990), 241-55. The paper had circulated since 1987.

[16] Francesca Francesconi, *Tra speculazione e oratoria. Un commento al* Palamede *di Gorgia* (MA Thesis, University of Perugia, 1990).

[17] We have a "parallel connection" when a set of bulbs can continue to work even if one or two of them burned out, and a "serial connection" when either all of them work correctly or the whole set goes out. Despite its creativity, little has been written on this *amarturos logos*.

analytically examined in the speech)[18] and, furthermore, that he (Palamedes) was portrayed (by Odysseus) as being simultaneously cunning (because involved in a sophisticated attempt to betray) and also stupid, if not insane (since he would have acted to his own detriment), which is manifestly impossible, these claims being patently contradictory (§25).[19] Therefore, Odysseus cannot be reliable in his accusation.

This is a model, quite unparalleled, of how to get around the difficulty of providing direct evidence to establish a fact. It consciously relies on the sole force of reasoning without any support from eyewitnesses. The *Palamedes* is a dizzying *amarturos logos* —one of the best *logoi amarturoi* among those written in the second half of the 5th century BCE—in which reasons are capable of convincing despite the supposed absence of "objective" proof.[20] It is an epideictic speech where each element shows an uncommon degree of functionality from the point of view of its overall (architectonic) project. Precisely because of the high level of functionality of each part, a truly argumentative vertigo is attained, and it is easy to grasp how demanding it must have been to reach excellence in these conditions.

There would be more to say about the *Palamedes*, but the point made so far is crucial, since its supreme mastery had escaped attention until a few decades ago.

New Ideas on the *Encomium of Helen*

As for the *Helen*, what I notice first is how difficult it has been to capture its main point. Scholars enjoyed debating Gorgias's ideas on truth, "poetical truth," poetry and prose, love and seduction,

---

[18] On the refined legal culture at work in Gorgias's *Palamedes,* see Giombini, *Gorgia epidittico.*

[19] An implicit assumption of this argument is that if you say I am simultaneously cunning and stupid, it is rather your mental sanity to be doubted. The implicit inference amounts to a powerful rhetorical (and juridical) argument.

[20] Despite its fascination, little has been written on the *amarturos logos*. See Livio Rossetti, "Il logos amarturos," *Journal of Classical Studies of Matica Srpska* 14 (2012): 49-72, and Giombini, *Gorgia epidittico*, 222-24.

pleasure and persuasion, play and game (*paignion*), *kairos*, his *gorgiazein*, his theories of speech and use of definition.[21] This *Helen* is, indeed, a surprisingly rich whole, and other points of detail, such as his use of the notion of *pharmakon*, are no doubt entitled to attract attention. But is there a governing idea in the *Helen*? In principle, one should first examine something of the sort and only then consider a number of "minor" points.

Indeed, there is a leading idea. Consider the systematic attention paid to the limits of the will (and therefore also to the limits of freedom and responsibility), i.e., to the ways one's behavior may be conditioned—and Helen's behavior is said to have actually been conditioned in her decision to leave Sparta for Troy. The whole *Encomium* deals with this topic, and nobody else before or after Gorgias is known to have dealt with the limits of the will with comparable systematicity. Moreover, there are clues that encourage us to treat the work as a disguised treatise on the limits of the human will. Consider, for example, how the *Helen* begins and ends. After some preliminaries, we read in §6:

> For it was either [*1a*] by the designs of Fortune, [*1b*] the plans of the gods, and [*1c*] the decrees of Necessity that she

[21] On these topics, see e.g., Jaume Pórtulas, "Lode poetica ed encomio sofistico: la verità di Pindaro e quella di Gorgia," *Lexis* 8 (1991): 99-112; Barbara Cassin, "Encore Hélène: une sophistique de la jouissance," *Littoral* 15-16 (1985): 161-76; Marie-Pierre Noël, "La persuasion et le sacré chez Gorgias," *Bulletin de l'Assoc. Guillaume Budé* (1989): 149-51; id. "L'enfance de l'art. Plaisir et jeu chez Gorgias," *Bulletin de l'Assoc. Guillaume Budé* (1994): 71-93; id. "Gorgias et l'invention des *gorgieia schemata*," *Revue des Etudes Grecques* 112 (1999): 193-211; Casertano, "L'amour;" P. Mureddu, "La parola che 'incanta': nota all'*Elena* di Gorgia," *Sileno* 17 (1991): 249-58; James I. Porter, "The Seductions of Gorgias," *Classical Antiquity* 12.2 (1993): 267-99; Giuseppe Tortora, "Il senso del kairos in Gorgia," in *Siculorum Gymnasium* 38 (1985): 537-64; Calboli, "Nota;" and MacDowell, *Encomium*; R. Velardi, "Parola poetica e canto magico nella teoria gorgiana del discorso," in *Tradizione e innovazione nella cultura greca da Omero all'età ellenistica,* ed. R. Pretagostini (Roma: Gruppo Editore Internazionale, 1993), 813-26.

> did what she did, or [2] because she was seized by force, or [3] persuaded by words, or [4] overcome by love.
>
> ἢ γὰρ Τύχης βουλήμασι καὶ θεῶν βουλεύμασι καὶ Ἀνάγκης ψηφίσμασιν ἔπραξεν ἃ ἔπραξεν, ἢ βίαι ἁρπασθεῖσα, ἢ λόγοις πεισθεῖσα, <ἢ ἔρωτος ἡττηθεῖσα>.[22]

In §20 (i.e., towards the conclusion) we read:

> How then ought one consider the blame for Helen as being just, given that, if she did what she did because [*1*] she had fallen in love or [2] had been persuaded by speech or [*3*] had been seized with force or [*4*] had been constrained by divine constraint, on every count she is acquitted of the accusation?
>
> πῶς οὖν χρὴ δίκαιον ἡγήσασθαι τὸν τῆς Ἑλένης μῶμον, ἥτις εἴτ' ἐρασθεῖσα εἴτε λόγωι πεισθεῖσα εἴτε βίαι ἁρπασθεῖσα εἴτε ὑπὸ θείας ἀνάγκης ἀναγκασθεῖσα ἔπραξεν ἃ ἔπραξε, πάντως διαφεύγει τὴν αἰτίαν;

Gorgias quite clearly lists four possible sorts of conditions that may have affected Helen and can affect everybody else. He does not say openly that the story of Helen is a sort of paradigm suitable to be generalized. He just gives his list in a certain order at the beginning, and in the reverse order at the end, while devoting the body of his speech to each of the four possible conditions in an orderly fashion, i.e., *as if it were* a treatise on the limits of the will.

Besides, Gorgias lived in a society where it was common to claim the involuntariness of criminal behavior. It is enough to browse the texts of the Greek orators to see how often they claim that their clients were momentarily blinded by a god, or at least by an overwhelming emotion, and therefore cannot bear responsibility for what they did in those conditions. These speeches do not even try to explain why one did what he did in such a state.

---

[22] Text and translation are from André Laks and Glenn W. Most, *Early Greek Philosophy, Volume VIII: Sophists Part 1* (Cambridge, MA: Harvard University Press, 2016), 170.

A further point is that from Homer to Aristotle a number of texts openly invite the audience to see in such appeals to non-governable contributing causes not facts but, rather, unreliable excuses and unmistakable forms of opportunism. This occurs on the very first page of the *Odyssey* (verses 32ff.) when Zeus opens the council of the gods and complains that too often men attribute the responsibility for their faults to them. The same kind of remarks surface, for example, in Democritus's fragment 19 DK ("Men devised the phantom of fortune in order to mask their recklessness"), Aristophanes's *Clouds* 1080 ("then you can put the blame on Zeus"), Euripides's *Iphigenia in Tauris* 389 ("they are murderers, nevertheless they shift their guilt on divinity"), Euripides's *Trojan Women* in two interconnected passages: 948 ("blame the goddess as well") and 982ff. ("don't tell me goddesses are stupid for the sole purpose of embellishing your misdeeds!"), Sophocles's *Philoctetes* 991 ("Are you making up that gods are liars?"), and Aristotle's *Nicomachean Ethics* 3.1, 1111a27-9 ("Isn't it laughable to say that we do noble acts voluntarily and base acts involuntarily?"). These sample references show that in Gorgias's time denials of responsibility were common practice but, at the same time, raised serious suspicions of bad faith. So, for Gorgias it was far from impossible to offer an ordered survey of all these denials, not without adding, for his part, a smile.[23]

On the other hand, a step Gorgias did not even try to make is the connection between female beauty, men falling in love, and speeches aimed at attracting the attention of a girl or woman. On so topical a connection Gorgias has nothing to say, and this offers additional (though perhaps not decisive) evidence for the prevailing attitude of outlining a survey of the circumstances suitable to condition one's will. It is therefore likely that the *Helen* remained for a long time unique in the field. Its character as a disguised treatise on the will

[23] What I here label "a smile" (to account for both the word *enkomion* in the title, and the final reference to *paignion*) may open the avenue to a meaningful inference: that the *Helen* does not outline what Gorgias believed, i.e., that he was considering only some parts of the whole issue, some sides of the polygon "will-responsibility-conditioning." Indeed, in the *Helen*, suspicion of bad faith is never considered.

becomes apparent at the same time as its intrinsic importance as a unique treatise.

It follows that the very core of the *Helen*, its true nature, went unnoticed for a while. As a matter of fact, every other feature of this writing should be downgraded to a mere ingredient of a more comprehensive whole. But when did the idea that the *Helen* might be a disguised treatise on the will begin to be considered? As far as I know, only in Giombini, *Gorgia epidittico* 113ff., due attention was paid to the *tractatio* as a salient feature of the speech. Are there serious alternatives, however, to acknowledging that in the *Helen* Gorgias wrote, in a slightly camouflaged form, the very first treatise *de servo arbitrio*[24] of western civilization?

New Ideas on *On Not Being*

A third writing by Gorgias has even greater ambitions. It is the work known as the *PTMO*, i.e., the *Peri tou mē ontos ē peri physeōs* (*On Not Being, or On Nature*). It failed to come down to us, but good luck preserved two detailed and surprisingly competent summaries, one anonymous (wrongly included in the *Corpus Aristotelicum*), the other due to Sextus Empiricus—both largely complementary,[25] and both available in current collections of Gorgianic texts. As a consequence, we can rely on them to form a definite idea of what cannot be properly read. Gorgias's argument is notoriously governed by the following series of claims:

> nothing exists; but supposing that my argument fails, you will concede at least this, that nothing of what exists can be known; and supposing that even my second claim will be taken for unconvincing, you will acknowledge at least

---

[24] Martin Luther's treatise bearing this title is a work of 1525. Let me add that here Gorgias is satisfied to offer a survey of reasons in support of weakness of will, while saying nothing in support of a stronger ego, able to resist several kinds of pressure, nor on the identity of what is expected to resist. See also my tentative conclusion below.

[25] On these texts, see Giombini, *Gorgia epidittico.* and L. Rossetti, "Trilemmi: il *PTMO* di Gorgia tra Zenone e Melisso," *Peitho. Examina Antiqua* 6, (2017): 155-72.

> this, that nothing of what exists and is known can be communicated.[26]

An *implicit cauda* is as follows:

> Now let us suppose you will concede my third claim. Well, because of that, you should be prepared to reconsider my second claim too and, as a consequence, my first claim too, that nothing exists.[27]

Clearly, what Gorgias mounted was an extremely ambitious *tour de force*. Just consider: "nothing exists," "nothing can be known," "nothing can be communicated." One is tempted to continue with Leibniz (who lived a little more than two thousand years later): "Each of us is a Monad, totally closed in on itself." If we are totally closed in ourselves, how could we know something that is totally exterior, other, not part of us?

A couple of further remarks may be in order. Gorgias's primary claim, that nothing exists, is clearly meant as a destruction of the Parmenidean "orthodoxy" on being (established, *de facto*, by Melissus). But what does it mean? That "for the reasons to be given, neither I, nor you, nor whatever other thing does exist." Despite its attractiveness, this clearly is the most untenable of all statements, since it is affected by a patent pragmatic contradiction: I am telling you something about us, and there are signs that you are understanding me, therefore how could I, or you, be nonexistent? Gorgias was hardly unaware of this potential contradiction, but he probably enjoyed leaving to each hearer or reader the opportunity of discovering this (self-destructive) implication for him- or herself. Clearly, it could escape one's attention, but hopefully not everyone's attention.

An almost unilateral admiration for Parmenides as the father of metaphysics spanned the millennia and met unexpected prosperity

---

[26] This translation is my own free paraphrase of Sextus Empiricus, *Adv. Math.* VII 65 (88B3 DK).

[27] For an expanded version of these remarks, see Livio Rossetti, "Lo scambio simpliciter/secundum quid nel *Peri tou me ontos*," in *Siculorum Gymnasium* 38 (1985): 107-18.

thanks to Heidegger, Sartre, and many other scholars (notably the late Gwilym Owen)[28] during the 20th century. This occurred without the least suspicion of how penetrating Gorgias's objections were to Parmenides's basic assumption, that nonbeing cannot exist. Indeed, who could deny at least this, that nonbeing is a well-identified notion? But there is a problem, raised for the first time by Gorgias. He insisted that nonbeing can only be nonexistent and, at the same time, existent. As such, a contradiction surfaces since it cannot both be nothing and, at the same time, something.

Let me expand this point a little. Gorgias seems to have clearly claimed that although nonbeing does not exist by definition, as its name shows, it is a notion known to us, and many among us have a definite idea of it no matter how different our opinions about it may be (indeed there is wide discussion about it, with sustained arguments, speeches, disagreements). The existence of nonbeing has something in common with the existence of centaurs, cyclopes, sphinxes, etc., namely that each is often the subject of definite tales, despite their ascertainable nonexistence as physical objects. Because it is a matter we sometimes talk about, it does exist as the unmistakable subject of many talks, arguments, and comments—enough to establish itself as something quite definite—to the point that in encyclopedias there are entries on it.

The latter point evokes what in our times is known as "noetic existence," i.e., what we identify only mentally, and nevertheless this is enough in order to speak about them in pertinent ways. The idea of noetic existence was a creation of Alexius Meinong in his *Gegenstandstheorie* (theory of objects) of 1904. According to Meinong, the set of existing objects includes a great variety of merely mental objects, not only the monsters of Greek and non-Greek mythologies, but also the square circle, Odysseus, and everything that materializes only if and when it is evoked or portrayed one way or another by one or more humans. This illustrates how far forward Gorgias was able to look (and see). Students of Meinong should not ignore what occurred little more than 2,400 years before his *Gegenstandtheorie*.

---

[28] Gwilym Ellis Lane Owen, "Eleatic Questions," *Classical Quarterly* 10 (1960): 84-102.

Moreover, when claiming that nonbeing is totally nonexistent (and therefore being enjoys universality from various points of view), Parmenides dared to assume that such a "rational" discipline was entitled to prevail not only over language, but also over what exists or does not exist (or, what is entitled to exist and what is not). So, his doctrine of being operated as a powerful ontological argument. But is it able to resist Gorgias's remarks on the "noetic existence" of what in a sense is not? Unless I am seriously wrong, these remarks of his have the power to literally crack the force of the most basic Parmenidean assumption. But they passed unnoticed until our time, nobody acknowledged their force, and such widely shared unawareness greatly contributed to the "universal" prestige of Parmenides as well as of every expansion of his claims.

Enough for the first point made in the *PTMO*. Now, let us postpone discussing Gorgias's second claim and concentrate on the third one: that no communication between two people is possible. In order to convince us that this claim is tenable and, perhaps, unobjectionable, Gorgias submits that he entertains a communication with us where we understand him, and possibly acknowledge the force of his argument, although the content of this communication is that we are not communicating at all, since (this is his claim) no communication is possible. Why on earth? Because, Gorgias suggests, we pretend to share thoughts by means of audible words, and at the most words can give a rough idea of our thoughts, i.e., a structurally unfaithful rendering.

To say that he enters a contradiction here would be too much, but it is difficult not to acknowledge that spoken or written words, not unlike pictures, video clips, etc., can only offer approximations of what one has in mind and wants to communicate. There is always a gap between what one wants to say and what one actually says. Even when we admire the quality and effectiveness of a certain piece of communication, it is easy to see what has been simplified, passed over, or only approximately well done. Gorgias, without being a sceptic, was able to make a strong case for this.

Indeed, according to Gorgias's second claim, our perception of what we see, hear, taste or otherwise understand reflects real states of affairs only approximately, if not in distorted ways. One could add, for instance, how easily it happens that one thing passes unnoticed, while another detail acquires undeserved prominence. By now, such issues are widely recognized, but ancient, medieval, and modern philosophy found it difficult to acknowledge them. Besides, Gorgias hardly had the idea of philosophy in the Platonizing way it has been commonly shared for centuries, and still is in our times. Moreover, nobody took what Gorgias said (or what is known of certain writings of his) seriously for whole millennia. Nevertheless, his perspicacity was unique, and it is probably time to offer unto Caesar what belongs to Caesar.

Judging from the summaries still available, another important feature of the *PTMO* is its provocative attitude. Indeed, it is hardly conceivable that Gorgias could seriously believe that nothing exists, no knowledge is possible, and no communication either. He seems rather to behave as a playwright (or director) who stays behind the scenes during the spectacle: he just launches some suggestions meant to leave us perplexed and, possibly, unable to find immediately the key to a better understanding. His goal is to let us continue to think about what is true and what is false in his claims without giving his own advice. Indeed, he seems to want to put us in a position where we are unable to understand what he really thinks of the three fundamental statements. His own opinion remains concealed.

This should come as no surprise, since several enlightened contemporaries of Gorgias (not only the so-called sophists, but also Thucydides, for example) enjoyed writing antilogies (couples of speeches where every speaker seems to be right) and theaters enjoyed portraying dramatic *agōnes* (verbal competitions) where everyone equally seems to be right. Properly speaking, *PTMO* is not an antilogy, but only because nobody is there to claim the opposite. However, one should consider that both the *Helen* and the *Palamedes* suppose another speech where somebody argues that Helen is to be blamed for what she did, or Odysseus claims that Palamedes is clearly guilty of high treason. Likewise, the *PTMO* clearly supposes that "everybody" is prepared to argue that something does certainly exist, that we normally know a lot, and also that, generally speaking, we don't meet serious obstacles in our efforts to enact a rather efficient communication. This means that it would be out of place to try to identify Gorgias's personal beliefs among the set of main claims made in the *PTMO* (or in the *Helen* or *Palamedes*). None of these texts gives us his tenets. Likewise, from the great tragedies of Gorgias's time one can tentatively extract some hints about the poets' personal opinions, but not from the verses devoted to this or that dramatic *agōn*.

Moreover...

At least two further sentences by Gorgias were preserved but left without context. They too deserve our attention. Fragment 26 DK is markedly "philosophical" in character. Here we read that

> being is without evidence if it does not encounter appearing, and appearing is without force if it does not encounter being.
>
> τὸ μὲν εἶναι ἀφανὲς μὴ τυχὸν τοῦ δοκεῖν, τὸ δὲ δοκεῖν ἀσθενὲς μὴ τυχὸν τοῦ εἶναι.[29]

The lack of a context leaves us in the dark; however, this sentence could pertain to the *PTMO*, possibly as a corollary of one of its main claims. Gorgias seems to be saying that, if we are left with mere appearances, we can at least add some force to them with the help of what may pass for a being.

Analogous conjectures can be made with reference to fragment 32 DK, a rather well-known sentence dealing with tragedy. Tragedy, Gorgias is told to have said, enacts

> … a deception in which the one who deceives is more just than the one who does not deceive, and the one who is deceived is more intelligent than the one who is not deceived.

[29] Text and translation from Laks and Most, *Early Greek Philosophy Volume VIII: Sophists Part 1*, 250ff.

> ἀπάτην ... ἣν ὅ τ' ἀπατήσας δικαιότερος τοῦ μὴ ἀπατήσαντος καὶ ὁ ἀπατηθεὶς σοφώτερος τοῦ μὴ ἀπατηθέντος.[30]

Its primary meaning is immediate. The fascination of drama is a sort of noble *apatē*, a play of imagination that is a form of excellence in which author, choir, and actors together get their spectators to figure out a certain situation while spectators let themselves be influenced by the show. Nothing of the sort would happen if choir, actors, and players, as well as spectators, weren't all willing to encourage rather than discourage the play of imagination. So, to say that the author, actors, etc., are "more just" when they do their best to create a theatrical suggestion (in a sense, when they try to deceive) should be a way of pointing out that they certainly do not incur blame for that. In the same spirit, spectators are said to be "intelligent" if and when they accept what the spectacle is trying to evoke and, for a while, allow their sense of reality cede to imagination, i.e., they allow themselves to be "deceived" since to do the contrary would be silly (if not stupid).

In this way Gorgias creatively draws our attention to the cooperative attitudes thanks to which a play can be successful and meaningful. Although in his time, and certainly not only in Athens, thousands of people went many times to the theatre, nobody before or after Gorgias is known to have captured so perspicaciously the "secret" of theatrical events. This passage, too, *could* pertain to the *PTMO* as a marginal corollary since, again, we have to deal with appearances, not reality. For this reason, it is at least possible that Gorgias evoked deception and appearance to attach some value to them, at least in the context of the theatrical practices of contemporary Athens. But it is not so important to establish this particular connection. Besides, were it confirmed, we should perhaps stop seeing in the *PTMO* a sort of antilogy.

Another relevant feature of this passage is the sort of society it evokes, one where communication is central, as in ours today, and where spectators are encouraged to experience intensely what

[30] Text and translation from Laks and Most, *Early Greek Philosophy Volume VIII: Sophists Part 1*, 250ff.

happens on the stage. That such a shared attitude could be identified and commented on in those times is impressive. No other mind could have conceived it over twenty-four centuries ago! And there must be more: we are basically unable to identify other writings by Gorgias. Therefore, we cannot know whether the writings we have, at least in part, were his best work or not.

Towards a Conclusion

As I stated previously, Gorgias showed no hurry (and thus no need) to establish a doctrine of his own. Rather, he did his best to ensure that his ideas were creative and stimulating, while remaining uninterested in the possibility that this or that claim would be taken as a reliable portrayal of his beliefs. Therefore, despite their attractiveness, his explicit claims should not be taken at face value. He did not pretend to persuade us of Helen's or Palamedes's innocence, nor of the impossibility of communication or knowledge, nor (to a greater degree) of a supposed universal nonexistence. In the main texts available to us we discover a great mind doing his best to persuade us *"only" of patently false claims*, looking forward to see how we react, what we begin to think and counter-argue, what we discover thanks to his very sustained intellectual provocations.

This is, at the same time, a very high evaluation of Gorgias as an intellectual and an equally high evaluation of him as a genial master of communication, for he did his best to inculcate the misleading idea that he was really seriously convinced that Helen fell victim to the circumstances (and the gods), that Palamedes was completely innocent, and so on. But why on earth should he have unilaterally sided with Helen or Palamedes? His *Helen*, in addition to being a disguised treatise (a sort of *de servo arbitrio*), does not consider in any detail what she did or failed to do; his *Palamedes*, in addition to being a superb *logos amarturos*, does not discuss any of the arguments Odysseus is supposed to have adduced. But a real examination of Helen's and Palamedes's behavior would have requested, no doubt, much more comprehensive discussions.

And now a note on Gorgias and Zeno of Elea. The point is probably unknown in the scholarly literature, but consider this: Zeno is known for having done his best to claim that Achilles will never reach the tortoise, that a runner will never be able to begin his run, that the flying arrow is actually standing still and so on, and he too expected to encounter some smart people wanting to do their best to untie his knots and dissolve his arguments, and finally claim that in reality Achilles is perfectly able to reach a tortoise and so on. Gorgias, too, adopted an antiphrastic mood and expected us to be careful to avoid taking his claims at face value. He also did his best to put people in serious trouble, and was seemingly satisfied. Zeno is sometimes labelled "a philosopher without a philosophy." Should we label Gorgias this way too? The word "philosopher: is misleading, since it was a neologism coined by Plato, and the question goes well beyond names. It seems that Gorgias was tremendous in his subtle intellectual provocations, and if he wanted his personal opinions to remain hidden, he was totally successful. But he was a great virtual philosopher who launched ideas worth being explored in depth: freedom of the will, noetic existence, notions of being and nonbeing, gnoseology, theory of communication, and contradiction—to mention a few being studied in depth even now. It is not by chance that these topics are listed in every philosophical encyclopedia.

At the same time, Gorgias made us progressively aware of the infinitely small intricacies of language, but we cannot say exactly what ends are served by the doubtful innocence of Helen and Palamedes, the impossibility of communication, the impossibility of knowledge, and a supposed universal nonexistence. I dare to conclude that in comparison with Zeno, the Gorgianic riddles are much more insidious. And this means that he had a superb command of communication strategies as well as of a number of detailed precautions meant to reinforce what his speeches suggest. We note excellence in each of his communication projects as well as in the refinement of each passage. From this point of view, it is of little help to mention his celebrated "*gorgiazein,*" since this term captures only some exterior features (balance and opposition) of his way of structuring sentences.

All in all, it is not easy to account for what was devised and put into writing by Gorgias. His mind went in many directions, and each time it travelled very far, but how much of that is acknowledged in current accounts of Gorgias's work? So far as I know, his superior creativity has yet to be accounted for, and I myself have written papers where I tried in vain to do so.[31] So, my final conclusion can only be that there probably is still a lot to discover about this Sicilian thinker and writer.[32]

---

[31] Rossetti, "Lo scambio," 18; Rossetti, "Trilemmi."

[32] Additional sources that I did not cite directly include: F. Donadi, ed., *Gorgias: Helenae encomium. Petrus Bembus: Gorgiae Leontini in Helenam laudatio* (Berlin: De Gruyter, 2016); S. Giombini, "Why Sextus? The *Pros logikous* as Reliable Source for Gorgias's *Peri tou me ontos*," *Studia Philosophica Wratislaviensia* 14 (2019): 83-96; S. Giombini, "Il processo come pretesto. Sul *Palamede* di Gorgia," *Archive of history, philosophy and social thought* 65 (2020): 143-56; R. Joli, *Gorgia. Testimonianze e frammenti* (Ropa: Carocci, 2013); G. Mazzara, "Gorgia. Origine e struttura materiale della parola," *L'Antiquité classique* 52 (1983): 130-40; G. Mazzara, *Gorgia. La retorica del verosimile* (Sankt Augustin: Academia, 1999); J. Schollmeyer, *Gorgias' "Lobrede auf Helena," Literatur-geschichtliche Untersuchungen und Kommentar. Untersuchungen zur antiken Literatur und Geschichte* (Berlin: De Gruyter, 2020).

François Renaud[1]

Defining Poetry, Defending Prose: Gorgias's *Encomium of Helen* §9 and Its Reception

Gorgias is generally regarded today as the first theoretician of artistic prose in a period when poetry was far more prestigious. His theory of prose in connection with his definition of poetry is usually neglected in studies of his theory of language, despite the notable influence it exerted on Plato, Aristotle, and the rhetorical tradition, including his student Isocrates.

In the *Encomium of Helen* (§9), Gorgias characterizes all poetry as speech with meter (τὴν ποίησιν ἅπασαν καὶ νομίζω καὶ ὀνομάζω λόγον ἔχοντα μέτρον). Many of the difficulties involved in interpreting this definition, and other statements surrounding it, are related to implications that Gorgias does not explicitly draw. He describes both the power of poetical speech and the similar power of speech (*logos*) as though he was arguing that the emotional power of oratory on the soul (fear, pity, longing, etc.) is equal in power to that of poetic speech. Indeed, he subsumes poetic speech under the larger category of *logos*. Does this imply a rivalry between prose and poetry? Other difficulties include the meaning of the word "meter" (*metron*) as employed here and its relationship with poetry (*poiēsis*). Is meter a mere external ornament? If so, does this underlying conception of speech do full justice to poetry's specificity? Where does the originality of Gorgias's definition lie? More generally, why is the rapprochement between poetry and prose of historical and philosophical importance?

In what follows I will first sketch the larger historical question concerning the transition from poetry to prose, then discuss Gorgias's definition of poetry, after which I will turn to its reception: first in Plato, then Aristotle, then in Gorgias's student Isocrates. In the following section I will argue that Gorgias's definition of poetry

[1] François Renaud is Professor of Philosophy at the Université de Moncton, Canada. His publications include *The Platonic Alcibiades I: The Dialogue and Its Ancient Reception*, co-authored with Harold Tarrant (Cambridge: Cambridge University Press, 2015) and *La justice du dialogue et ses limites: étude du* Gorgias *de Platon* (Les Belles Lettres, 2022).

includes not only tragedy, but also epic, especially Homer. Finally, I will return to the larger question concerning the transition from poetry to prose by briefly examining Strabo's account of it. But first the immediate context of Gorgias's definition.

In the *Encomium of Helen,* Gorgias defends the mythological figure against her accusers, and in so doing discusses and illustrates the power of *logos*. He provides four arguments in favor of Helen's case: she left her husband with Paris because she was the victim of either (i) the will of Fate and of the gods, (ii) physical force (*bia*), (iii) seducing speech (*logos*), or (iv) love (*erōs*). He explains the third reason, the irresistible power of speech, in the most detail (§8-14). To provide the immediate context of Gorgias's definition, I quote sections 8, 9 and part of 10 in Sprague's translation:

> [8] But if it was speech [λόγος] which persuaded her and deceived [ἀπατήσας] her heart, not even to this is it difficult to make an answer and to banish blame as follows. Speech is a powerful lord [δυνάστης μέγας], which by means of the finest and most invisible body [σώματι] effects the divinest works: it can stop fear and banish grief [φόβον παῦσαι καὶ λύπην ἀφελεῖν] and create joy and nurture pity [ἔλεον ἐπαυξῆσαι]. I shall show [δείξω] how this is the case, since [9] it is necessary to offer proof to the opinion [δόξηι] of my hearers [τοῖς ἀκούουσι]: I both deem and define all poetry as speech with meter [τὴν ποίησιν ἅπασαν καὶ νομίζω καὶ ὀνομάζω λόγον ἔχοντα μέτρον]. Fearful shuddering [φρίκη περίφοβος] and tearful pity [ἔλεος πολύδακρυς] and grievous longing [πόθος φιλοπενθής] come upon its hearers, and at the actions and physical sufferings of others [ἀλλοτρίων] in good fortunes and in evil fortunes, through the agency of words [διὰ τῶν λόγων], the soul is wont to experience a suffering of its own. [10] Sacred incantations [ἐπωιδαὶ] sung with words are bearers of pleasure [ἡδονῆς] and banishers of pain, for, merging with opinion in the soul, the power [δύναμις] of the incantation is wont to beguile [ἔθελξε] it and persuade it and alter it by witchcraft [γοητείαι].

The historical and philosophical importance of Gorgias's theory of speech (*logos*) as expounded in the *Encomium of Helen* is generally recognized. Edward Schiappa, for instance, considers it the "most theoretical in its treatment of persuasive *logos*" of the 5th century. Schiappa also notes the absence of the term *rhētorikē*, which we would expect here, as an indication of both the terminological and conceptual uncertainty in the 5th century about rhetorical theories, and therewith the slow transition "from *logos* to *rhētorikē*."[2] My paper has at once a more modest and more ambitious aim than that of following the fortune of concepts such as rhetoric or prose. I would like to concentrate on the meaning and implications of Gorgias's definition of poetry, in connection to both the larger question of the "move from poetry to prose" and the reception of that definition in few later writers, namely Plato, Aristotle, Isocrates, and Strabo.

The Larger Question: The Transition from Poetry to Prose

Let me begin, then, with the "big picture" concerning the transition from poetry to prose. It is generally agreed that there are important connections between the emergence of artistic prose and the emergence of a more rational, secular, scientific outlook, often called the Greek Enlightenment, associated among others with the Sophists. This turn would involve the slow replacement of the traditional, mythic-poetic mode of thinking by the prose of the historians, orators, philosophers, etc.[3] Gorgias's *Encomium of Helen* explicitly claims to prove Helen's innocence by means of reasoning (*logismos* §2) and demonstration (*deixō* §8). He examines analytically the form and workings of speech.[4] His analysis of the emotional impact of speech is based on a rational psychology making no appeal to divine will. While performing this analysis, however, he

---

[2] Edward Schiappa, "Did Plato Coin *Rhētorikē*?" *American Journal of Philology* (1990): 459, 463, 470. Cf. Thomas Cole, *The Origin of Rhetoric in Ancient Greece* (Baltimore: John Hopkins University Press, 1991), 2, 12, 98-9.

[3] Cf. Eduard Norden, *Die antike Kunstprosa: Vom VI. Jahrhundert v. Chr. bis in die Zeit der Renaissance*, erster Band, dritter Abdruck (Leipzig, Berlin: Teubner, 1915), 20.

[4] Edward Schiappa, *The Beginnings of Rhetorical Theory in Classical Greece* (New Haven, London: Yale University Press, 1999), 114-32.

simultaneously illustrates the power of his own performance-prose. His prose refers emphatically to, and depends upon, the spoken word. His prose composition is still very much part of an oral culture. He addresses his audience as "my hearers" (§9). The young Friedrich Nietzsche in his lecture notes on the *History of Greek Literature* (1874-1876) defends a theory which finds approval only later, such as in Eric Havelock's work,[5] namely that poetry is the expression of an oral culture, while prose is based on a literate culture. Nietzsche unduly insists, however, on the opposition of two types of culture, supposing that some kind of radical break separated them, a view for which Havelock has also been criticized. Ultimately the replacement of poetry means the replacement of orality.[6] This movement was, however, gradual and slow in the 5th and 4th century BCE. Gorgias's written prose is part of the transitional period leading from one to the other.[7]

Gorgias's Definition of Poetry and Its Difficulties

Gorgias's definition of poetry raises several questions. What is the relationship between poetry and prose? What are the boundaries between them? What is the significance and novelty of his definition? And does it do justice to poetry's specificity? Let us recall that the concept of prose, in Gorgias, is expressed simply by the term *logos*. Later the notion will be specified as *pezos logos*, *pezos* meaning "on foot, walking," hence prosaic, ordinary. Contrary to many later writers, Gorgias establishes a prose-poetry distinction, although he does not maintain it consistently. As we have seen in *Encomium* §9, Gorgias defines poetry as speech containing "meter": "I both deem and define all poetry as speech with meter [τὴν ποίησιν ἅπασαν καὶ νομίζω καὶ ὀνομάζω λόγον ἔχοντα]."

---

5 Havelock oddly enough never quotes Nietzsche in his 1963 book, *Preface to Plato* (Cambridge, MA, London: Harvard University Press, 1963), although he does so in *The Literate Revolution in Greece and Its Cultural Consequences* (Princeton: Princeton University Press, 1982), 266; cf. 312.

6 Eric A. Havelock, *The Muse Learns to Write* (New Haven: Yale University Press, 1986), 8.

7 Cf. Edward Schiappa, "Twenty-Five Years after 'Did Plato Coin *Rhētorikē*?': An Episodic Memoir," *Rhetoric Review* 35 (2016): 6.

MacDowell in his commentary writes: "Scholars who object that poetical style differs from oratorical style are making too much of the passage; Gorgias does not here enter into the question of style, but is just saying—what is undeniably true—that poetry, like oratory, uses words."[8] This means that poetry has the powerful effects it has not *qua* poetry but *qua logos*.[9] What is the exact meaning of *metron*? Liddell and Scott say: "meter," and "[in opp[osition to] μέλος (music) and ῥυθμός (time)." This lexical entry includes references to Aristophanes's *Clouds* (v. 638, 641) and Plato's *Gorgias* (502c).[10] Greek meter differs from modern verse in being quantitative, based on patterns of long and short syllables, such as in the dactylic hexameter of Homeric poetry. The relationship between *metron* and *rhythmos* would thus consist in the fact they are the two necessary components for a complete formal classification of a verse.

Is this definition new or does it rather reflect the common conception at the time? There are reasons to suppose it is meant as intentionally novel. Gorgias's emphatic phrasing "I both deem and define [καὶ νομίζω καὶ ὀνομάζω]" does seem to insist with pride on his originality.[11] Moreover, it might be the very first example of a definition as procedure.[12] Some commentators claim, on the contrary, that Gorgias is here referring to a traditional (or conventional) understanding of poetry. Gorgias would be appealing to "his

---

[8] Douglas Maurice MacDowell, ed., *Gorgias, Encomium of Helen* (Bristol: Classical Press, 1982), 37; likewise, Penelope Murray, "Introduction," in *Classical Literary Criticism*, tr. P. Murray and T.S. Dorsch (London, New York: Penguin, 2000), xxi.

[9] Andrew Ford, *The Origins of Criticism: Literary Culture and Poetic Theory in Classical Greece* (Princeton: Princeton University Press, 2002), 178.

[10] Aristophanes, *Clouds*, ed., trans. and commentary Kenneth J. Dover (Oxford: Clarendon Press, 1968), 178-9 on *Clouds* v. 638.

[11] Cf., e.g., Mario Untersteiner, *I Sofisti*, presentazione di Fernanda Decleva Caizzi (Milano: B. Mondadori, 2008 [1968]), 99.

[12] Cf. Edward Schiappa, "Toward a Predisciplinary Analysis of Gorgias' *Helen*," in *Theory, Text, Context. Issues in Greek Rhetoric and Oratory*, ed. C. Johnstone (Albany: State University of New York Press, 1996), 82, id. "Rethorical Theory," 127; Giombini, *Gorgia epidittico*, 132-3; Roberta Ioli, *Gorgia, Testimonianze e frammenti* (Roma: Carocci, 2013), 228.

audience's shared preconceptions."[13] Immediately before giving that definition, Gorgias says "it is necessary to offer proof to the opinion (δόξῃ) of my hearers" (§9).[14] At any rate, his definition differs from the traditional understanding of poetry in at least two respects: it is purely formal and sets aside truth claims as well as morality, and it excludes inspiration from the Muse.[15] Indeed, this definition is the first attempt at describing the whole of poetry from a formal point of view, highlighting what according to Gorgias constitutes poetry's specific difference from other forms of discourse.[16] Plato's Socrates in the *Gorgias* takes up this definition in very similar words: "Well then, if one stripped away from the whole composition [τῆς ποιήσεως πάσης] both melody [μέλος], rhythm [ῥυθμὸν], and meter [μέτρον, does it turn out that what's left is only speeches [λόγοι]?" (*Gorgias* 502c5-7; ed. Burnet; trans. Zeyl).[17]

In Plato's rendering, too, poetry is equated with *logos* without meter. The difference in formulation, in comparison to that of Gorgias, might be helpful, even if from a later date. Socrates lists *metron* in company with *melos* and *rhythmos*. The exact relationship between *metron* and *rhythmos* is not so easy to determine. *Melos* means "song," which includes words, tune, and rhythm. In general, as Gerald Else notes, "*metron* means 'verse,' including speech and rhythm." So *metron* could be translated as "verse," bearing in mind,

[13] Denis C. Feeney, *The Gods in Epic: Poets and Critics of the Classical Tradition* (Oxford: Clarendon Press, 1991), 25.

[14] Cf. Donald Andrew Russell, *Criticism in Antiquity* (Berkeley: University of California Press, 1981), 23.

[15] Cf. Jacqueline de Romilly, "Gorgias et le pouvoir de la poésie," *Journal of Hellenic Studies* 93 (1973): 155-62.

[16] Jonas Schollmeyer, *Gorgias' ›Lobrede auf Helena‹ Literaturgeschichtliche Untersuchungen und Kommentar* (Berlin, Boston: de Gruyter, 2020), "§ 9 Funktion und Gedankengang" (Kindle edition, 2021).

[17] Cf. *Republic* X, 601b1-b4: "so great [μεγάλην] is the natural charm of these things—that he [*scil.* the poet] speaks with meter, rhythm, and harmony [ἐν μέτρῳ καὶ ῥυθμῷ καὶ ἁρμονίᾳ] for if you strip [γυμνωθέντα] a poet's works of their musical colorings [τῶν τῆς μουσικῆς χρωμάτων] and take them by themselves, I think you know what they look like" (trans. Grube rev. Reeve).

however, that its meaning changes according to context.[18] I will come back to the question of rhythm.

Other difficulties in Gorgias's *Encomium* concern its unstated implications. Is polemic implied on his part? When he declares that meter distinguishes poetry from prose, does he mean "and nothing else," with the intention of enhancing the prestige of oratory?[19] Moreover, is Gorgias implying that oratory, that is simple speech without music or meter, can be as powerful as poetry?[20] If this is so, as seems to be the case, it would be the first time such a claim is made on behalf of oratory. Furthermore, does Gorgias's definition of poetry and his praise of its power imply that prose writers are entitled to exploit all the resources of the poet's language, except meter? Gorgias does seem to put prose in direct rivalry with poetry in that fashion.[21] Contrary to his pupil Isocrates's strict rule that prose must only use common words, Gorgias uses poetic words, as well as figures of speech (*schēmata*),[22] presumably as substitutes for meter.[23]

---

[18] Gerald F. Else, *Aristotle's Poetics: The Argument* (Cambridge MA: Harvard University Press, 1957), 62, 66. *Metron* is generally translated as "meter" (*Versmaß*). But for Schollmeyer, *Gorgias*, "§ 9 Funktion und Gedankengang," *metron* as meter is rare in the 5th century. Aristotle seem to see *metron* as including both *logos* and *rhythmos*. Charles P. Segal, "Gorgias and the Psychology of the Logos," *Harvard Studies in Classical Philology* 66 (1962): 150n102 regards as possible that *metron* has "a wider range of meaning [...] referring to all the measured qualities, of which Greek poetic expression [...] is capable." Gorgias does not make that claim but affirms, in the case of both poetry and prose, an intimate relationship between form and effect.

[19] Cf. Victor Bers, *Greek Poetic Syntax in the Classical Age* (London, New Haven: Yale University Press, 1984), 1.

[20] Cf. Rudolf Pfeiffer, *History of Classical Scholarship: from The Beginnings to the End of The Hellenistic Age* (Oxford: Clarendon Press, 1968), 48.

[21] Cf., e.g., Schollmeyer, *Gorgias*, "§ 9 Funktion und Gedankengang."

[22] Such as antithesis, assonance and alliteration, as well as poetic vocabulary made of rare, foreign words and neologisms.

[23] Cf. Friedrich Blass, *Die attische Beredsamkeit. Erste Abtheilung: von Gorgias bis zu Lysias* (Teubner, Leipzig: Zweite Auflage, 1887), 63.

Aristotle: Meter as Non-Essential Difference

Aristotle claims at the beginning of his *Rhetoric* (III, 1404a24) that artistic prose began with a poetic style, and he cites the example of Gorgias. Aristotle is critical of the use of rare, poetic words in prose:

> And as the poets, although their utterances were devoid of sense [εὐήθη], appeared to have gained their reputation through their style [λέξις], it was a poetical style [ποιητική] that first came into being, as that of Gorgias.[24] Even now, the majority of the uneducated think that such persons express themselves most beautifully, whereas this is not the case, for the style of prose is not the same as that of poetry [αλλ' ἑτέρα λόγου και ποιήσεως λέξις ἐστίν] (*Rhetoric* III, 1404a24-29; ed. Ross; trans. Freese mod.).

A little later, Aristotle expresses partial agreement with Gorgias about meter as a distinct trait of poetry: "this is why prose must be rhythmical [ῥυθμὸν δεῖ ἔχειν], but not metrical [μέτρον δὲ μή], otherwise it will be a poem" (*Rhetoric* III, 1408b30; ed. Ross; trans. Freese mod.). Thus, according to Aristotle, prose may and even must have rhythm, as in the case of Thrasymachus's prose, as he mentions a little later (1409a2). Aristotle argues, however, that poetry's specific diction is distinct from that appropriate to prose.

In the *Poetics,* on the other hand, he opposes the received view that meter is the essential element in poetry (without referring to Gorgias): the *fundamental* distinction between the two would *not* lie in the meter, that is, in its form, but in its content, namely in mimesis, its mimetic object (1447b16-20). Is Aristotle's premise here that meter is a mere veil concealing the essence of poetry, that is its subject, mimetically portrayed? If *logos* is to have the same power as poetry, as Gorgias argues, the *specific* feature of poetry must be minimized, which implies treating *metron* "as an external ornament, not affecting the intrinsic qualities of the whole."[25] In other words, *metron* is superficial. Yet, from Gorgias's own formal viewpoint, does the

---

[24] See also Philostratus, *Lives of Sophists,* I, 9; Diodorus of Sicily XII, 53, 1-5; Dionysius of Halicarnassus, *Composition* VI, 25, 7.

[25] Russell, *Criticism in Antiquity,* 23.

power of poetry, just as that of prose, not lie in its form? Gorgias, as Plato after him, regards the overpowering influence of poetry, rhetoric, and music on the soul as residing in the force of sheer sound. Generally, there is a tension in rhetorical and philosophical criticism in antiquity between content (mostly ethical) and form, that is between sense and sound, or between ethics and techniques. The latter is apparently rooted in Gorgias's case in materialistic conceptions of language, such as that of his teacher Empedocles and Democritus, who possibly influenced him. As Andrew Ford observes, the "classical approach to the split between sound and sense is, ideally, to harmonize the two."[26] This position is expressed, e.g., in Plato's *Cratylus* (387d4-7), which supposes a *natural* correspondence between name and meaning.

Isocrates: Meter for Poetry Alone, Rhythm for Prose Also

Gorgias's best-known student, Isocrates, takes a different view from Aristotle concerning the role of meter. Isocrates argues that meter *is* the essential, distinctive trait of poetry, that it is not an external feature, but is intrinsic to it. Without meter poetry would lose its power (*dynamis*).[27] This seems to contradict Gorgias's thesis according to which *logos*, by itself, is a great master. While Gorgias places poetry within prose, Isocrates keeps them apart. In addition to meter, other devices are poetry's prerogative alone.[28] In the *Antidosis* Isocrates discusses political, as opposed to private, forms of discourse, such as panegyric, to be delivered at the Pan-Hellenic assemblies (explicitly referring to his own):

> [these] discourses which, as everyone will agree, are more akin to works composed in rhythm and set to music [ὁμοιοτέρους εἶναι τοῖς μετὰ μουσικῆς καὶ ῥυθμῶν πεποιημένοις] than to the speeches which are made in court [ἢ τοῖς ἐν δικαστηρίῳ λεγομένοις]. For they set forth facts in a style more imaginative and more ornate [ποικιλωτέρᾳ]; they employ thoughts which are more lofty

[26] Ford, *Origins of Criticism*, 186-7.

[27] Isocrates, *Evagoras*, §11.

[28] Schollmeyer, *Gorgias*, "§ 9 Funktion und Gedankengang."

> and more original [ὀγκωδεστέροις καὶ καινοτέροις χρῆσθαι ζητοῦσιν], and, besides, they use throughout figures of speech in greater number and of more striking character. All men take no less pleasure [χαίρουσιν οὐδὲν ἧττον] in listening to this kind of prose than in listening to poetry [ἢ τῶν ἐν τοῖς μέτροις πεποιημένων] (*Antidosis* 46-47; ed. and trans. Norlin mod.).

Isocrates thus presents a more complex account of the relationship between poetry and prose. According to him, artistic prose can enchant the audience just as much as poetry does, but its task is more difficult, because it lacks the psychagogic power of meter.

The challenge of writing prose would mainly lie in capturing the power of poetry while respecting the boundaries between the two forms. To that end, it has rhythm, as Aristotle also says.[29] Isocrates takes pride in his own use of harmonious rhythm (εὐρυθμία).[30] He underscores rhythm as prime condition of the power and charm of prose. In *Evagoras* he writes, "Nevertheless, although poetry has advantages so great [πλεονεκτούσης τῆς ποιήσεως], we must not shrink from the task, but must make the effort and see if it will be possible in prose to eulogize good men in no worse fashion [μηδὲν χεῖρον] than their encomiasts do who employ song and verse [τῶν ἐν ταῖς ᾠδαῖς καὶ τοῖς μέτροις ἐγκωμιαζόντων] (*Evagoras* 11; ed. and trans. Norlin). Isocrates thus maintains poetry's superiority, due to meter, but considers rhythm as the principal means to approach its power of expression.[31] Plato too, as we have seen, refers to the close connection among *metron, melos,* and *rhythmos*. The rhetorical tradition will largely maintain the position that prose should be rhythmical, but not metrical.[32]

---

[29] Aristotle, *Rhetoric,* III, 1408b30-31; cf. Schollmeyer, *Gorgias,* "§ 9."

[30] *To Philip,* 27. *Against the Sophists,* 13: εὐρύθμως καὶ μουσικῶς.

[31] See Friedrich Nietzsche, "Geschichte der griechischen Literatur," in *Werke Kritische Gesamtausgabe* II/5, ed. G. Colli, M. Montinari (Berlin: de Gruyter, 1993), 27-32: "Prosa und Poesie in ihrem Unterschiede."

[32] Dionysius of Halicarnassus, *Demosthenes* 50, *On Composition* 25 (cf. 11); Demetrius, *On Style* 180-81 (cf. 118); Cicero, *Orator* 187-88, 194, 198; Quintilian, *Institutio oratoria* IX, 4, 56-57, 60-61, 72, 77.

The Epic Tradition: Homer

In his account of the psychagogic power of speech, Gorgias includes references to the emotions of pity and fear, which has led many commentators to suppose that he had tragic rather than epic poetry in mind. Tragedy is certainly a key form of poetry in his account. His influence on Aristotle's understanding of tragedy, in terms of these two emotions, is also quite probable. Whether Gorgias, like Aristotle, associated pity and fear with purgation (*katharsis*), is another question. It is, however, a mistake to suppose that Gorgias is concerned exclusively with tragedy.

First, Gorgias's definition is meant to be universal: it includes all poetry. Second, as in the case of other sophists, Gorgias's oratory appeals to mythological narrative related to the Trojan war and thus to Homeric characters (Helen, Palamedes, etc.).[33] Third, the powerful emotions Gorgias evokes, such as grievous longing, are already portrayed in Homer. As Rana Saadi Liebert points out, the phrase "longing for lamentation" (Ἵμερος γόοιο) is frequent in Homer.[34] Fourth, the emotion of pleasure or delight (*terpsis*), the exclusive privilege of the poets until then, is typical of Homeric poetry (cf. *Od.* I, 347; VIII, 45). Fifth, Plato's view that epic and tragic poetry are fundamentally synonymous may derive from Gorgias or may be a common view at the time.[35] Both genres belong to high art capable of elevating the mind, and Aristotle too considers Homer's epic to be the first form of tragedy in its dramatic quality.[36]

Finally, Plato's description of the rhapsode's emotional state and impact on the audience in the *Ion* (535c), when reciting Homer,

---

[33] See Paola Bassino and Nicolò Benzi (eds.), *Sophistic Views of the Epic Past from the Classical to the Imperial Age* (London: Bloomsbury, 2021).

[34] Rana Saadi Liebert, *Tragic Pleasure from Homer to Plato* (Cambridge, New York: Cambridge University Press, 2017), 109: Homer, *Iliad* XXIII, 14, 108, 153; XXIV, 507; *Odyssey* IV, 113, 183; X, 398; XVI, 215; XIX, 249.

[35] Plato, *Republic* 595a, 598d, 607a; *Theaetetus* 152e.

[36] *Poetics* 1448b35-37, 1449b9-10. Cf. Fritz R. Wehrli, "Der erhabene und der schlichte Stil in der poetisch-rhetorischen Theorie der Antike," in *Phyllobolia für Peter von der Mühll*, ed. Olof Gigon et al. (Basel: Schwabe, 1946), 17-8; Giuliana Lanata, *Poetica pre-platonica* (Firenze: Nuova Italia, 1963), 197.

involves very similar emotions to those to which Gorgias refers.[37] The importance of epic, Homeric poetry in Gorgias's oratory raises the larger question about his relationship to the oral-mythic tradition as a whole. Gorgias does not contest the stories about Helen's life; he uses them without changing them. As Stephen Halliwell suggests, it "looks, therefore, as though Gorgias is not simply rejecting poetic tradition but competing with it on its own terms. [...] He may adopt a stance of analytic 'reasoning' (*logismos*), but he nonetheless signals his wish to give his audience a deep pleasure which can match that to be expected of poetry itself."[38]

Conclusion: Strabo's Account of the Transition

To conclude, let us return to the larger question concerning the overall transition from poetry to prose. The use of writing without meter has been felt and judged in antiquity as a daring enterprise, indeed by some, as a radical breach with tradition, that nevertheless established itself with time.[39] A very interesting account of the long and slow transition from poetic discourse to artistic prose can be found in the writings of the historian and geographer Strabo (c. 60 BCE-20 CE), who happens to be an unconditional admirer of Homer. After criticizing Eratosthenes's view of poetry as entertainment, Strabo defends poetry as a source of knowledge as well as of pleasure. He then presents his account of how poetry first reigned supreme, then competed with prose, until it was replaced by it.

---

[37] 535c5-8: (Ion) ἐγὼ γὰρ ὅταν ἐλεινόν τι λέγω, δακρύων ἐμπίμπλανταί μου οἱ ὀφθαλμοί· ὅταν τε φοβερὸν ἢ δεινόν, ὀρθαὶ αἱ τρίχες ἵστανται ὑπὸ φόβου καὶ ἡ καρδία πηδᾷ. Cf. Russell, *Criticism in Antiquity*, 23.

[38] Stephen Halliwell, *Between Ecstasy and Truth: Interpretations of Greek Poetics from Homer to Longinus* (Oxford: Oxford University Press, 2011), 271-2. On Gorgias's stylistic borrowings from Homer, see A. Nieschke, *De Thucydide Antiphontis discipulo et Homeri imitatore* (Münden: Klugkist, 1885), A. Nieschke, *De figurarum, quae vocantur* σχήματα Γοργίεια, *apud Herodotum usu* (Münden: Klugkist, 1891), and Karl Reich, *Der Einfluss der griechischen Poesie auf Gorgias den Begründer der attischen Kunstprosa* (Würzburg: Universitätsdruckerei, 1907-1909), 19-27.

[39] Michael Erler, "Philosophie," in *Handbuch der griechischen Literatur der Antike,* ed. Bernhard Zimmermann (München: Beck, 2011), 261.

But is not language a generality [ὁ λόγος ἐστὶ γενικός], of which poetry and prose are forms [οὗ εἴδη ὁ ἔμμετρος καὶ ὁ πεζός]? Yes, language is; but are not the rhetorical, the eloquent, and the florid styles also? I answer, that flowery prose [ὁ πεζὸς λόγος, ὅ γε κατεσκευασμένος] is nothing but an imitation of poetry [μίμημα τοῦ ποιητικοῦ]. Ornate poetry [ἡ ποιητικὴ] was the first [πρώτιστα] to make its appearance in our midst [εἰς τὸ μέσον], and was well regarded [εὐδοκίμησεν]. Afterwards [εἶτα] it was closely imitated by writers in the time of Cadmus, Pherecydes, and Hecatæus. The metre [μέτρον] was the only thing dispensed with [λύσαντες], every other poetic grace being carefully preserved. As time advanced [ὕστερον], one after another of its beauties was discarded, till [εἰς τὸ νῦν] at last it came down from its glory into our common prose. In the same way we may say that comedy took its rise from tragedy, but descended from its lofty grandeur into what we now call the common parlance of daily life [τὸ λογοειδὲς νυνὶ]. And when [we find] the ancient writers making use of the expression 'to sing,' [τὸ ἀείδειν] to designate eloquence of style, this in itself is evidence that poetry is the source and origin [πηγὴ καὶ ἀρχὴ] of all ornamented and rhetorical language [φράσεως κατεσκευασμένης καὶ ῥητορικῆς ὑπῆρξεν ἡ ποιητική]. Poetry in ancient days was on every occasion accompanied by melody. The song or ode [ᾠδὴ] was but a modulated speech [λόγος μεμελισμένος], from whence the words *rhapsody, tragedy, comedy,* are derived; and since originally eloquence was the term made use of for the poetical effusions which were always of the nature of a song, it soon happened [that in speaking of poetry] some said, to sing, others, to be eloquent [τὸ ἀείδειν αὐτοῖς τὸ αὐτὸ τῷ φράζειν]; and as the one term was early misapplied to prose compositions, the other also was soon applied in the same way. Lastly, the very term prose [τὸ πεζὸν], which is applied to language not clothed in metre [τὸν ἄνευ τοῦ μέτρου λόγον], seems to indicate, as it were, its descent from an elevation or chariot to the ground [τὸν ἀπὸ ὕψους τινὸς καταβάντα καὶ ὀχήματος εἰς τοὔδαφος] (*Geography* I, 2, 6; Meineke; tr. Hamilton, Falconer, mod.).

Incidentally, a very similar history of literature, presented in very similar terms, can be found in Plutarch.[40] Both are generally thought to go back to the Stoic philosopher Posidonius (c. 135-51 BCE). Prose style, or *pezos logos,* would be a mere imitation of poetic diction. Strabo distinguishes with clarity the various steps leading from one to the other. Initially poetry stood alone with prestige. Later the first prose writers imitating the poetic model appeared—they set meter aside but otherwise retained the poetic character. The later prose writers disposed more and more of the poetic means, which led prose as it were down from its heights to contemporary character. This theory of the gradual emergence or prose from poetry certainly deserves to be pondered.[41] It can be read in part as a reply to Gorgias, especially around the generic notion of *logos* (*genikos*), although Strabo does not mention him by name. Gorgias would belong to the first prose writers who still preserved the inner stylistic form of poetry, except for the meter. Next, the gradual dissociation from the poetic character, which finally led to the further descent to the ground, where prose became fully prosaic, not to say pedestrian in the modern sense. This account of the history of literature ultimately raises the question of the value of poetry with respect to prose, to the clear advantage of poetry. It depicts poetry as the mother-tongue of humanity, capable of providing pleasure and instruction, and as the source of prose, which will gradually depart from its source, and not for the better. In this account Gorgias's practice would thus appear to stand close to the initial heights.

---

[40] Plutarch, *De Pythiae oraculis,* 406b-d.

[41] Wolfgang Schadewaldt, "Heraufkommen der Prosa," in *Die Anfänge der Geschichtsschreibung bei den Griechen: Herodot-Thukydides,* ed. Ingebort Schudoma (Frankfurt am M.: Suhrkamp, 1982), 31, firmly defends the soundness of this account.

R.J. Barnes[1]

Gorgias on Speech and the Soul

In his *Encomium of Helen* and *On Not Being*, Gorgias of Leontinoi discusses the nature and function of speech more extensively than any other surviving author before Plato. His discussions are not only surprising in the way they characterize the power of *logos* and its effects on a listener but also in how the two descriptions of speech seem to contradict one another. In the *Helen*, Gorgias claims that *logos* is a very powerful entity, capable of affecting a listener in whatever way it wants. In *On Not-Being*, he makes the very different (but no less exaggerated) claim that *logos* is a non-entity, incapable of referring to anything other than itself. In this essay I show how these apparently contradictory accounts might be brought into harmony with one another.[2] In the first part I address some of the interpretive difficulties with the text of Gorgias's *On Not Being* (henceforth *ONB*) and the role that irony plays in the work. In particular I argue (as others have before) that Gorgias's remarks about the impotency of speech are not meant to be taken seriously. Instead, they are aimed more squarely at raising questions about how exactly speech is thought to function and, more specifically, how linguistic reference works—i.e., how words somehow correspond to things, on one level, and to our ideas about things, on another.

In the second and third parts of this paper, I illustrate how Gorgias's concern with linguistic reference in *ONB* goes on to inform his notion of *logos* in the *Encomium of Helen*. I point specifically to evidence found in an important and often overlooked exit clause at

---

[1] R.J. Barnes completed his Ph.D. in Greek, Latin, and Classical Studies at Bryn Mawr College in 2022. He served as a Visiting Instructor in Classics at Haverford College and is currently an Instructor in Classics at Wabash College, in the United States.

[2] For other attempts to synthesize the two accounts, see Jacques Brunschwig, "Gorgias et l'incommunicabilité," in *La communication, Actes du XVe Congrès de l'Association des Sociétés de Philosophie de langue française*, v. 1 (Montreal: Éditions Montmorency, 1971), 79–84, and Alexander Mourelatos, "Gorgias on the Function of Language," *Philosophical Topics* 15, no. 2 (1987): 135–70.

the close of *ONB* regarding the difference between words and things. There, Gorgias insists that if words manifest meaning at all, they must appeal to their own sort of sense organ. In the *Helen*, he draws on the concepts of soul (*psychē*) and opinion (*doxa*) in order to construct this alternative, psychagogic account in which utterances are actually apprehended in ways akin to sense perception. Whether or not one is convinced by Gorgias's alternative account of how speech works, the description he gives of *logos* does notionally circumvent the problem of linguistic reference and, in doing so, pushes one to think beyond the potentially constrictive framework of *nomen et nominatum*. I argue that, when read in this way, these two early discussions of *logos* represent a unified progression of serious thought about how speech works.

Approaching *On Not-Being*

The text and tone of Gorgias's *ONB* pose several important interpretative difficulties that must be addressed at the outset. For one, the text we have survives in paraphrase from two sources—Sextus Empiricus's *Against the Logicians* and a pseudo-Aristotelian text titled *On Melissus, Xenophanes, and Gorgias* (henceforth *MXG*). The versions differ markedly from one another in several respects, and the tides of scholarly opinion over the past century have ebbed and flowed over which text is closer to the original. Since Sextus's version is in much better shape materially and easier to follow than *MXG*, it was once strongly preferred—so much so that Hermann Diels declined even to print the latter in *Die Fragmente der Vorsokratiker*.[3] Over the last half-century, scholars have increasingly tended to prefer *MXG*, largely because it appears to cleave more closely to the verbiage of Gorgias's own day than Sextus's version, which incorporates a greater amount of later philosophical jargon.[4]

---

[3] In addition to Diels, see Heinrich Gomperz, *Sophistik und Rhetorik* (Leipzig: Teubner, 1912), 18; Wilhelm Nestle, "Die Schrift des Gorgias 'über die Natur oder über das Nichtseiende,'" *Hermes* 57 (1922): 554-5.

[4] Walter Bröcker, "Gorgias contra Parmenides," *Hermes* 86 (1958): 425–40; Jaap Mansfeld, "Aristotle, Plato, and the Preplatonic Doxography and Chronography," in *Studies in the Historiography of Greek Philosophy*

Although it is true that *MXG* is preferable in this respect, there are other aspects in which Sextus's version may better reflect Gorgias's original work—one being the overall structure of its arguments which more closely echoes other surviving Gorgianic works.[5] In this paper I refrain from absolutely privileging one version over the other and instead take a more synthetic approach.[6]

What is fundamentally clear from both versions of the text is that Gorgias structured his work around a series of three interlocking claims:

1. Nothing is.
2. Even if something is, what is cannot be known.
3. Even if something is and can be known, the thing known cannot be communicated.

The concessive structure of this argument (not x, and even if x, not y, and even if y, not z) is, by all accounts, authentically Gorgian. It is closely paralleled in the *Defense of Palamedes* and never quite catches on with other authors as an argumentative form until the Pyrrhonist philosopher Aenesidemus includes it as one of his five tropes.[7] It is

(1986; repr., Maastricht: Van Gorcum, 1990), 22–83; Jaap Mansfeld, "*De Melisso Xenophane Gorgia*: Pyrrhonizing Aristotelianism," *Rheinisches Museum für Philologie* 131 (1988): 239–76; Richard Bett, "Gorgias' Περὶ Τοῦ Μὴ Ὄντος and Its Relation to Skepticism," *International Journal for the Study of Skepticism* 10 (2020): 187–208.

[5] Evan Rodriguez, "Untying the Gorgianic 'Not': Argumentative Structure in Gorgias's *On-Not-Being*," *Classical Quarterly* 69 (2019): 87-106.

[6] On the need for a synthetic approach, see Mario Untersteiner, *The Sophists*, tr. K. Freeman (New York: Philosophical Library, 1954), 97; G.B. Kerferd, "The Interpretation of Gorgias' Treatise: Περί Του Μη Όντος ή Περί Φύσεως," *Deucalion* 9 (1981), 321; Kerferd, "Meaning and Reference: Gorgias and the Relation between Language and Reality," in *The Sophistic Movement*, ed. K.J. Boudouris (Athens, 1984), 215; Rodriguez, "Untying the Gorgianic 'Not'," 103.

[7] A.A. Long, "Methods of Argument in Gorgias' *Palamedes*," in *The Sophistic Movement*, ed. K.J. Boudouris (Athens, 1984), 235; David Sedley, "Sextus Empiricus and the Atomist Criteria of Truth," *Elenchos* 13 (1992), 25-26n8.

more difficult to determine whether this thesis authentically reflects Gorgias's own opinion, however, or whether it is meant ironically.

The three claims Gorgias makes are not only outlandish but also self-refuting in their very enunciation. How is it not paradoxical, for instance, to use speech in order to communicate the idea that our speech cannot communicate our ideas? Problems like this one have naturally caused readers to wonder whether Gorgias's claims are meant to be taken at face value or with some degree of irony. If we imagine that Gorgias was genuinely committed to them, we would be condemning him to some truly tangled reasoning. A more charitable approach, and one which other interpreters have taken, would be to say that Gorgias (a showman by all accounts) makes this argument as a way of surprising his audience and showing off his cleverness.[8]

This practice of constructing elaborate arguments for unlikely premises was, to be sure, not uncommon for intellectuals in Gorgias's day. One is reminded of Plato's *Euthydemus* (where the titular character argues that Ctesippus's father is a dog),[9] Aristophanes's Pheidippides (who argues that it is a just thing for a son to beat his father),[10] or the various mock-encomia which were written in praise of salt, mice, pebbles, death, and the like.[11] The proper response to these sophistic displays was not, of course, to assent to the arguments themselves but rather to delight in the cleverness involved in their

---

[8] Gisela Striker, "Methods of Sophistry," in *Essays on Hellenistic Epistemology and Ethics*, ed. Gisela Striker (Cambridge: Cambridge University Press, 1996), 13-14; Kurt Lampe, "The Logos of Ethics in Gorgias' *Palamedes, On What Is Not*, and *Helen*," in *Early Greek Ethics*, ed. David Wolfsdorf (Oxford: Oxford University Press, 2020), 113.

[9] Plato, *Euthydemus*, 298d-e.

[10] Aristophanes, *Clouds*, 1405.

[11] On salt: Plato (*Symposium* 177b) and Isocrates (*Helen* 12); on mice offered by Gorgias's pupil Polycrates, see Aristotle, *Rhetoric*, 2.24 1401b15; on pebbles offered by Polycrates, see *Rhetoric to Alexander*, 3.10-2; on death offered by Gorgias's pupil Alcidamas, see Cicero, *Tusculan Disputations*, 1.116 cf. Athenaeus, *The Learned Banqueters*, 592c. On these sorts of encomia more generally, see Arthur Pease, "Things without Honor," *Classical Philology* 21 (1926): 27–42.

invention and, perhaps also, to reflect on the deeper questions they may raise *sotto voce*.[12] In fact, Gorgias already lays out this principle quite clearly in his own playful encomium: "telling those who know the things that they already know is persuasive but it does not bring delight [τὸ γὰρ τοῖς εἰδόσιν ἃ ἴσασι λέγειν πίστιν μὲν ἔχει, τέρψιν δὲ οὐ φέρει]."[13]

According to early sources, Gorgias often wielded his wit with purpose. Aristotle, for instance, cites Gorgias's famous observation that seriousness can be diffused by a dose of humor, just as humor is diffused by seriousness.[14] He also notes how Gorgias was adept at using humor and irony (*eirōneia*) as a means of honing in on serious questions.[15] In the *Politics*, for example, Aristotle recalls how Gorgias made the punning remark that the craftsmen (*dēmiourgoi*) of Larisa are not just pot-makers (*holmopoioi*) but also Larisa-Makers (*larisopoioi*) when they bestow citizenship on foreigners. The pun partly hinges on the term *dēmiourgos,* which means "craftsman" but looks like "people-maker." As Aristotle recognizes, the humorous equivalence is not just a pun but also an invitation to ask serious questions about the issue of citizenship and how it is bestowed—e.g., is citizenship something that can be produced (like a pot) or is it something that must be inherited naturally at birth? Importantly, Gorgias's joke only raises questions and never provides answers. This dodginess also seems to have been characteristically Gorgian.

---

12 See also Jonathan Pratt, "On the Threshold of Rhetoric: Gorgias' *Encomium of Helen,*" *Classical Antiquity* 34 (2015): 169-70, who warns against the tendency of dismissing these displays as τὸ ψευδολογεῖν when they "could more fruitfully be seen as intellectual experiments, protests against convention, or attempts to address the demands of unusual situations."

13 Gorgias, *Helen*, 5.

14 Aristotle, *Rhetoric,* 3.18 1419b3-5 = DK 82B12.

15 Aristotle praises Gorgias's capacity to produce comic metaphors that are neither too ridiculous (γελοῖον) nor too solemn and tragic (σεμνὸν ἄγαν καὶ τραγικόν), nor even far-fetched (πόρρωθεν) or obscure (ἀσαφεῖς, Aristotle, *Rhetoric,* 3.3 1406b4-19 = DK 82A23). He also compares the ironic bombast of Gorgias's speeches to the display speeches in Plato's *Phaedrus* (Aristotle, *Rhetoric,* 3.7 1408b17-20).

As Aristotle puts it, Gorgias makes the joke "partly out of aporia and partly with irony [τὰ μὲν ἴσως ἀπορῶν τὰ δ᾽ εἰρωνευόμενος]."[16]

It is not hard to imagine that a similar dynamic might be at play in *ONB*. Gorgias raises serious questions about ontology, epistemology, and human communication; however, he does so partly out of *aporia* and partly with irony. His claims that nothing exists, nothing can be known, and nothing can be communicated may not convince anyone—and may not be meant to. But once we confidently sweep them aside as ridiculous, we are faced with the question of what to put in their place. We must ask how to account for our own suppositions about speech, knowledge, being, and, importantly, whether or not other contemporary theories resembling Gorgias's own extreme version have any more or any less credence.

As scholars have long recognized, one lightly veiled agenda of *ONB* is to take a potshot at the Eleatics who, in Gorgias day, were making influential claims about what can exist, what can be known, and what can be communicated through speech.[17] The three central pillars of Eleatic philosophy are that not-being is (1) unreal, (2) unthinkable, and (3) unspeakable. Gorgias's triple-tiered thesis in *ONB* undermines these claims all too neatly by trading not-being for being and constructing an argument for why the latter is (1) unreal, (2) unthinkable, and (3) unspeakable. By arguing flatly against the Eleatic position on these issues, Gorgias calls into question an influential strand of contemporary thought. Although he may not shake anyone's instinctive confidence that things in the world are, can be known, and can be communicated, he raises doubts about popular ways of explaining these things and challenges his audience

---

[16] Aristotle, *Politics*, 3.1 1275b26-30 = DK 82A19. For a broader discussion of this passage and other examples of Gorgianic irony, see Marie-Pierre Noël, "L'enfance de l'art: Plaisir et jeu chez Gorgias," *Bulletin de l'Association Guillaume Budé* 1 (1994): 71–93.

[17] George Grote, *Plato and the Other Companions of Sokrates*, 2nd ed., vol. 1, 3 vols. (London: John Murray, 1867), 107-9; Bröcker, "Gorgias contra Parmenides." For a more recent study of this anti-Eleatic aspect of *ONB*, see Patricia Curd, "Gorgias and the Eleatics," in *La construzione del discorso filosofico nell'eta dei presocratici*, ed. Maria Sassi (Pisa: Edizioni della Normale, 2006), 183–200.

to find better ways of accounting for their own suppositions about the nature of being, knowledge, and *logos*.[18] With this in mind, let us turn now to what Gorgias has to say specifically about *logos* in *ONB*.

Speech and the Senses in *On Not Being*

Gorgias's initial argument regarding the impossibility of communication rests on the observation that words do not manifest meaning in the same way as things do.[19] By "thing" (*pragma* in *MXG*) or "things that exist externally" (ἅπερ ἐκτὸς ὑπόκειται in Sextus), Gorgias has in mind phenomenal objects. Most objects present themselves quite naturally to our faculties of perception. That is, visible objects are apprehended by our eyes, audible objects by our ears, and so on. Words function differently. They do not present themselves to our eyes or ears like other visible or audible objects. Instead, they *re-present* other things. That is to say, speech somehow points beyond itself, beyond its own perceptible content, and toward something else without appealing to our eyes or ears in quite the same manner as other perceptible objects do. As Gorgias puts it, speech is not something one hears or sees any more than colors are heard or sounds are seen:

> For if things that are—i.e., things that truly exist externally—are visible and audible and, broadly speaking, perceptible, and if visible things are apprehended by sight, audible things by hearing and not vice versa, how then is it possible to indicate these things by some other means.[20] For

---

[18] I agree with Rachel Barney, "Gorgias's *Encomium of Helen*," in *Ten Neglected Classics of Philosophy*, ed. Eric Schliesser (Oxford: Oxford University Press, 2016), 24, who suggests that Gorgias's brand of philosophy (if we can call it that) is characterized by "provocation and challenge." It is comparable to Plato's aporetic dialogues.

[19] For the best overall discussions of Gorgias's third thesis of *ONB*, see Kerferd, "Interpretation," and "Meaning." Mourelatos, "Gorgias on the Function" is also helpful on certain details.

[20] Here I take ἑτέρῳ as instrumental. Most read it as an indirect object: "to someone else." However, this overlooks the parallelism with ὁράσει and ἀκοῇ as well as the later explaination that speech is the "other means" by which we must somehow indicate things seen and heard.

> speech is the means by which we indicate [things] and speech is not the things that are and exist [externally].
>
> εἰ γὰρ τὰ ὄντα ὁρατά ἐστι καὶ ἀκουστὰ καὶ κοινῶς αἰσθητά, ἅπερ ἐκτὸς ὑπόκειται, τούτων τε τὰ μὲν ὁρατὰ ὁράσει καταληπτά ἐστι τὰ δὲ ἀκουστὰ ἀκοῇ καὶ οὐκ ἐναλλάξ, πῶς οὖν δύναται ταῦτα ἑτέρῳ μηνύ-εσθαι; ᾧ γὰρ μηνύομεν, ἔστι λόγος, λόγος δὲ οὐκ ἔστι τὰ ὑποκείμενα καὶ ὄντα.[21]

This passage points to the categorical difference in how we apprehend words and how we apprehend perceptible objects.[22] It maps this distinction onto the categorical difference between how specific sense organs apprehend specific forms of sense data—a claim that may loosely riff on an Empedoclean model of perception in which specific sense organs function as pores that admit only specific effluences of sense data.[23] Either way, in making this argument, Gorgias raises an important linguistic question that he pointedly never answers: How can speech indicate something other than itself? He concludes (as he must for the sake of the argument of *ONB*) that speech cannot indicate anything other than itself and, for this reason, communication must be impossible.

After reaching this point, the two versions of *ONB* diverge. *MXG* launches into an additional argument against the possibility of

---

21 Sextus Empiricus, *Against the Logicians*, 7.83-4 cf. *MXG* 6 980b1-3. All translations are my own.

22 It does not tacitly concede that communication may be possible through "onomatopoeia" or "ideographic supplements" as is argued by Mourelatos, "Gorgias on the Function," 137.

23 See Plato, *Meno*, 76a8-e2 with Kerferd, "The Interpretation," 323-4. It is quite clear (*pace* Mourelatos, "Gorgias on the Function," 137-8, 148-9) that Gorgias's writings draw on many contemporary strands of intellectual thought, be it Hippocratic, Eleatic, Empedoclean, or otherwise: Andrew Ford, *The Origins of Criticism: Literary Culture and Poetic Theory in Classical Greece* (Princeton: Princeton University Press, 2002), 172-87; Brooke Holmes, *The Symptom and the Subject: The Emergence of the Physical Body in Ancient Greece* (Princeton: Princeton University Press, 2010), 211-6.

communication, focusing this time on the categorical difference between words and thoughts.[24] Sextus's version, however, continues with the argument we just summarized and adds two striking qualifications. The first has been read by Alexander Mourelatos as representing an alternative theory of communication that Gorgias explores further in the *Helen*.[25] However, as I will argue, it is actually the second and final qualification that acts as the exit clause from Gorgias's *elenchos* and provides the groundwork for thinking about speech in an alternative way.

The first qualification makes a concession regarding the correspondence between words and things. It states that even if speech corresponds to things in the world, it must be the case that *speech* is expressed by *things* and not vice versa.

> To be sure, speech, [Gorgias] says, is for us composed of things that strike us from the outside—i.e., perceptibles. For instance, from contact with flavor, there arises within us speech expressed by that quality, and, from the encounter with color, the [speech expressed] by that color. But, if this is the case, speech is not an indicator of the external, rather the external is revelatory of speech.
>
> ὅ γε μὴν λόγος, φησίν, ἀπὸ τῶν ἔξωθεν προσ-πιπτόντων ἡμῖν πραγμάτων συνίσταται, τουτέστι τῶν αἰσθητῶν· ἐκ γὰρ τῆς τοῦ χυλοῦ ἐγκυρήσεως ἐγγίνεται ἡμῖν ὁ κατὰ ταύτης τῆς ποιότητος ἐκφερόμενος λόγος, καὶ ἐκ τῆς τοῦ χρώματος ὑποπτώσεως ὁ κατὰ τοῦ χρώματος. εἰ δὲ τοῦτο, οὐχ ὁ λόγος τοῦ ἐκτὸς παραστατικός ἐστιν, ἀλλὰ τὸ ἐκτὸς τοῦ λόγου μηνυτικὸν γίνεται.[26]

---

[24] It is argued that a word cannot represent the same idea to all persons or even to a single person at different times (*MXG* 6 980b8-b21).

[25] Mourelatos, "Gorgias on the Function," followed by Juan Pablo Bermúdez, "Truth and Falsehood for Non-Representationalists: Gorgias on the Normativity of Language," *Journal of Ancient Philosophy* 11 (2017): 1–21. Mourelatos's thesis is critiqued by Erminia Di Iulio, "Gorgias' Account of Truth: Mourelatos and Bermúdez between Behaviorism and Coherence," *Fogli Di Filosofia* 11 (2019): 73–91.

[26] Sextus Empiricus, *Against the Logicians*, 7.85.

Although interpretations of this passage may vary in detail, the basic message is clear enough: even if there exists a particular avenue of correspondence between words and things, we can be sure that things—not words—are still responsible for manifesting meaning.[27] The primary reasoning for this seems to be that even if speech arises through the interaction with objects, the speech that arises from this interaction still has no way of referring back to the object that generated it. Speech is categorically distinct from that to which it refers, and Gorgias has not yet resolved his aporia about how it might indicate something other than itself without appealing to sense perceptions. So, on the face of it, what we end up with is another strike against the possibility of communication.

Alexander Mourelatos has influentially argued that this passage hints at an alternative theory of communication. For him, this alternative theory is equivalent to the behavioral conception of language popular in the mid-twentieth century, in which words are regarded as substitutes for experiences and thereby act as surrogate stimuli for those experiences. Although Mourelatos is not far from the mark in his conclusion about what Gorgias's alternative theory of communication might look like and how well that alternative theory squares with Gorgias's notion of *logos* in the *Helen,* this passage alone cannot sufficiently support his conclusion since it nowhere indicates that *logos* acts as a stimulus in its own right or somehow generates experiences in a way comparable to how perceptible objects generate experiences.[28] Like Mourelatos, I think that Gorgias's *ONB* does open the door to an alternative model of communication and that, according to this alternative model, speech would function as a sort of stimulus, capable of conveying meaning in ways similar to perceptible objects. However, this observation that sensible objects trigger utterances only becomes interesting once Gorgias concedes the possibility that speech might be thought of as its own type of object corresponding to its own faculty of perception.

---

[27] Similarly, Kerferd, "Meaning and Reference," 218.

[28] To call this a behavioral conception of language is also, in my mind, unnecessarily anachronistic (cf. Bett, "Μὴ Ὄντος," 194n22, 204n35).

This latter concession is made only with a second qualification which effectively serves as an exit clause to the foregoing elenchus. It states that even if speech can be thought of as something that exists, it must (1) exist differently from other things that exist and (2) be apprehended differently from other things that exist:

> For even if speech exists, [Gorgias] says, it at the very least differs from the rest of things that exist, and visible bodies would differ most of all from things spoken. For the visible is apprehensible through one organ and speech through another.
>
> εἰ γὰρ καὶ ὑπόκειται, φησίν, ὁ λόγος, ἀλλὰ διαφέρει τῶν λοιπῶν ὑποκειμένων, καὶ πλείστῳ διενήνοχε τὰ ὁρατὰ σώματα τῶν λόγων· δι᾽ ἑτέρου γὰρ ὀργάνου ληπτόν ἐστι τὸ ὁρατὸν καὶ δι᾽ ἄλλου ὁ λόγος.[29]

In this passage, Gorgias entertains the possibility that speech might exist as its own sort of entity under two related conditions: *logos* must differ from all other things and must be apprehended differently from other things (especially sight). Mourelatos dismisses this passage, assuming that the contrast drawn between speech perception and sight perception entails an implicit (non-Gorgian) concession that the meaning of speech can be communicated to the faculty of hearing alone (as opposed to sight).[30] However, this need not be the case. The assumption that speech conveys its meaning to the faculty of hearing alone was already explicitly denied earlier on in both versions of the *ONB*.[31] Moreover, one should ask what purpose Gorgias would have for granting the possibility that speech may be apprehensible through hearing while denying the possibility that speech may be apprehensible through sight (i.e., writing). It would be more consistent and more charitable to assume that when Gorgias says that speech, as a thing that exists, must differ from the

---

[29] Sextus Empiricus, *Against the Logicians*, 7.86.

[30] Mourelatos, "Gorgias on the Function," 137 cf. Kerferd, "Meaning and Reference," 219.

[31] *MXG* 6 980b1-3; Sextus Empiricus, *Against the Logicians*, 7.83-4 quoted and discussed above.

rest of the things that exist, he means simply that it must differ from all perceptible objects that exist, including audible things. In other words, he abstracts *logos* from all of its perceptible manifestations that may be available to sight, hearing, or the like and treats it as its own entity—an entity that, if it has any effect on a listener at all, must be apprehended by something like a sixth sense.

What makes this final exit clause remarkable is that it grants a starting point for an alternative framework for communication. If speech is understood as a thing that exists, it may, like other things that exist, manifest meaning to the one apprehending it. The only conditions to this are that speech must (1) be radically different from all other objects of perception and (2) must be apprehended differently from them as well. Once these conditions are met, a form of communication may take place in which speech functions analogously to (but still differently enough from) perceptible objects. In the next section, we shall see how this alternative theory is developed in Gorgias's *Encomium of Helen*.

Speech and the Soul in the *Encomium of Helen*

In sections 8-14 of the *Encomium of Helen*, we find a very different, though no less surprising, picture of *logos* than we had in *ONB*. It must be said at the outset that this account is probably not meant to be taken as Gorgias's final word on how words work. By Gorgias's own admission, the *Helen* was written as a plaything (*paignion*) and thus not as something to be taken all too seriously.[32] I suggest simply that sections 8-14 of the *Helen* may be regarded as a playful and provisional sketch of an alternative theory of communication, one that specifically sidesteps the problems of linguistic reference that Gorgias underscores in *ONB*. In particular I show how the *Helen* picks up where the final exit clause of *ONB* leaves off and fulfills its conditions by presenting *logos* as (1) something different from all things (especially visible things) and (2) something that is apprehended differently from (but analogously to) perceptible things.

---

[32] "I wanted to write this speech as an encomium of Helen and as plaything for myself [ἐβουλήθην γράψαι τὸν λόγον Ἑλένης μὲν ἐγκώμιον, ἐμὸν δὲ παίγνιον]" (*Helen*, 21).

Gorgias fulfills the first condition by carving out a new conceptual space in which speech may exist. As he put it, speech is a mighty dynast (*dunastēs megas*) that performs divine deeds with the smallest and most imperceptible (*aphanestatos*) body.[33] By locating speech beyond human perception, he marks *logos* out as categorically distinct from other perceptible objects. The word *aphanestatos* is, of course, derived from *phainō,* which denotes all types of disclosure and revelation but, at its core, bears a strong visual sense. To call speech physically minute and *aphanestatos,* Gorgias is especially stressing the difference between speech objects and visible objects while at the same time categorically distinguishing speech from all other perceptible things. This move harmonizes well with what is said in *ONB* about the necessary difference between words and all other perceptible things in the world (especially visible things).[34] Thus, already from the outset of Gorgias's description of speech in the *Helen,* we find that *logos* is not only an object that exists in the world but also one that exists in the world differently from other things we might see or hear.

The fulfillment of the second condition left open in *ONB* is slightly more complex. In order to show that speech is apprehended differently from other things, Gorgias creatively coordinates the concepts of opinion (*doxa*) and soul (*psychē*) in order to construct something that resembles a faculty of speech perception. He models this new idea of speech perception directly on the idea of sense perception—in particular, the faculty of sight (*opsis*), which he describes in sections 15-20. As I shall illustrate in what follows, Gorgias offers a two-tier model of both speech and sight perception in which just as visible things impact the soul (*psychē*) through the intermediary of sight (*opsis*), thingified speech impacts the soul (*psychē*) through the intermediary of human opinion (*doxa*). The two faculties of speech perception and sight perception are categorically

---

[33] Gorgias, *Helen,* 8.

[34] "The contrast between the diminutive substance of *logos* and the magnitude of its effects reaffirms the categorial gulf between words and things—an echo of the third part of *Not Being*" (Mourelatos, "Gorgias on the Function," 156).

distinct (as they must be) yet parallel in how they function. To grasp this, it helps to take a closer look at what Gorgias has to say specifically about the workings of speech and sight and, importantly, the role that *psychē* plays in both.

Gorgias makes it quite clear that both speech and vision work by shaping the soul in one way or another. He writes, for instance, that "persuasion joining with speech shapes the soul too in the ways it wants [ἡ πειθὼ προσιοῦσα τῷ λόγῳ καὶ τὴν ψυχὴν ἐτυπώσατο ὅπως ἐβούλετο]"[35] and that "the soul is shaped in its very character through sight [διὰ δὲ τῆς ὄψεως ἡ ψυχὴ κἀν τοῖς τρόποις τυποῦται]."[36] Moreover, both vision and speech affect the soul in similar ways. The faculty of vision works by transmitting mental states directly to the soul. For instance, Gorgias notes how, at the sight of an enemy army, *opsis* "becomes perturbed and perturbs the soul [ἐταράχθη καὶ ἐτάραξε τὴν ψυχήν]."[37] Later, he describes how the eye of Helen, when it caught sight of Paris, "transmitted to the soul a desire and eagerness for eros [προθυμίαν καὶ ἅμιλλαν ἔρωτος τῇ ψυχῇ παρέδωκε]."[38] Speech functions somewhat similarly. As Gorgias puts it, speech affects the soul just as drugs (*pharmaka*) affect the body (*sōma*).[39] When drug-like speech comes into contact with the soul, it causes it to experience a wide variety of emotions/illusions:

> For just as different drugs extract different fluids from the body, some stop sickness, others life, so too some utterances create pain, others delight, others fear, others instill auditors with courage, and still others intoxicate and bewitch the soul with evil persuasion.

---

[35] Gorgias, *Helen*, 13.

[36] Gorgias, *Helen*, 15.

[37] Gorgias, *Helen*, 16.

[38] Gorgias, *Helen*, 19.

[39] Gorgias, *Helen*, 14: "The power of speech has the same relation to the composition of the soul as the composition of drugs has to the nature of bodies [τὸν αὐτὸν δὲ λόγον ἔχει ἥ τε τοῦ λόγου δύναμις πρὸς τὴν τῆς ψυχῆς τάξιν ἥ τε τῶν φαρμάκων τάξις πρὸς τὴν τῶν σωμάτων φύσιν]."

> ὥσπερ γὰρ τῶν φαρμάκων ἄλλους ἄλλα χυμοὺς ἐκ τοῦ σώματος ἐξάγει, καὶ τὰ μὲν νόσου τὰ δὲ βίου παύει, οὕτω καὶ τῶν λόγων οἱ μὲν ἐλύπησαν, οἱ δὲ ἔτερψαν, οἱ δὲ ἐφόβησαν, οἱ δὲ εἰς θάρσος κατέστησαν τοὺς ἀκούοντας, οἱ δὲ πειθοῖ τινι κακῇ τὴν ψυχὴν ἐφαρ-μάκευσαν καὶ ἐξεγοήτευσαν.[40]

Like visible objects, things spoken instill a wide variety of mental states within the soul. In this capacity, speech, in Gorgias's words, coerces the soul (*ēnagkase*) to do and believe whatever it wants.[41]

The chief similarity between vision and speech is that they both ultimately affect *psychē*—that is to say, they are at bottom psychological or, perhaps better, *psychagogic* experiences. This fact becomes especially important when we realize that Gorgias is one of the first extant authors to speak about *psychē* in a psychological sense and that, throughout his extant writings, the term for soul only appears in the *Encomium of Helen*. In Gorgias's lifetime, the meaning of *psychē* was evolving (somewhat messily) from a smokey substance that drifts apart from the body at death to the unifying seat of sensation, thought, and emotion.[42] In the *Helen*, Gorgias capitalizes

---

[40] Gorgais, *Helen*, 14. See also *Helen*, 9: "To those who hear it [i.e., poetic speech] comes fearful shuddering, tearful pity, grief-loving desire, and, based on the fortunes and misfortunes of the actions and bodies of others, the soul experiences, through speeches, a certain experience of its own [ἧς τοὺς ἀκούοντας εἰσῆλθε καὶ φρίκη περίφοβος καὶ ἔλεος πολύδακρυς καὶ πόθος φιλοπενθής, ἐπ' ἀλλοτρίων τε πραγμάτων καὶ σωμάτων εὐτυχίαις καὶ δυσπραγίαις ἴδιόν τι πάθημα διὰ τῶν λόγων ἔπαθεν ἡ ψυχή]."

[41] "For speech, after persuading the soul, coerces what it persuaded to obey what is said and approve what is done [λόγος γὰρ ὁ τὴν ψυχὴν πείσας, ἣν ἔπεισεν, ἠνάγκασε καὶ πείθεσθαι τοῖς λεγομένοις καὶ συναινέσαι τοῖς ποιουμένοις]" (*Helen*, 12).

[42] See David Claus, *Towards the Soul: An Inquiry into the Meaning of Ψυχή before Plato* (New Haven: Yale University Press, 1981), esp. 148-50; André Laks, "Soul, Sensation, and Thought," in *The Cambridge Companion to Early Greek Philosophy*, ed. A. A. Long (Cambridge: Cambridge University Press, 1999), 250–70.

on this new sense of the word, using it fourteen times, mostly in reference to the function of speech and sight.[43]

What must have appealed to Gorgias about the psychological sense of the word *psychē* is that it provides a neat way of marrying the physical domain of sense perception with the cognitive domain of speech perception. As we saw earlier in *ONB*, Gorgias's main problem with speech is that it does not seem to convey meaning to the senses in the same way that other things do. And, if it does not do this, it is difficult to articulate how speech conveys meaning at all. With the addition of the new concept of *psychē*, the situation changes. Sense perceptions are no longer the ultimate receptors of external content and, instead, become intermediaries that ultimately inscribe what they perceive directly onto the soul.[44] With sense perception serving this subsidiary role, it becomes less problematic that speech cannot manifest meaning to the senses directly since it becomes theoretically possible to imagine a scenario in which speech might somehow bypass the senses entirely and communicate with the soul by some other avenue. As we saw already, this is essentially how Gorgias conceives of speech as working in the *Helen*.

So far, we have noticed that in Gorgias's *Helen* things seen and things spoken function in similar ways; they are imagined as external stimuli that ultimately affect the same terminus—namely, the soul. They differ, however, in the faculties through which they are apprehended and conveyed to the soul. Gorgias is quite clear that visible objects pass through the intermediary of sight (*opsis*) or the eye (*omma*) before affecting the soul. He is also clear that speech is not apprehended by sight or hearing or any of the five senses.

[43] The only time it is not specifically used in reference to vision or speech is in the opening sentence (κόσμος […] ψυχῇ δὲ σοφία; *Helen*, 1) which can be translated in various ways depending on how one reads the predication: "*sophia* is *kosmos* for the soul" or "*kosmos* is *sophia* for the soul." Either way, Gorgias is using *psychē* with its psychological meaning.

[44] Gorgias uses the concept of *psychē* similarly to how medical writers speak of *sōma* where it functions as "a kind of interval" fitted conceptually between the "external catalyst and a (visible) outcome" (Holmes, *The Symptom*, 214).

Instead, it appeals to what Gorgias calls the eyes of opinion (τοῖς τῆς δόξης ὄμμασιν).[45] In this role, opinion (*doxa*) functions analogously to sight as an intermediary between the external stimulus (i.e., *logos*) and the internal terminus of human experience (i.e., *psychē*). In the tables below, I map out the conceptual difference between *ONB*, which omits any idea of *psychē* and *doxa*, and the *Helen*, which includes them as a way of mapping speech perception onto sense perception while still allowing each to remain categorically distinct:

***On Not-Being* (without *psychē/doxa*)**

	Stimulus	Terminus
Sense perception	visible objects	sight (*opsis*)

***Encomium of Helen* (with *psychē/doxa*)**

	Stimulus →	Intermediary →	Terminus
Sense perception	visible objects	sight (*opsis*)	soul (*psychē*)
Speech perception	speech (*logos*)	opinion (*doxa*)	soul (*psychē*)

This mediating role of *doxa* is crucial for understanding Gorgias's discussion of magic in §10:

> For the power of the incantation, joining with the opinion of the soul, enchants and persuades and alters it with magic. And the arts of enchantment and magic are found to be twofold—namely, the errors of the soul and the deceptions of opinion.
>
> συγγινομένη γὰρ τῇ δόξῃ τῆς ψυχῆς ἡ δύναμις τῆς ἐπῳδῆς ἔθελξε καὶ ἔπεισε καὶ μετέστησεν αὐτὴν γοητείᾳ. γοητείας δὲ καὶ μαγείας δισσαὶ τέχναι εὕρηνται, αἵ εἰσι ψυχῆς ἁμαρτήματα καὶ δόξης ἀπατήματα.

[45] Gorgais, *Helen*, 13. As far as I can tell, the phrase is unparalleled in archaic and classical Greek.

Here, *dissai technai* does not refer to two types of verbal magic,[46] nor does it refer to two separate arts of speaking—be they poetry and incantation,[47] oratory and incantation,[48] or poetry and prose.[49] Rather, what Gorgias is saying is that the magic inherent to all of the arts of speech involves a *"twofold" process* (*dissai*): speech deceives opinion, and opinion, in turn, misleads the soul.[50]

This difference in how things spoken and things seen are apprehended leads to differences in how each phenomenon is experienced. Unlike the intermediary of *opsis*, *doxa* can be especially deceptive. Gorgias stresses that *doxa*, in its role as the "counselor to the soul" (σύμβουλον τῇ ψυχῇ), is especially slippery and unstable (σφαλερὰ καὶ ἀβέβαιος) and capable of casting people into slippery and unstable fortunes.[51] The reason for this heightened instability has to do with the imperceptible quality of speech. Gorgias notes how "the things we see do not have the nature we wish, but the one each happened to have" (ἃ γὰρ ὁρῶμεν, ἔχει φύσιν οὐχ ἣν ἡμεῖς θέλομεν, ἀλλ' ἣν ἕκαστον ἔτυχε).[52] *Logos*, on the other hand, is apparently unmoored from any sensible manifestation and could putatively communicate a much wider range of things to the faculty of *doxa* than the visible domain can to the faculty of sight. For this reason, skilled speakers can, as Gorgias puts it, "cause things both unbelievable and unclear to appear to the eyes of opinion [τὰ ἄπιστα

---

[46] D.M. Macdowell, *Gorgias: Encomium of Helen*, 2nd ed. (1982; repr., London: Bristol Classical Press, 1993), 33, thinks that δισσαὶ τέχναι suggests a distinction between the synonyms μαγεία and γοητεία.

[47] Jacqueline de Romilly, *Magic and Rhetoric in Ancient Greece* (Cambridge, MA: Harvard University Press, 1975), 3-22.

[48] W.J. Verdenius, "Gorgias' Doctrine of Deception," in *The Sophists and Their Legacy*, ed. George B. Kerferd (Wiesbaden: Franz Steiner, 1981), 122n37.

[49] Thomas Duncan, "Gorgias' Theories of Art," *The Classical Journal* 33 (1938): 406; Untersteiner, *The Sophists*, 116.

[50] See also Charles Segal, "Gorgias and the Psychology of the Logos," *Harvard Studies in Classical Philology* 66 (1962), 112; Mikhail Pozdnev and Viktor Streicher, "'Die doppelten Künste der Magie'? Zu Gorgias von Leontinoi, Helena c. 10," *Wiener Studien* 123 (2010): 11-18.

[51] Gorgias, *Helen*, 11.

[52] Gorgias, *Helen*, 15.

καὶ ἄδηλα φαίνεσθαι τοῖς τῆς δόξης ὄμμασιν] simply by dispelling and instilling one opinion instead of another [δόξαν ἀντὶ δόξης τὴν μὲν ἀφελόμενοι τὴν δ' ἐνεργασάμενοι]."[53]

With this twofold process in mind, we can see how the description of speech in Gorgias's *Helen* carries forward strands of thought left undeveloped in *ONB*. In the latter work, we saw how Gorgias calls into question whether speech is capable of referring to anything other than itself without appealing to sense perceptions. In an important passage at the close of Sextus's version of *ONB*, a concession is made that if speech could potentially exist as a thing in the world, it would differ from all perceptible things and, therefore, would be apprehended differently from perceptible things as well. This concession is not explored further in *ONB*. Instead, Gorgias concludes absurdly (and, I take it, ironically) that a thought cannot be indicated to others (οὐ δηλωτὸν ἄλλοις).[54] I have argued that, in the *Helen*, Gorgias picks up where the final concession left off in *ONB*. Gorgias conceives of speech as something that differs from all perceptible things and is apprehended in a way unlike (but analogous to) perceptible things. In particular, just as visible objects affect the soul by appearing to the eyes, speech affects the soul by appealing imperceptibly to the "eyes of opinion" (τοῖς τῆς δόξης ὄμμασιν) and, in doing so, it even communicates things that are unbelievable and unapparent (τὰ ἄπιστα καὶ ἄδηλα).[55]

There, of course, remain many pockets of obscurity in the way Gorgias presents this alternative theory of communication. It is difficult to know, for instance, how exactly opinion communicates with the soul or how exactly speech communicates with opinion. It is correspondingly unclear what kind of thing speech is exactly or, for that matter, what kind of things the soul and opinion are. Speculating further about these and other details of Gorgias's description of *logos* in the *Helen* can be a ticklish endeavor even in the best of circumstances: our evidence is slim, and there is the ever-

---

[53] Gorgias, *Helen*, 13.

[54] *MXG* 5 979a13, cf. πῶς ἄν τις…δηλώσειεν ἄλλῳ, *MXG* 980a20; οὐδεὶς… ἑτέρῳ δηλώσειεν, *MXG* 980b17-8.

[55] Gorgias, *Helen*, 13.

present danger of treating Gorgias's game (*paignion*) as something more serious than it was meant to be. At the very least, I have tried to explain the basic elements of Gorgias's intriguing, non-referential picture of *logos* in the *Helen* and how these basic elements can be seen to complement (rather than contradict) Gorgias's picture of *logos* in *ONB*. On a broader view, I hope to have shown how Gorgias's musings about speech contain serious reflections on the nature of human communication, even if these reflections are not always presented in a serious way.

Mauro Serra[1]

The Violence of *Logos*: A Political Reading of Gorgias's *Helen*

Over recent decades there has been a great deal of work to rehabilitate the sophists and Gorgias in particular.[2] In this very recent rediscovery of Gorgias,[3] the *Encomium of Helen* has naturally received the most attention—to the point that, today, we might even say that it has become a classic (of philosophy). In 2016, Rachel Barney wrote a challenging paper about the *Helen* as part of a book whose significant title was *Ten Neglected Classics of Philosophy*,[4] and just the same year Gorgias's text received the honor of an independent

---

[1] Mauro Serra teaches Philosophy of Language at the University of Salerno, Italy. He mainly deals with rhetoric, both ancient and modern. He is currently working on a book about the relationship between language and violence which is expected to be published in 2023.

[2] For Gorgias, although some earlier work should not be overlooked, such as a seminal paper of Charles Segal (1962), 1980 can be considered a good starting point for this rehabilitation. That year saw the publication of Cassin's monograph on *On Not Being*. The following year it was the turn of Kerferd's book, *The Sophistic Movement*. See Kurt Lampe "The *Logos* of Ethics in Gorgias's *Palamedes, On What is Not*, and *Helen*" in *Early Greek Ethics*, ed. D. Wolfsdorf (Oxford: Oxford University Press, 2020), 128-29.

[3] Here I paraphrase Livio Rossetti's keynote speech from the conference. Notwithstanding this rediscovery, there is a lot more to be discovered about Gorgias. See also Maria M. Sassi, "Socrate salvato dal suo isolamento. La 'discussione' con Simonide, Euripide e Gorgia sulla volontà morale," in *La volontarietà dell'azione tra Antichità e Medioevo*, ed. Fulvia de Luise and Irene Zavattero (Trento: Università degli Studi di Trento, 2019), 80n23: "Per quanto riguarda non solo il campo problematico del discorso e del linguaggio, ma anche quello dei processi cognitivi, emotivi e rappresentativi, l'opera di Gorgia e segnatamente *l'Encomio di Elena* costituiscono una vera miniera, *di cui alcuni filoni sono probabilmente ancora da esplorare*, di spunti teorici che verranno variamente raccolti e sviluppati nel pensiero platonico e aristotelico" (my emphasis).

[4] Rachel Barney, "Gorgias's *Encomium of Helen*," in *Ten Neglected Classics of Philosophy*, ed. Erich Schliesser (New York: Oxford University Press, 2016), 1-26.

critical edition in the prestigious *Bibliotheca Teubneriana*.[5] Therefore, we are now provided with plenty of interpretations of the *Helen*, which, in some cases, are sophisticated and challenging, but we find little attention paid to its potential political dimension. Although it is, of course, very difficult to say why may be, I put forward two possible reasons, naturally leaving aside a third, which is that I'm simply wrong to propose a political reading of the *Helen*.

The first is the paradoxical nature of text. Taken as a whole, the text seems enigmatic, starting from its subject, Helen. Among the writers of the 5th century BCE, Helen was often treated as the paradigm of the adulterous woman, who with her wrong actions gave rise to one of the greatest conflicts of the Mediterranean world. Incredibly—only the first paradoxical cue of the text—Gorgias sets out to defend her as not having been responsible for these actions. Moreover, looking beyond his treatment of Helen, one notices immediately that in the largest section of the text (about one third of it, or seven paragraphs), Gorgias turns his attention to the effect of persuasion and to the power of *logos*—and it is often thought that rhetoric is, in fact, the work's primary concern. Other scholars, however, have thought other themes to be more important. Thus, the *Encomium of Helen* has been read as an extended analysis of language's functioning, as a reflection on agency and responsibility, or even as a work on the nature of knowledge and the irrational role of emotions. It would be a mistake, however, to think that only one of these accurately describes what the text is fundamentally about; all the issues should have some weight in one's overall interpretation. All in all, it is difficult to escape the impression that Gorgias's text is a Russian nesting doll, as, for example, Barney's description—the best, in my opinion—suggests: "the *Helen* presents a bold thesis about the nature of language and persuasion, *nested within* a valid and disturbing argument about moral responsibility, *wrapped up* in a spectacularly self-undermining showpiece of rhetorical display."[6]

---

[5] Gorgias, *Helenae Encomium*, ed. F. Donadi (Berlin: de Gruyter, 2016).
[6] Barney, "Gorgias's *Encomium*," 24 (my emphasis).

Let us now turn to the second reason, which seems to me a little more probable. At first sight, the *Helen* presents a view of *logos* and its actions that is actually at odds with the classical Greek democratic conception of political life. Among the many texts that it would be possible to quote, I have chosen a passage from the *Funeral Oration* by Lysias, which clearly emphasizes that the distinction/opposition between force (*bia*) and persuasion (*peithō*) is the real distinguishing feature of a democratic political life:

> [They, the ancestors] were the first and only people in that time to drive out the ruling classes of their state and to establish a *democracy*, believing the liberty of all to be the strongest bond of agreement; by sharing with each other the hopes born of their perils they had freedom of soul [ἐλευθέραις ταῖς ψυχαῖς] in their civic life, and used the law for honoring the good and punishing the evil. For they deemed that *it was the way of wild beasts to be held subject to one another by force* [ὑπ᾽ ἀλλήλων βίᾳ κρατεῖσθαι], but the duty of men to delimit justice by law, to convince by argument [λόγῳ πεῖσαι], and to serve these two in act by submitting to the sovereignty of law and the instruction of reason.[7]

It is a somewhat later text than Gorgias's *Helen* (by about thirty years), but there is no doubt that it reflects a conception that was also canonical in 5th century BCE thought, at least from the middle of the century.[8] Taking into account this conceptual framework, if one sticks to the letter of the statements made by Gorgias, it becomes really difficult to imagine that he is speaking seriously and that the text reflects a serious political concern. As Jonathan Pratt says: "If the notion that persuasion is reducible to compulsion were to gain wide currency, it would not only obliterate an entrenched opposition

---

[7] Lysias, *Funeral Oration* 18–19, trans. Lamb (my emphasis).

[8] Aeschylus's *Oresteia* and the myth of Prometheus, attributed in Plato's dialogue to Protagoras, could be considered milestones in the elaboration of this conception. On this topic, it is always useful to see R. Buxton, *Persuasion in Greek Tragedy: A Study in* Peithō (Cambridge: Cambridge University Press, 1982), 5-66.

within Greek thought but would also pull the rug out from under any consensual or egalitarian political regime."[9]

Having said that, it would be unfair to say that my own reading emerges completely out of the blue. I have found three different scholars who explicitly address the topic of the *Helen*'s political interpretation.[10] For reasons of space, I will not comment in detail on each of them. Instead, I will limit myself to highlighting what seems to me the most significant aspects of each, followed with a very short comment. I hope that the remainder of my paper will show enough points of contact and points of divergence.

For Diego Lanza,[11] the rhetorician in Gorgias's representation appears to be completely different from the Athenian speaker. A teacher of paradoxes and enigmas rather than of the just and unjust, Gorgianic rhetoric develops in a non-political dimension. For Takis Poulakos,[12] however, the *Helen* should be read as a signal of a crisis in the aristocratic networks of power and as an effort to fill the lack that had caused the crisis, "redirecting the art of rhetoric away from the probable and toward the performative."[13] Finally, for Michael Pfau,[14] the *Helen* allegorically represents a barbarian view of politics, a perspective of someone who was neither Athenian nor democratic and therefore did not share a belief in the potentially liberating aspects of political speech.

---

[9] Jonathan Pratt, "On the Threshold of Rhetoric: Gorgias' *Encomium of Helen*," *Classical Antiquity* 34. 1 (2015): 168.

[10] To these should be added the paper by Jonathan Pratt quoted in the previous note. I agree with it in many respects, even if it proposes, strictly speaking, an ethical rather than a political interpretation.

[11] Diego Lanza, *Lingua e discorso nell'Atene delle professioni* (Napoli: Liguori, 1979), 45-49.

[12] Takis Poulakos, "Human Agency in the History of Rhetoric," in *Writing Histories of Rhetoric*, ed. Victor J. Vitanza (Carbondale: Southern Illinois University Press, 1994), 59-80.

[13] Poulakos, "Human Agency," 70.

[14] Michael W. Pfau, "Encomium on Helen as Advertisement: Political Life According to Gorgias the Barbarian," in *Advances in the History of Rhetoric: The First Six Years*, ed. Richard L. Enos and David E. Beard (West Lafayette: Parlor Press, 2007), 154-166.

Let us turn to a brief comment on these three interpretations. Lanza's is meaningfully conditioned by the paradoxical nature of the text and by the difficulty of satisfactorily explaining the relationship between its form and its content.[15] There is no space in the social context of the *polis* for a rhetoric that is interpreted as a magical tool on the basis of its formal characteristics alone. Therefore, we have no space for politics at all. Poulakos and Pfau, however, share the conviction that Gorgias's rhetoric is not representative of a democratic conception of political life, but of an aristocratic effort to use a new technical knowledge to maintain its power.[16] In both cases, this line of interpretation presents serious difficulties. On the one hand, the "probable," corresponding to the Greek word *eikos*, is an essential element of the conceptual framework delineated in Gorgias's *Helen*;[17] on the other, I don't really understand in what

---

[15] This difficulty is not new, see, e.g., the ungenerous judgement of J.D. Denniston in *Greek Prose Style* (Oxford: Clarendon Press, 1952), 12: "Starting with the initial advantage of having nothing in particular to say, he [Gorgias] was able to concentrate all his energies upon saying it." It has been definitively overcome by the idea of a "prose rhapsode" introduced by Edward Schiappa, *Beginnings of Rhetorical Theory in Classical Greece* (New Haven: Yale University Press, 1999), 101-2. "Accordingly, I propose that Gorgias be understood as a *prose rhapsode*. By calling Gorgias a rhapsode I wish to emphasize the fact that his speeches were composed to be performed and to underscore his debt to the oral poetic tradition." Seen from this perspective, there is no gap between form and content in Gorgias's *Encomium*.

[16] For an analogous and, in my opinion, paradoxical position, see also Michael Kochin, *Five Chapters on Rhetoric* (University Park: Pennsylvania State University Press, 2009), 136-137: "[...] Gorgias's rhetoric is to be used within "democratic" institutions, but is intended to serve those whose capacity for violence does not depend on speech but rather on familial wealth and on familial relations."

[17] I have tried to show elsewhere that the probable and the performative, to use Poulakos's terminology, are coexisting elements in Gorgias's thought. See Mauro Serra, "Narrare ed argomentare: percorsi della verità nella Grecia antica," *Testi e linguaggi* 6 (2012), 253-268; Idem, "La performance retorica: l'*Encomio di Elena* di Gorgia tra improvvisazione e metalinguaggio," *Testi e linguaggi* 9 (2015): 85-98.

sense it could be said that Gorgias was a "barbarian."[18] After all, not only was he chosen for the diplomatic mission to Athens in 427 BCE during the most Greek of the wars, so to speak, but "during the middle decades of the 5th century, the time when Gorgias was presumably beginning to develop his talents and reputation, the cities he dwelled in and travelled to were democratically governed."[19] To provide a political interpretation of Gorgias's *Helen* we need obviously to follow a different path. However, before doing this, and in order to outline the background of my own interpretation, I need to introduce another, completely different, perspective.

According to two leading scholars, if we take into consideration the homonymous Platonic dialogue, the teaching of Gorgias—that teaching to which the Sophist gives the name rhetoric—would be nothing other than politics. In a seminal paper of 2011, Yosef Z. Liebersohn says that

> in the consciousness of those who teach it (represented by the Platonic character Gorgias), rhetoric is nothing but politics. The speaker is a politician who knows how to speak. Its sphere—if we are careful enough not to use the term *materia*—is the affairs of the *polis*, and its evaluation concerning its beneficence is wholly political.[20]

More recently, in 2020,[21] Maria Tanja Luzzatto, looking again at one of the hot questions of the secondary literature (i.e., the origins of

---

[18] I don't think Isocrates's observation that Gorgias, moving from place to place, did not become attached to any particular city state, neither paying taxes nor providing for public benefits, is "one piece of corroborating evidence," as Pfau thinks. See Pfau "Encomium," 163.

[19] Eric W. Robinson, "The Sophists and Democracy Beyond Athens," *Rhetorica* 25.1 (2007): 115. The cities Robinson refers to are Leontinoi, Acragas, and Syracuse.

[20] Yosef Z. Liebersohn, "The Problem of Rhetoric's *Materia* in Plato's *Gorgias* (449c9-d9)," *Rhetorica* 29 (2011): 21-22.

[21] Maria T. Luzzatto, "Did Gorgias Coin *Rhētorikē*? A Rereading of Plato's *Gorgias*," *Lexis* 38, (2020): 200.

technē rhetorikē),[22] states resolutely two complementary theses: 1) Gorgias is the inventor of rhetoric both as a discipline and as a name; and 2) "*rhetorikē* [is] the perfect word for an eminently Greek discipline combining skilled public speech with leadership and personal *doxa*, and the term bears the distinctive mark of the free citizen pursuing success in the ancient city-state."[23] Therefore, again, rhetoric would be nothing other than politics. In this way, we come to outline what I will call the "two Gorgias thesis"—a thesis which, I need to specify, is explicitly endorsed by Luzzatto. According to her, we have, on the one side, Gorgias as a teacher of rhetoric, for whom rhetoric is politics, so that we can even say that his school is a school of politics. On the other side, however, we have Gorgias as the author of the *Helen*, a text which is neither a general theory of *logos* nor the sophist's manifesto, but which contains a paradoxical theory that is at least seemingly at odds with a democratic (and perhaps even Greek) view of political life.

In my opinion, this view faces at least two problems. According to Luzzatto, Gorgias's choice of *logoi* in *Helen* (8-14) strongly suggests the need for a different and distinctive "term of art," since the peculiar list entirely leaves out the political speeches that properly belong to rhetoric.[24] There would be, therefore, a sort of relation of complementarity between the teaching of rhetoric and the framework delineated in the central part of the *Helen* with its different examples of the power of *logos*. I am not sure, however, if the second example of §13 doesn't really refer to the speeches given in the political sphere. Here is the text of example:

---

[22] The question was raised, as is widely known, by Schiappa's paper "Did Plato Coin *Rhētorikē?*" (*American Journal of Philology* 111.4 (1990): 457-470) whose conclusions are questioned by Luzzatto. Fortunately, to support my interpretation, I don't need to go into this debate. It seems to me, however, that my interpretation of *Encomium* presents a possible synthesis of the two different perspectives put forward respectively by Schiappa and Luzzatto.

[23] Luzzatto, "Did Gorgias Coin *Rhētorikē*?," 200.

[24] Luzzatto, "Did Gorgias Coin *Rhētorikē*?," 205.

> second [consider] the compelling agonistic arguments in which one speech, artfully written not truthfully said, delights and persuades a numerous crowd.
>
> δεύτερον δὲ τοὺς ἀναγκαίους διὰ λόγων ἀγῶνας, ἐν οἷς εἷς λόγος πολὺν ὄχλον ἔτερψε καὶ ἔπεισε τέχνῃ γραφείς, οὐκ ἀληθείᾳ λεχθείς.

Its interpretation is notoriously difficult, first of all because the meaning of the adjective *anagkaious* is not clear. Most interpreters, in fact, translate it as "compelled," suggesting a reference to forensic oratory that would be confirmed by the word *agōnas,* which may of course very naturally refer to the law-courts. However, Doreen Innes has persuasively shown, with close parallels from Homer to Plato, that the adjective's correct meaning is "compelling," and that with this example the sophist was not only referring to all public oratory but was also using "a cluster of key vocabulary, through which Gorgias invites us to identify his own oratory and gives a metaliterary description of the *Helen* itself."[25] In any case, the use of the word *ochlos* (crowd) in the same passage cannot be overlooked, since it is a key word on which Plato constructs his image of Gorgias as a teacher of rhetoric or, what amounts to the same, as a teacher of politics (e.g., 453d7; 455a4).

We can now move on to the second difficulty, which has to do precisely with the relationship between Gorgias's *Helen* and the homonymous Platonic dialogue or, to put it in another way, with the relationship between the historical Gorgias and the character of the Platonic dialogue. According to Luzzatto:

> there are serious problems with the widespread belief that *Helen* 8-14 expounds a general theory of *logos,* and it is my opinion that we should resist the temptation to view the celebrated passage as the sophist's manifesto: rather, all our pieces of evidence, *including* the statements made by Gorgias in Plato, should be understood as complementing

[25] Doreen Innes, "Gorgias, *Helen* 13," in *Sygkharmata. Studies in Honor of Jan Fredrik Kindstrand* (Uppsala: Uppsala Universitet 2006), 129.

each other by supplying separate parts of a final picture that will only result by fitting all the available pieces together.[26]

If this perspective is adopted, however, it is difficult to explain why the conceptual framework that we find associated with the Gorgianic political teaching in the Platonic dialogue is substantially congruent with what Gorgias himself says in the central part of the *Helen*. Of course, I don't have the space here to develop a detailed demonstration of this; I will therefore limit myself to highlighting a few significant aspects that may support my observation. First of all, in the Platonic dialogue, Gorgias makes repeated use of the vocabulary of *dynamis/dynamai* in the preliminary conversation with Socrates (especially in 452c and 456a-c), with an undeniable reference to the exaltation of *logos'* power contained in his *Helen*. Second, and more importantly, under pressure by Socrates to define his art, Gorgias not only identifies it with the art of *logoi* that has persuasion as its object or end, but boldly claims that "persuasion is the greatest possession since it is at the same time the reason why men are free and manage to dominate the others in their city" (*Gorgias*, 452d6-8).

In this way, Plato's *Gorgias* is taking up, in a slightly different way, the *Helen*'s paradoxical thesis on the identity of persuasion and force or compulsion. Moreover, as Barney rightly says, "that this disturbing claim to powers of 'enslavement' is seriously meant—and is Gorgias's own—is confirmed by a remark in Plato's *Philebus* (a very late dialogue with no obvious anti-sophistic agenda)."[27] There, in fact, the character Protarchus claims to have often heard Gorgias repeat that the art of persuasion is greater than all others because it permits you to enslave others with their consent (58a-b).[28] In short, it seems to me that it is difficult to escape the impression that Plato, in creating the portrait of Gorgias as teacher of rhetoric and politics, drew heavily on what Gorgias himself claimed in the *Helen*.

---

[26] Luzzatto, "Did Gorgias Coin *Rhētorikē*?," 206.

[27] Barney, "Gorgias's *Helen*," 22.

[28] I am not convinced, however, by Barney's claim that Gorgias would be depicted by Plato (probably accurately) as genuinely torn between two different conceptions of rhetoric, cooperative and manipulative.

What I would like to do, then, is show why a political reading of the *Helen* could bring together these two faces of Gorgias. To do this, I propose an interpretation in three steps roughly corresponding to the three layers of Gorgias's text highlighted by Barney.[29] My starting hypothesis is that the *Helen* is an example of "meta-rhetoric" attempting to theorize about rhetoric understood as political oratory, a sort of paradoxical model of democratic politics (and perhaps politics in general) that represents democratic citizens acting in their deliberative capacity.[30]

Let us start with the general structure of the *Helen*. It is often considered to have a design of the following form: Gorgias uses Helen as a paradigmatic example to reflect on the philosophical topic of moral responsibility—a topic, as is well-known, that was at the heart of then contemporary tragic poetry.[31] The text is thus guided

---

[29] I quote again the definition by emphasizing the three layers that I will address (in different order) in my following interpretation: "the Helen presents a bold thesis about the nature of *language and persuasion*, nested within a valid and disturbing argument about *moral responsibility*, wrapped up in a spectacularly *self-undermining showpiece of rhetorical display*" (Barney, "Gorgias's *Helen*," 24, my emphasis). While Barney in her interpretation also ends up presenting these elements as possible alternatives, complementary but autonomous, my aim is to show how a better understanding of Gorgias's text can be obtained precisely by highlighting the tight relationship between the three layers identified by Barney.

[30] On this point, I am very sympathetic with Pfau's perspective, while obviously arriving at a completely different conclusion.

[31] See Alonso Tordesillas, "Gorgias et la question de la responsabilité d'Hélène" in *Anthropinē sophia. Studi di filologia e storiografia filosofica in memoria di Gabriele Giannantoni*, ed. Francesca Alesse et alii (Napoli: Bibliopolis, 2008), 46: "D'où vient donc qu'Hélène soit peu à peu apparue comme une sorte d'incarnation de la faute morale? Très probablement de la réflexion que la tragédie mène sur la question de la reponsabilité en matière d'actions. C'est en effet par la tragédie que se forge progressivement une image négative d'Hélène." On the important relationship between Gorgias and tragedy, see Roberta Ioli, *Il felice inganno* (Milano: Mimesis, 2018); Simon Critchley, *Tragedy, The*

by an attempt at exoneration: a radical reconsideration of the blame ascribed to Helen. But while some of the tradition (e.g., Stesichorus, Euripides) had tried to exonerate Helen by assuming that she had never gone to Troy, Gorgias follows a completely different path. Helen did what she was accused of (*Helen* 5), but should not be blamed for what she did, because she was not responsible for it. Whatever the cause of her action was, Helen was forced to go to Troy and therefore cannot be held responsible. The argumentative structure that thus unfolds appears quite clear: all the possible causes of Helen's decision are identified[32] and the argument proceeds to show that, for each of them, Helen must be considered innocent as a victim of compulsion. According to this line of thought, "one might well infer that Gorgias's view destroys the possibility of personal responsibility."[33] If the argument put forward by Gorgias works, in fact, it works for all agents and all actions, and no one is ever responsible for anything. Take the Trojan war (to continue with the same Homeric context). Responsibility for starting the war cannot be attributed to Paris (for one may construct a very similar argument), or Agamemnon (for the same reason), or any other person. Simply, no one can be held morally responsible for anything. A similar argumentation could be applied to all actions by all people. We could find a way out of this paradoxical and disturbing conclusion by reducing the size of the domain that Gorgias is discussing. In this

---

Greeks and Us (New York: Pantheon, 2019) and, more recently, Jonas Grethlein, *The Ancient Aesthetics of Deception: The Ethics of Enchantment from Gorgias to Heliodorus* (Cambridge: Cambridge University Press, 2021), Chapter 1.

[32] Actually, Gorgias says "I will set forth the causes because of which it is plausible (*eikos*) that Helen's journey to Troy took place" (*Helen* 5). Therefore, logically speaking, Gorgias does not really claim to exclude all other explanations of Helen's flight. I don't think, however, that "Gorgias seems to forget or ignore this major qualification as the argument proceeds" (Barney, "Gorgias's *Encomium*," 6). Rather, this qualification is fundamental to correctly interpreting the role of truth—a question that I cannot address here.

[33] David Roochnik, "Responsible Fictions," in *Responsibility*, ed. Barbara Darling-Smith (Lanham: Lexington Books, 2007), 19.

way, one can see that the consequences of his thought apply only to a more limited range of actions. If we adopt a narrow reading, as, for example, Rachel Barney has done, Helen's action could be seen as a paradigmatic case of irrational and self-destructive action, an example of actions predictably ruinous or disastrous. From this perspective we could think that, when people act irrationally and self-destructively, they will always be found, on closer scrutiny, to have been compelled to do so by some external force. Therefore, their actions will be involuntary and the agents will be not morally responsible. There is also another possible way to narrow the range of actions to which Gorgias's example applies. Helen's action could, in fact, be understood as a paradigmatic example of a morally wrong action.[34] Unfortunately, however, there does not seem to be any straightforward evidence to support either of these readings, and it is no coincidence, in my opinion, that Barney's interpretation is based on a comparison between the *Helen* and the *Palamedes*. Remaining within the argument put forward in Gorgias's *Helen*, we have, however, what seems to me to be a more promising way out of this difficulty. We must not forget that moral responsibility, in Gorgias's text, cannot be discussed separately from a discussion of *logos* or persuasion (or any model of belief-formation). Here we have my second step.

One central, and paradoxical, feature of Gorgias's account of persuasion is surely that it is capable of explaining how Helen was (non-culpably) persuaded to leave her husband to go to Troy with Paris. At first sight, this argument seems to be implausible. If, in fact, there is a clearly defined opposition in Greek thought (but not only), it is that between force and persuasion, *bia* and *peithō*. The presence of one implies the absence of the other. The concept of persuasion, however, has a basic ambiguity. In English, as in ancient Greek (but also in Italian and other modern languages), the verb "to persuade" has two primary uses, the first having to do with action, and the

[34] In this way, Gorgias's argument would come close to the famous Socratic principle, according to which "no one does wrong voluntarily." See Barney, "Gorgias's *Encomium*," 19-20.

second with belief.[35] This distinction is to some extent reflected in English grammar in that one can be persuaded to do something, or that something is the case. While there is an obvious relationship between these two kinds of persuasion in that one can persuade someone to do something by persuading him that something is the case, belief-persuasion is primarily related to truth, not action. The apparent contradiction comes from describing persuasion as both voluntary and necessary, and may be resolved by understanding "voluntary" as referring to action, while "necessary" as referring to belief or judgement. Voluntary actions occur once one's beliefs have been changed; but the force of persuasion on the beliefs themselves has (or at least, may have) the same power as compulsion, as Gorgias himself says (*Helen* 12). According to this distinction, we have the possibility of affirming that the action of the person persuaded is voluntary as regards the action but necessary as regards the belief. On the one hand, therefore, Helen voluntarily went to Troy; on the other hand, however, her action can be understood as the necessary consequence of belief (*doxa*) and of the state of conviction (*pistis*) produced in her by the persuasive speech of Paris. I am convinced that this line of thought, which makes Gorgias's argument less paradoxical and more philosophically defensible, is correct. It is, however, also incomplete because we need to explain why the hearer's belief-change is considered by Gorgias to be out of his or her control.

Here we need a speculative leap, I think, since we don't find an explicit explanation of how this is possible in Gorgias's text. The best explanation of the argument at work in Gorgias's *Helen* is provided, in my opinion, by Aristotle in *On the Soul*,[36] where he traces a

---

[35] The first scholar to highlight the importance of this ambiguity for Gorgias's argument was, to the best of my knowledge, David Futter, whom I paraphrase here. The conclusions he draws, however, are different from mine. See David Futter, "Gorgias and the Psychology of Persuasion," *Akroterion* 56 (2011): 3-20, especially 9-10.

[36] I need to specify that I am not in any way assuming an intention on Aristotle's part to refer to Gorgias. Nevertheless, it seems to me that the Aristotelian framework helps to make Gorgias's argument more

difference between *phantasia* and *doxa*, on the one hand, and between *phantasia* and *hypolepsis*, on the other:[37]

> It remains, then, to see if it is belief, since belief too is both true and false. But conviction follows upon belief (since no one can believe something which does not seem convincing); yet no beast has conviction, though many of them have imagination. Further, every case of belief implies conviction, while conviction implies being persuaded, and persuasion implies *logos*; yet among the beasts some have imagination, but none has *logos*. (3.3, 428a18-24)[38]

---

understandable. It is interesting to observe that Aristotle might also be thinking of Gorgias's argument, when, in the *Nicomachean Ethics* (1110b), he addresses the question of the agent who can be deemed morally responsible and thus legitimately subject to praise or blame for his actions. See Xavier Echenique, *Aristotle's Ethics and Moral Responsibility* (Cambridge: Cambridge University Press, 2012), 107-111.

[37] This is a notoriously tricky chapter, and I will just point out a few aspects that, in my opinion, may shed some light on Gorgias's argument. I need, however, to add a few considerations on the translations of the key words of the two passages, because almost all of them are controversial. I start with *doxa*. It is generally translated as 'opinion' or as 'belief.' Recently, however, Jessica Moss and Whitney Schwab, "The Birth of Belief," *Journal of the History of Philosophy* 57.1. (2019), 1-32 have persuasively argued that *doxa* is not the word corresponding to what we moderns mean by 'belief.' This would rather apply to *hypolepsis*. Since, however, "the common element in *doxa*, knowledge, and practical wisdom that makes them all count as *hypolepseis* is conviction or taking to be true" (Moss-Schwab, "The Birth of Belief," 23), I think that in the context of my argument and of my comparison with Gorgias I can continue to use 'belief,' which I prefer to 'opinion' for the derogatory meaning it generally assumes. The second question is the translation of *pistis*, which in turn can also translated with 'belief.' I adopt Shield's translation, 'conviction,' limiting myself to emphasizing that the really relevant aspect is that *pistis* admits of degrees. As for *logos*, finally, I leave it mostly untranslated, so as not to be forced to justify my preference for 'speech' instead of 'reason.'

[38] Aristotle, *De Anima*, Trans. Cristopher Shields (Oxford: Clarendon Press, 2016), 57 (modified).

According to Aristotle, the fundamental difference between *doxa* and *phantasia* depends on the fact that it is not possible to have a belief without being convinced at the same time. While it is possible to have mental representations without necessarily believing that they are true, the same is not possible in the case of *doxa*. Every belief depends on conviction; conviction in turn depends on having been persuaded (*pepeisthai*), and persuasion (*peithō*) depends on *logos*. *Doxa* is the point of arrival in a process whose origin is *logos* and necessarily passes through persuasion, namely in the double aspect of persuading and being persuaded. Ronald Polansky rightly observes in his commentary that "the claim that opinion involves conviction from being persuaded by *logos* joins Aristotle with the Socratic-Platonic tradition."[39]

It seems to me, however, that we are also in a decidedly Gorgianic landscape. Aristotle's correlation seems, in fact, to be largely analogous to the Gorgianic one in *Helen*. Both think that having a belief depends on a state of conviction whose changes depend on having been persuaded, which is primarily effected through *logos* or speech. Thus, if *logos* is able to change the belief of an individual (the act of persuasion), it will lead him to believe a certain thing (to be the case). For this reason, beasts who lack *logos* but have *phantasia* cannot be persuaded, cannot have conviction, and cannot have belief. This analogy appears to be further emphasized by Aristotle's statement in a passage a little earlier, which traces a difference between *phantasia* and *hypolēpsis*:

> That [imagination] is not the same kind of thinking as *hypolēpsis* is clear. For this affection [imagination] is up to us whenever we wish (for we can put something before our eyes, just like those who place and form an image in mnemonics), but *doxazein* is not up to us, because it is necessary either to be true or to be false. Further, whenever we *doxazein* something terrible or fearful, we are immediately affected, and similarly with something encouraging; but with respect to imagination we are in the

39 Ronald Polansky, *Aristotle's* De Anima (Cambridge: Cambridge University Press, 2007), 422.

> same condition as if we were observing terrible or encouraging things in a painting. And there are *differentiae* of *hypolēpsis* itself: knowledge, *doxa*, practical wisdom and the opposites of these; of these *differentiae* I must speak elsewhere. (Aristotle, *On the Soul*, 427b16-27)[40]

While *phantasia* can be recalled voluntarily, the same cannot apply to belief (*doxa*).[41] In fact, this does not depend on us since in the case of belief it must be true or false. We only tend to hold a belief when, as we have seen, we are convinced and thus believe that it is true. Aristotle's claim cannot be taken, however, to refer to the fact that all *doxai* necessarily have a truth-value. In this way, the argument would be unsuccessful because, for Aristotle, imagination too has truth-value. A more charitable reading is possible, supported by the widespread use of *aletheuein* and *pseudesthai* to mean to speak truly/falsely. According to this reading, "[...] *doxa* but not imagination asserts its content as true: to have a *doxa*, in other words, entails taking something to be true, and it is not up to us whether we take something to be true (or false)."[42] Aristotle would then mean that belief is not under our control from a causal or conative point of view. Unlike imagination, we cannot believe "at will," because belief aims at truth.[43] According to a slightly different hypothesis, the expression "up to us" used by Aristotle would have, however, a normative sense. We cannot believe "as we please" because "[...] believing is TRUTH-NORMED, which means that beliefs are in their right state when they are true, and in the wrong state when they are false."[44] In any case, the conclusion is roughly the same: we are not at liberty to form any belief at any given moment in our lives. We do

---

[40] Translation by Moss and Schwab, "The Birth of Belief," 20.

[41] Aristotle uses the verb *doxazein* ('to hold belief') as one possible example of a larger *genus* constituted by *hupolepsis*.

[42] Moss and Schwab, "The Birth of the Belief," 17.

[43] In modern times it was Bernard Williams who drew attention to this specific characteristic of "belief" in *Problems of the Self* (Cambridge: Cambridge University Press, 1970), 136-151, Chapter 9.

[44] Ian McCready Flora, *Belief and Rational Cognition in Aristotle*, PhD Thesis, University of Michigan, 2011, 115.

not form any given belief because we want that particular belief, but because of some compulsion.

Whichever solution is adopted, the Aristotelian formulation seems to me to bring back, without necessarily sharing it, Gorgias's intuition according to which the individual's capacity to act on *doxa* can be interpreted as a form of constriction on others. In particular, if we think about the relationship between *pistis* and *doxa*, I find the explanatory model proposed by Ian McCready-Flora very interesting.[45] According to this model, which he calls "pneumatic," the process of belief formation depends on the epistemic pressure exerted on the subject by his conviction: "given enough pressures, things pop, and belief results."[46] Since *pistis* is primarily the result of an act of communication that leads someone to some action,[47] this assessment will have to be understood as a linguistic, fallible (and sometime dangerous) activity. While it is obviously not possible to apply this model to Gorgias fully, I suspect that something like this is what the he means when he says, for example (in *Helen* §13), that *logos* makes what is incredible and unclear (*ta apista kai adēla*) seems true to the eyes of belief.

In any case, there is an obvious objection to my reconstruction: Aristotle, unlike Gorgias, does not say anywhere that persuasion is a form of compulsion and, most important of all, does not think that such an explanation of the belief formation leads to the conclusion that, although indirectly, an individual cannot exercise control over his beliefs.[48] Even for Gorgias, however, the situation is a little more

---

[45] McCready Flora, *Belief and Rational Cognition*, 168.

[46] Owen Goldin, "*Pistis*, Persuasion, and *Logos* in Aristotle," *Elenchos* 41.1 (2020), 56. McCready Flora's translation of *pistis* is not "conviction" but "credence," though it is not clear what exactly this credence is, "it seems to be—as Goldin ("*Pistis*," 55) rightly observes—something like a disposition or inclination to believe a proposition."

[47] Goldin, "*Pistis*," 64.

[48] Another, more poignant, objection could be raised. According to a widespread tradition, there is in Gorgias's thought and particularly in his *Encomium* no space at all for truth. It would therefore make no sense to understand *doxa* as "belief" aiming at truth. I think that this

complicated than it seems. I noted previously Polansky's observation regarding Aristotle's link to the Socratic-Platonic tradition. I return to this tradition because within it we find our possible solution. Long ago, in a seminal paper, Guido Calogero put forward the hypothesis that both of Gorgias's orations, *Helen* and *Palamedes*, presupposed the Socratic principle "no one does wrong voluntarily" (*nemo sua sponte peccat*).[49] Although Calogero concentrated mainly on *Palamedes*, his considerations seem to me to apply to *Helen* as well.[50] I don't have the space here for a complete demonstration of this, but it will be enough to emphasize that, at the beginning of *Helen* (1), Gorgias says explicitly that error (*amartia*), consisting in blaming the praiseworthy and praising the blameworthy, is equal to ignorance (*amathia*), and that at the end (21) he takes up the same line of reasoning, claiming to have tried to put an end to the injustice of blame and ignorance of opinion (*tēs doxēs amathian*). What is more important is the conclusion of Calogero's argument, which is worth quoting in full:

> [...] the idea of the irresistible power of *logos* and *peithō*, so brilliantly outlined in the *Helen*, coincided with the *oudeis ekōn kakos* of Socrates, but also confronted him with the most important problem of moral conduct. In fact, Gorgias, envisaging the *nemo sua sponte peccat* in its most elementary form, might fall into a sort of moral indifference. Everybody could act only according to his persuasions: so everybody could dominate the others if he was able to persuade them!

---

interpretation is decidedly wrong, though I cannot here explain the role and meaning of truth in Gorgias's *Encomium*. I therefore refer to another paper of mine: "The Efficacy of True Speech: Gorgias between Rorty and Foucault," in *The Journal for the Philosophy of Language, Mind and the Arts* 3.1 (2022): 33-50.

[49] Guido Calogero, "Gorgias and the Socratic Principle *Nemo Sua Sponte Peccat*," *The Journal of Hellenic Studies* 77 (1957): 12-17.

[50] Sassi, "Socrate salvato," 82n25 argues rightly that this important work now seems forgotten, probably because Calogero hypothesized that the Socratic principle was inspired by Gorgias himself. As Sassi herself points out in her paper, what is most important is the "dialogue" between the Socratic thesis and the reflections of Gorgias (as well as Simonides and Euripides) about a similar topic.

> Against this new tyranny of the *logos*, which was both threatening the independence and directing the behavior of the *psychē* in her most intimate realm (by the way, even this idea of the soul as the seat of consciousness and moral conduct, in which Burnet and Taylor saw the most important element of Socrates's philosophy, has been found present in Gorgias's discourses), Socrates had to find a remedy. And this was not a repudiation of the *nemo sua sponte peccat*, but the discipline of the *peithō* by the *dialogos*.[51]

The discipline of *dialogos*—or, to say it differently, "dialogicity"—represents one of Plato's main concerns throughout the dialogues. According to Plato, in fact, everyone acts according to his private reasons, but everybody has to *didonai logon*, i.e., give reasons that could also be accepted by others. And this action consisting in giving and taking of argument is the main characteristic of persuasion understood as a rational activity. Moreover, as is well-known, Plato holds that discursive thought (*dianoia*) can be considered as internal speech or inner dialogue, alluding to the dialogic relationship that the *psychē* entertains with itself.[52] In this perspective *doxa* is defined by Socrates as a silent statement (*logos*), the final output of this inner dialogue, a process that moves from a set of doxastic states to a final doxastic state, in which "the soul, when thinking (*dianooumenē*) does nothing other than discuss (*dialegesthai*), asking itself questions and answering them, both affirming and denying" (*Theaetetus*, 190a1-2).

---

[51] Calogero, "Gorgias and the Socratic Principle," 16.

[52] In *Theaetetus* (189e4-190a6) and *Sophist* (263d6-264b4). For a recent overview of this topic, see Franco Trabattoni, *Essays on Plato's Epistemology* (Leuven. Leuven University Press, 2016), 1-12; Matthew Duncombe, "Thought as internal speech in Plato and Aristotle," in *Logical Analysis and History of Philosophy* 19 (2016), 105–125; Alexandru-Ovidiu Garcea, "Plato and the "Internal Dialogue": An Ancient Answer for a New Model of the Self," in *Psychology and Ontology in Plato*, eds. Luca Pitteloud and Evan Keeling (Champaign and Urbana: Springer, 2019), 33-54.

We can now turn our attention back to Gorgias, in which we find a significantly different model describing the soul's activity. In §11, Gorgias says, in fact, that "most people on most subjects furnish themselves with *doxa* as advisor (*symboulos*) to the soul. But opinion, being slippery and unsteady, surrounds those who rely on it with slippery and unsteady successes."[53] The word chosen by Gorgias can hardly be considered casual, because in the second half of the 5th century *symboulos* was an almost technical word referring to an orator giving advice to the *dēmos* in an assembly. We could say, then, that both for Gorgias and Plato the relationship a soul entertains with itself can be described through *logos*' action. For Plato, this action corresponds to a conversational or dialogical model in which *doxa* is the output of an inner speech, understood in turn as a somewhat symmetrical and equal dialogue. In Gorgias, however, we find an oratorical model, according to which *doxa* is more directly the output of the persuasive action of the *logos*. This model corresponds significantly to what happened in ancient Greek democratic assemblies. According to Daniela Cammack,[54] in fact, assembly deliberation was almost always represented in ancient sources as guided deliberation in which speaking and deliberating were performed by advisers and decision-makers respectively. The *dēmos*—i.e., the audience—deliberated (*bouleuō*), while those who spoke before it advised (*symbouleuō*). This fact has an important consequence for the conceptual framework in which we have to insert the action of *logos*. Speakers and audience are not identical, as in conversation, but distinct in that few are speakers and most are listeners; orators, in turn, are not cooperative but agonistic, aiming to prove their own case and demolish the adversary's. From this perspective, the power *logos* exerts is relativized by its plural nature. We can always oppose one *logos* to another.

If we take, for example, §13, where the efficacy of persuasion is mostly underlined, we find a series of activities and contexts which

[53] A different question is whether Gorgias thinks this condition affects all men or allows exceptions. In my opinion the right answer is the first.

[54] Daniela Cammack, "Deliberation in Ancient Greek Assemblies," *Classical Philology* 115 (2020), 486-522.

revolve around rational argumentation. Rather, we could say that all contexts that could spring to the mind of a 5th century Greek where rationality is used are recalled here. Therefore, it is evident that the idea of persuasion being violent because it is irrational and 'manipulative' does not work. It is necessary to find a different explanation. I think that we can find our solution if we consider the agonistic dimension of speech underlined by Gorgias. Within this competitive model of the functioning of speech, disagreement and opposition appear to be the elements of a struggle for predominance where *logos* is in opposition to another *logos* and aims to supersede it. The three examples in §13 underscore this aspect very clearly. Therefore, the emerging situation is sufficiently homogeneous and can be reformulated in the following way. *Logos* does seem to have such a strong, binding power as to justify the parallel with and even the substitution by force, but such power emerges in the context of a general contrast where *logos* is always opposed to another *logos*. As Takis Poulakos rightly says,

> partly expressed in the metaphoric language of a combat in war, partly in the spirit of a wrestling match in the *palaestra*, arguments in the text enact symbolically the rituals of competition. [...] *The locus of resistance to the power of logos lies for Gorgias in logos itself:* since the human soul has no better guide than opinion, one speaker's *logos* can counteract another's *logos* in exactly the same way that the words of astronomers 'substitute one opinion with another [...].'[55]

In this agonistic perspective, the use of a woman to explore the limits of agency is significant. The exemplification of the powers available to speech, besides being reduced to an agonistic context, revolves around a woman whose submission to such powers is expressed in terms of passivity, so much so that one scholar has talked of a true "psychic rape"[56] perpetrated against her. This statement is not as extravagant as it might seem at first glance.

[55] Poulakos, "Human Agency," 71 and 75 (my emphasis).

[56] Robert Wardy, *The Birth of Rhetoric* (London: Routledge, 1996), 43.

On one hand, in fact, while our own particular system divides people into two major classes on the basis of whether they have sex with others of the same sex or not (heterosexuals versus homosexuals), "the system shared by the ancient Greeks and Romans was quite different and divided acts and people on the axis of active versus passive."[57] For this reason, sexual activity was symbolically considered a "zero-sum competition [with a] relentless conjunction of winners and losers."[58]

On the other hand, however, oratorical performance was the most important opportunity for the elite man to express his identity in terms of gender, primarily through the construction and maintenance of a verbal and bodily practice conventionally associated with his status of citizen. As the cultivated outgrowth of the natural capacity for speech that is the distinguishing characteristic of humanity, rhetoric represents the unique human ability to form communities, establish laws, and regulate all kinds of social and political interaction. But while rhetoric was potentially available to all members of humanity with the power of speech, including the morally objectionable and the ethically unsound, women (but also slaves, foreigners, and generally the disenfranchised of antiquity) were excluded from rhetorical discourse,[59] and it is precisely for that reason that "[...] their physical

---

[57] H.N. Parker, "The Myth of Heterosexual: Anthropology and Sexuality for Classicists," *Arethusa* 34.3 (2001): 314.

[58] John J. Winkler, *The Constraints of Desire: The Anthropology of Sex and Gender in Ancient Greece* (New York: Routledge, 1990), 54. Erotic pleasure in being penetrated was thought socially unacceptable for a citizen male, because such behavior did not offend *erōs* but, rather, honor. See John Boswell, "Concepts, Experience, and Sexuality," in *Sexuality in Greek and Roman Society*, eds. David Konstan and Martha Nussbaum, 72: "This 'penetration code' [...] was clearly not related to a dichotomy of sexual preference, but to issues of *power, dominance, and submission*" (my emphasis).

[59] The relationship between women and language in ancient Greek thought is actually much more complex and is another "subtext" of Gorgias's *Helen,* that I cannot explore here. See, at least, Laura McClure, *Spoken*

and verbal comportment was consistently offered as an example of what not to do, due to the complex mechanism of social structure that consistently transforms the inferior member of the binary hierarchy into the negative reflection of the superior."[60] Helen's story, then, functions as an inverted paradigm of behavior, to which the citizen is called within the community to which he belongs. If it is true, in fact, that Helen can be exonerated, this is done only by virtue of her passivity and her consequent denial of moral responsibility for the actions committed. Although this condition in ancient Greek imagery can be suitable for a woman, it is not for a man, nor, above all, for a citizen. Each of them, in order to avoid being a victim of the violence that can be exerted through the speech, is called to acquire a similar capacity and to use it in the political sphere. In this case also it is useful to compare Gorgias's thought with Plato's reflection. It is, in fact, clear that the two are using the same conceptual framework but in decidedly different ways. While Plato (like Aristophanes and Euripides) addresses the central *ethical* concern of rhetorical persuasion in terms of its relation to femininity, linking the epistemological and ethical problems generated by the practice of rhetoric to the pervasive moral failings of women,[61] Gorgias

---

Like a Woman: Speech and Gender in Athenian Drama (Princeton: Princeton University Press, 1999); Ann Bergren, *Weaving Truth. Essays on Language and the Female in Greek Thought* (Cambridge, MA: Harvard University Press, 2008); John Heath, *The Talking Greeks: Speech, Animals, and the Other in Homer, Aeschylus, and Plato* (Cambridge: Cambridge University Press, 2005), 185-192.

[60] Joy Connolly, *Vile Eloquence: Performance and Identity in Greco-Roman Rhetoric*, PhD Dissertation, University of Pennsylvania, 1997, 3 (my emphasis).

[61] Connolly, *Vile Eloquence*, 12. "The mimetic capacity to assume another's voice, to disregard reason as a basis for decision making, to speak pleasure out of ignorance, to persuade with passion rather than reason, to substitute an ornamental surface for rational content: all these things are understood as womanly ways of speech and thought, and criticized as such, by Athenian observers." Connolly's first chapter, to which I am indebted for these considerations, is a rich illustration of this point.

addresses the same question in *political* terms, using the image of a woman as the inversion of the rhetorical ability required for citizens to exercise their functions and to construct and proclaim their identity.

Therefore, Gorgias's *Helen* can be considered, as many scholars have suggested, as an advertisement of Gorgias's rhetorical teaching, but this advertisement is more sophisticated, challenging, and above all, much more politically driven than one might have thought.

Stamatia Dova[1]

Aggressive Contrafactuals in Gorgias's *Palamedes*[2]

This paper examines the argument from implausibility as it is constructed through conditional sentences and especially contrary-to-fact conditions in Gorgias's *Defense of Palamedes*. Through close readings of all relevant passages, this analysis illustrates how Gorgias has the defendant employ a series of powerful hypotheses in order to destabilize his accuser's argument. By establishing a conjectural reality in which Odysseus prosecutes him with the honorable intention of protecting Hellas from treason, Palamedes embarks on a masterful attack against the case for the prosecution. Expanding to address the likelihood of malicious persecution, this attack draws on the mythographical tradition, which casts Palamedes as the victim of judicial injustice caused by Odysseus's manipulative rhetoric. Fully aligned with this traditional characterization, Gorgias's exercise in forensic oratory tests the limits of the genre, as Palamedes's defense, despite its brilliant formulation, remains inextricably intertwined with the hero's wrongful conviction in myth.

As Plato put it in the *Meno*, Gorgias's area of expertise is to make people "great speakers."[3] In his *Palamedes*,[4] Gorgias presents us with

---

[1] Stamatia Dova is Professor of Classics and Greek Studies at Hellenic College in Brookline, Massachusetts USA, and an Associate in Athletics, Hellenism, and Poetics at the Center for Hellenic Studies in Washington, D.C. Her publications include *Greek Heroes in and out of Hades* (Lanham, MD: Rowman and Littlefield, 2012) and *The Poetics of Failure in Ancient Greece* (Routledge, 2020).

[2] The author would like to thank Shane Ewegen, Heather L. Reid, and Coleen Zoller for their insightful feedback as well as the *Fonte Aretusa* Gorgias translation seminar for many inspiring discussions.

[3] δεινοὺς λέγειν, Plato, *Meno*, 95c1-4. All translations are my own. Cf. also Nancy Worman, *The Cast of Character: Style in Greek Literature* (Austin: University of Texas Press, 2002), 179.

[4] On the significance of this speech in the extant Gorgianic corpus, see Kurt Lampe, "The *Logos* of Ethics in Gorgias' *Palamedes, On What is Not*, and *Helen*," in *Early Greek Ethics*, ed. David C. Wolfsdorf (Oxford University

the implicit duel between two masters of speech,[5] both of whom are also renowned for their intelligence. An imaginative combination of myth and oratory,[6] Gorgias's *Palamedes* constitutes a *tour de force* in scrutiny for the purposes of refutation. Indeed, it can be said that the relationship between Odysseus and Palamedes is a continuous *élenchos*. According to the epic tradition, this *élenchos* started when Palamedes came to Ithaca to ask Odysseus to honor the oath taken by all of Helen's suitors and to recruit him for the Trojan expedition. As we learn from Apollodorus, who, in turn, echoes a variety of sources,[7] "Odysseus, not wishing to go to the Trojan war, feigned

---

Press, 2020), 110-31; Stefania Giombini, *Gorgia Epidittico* (Passignano sul Trasimeno: Aguaplano, 2012), 147-53, 199-228; Scott Porter Consigny, *Gorgias, Sophist and Artist* (Columbia, S.C.: University of South Carolina Press, 2001), 60-94; Dimos G. Spatharas, *Gorgias: An Edition of the Extant Texts and Fragments with Commentary and Introduction* (Ph.D. Dissertation, University of Glasgow, 2001), 17-34, and "Patterns of Argumentation in Gorgias," *Mnemosyne* 54.4 (2001): 393-408; Edward Schiappa, *The Beginnings of Rhetorical Theory in Classical Greece* (New Haven: Yale University Press, 1999), 85-112; Bruce McComiskey, "Gorgias and the Art of Rhetoric: Toward a Holistic Reading of the Extant Gorgianic Fragments," *Rhetoric Society Quarterly* 27.4 (1997): 5–24, especially 17-21; Charles P. Segal, "Gorgias and the Psychology of the *Logos*," *Harvard Studies in Classical Philology* 66 (1962): 99-155; Friedrich Blass, *Die attische Beredsamkeit* (2nd edn, Leipzig: B.G. Teubner, 1887), 47-91.

[5] In Plato, *Phaedrus*, 261b7-8, both men are said to have authored treatises on rhetoric during their leisure time in Troy.

[6] On the sophistic reception of Palamedes's myth, see Paola Bassino, "Palamedes, The Sophistic Hero," in *Sophistic Views of the Epic Past from the Classical to the Imperial Age*, eds. Paola Bassino and Nicolò Benzi (Bloomsbury Academic, 2022), 41-63. On Gorgias's *Defense of Palamedes* as a "mytho-forensic" speech examined in parallel with Alcidamas's *Odysseus* and Antisthenes's *Ajax* and *Odysseus*, see Rachel Ahern Knudsen, "Poetic Speakers, Sophistic Words," *American Journal of Philology* 133.1 (2012): 31-60, especially 31-43.

[7] Apollodorus, *Library*, 3.7a, Scholia to Euripides's *Orestes* 432, Hyginus, *Fabulae*, 95 and 105, *Cypria*, argumentum 5, 12, fr. 27, *Nostoi* 11. See also Timothy Gantz, *Early Greek Myth* (Baltimore: Johns Hopkins University Press, 1993), 576-80, 603-6.

madness. Nevertheless, Palamedes, son of Nauplius, *proved* his madness to be untrue [ἤλεγξε τὴν μανίαν ψευδῆ]."[8] Odysseus pretended to be mad by trying to plow a field with a horse and an ox yoked together, but Palamedes placed Odysseus's infant son Telemachos in front of his father's yoke, whereupon Odysseus stopped pretending and rushed to save the baby.[9] It is noteworthy that the verb *elénchō* here is a *hapax* in Apollodorus;[10] furthermore, I would venture to suggest that a 1st or 2nd century CE encyclopedic mythographer like Apollodorus is echoing a tradition in which Palamedes exercised life-changing *élenchos* over Odysseus and thereby became his arch-nemesis. It is not by coincidence, I submit, that Apollodorus employs the verb *elénchō,* with its semantic range from "questioning" to "exposing," to describe the inception of such a notorious rivalry. Interestingly, we can reconstruct Palamedes's *élenchos* and articulate his rationale into a future-more-vivid condition: "if Odysseus is insane, as he pretends to be, he will let me harm his child; if, however, he protects Telemachos, he will be proven sane and will be forced to join the Trojan expedition."

The consensus in the mythical tradition from which Gorgias draws is that Palamedes made a sworn enemy out of Odysseus. As the story goes, "[i]n Troy, Odysseus took prisoner a Phrygian man and forced him to write a letter, ostensibly sent by Priam, incriminating Palamedes of treason. And having buried gold in Palamedes's tent, he dropped the letter in the camp. Agamemnon read the letter, found the gold, and delivered up Palamedes to the allies to be stoned as a traitor" (Apollodorus, *Library*, 3.8). In addition to the revenge sought by Odysseus for Palamedes's *élenchos,* the mythical tradition reports an intense antagonism between the two men with respect to intelligence. According to the testimony of 2nd c.

8 Richard Wagner, *Apollodori Bibliotheca* (Leipzig: Teubner, 1894).

9 Martin L. West, *The Epic Cycle: A Commentary on the Lost Troy Epics* (Oxford: Oxford University Press, 2013), 101-4, 123-6.

10 Based on a lemma search at the *TLG,* the verb is well attested among classical prose authors, especially orators (48 attestations in Antiphon, 24 in Andocides, two in Isocrates and Antisthenes each, ten in Isaeus and Lysias each, and 75 in Demosthenes). It also occurs three times in Gorgias (*Defense of Palamedes* 30.2, *Encomium of Helen*, 2.2, 3.5).

CE orator Aelius Aristides (*Oration* 3, 477-8), Pindar acknowledged that Palamedes surpassed Odysseus in wisdom.[11] In fact, in Pindar fr. 260 Snell-Maehler, the crucial terms, "Odysseus" (5), "concerning the discourse on wisdom" (εἰς σοφίας λόγον, 7), and especially "scrutiny" (ἐλεγχο, 1), provide an early 5th century confirmation of later traditions of Odysseus's envy over the many manifestations of Palamedes's genius. As we will see, this "war of wits" is hinted at in Gorgias's *Palamedes*, 14, and undoubtedly constitutes the premise for Alcidamas fr. 2.113-17, quoted below. Entitled *Odysseus: Against the Treason of Palamedes*, it was presumably written by Gorgias's pupil Alcidamas in close dialogue with his teacher's *Palamedes*.

Nevertheless, Alcidamas's *Odysseus* has been attended by considerable doubt as to its authenticity, which remains, despite the speech's thematic relevance, outside the scope of this paper. As Neil O' Sullivan has demonstrated,[12] Alcidamas's *Odysseus* has linguistic discrepancies that confirm the suspicions over its questionable authorship, thereby disqualifying it as supporting evidence for Gorgias's speech. Still, we cannot help noticing the verb *elénchō* once more, here turned against Palamedes by Odysseus. Alcidamas's fr. 2, 113-17 should be taken, I posit, as a general acknowledgement of the unremitting *élenchos* between the two heroes:

> It is worth investigating how he [Palamedes] poses as an intellectual, deceiving the young and falsely persuading them [ἃ καὶ φιλοσοφεῖν ἐπικεχείρηκεν ἐξαπατῶν τοὺς

---

[11] κυριώτερον τοῦ Ὀδυσσέως εἰς σοφίας λόγον, "a greater master of intellect than Odysseus," Aelius Aristides, *Oration* 3, 478.2-3, quoted from: Michael B. Trapp, *Aelius Aristides: Orations*, Loeb Classical Library 533 (Cambridge, MA: Harvard University Press, 2017).

[12] Neil O'Sullivan, "The Authenticity of [Alcidamas] *Odysseus*: Two Linguistic Considerations," *Classical Quarterly* 58.2, (2008): 638-47; cf. Bassino, "Sophistic Hero," 52-57; Knudsen, "Poetic Speakers," 43; Douglas MacDowell, "Gorgias, Alkidamas, and the Cripps and Palatine Manuscripts," *Classical Quarterly* 11.1-2(1961): 113-24. On Alcidamas as inventor of oratorical style see also Evangelos Alexiou, *Greek Rhetoric of the 4th Century BC* (Berlin: De Gruyter, 2020), 43-52; Neil O'Sullivan, *Alcidamas, Aristophanes and the Beginnings of Greek Stylistic Theory* (Stuttgart: Steiner, 1992), 23-42.

νέους καὶ παραπείθων], also claiming that he invented military formations, letters, weights and measures, board games and dice, music, coin money, and even signal-fires. And he is not ashamed, when he is immediately **caught lying** openly to all of you [καὶ οὐδὲ αἰσχύνεται, ὅταν αὐτίκα **ἐλέγχηται** φανερῶς ἐν ὑμῖν **ψευδόμενος**].[13]

The author of the above passage proceeds to contest Palamedes's claim to all of these inventions except for weights and measures, board games and dice, and signal-fires. Even these, however, he connects to Palamedes's deceitful nature, accusing him of coming up with weights and measures to enable commercial fraud, board games and dice to encourage indolence, and signal-fires to facilitate treason. The bitterness with which Odysseus addresses Palamedes in the speech attributed to Alcidamas permeates all aspects of the argument, also bespeaking his preexisting enmity towards the accused. Although in Alcidamas's *Odysseus* the speaker insists that no such enmity existed (fr. 2, 17-20), it is evident that this disclaimer is made in adherence to rhetorical convention and does not reflect the true facts of the case even in their mythical dimension–one more argument, perhaps, against the speech's authenticity.[14]

Thus, it is very much in character that the *élenchos* exercised on Odysseus by Palamedes in Gorgias's speech should continue their pre-Trojan War rivalry. The problem is, however, that neither of them can present the court with factual evidence. As a result, a combination of argument from probability (*eikós*) and character proof (*ēthos*) will have to provide a convincing (enough) thesis.[15] This is

---

[13] Quoted from: Guido Avezzù, *Orazioni e frammenti*. Bollettino dell' Istituto di Filologia Greca, Supp. 6. (Rome: Bretschneider, 1982).

[14] Cf. Lysias 1, 4.4-5, where the defendant hurries to make clear that there was no pre-existing enmity between himself and his victim.

[15] As McComiskey, "Holistic Reading," 18, notes, "Gorgias exemplifies a topical method for inventing logical, ethical, and, when necessary, emotional arguments from probability (*eikos*); and these *topoi*, though presented in the narrative context of the Palamedes myth, are similar in many ways to the *topoi* for the invention of logical, ethical, and emotional arguments from probability described by Aristotle."

where conditional sentences come in, both as syntactical features and rhetorical devices guiding the argument towards a logical conclusion. Here I follow their classification by Smyth, as follows:[16]

> Contrary to Fact Present:
> Protasis: εἰ + imperfect indicative
> Apodosis: ἄν + imperfect indicative
> Translation formula: If were doing, would be doing.
>
> Contrary to fact past:
> Protasis: εἰ + aorist indicative
> Apodosis: ἄν + aorist indicative
> Translation formula: If had done, would have done.

Through his two opening contrafactuals, Gorgias's Palamedes offers three possible characterizations for Odysseus. The first, *áristos,* carries a wealth of epic connotations but receives only fleeting consideration. Tied to Odysseus's presumed good intentions, the Homeric superlative remains invalidated, as it depends on the hypothesis of Odysseus's genuine care for Hellas and his believable, fact-based or even conjectural allegations against Palamedes. Such a case for the prosecution would have earned him the title of *áristos.* As it soon becomes clear, however, earning this title is contingent upon some connection to the truth, and the contrary-to-fact present condition categorically denies him that in the here and now.

Furthermore, Palamedes does not wish to linger on this possibility, but hurries to dismiss it and quickly introduce the dominant binary *krátistos-kákistos* (most excellent-most wicked):

> If Odysseus, my accuser, were making the accusation [εἰ ἐποιεῖτο τὴν κατηγορίαν] on account of his goodwill toward Greece [δι' εὔνοιαν τῆς Ἑλλάδος]–either knowing clearly [σαφῶς ἐπιστάμενος] that I was betraying Greece to the barbarians, or supposing somehow [δοξάζων γ' ἁμῇ] that this was the case–then he would be the **best** of men [**ἄριστος** ἂν ἦν ὁ ἀνήρ]. But if he has fashioned this

[16] Herbert W. Smyth, *Greek Grammar*. Revised ed. (Cambridge, MA: Harvard University Press, 1984), §2302-20.

> accusation out of envy [*phthónos*], subterfuge [*kakotechnía*], or wickedness [*panourgía*], just as for those reasons [*ekeína*] he would be the most excellent [*krátistos*] of men, so too, for these reasons [*táuta*], he would be the most wicked [*kákistos*] of men (εἰ δὲ φθόνῳ ἢ κακοτεχνίᾳ ἢ πανουργίᾳ συνέθηκε ταύτην τὴν αἰτίαν, ὥσπερ δι' ἐκεῖνα κράτιστος ἂν ἦν ἀνήρ, οὕτω διὰ ταῦτα κάκιστος ἀνήρ, 3.6-8).[17]

I would suggest that the main reason for employing this binary instead of the possible (and customary) antithesis *áristos-kákistos* is that Palamedes prefers to disassociate his accuser from any Iliadic clout; even though Odysseus is not referred to individually as *áristos* in the *Iliad,* he shares in this distinction by virtue of his being a commander.

Since Gorgias's reconstructed dialogue between Palamedes and Odysseus takes us back to the time of the *Iliad,* when the trial is believed to have taken place, it would be far from advantageous to the defense to remind the court of the plaintiff's claim to excellence. Moreover, the superlative *krátistos,* never associated with Odysseus in Homer, appears rarely as the antonym of *kákistos* in extant Greek literature; with the exception of one attestation in Xenophon, Gorgias seems to be the only prose writer to have employed the pair.[18] Also, the fact that a different version of this pair of opposites, *áristos-chéiristos* (best-worst),[19] is well attested in classical Greek literature underscores the peculiarity of Gorgias's lexical choice. Thus, Palamedes wastes no time saying how unlikely it is for Odysseus to

---

[17] Quoted from André Laks and Glenn W. Most, eds. and trans., *Early Greek Philosophy, Volume VIII, Sophists, Part 1,* Loeb Classical Library 531 (Cambridge, MA: Harvard University Press, 2016).

[18] Xenophon, *Cyropaedia,* 2.2.20.5; κράτιστος is used interchangeably with βέλτιστος (best) in the Hippocratic Corpus (*De diaeta acutorum,* 18.62). Gorgias employs the binary twice in *Palamedes,* here and in 14.9.

[19] As in Xenophon *Memorabilia,* 3.1.8.2-3, Plato, *Timaeus* 89a3-5, Aristotle, *Metaphysics,* 1074b32, *Politics* 1289b8. On the antithesis noble-not noble (ἀγαθός-οὐκ ἀγαθός) as articulated by Odysseus disguised as a beggar in the context of his argument with the suitor Eurymachos (*Odyssey,* 18, 383), see Stamatia Dova, *The Poetics of Failure in Ancient Greece* (London: Routledge, 2020), 129-30.

be what is conventionally perceived as a truly noble person. At the same time, he states what he considers to be the true motives behind Odysseus's accusation: envy, subterfuge, and wickedness.

While in the first contrafactual Gorgias allows the defendant to explore the possibility that Odysseus is acting as a well-intentioned plaintiff, in the second he sets the stage for Odysseus's identification as an agent of *panourgía* (wickedness). This term is pivotal, given that the character typology (*ēthopoiía*)[20] which Gorgias's speech inherits from the epic tradition is one of Odysseus as *panoúrgos*, someone who is ready to do anything and will stop at nothing (18.6, 19.4-5), a person without moral scruples. As Nancy Worman has shown,[21] Odysseus is the embodiment of *panourgía* in the cast of poetic and oratorical characters; as the *panoúrgos* type *par excellence*, he concentrates in his persona a host of negative qualities, including untrustworthiness and falsehood. Most importantly, these qualities are not mutually exclusive with the attributes pronouncing him "extraordinarily clever" (*deinós*), since, according to oratorical practice, a gifted speaker *de facto* wields a potentially dangerous power.[22] Therefore, Palamedes's attempt to exonerate himself must focus on reminding the court, as eloquently as possible, of the fundamental difference in character between himself and Odysseus.

As part of this differentiation, it is also important for Gorgias's Palamedes to expose Odysseus's hypocrisy. Palamedes groups together in the accusative plural of the distant demonstrative pronoun *ekeína* (those things), all the possible honorable reasons for which Odysseus would be accusing Palamedes: he would be saving his fatherland, his parents, and all of Greece as well as punishing a criminal (3.5-7). At the same time, the much closer-to-home demonstrative *táuta* (these things), reminds us of Odysseus's *modus operandi*, which Palamedes's *élenchos* intends to expose. The first step

---

[20] Worman, *Cast of Character*, 150-51. On the evolution of Odysseus as a character in ancient Greek literature, see Silvia Montiglio, *From Villain to Hero: Odysseus in Ancient Thought* (Ann Arbor, MI: University of Michigan Press, 2011).

[21] Worman, *Cast of Character*, 173-6, 178-80, 189-90.

[22] On Odysseus as the combination of the *panoúrgos* and *deinós* types, see Worman, *Cast of Character*, 179, 185.

towards this exposure is, naturally, to ask the question whether or not it would have been possible for Palamedes to commit treason.[23] It is answered by two past contrary-to-fact conditions (5.6-8), which serve as the basis for his argument from inability. This argument encapsulates in elegant wordplay the conditionality of Palamedes's nefarious undertaking by capitalizing on the syntactical option of having a participle as the protasis: "For even if I wanted, I would not have been able to attempt such deeds [οὔτε γὰρ **βουληθεὶς ἐδυνάμην** ἂν], nor, if I had been able, I would have engaged in them [οὔτε **δυνάμενος ἐβουλήθην** ἔργοις ἐπιχειρεῖν τοιούτοις]" (5.6-8).

With its ability to compress, the participial protasis enables the speaker to go through conditional sentences more quickly and efficiently. Two questions ensue, carried out with future-less-vivid conditions consisting of optatives with ἂν and negative conditional participles: "How could there have been speeches [λόγοι δὲ πῶς ἂν γένοιντο] without a meeting taking place [μὴ συνουσίας τινὸς γενομένης]?" (6.5-6); "How could a meeting have taken place [γένοιτ' ἂν], without the enemy sending someone to me nor I to him [μήτ' ἐκείνου πρὸς ἐμέ πέμψαντος μήτε <του> παρ' ἐμοῦ πρὸς ἐκεῖνον ἐλθόντος;]?" (6.6-9). The examination of contingencies continues in the same spirit to encompass the presumed language barrier ("A Greek with a barbarian. Hearing and speaking in what way?" 7.3-4) as well as any guarantees such as oaths or hostages (8.2-6), only to conclude with a contrary-to-fact condition: "But if these things had taken place, they would have been manifest to all of you [ταῦτα δὲ γινόμενα πᾶσιν ὑμῖν ἂν ἦν φανερά]" (8.7-8).

Palamedes meticulously investigates any possible aspects of the treasonous transaction, namely how money could have changed hands, and how much of it, summarizing with a contrary-to-fact past condition: "For if many persons had brought the money over to me,

---

[23] Additionally, a mixed condition, consisting of a contrary-to-fact present protasis and a future-more-vivid apodosis introduces the two contrafactuals that answer the question: "if he were making the accusation because he believed that this is how things were [εἰ δὲ οἰόμενος οὕτω ταῦτα ἔχειν ἐποιεῖτο τὴν κατηγορίαν], I shall demonstrate [ἐπιδείξω] to you in two ways that he is not speaking the truth" (5.4-6).

there would have been many witnesses of the treachery; if, however, what was brought over was delivered by one person, it would not have been much [πολλῶν γὰρ κομιζόντων πολλοὶ ἂν ἦσαν μάρτυρες τῆς ἐπιβουλῆς, ἑνὸς δὲ κομίζοντος οὐκ ἂν πολύ τι τὸ φερόμενον ἦν]" (9.6-8). The next section follows the same pattern, with a torrent of questions about how the payment could have taken place, concluding again with two contrary-to-fact conditions: "If I had used the money, I would have revealed myself doing so; if, however, I had not used it, what good would that be for me? [χρώμενος δ' ἂν φανερὸς ἐγενόμην, μὴ χρώμενος δὲ τί ἂν ὠφελούμην ἀπ' αὐτῶν;]" (10.8-9). It is noteworthy that here the second conditional sentence has an apodosis carried out with the imperfect indicative. As the protasis is participial, we can take it to be past ("If I had not used the money") or present ("If I were not using the money"); still, the apodosis entertains the contrary-to-fact notion of the lasting benefits, up until the speech's actual time, derived from the money received in return for betrayal.

The argument continues with two sections debating the likelihood of Palamedes receiving assistance from others in carrying out his undertaking as well as in bringing into the Greek camp his Trojan co-conspirators (11-12). While the tone of these two sections is clearly one of sustained perplexity as to how his collaboration with the enemy would have been possible, Palamedes satisfies his *aporía* in the next section, where he addresses the judges and invites them to consider, together with himself, another contrafactual: "Why would it be appropriate [προσῆκε][24] for me to wish to do these things, if, first and foremost, I were able [εἰ ἐδυνάμην;]?" (13.1-3). By underscoring his previously established inability, Palamedes also emphasizes his lack of motive. This is an aspect of his defense that he approaches with the utmost diligence, going through each and every possible reason he could have had to commit treason. Paired with lack of opportunity, lack of motive helps to build a compelling

[24] Here the ἂν is omitted, as can be the case when the apodosis of a contrary-to-fact condition "consists of an imperfect indicative denoting unfulfilled obligation, possibility, or propriety," Smyth, *Greek Grammar*, §2313.

argument against Odysseus's accusations, all of which aim to portray Palamedes as a power-hungry and mercenary villain. All of these refutations are articulated by means of questions, to which there is a hypothetical background: "[Did I commit treason] in order to become a ruler? To rule over you or the barbarians?" (13.7).

After dismissing the likelihood of him gaining control over the Greeks, Palamedes explores the probability of the barbarians submitting to him willingly through persuasion or force, concluding: "But it would be utterly foolish to believe and accept that; for who would choose slavery over kingship, the worst [*kákiston*] over the best [*krátiston*]?" (14.6-9). The pair of opposites *krátistos-kákistos* (also discussed below) makes an impressive comeback here, echoing Odysseus's previous characterization (3.9-10). Though seemingly unrelated, the two passages maintain an implicit discourse on the binary best-worst, which manifests itself in the choices available to Odysseus and to the Trojans dealing with Palamedes; yet, while Palamedes's rhetorical question convinces us that no one in their right mind would choose slavery over kingship, doubt continues to hover over Odysseus, who is far from *krátistos*, as the defense will soon explicate. Furthermore, Palamedes's contrasting of slavery and kingship, unique in classical Greek literature, grants us the right to a brief digression.[25]

In intertextual conversation with Palamedes over this pair of opposites we find Achilles, another illustrious antagonist of Odysseus, albeit not his outright enemy. In fact, I would suggest that Gorgias here is making a masterful allusion to the famous passage from the *Nekyia*, where Achilles declares that he "would rather be the hired worker of a serf with little property than rule over all of the dead" (*Odyssey* 11.89-91).[26] The context in which this statement is made is perhaps as important as the statement itself. During his descent to the Underworld (*katábasis*), Odysseus encounters the

---

25 A full-corpus proximity search at the *TLG* within a 50-word context yielded no other results from the classical period.

26 On this passage in Homer and the katabatic tradition, see Stamatia Dova, *Greek Heroes in and out of Hades* (Lanham, MD: Rowman and Littlefield, 2012), 18-23.

shade of Achilles, whom he approaches with unduly inflated praise, extolling him as the most blessed (*makártatos*) of all men, even those before and after him. Odysseus bases his *captatio benevolentiae* on a twofold premise, that the Achaeans honored Achilles like a god when he was alive, and that after his death he rules over all of the dead; he concludes with a piece of unsolicited advice: "Therefore, do not grieve over your death, Achilles." (*Odyssey* 11.482-86). While he does not condescend to refuting Odysseus's distortion of the facts, Achilles hurries to express his resentment over his patronizing consolation, and with good reason: neither the *Iliad* nor the *Nekyia* corroborate Odysseus's version of events. As I argue elsewhere,[27] Achilles's passionate response is aimed at exposing Odysseus's hypocrisy and does not represent any revisionism over his heroic choice of *kléos* (heroic glory) over *nóstos* (heroic homecoming).

Nevertheless, the passage has often been interpreted as such over the past two-and-a-half millennia,[28] and one of the most influential discussions about it is, of course, the one between Socrates and Adeimantus in Plato's *Republic*. Indeed, this Homeric passage follows an interestingly contradictory journey in Plato, since in the third book of the *Republic* it is censored as unsuitable for the curriculum of the ideal *pólis* (Plato, *Republic*, 386b9-c7), only to be mentioned again in the seventh by virtue of its poetic ability to express the outspoken refusal of the former residents of the cave to go back to it (516c7-e3). Socrates's censoring of the passage is justified by the concern that these words of Achilles could give pupils the impression that he regrets his heroism, setting the dangerous example of choosing slavery over death.

It is very tempting to suppose that Gorgias was somehow aware of Plato's treatment of the Homeric passage during the composition of the *Republic* and despite the chronological difficulties (if not impossibility) in establishing such as connection between the two works.[29] Still, we may well interpret Gorgias's engagement with the

---

[27] Dova, *Greek Heroes*, 19, 144-45.

[28] See Dova, *Greek Heroes*, 154n89.

[29] Blass, *Die attische*, 80-81, considers the *Defense of Palamedes* the last of Gorgias's works.

passage from the *Nekyia* as an earnest literary *paignion*, through which he includes Achilles in the circle of Odysseus's victims by means of a pointed intertextual reference. Employed by Gorgias at the epilogue of his *Encomium of Helen*, the term *paignion* is usually rendered as "trifle" and may imply a playful spirit; however, as Edward Schiappa has demonstrated,[30] it rather highlights Gorgias's multi-faceted rhetoric, with all its potential of expressing both seriousness and playfulness. I would venture to add that Gorgias's successful reconstruction of the mythical context in which the characters of Palamedes and Helen originate requires such a combination of seriousness and playfulness.

As part of this intertextual richness, Gorgias's text may yield to us another connection between Palamedes and Achilles. Despite his total erasure from the *Iliad* and the *Odyssey*, the wrongfully convicted hero is mentioned in the lost to us epic poem *Cypria*, where, according to a summary by the 5th century CE philosopher Proclus, the wrath of Achilles and his decision to withdraw from battle follow immediately after the death of Palamedes: "Then comes the death of Palamedes. And the plan of Zeus to provide some relief to the Trojans by causing Achilles to remove himself from the Greek alliance" (*Cypria*, 5.7-12). Although this textual evidence does not establish a causal relationship between Palamedes's death and Achilles's anger, the visual record keeps reminding us of such a possibility. As Lucía Romero Mariscal points out, [31] the theme of Achilles and Ajax in full or partial battle-gear playing a board game, well-attested in 6th and 5th century vase paintings,[32] may echo an epic tradition according to which both heroes withdrew from battle in protest of Palamedes's death. Explicated by the sophist Flavius Philostratus (170-247/50 CE) in his *Heroicus* (25.16, 33.33-6),[33] this version makes clear that Palamedes's death, and not Chryseis's

---

30 Schiappa, *Beginnings of Rhetorical Theory*, 130-31.

31 Lucía Romero Mariscal, "Ajax and Achilles Playing a Board Game," *Classical Quarterly* 61.2 (2011): 394-401.

32 An estimated total of 150; cf. Romero Mariscal, "Ajax and Achilles," 394.

33 See also Romero Mariscal, "Ajax and Achilles," 397-9. On Palamedes's revenge in the visual record see Susan Woodford, "Palamedes Seeks Revenge," *The Journal of Hellenic Studies* 114 (1994): 164-9.

return to her father and its aftermath,[34] was the cause for Achilles's anger. It should also be noted that the abundant visual record consistently displays the two warriors playing a board game, which, as Palamedes's invention, could constitute an eloquent reference to the hero himself.

Having established that no king would become a slave at his behest, Palamedes turns next to the refutation of further possible motives such as money, honor, safety, and self-protection (15-19). At the beginning of the following section, the defendant invites the judges to consider what life after treason would have looked like for him: "How would my life have not been unlivable if I had committed such acts? [πῶς οὐκ ἂν ἀβίωτος ἦν ὁ βίος μοι πράξαντι ταῦτα;]" 20.1-2). Intensified by the powerful litotes "οὐκ ἀβίωτος," this past contrafactual entertains a scenario that is both weak and unreal. Underscored by the aphorism "life is not livable for a man who is deprived of trustworthiness [βίος δὲ οὐ βιωτὸς πίστεως ἐστερημένῳ]" (21.4-5), which follows soon, the implausibility of such a scenario expands to encompass Odysseus, who is endangering his own trustworthiness through his vengeful pursuit of Palamedes. In that sense, Odysseus is already *kákistos,* and runs the risk of being proven such, very much like the fictional character Palamedes puts forth in 13.3-5: "For no one wants to run the greatest risks and be the most wicked [*kákistos*] in respect to the greatest wickedness [τὴν μεγίστην κακότητα] for nothing [προῖκα]." And this is precisely why, following a brief summary evocative of 5.6-8,[35] Palamedes turns to his accuser and challenges his character, upon which depends entirely the credibility of his accusations.

Therefore, Palamedes's strategy is to discredit Odysseus, also reinstating the antithesis between their respective characters:

> *You* [Odysseus], being the sort of person *you* are [τοιοῦτος ὢν], accuse *me,* being the sort of person *I* am [τοιούτου], based on what? For it is worth examining closely [ἄξιον γὰρ

---

[34] Philostratus, *Heroicus,* 25.16: "not on account of the daughter of Chryses."

[35] "The fact that I would neither have been able [ἂν ἐδυνάμην] nor willing [ἂν ἐβουλόμην] to betray Greece, has been demonstrated by what I have said so far" (21.8-10); see also the discussion above.

> καταμαθεῖν] what sort of person you are and what sorts of aspersions you cast [οἷος ὢν οἷα λέγεις], since you are an unworthy man, saying these things against someone who does not deserve them [ὡς ἀνάξιος ἀναξίῳ]. (22.1-3)

Palamedes sets out to exercise *élenchos* once again, and this time the stakes are higher than ever. Here Gorgias is calling upon the mythical tradition of Palamedes as the arch-enemy and top victim of Odysseus; well-attested throughout the classical period and beyond, this tradition is also echoed in Polygnotos's lost painting *The Fall of Troy*,[36] which Pausanias (and maybe Gorgias himself) saw at the Lesche of the Knidians at Delphi. According to Pausanias (10.31.1-2), the famous painting depicted, along with Palamedes, several enemies-victims of Odysseus such as Ajax, the son of Telamon, Ajax, the son of Oileus, and Thersites.[37] Most importantly, as we saw above, the same mythical tradition reported that Odysseus had framed Palamedes for treason.[38]

With such a tradition behind him, Palamedes can build his argument about his accuser's character on solid ground. First, the pair of correlative pronouns τοιοῦτος (22.3) and οἷος (22.4), demonstrative and specific relative respectively,[39] links the defense speech to the rich intertext of literary and artistic production featuring Odysseus's victimization of Palamedes. Second, the binary knowledge-opinion (εἰδώς-δοξάζων, 22.6-7), already introduced at the beginning of the speech (σαφῶς ἐπιστάμενος-δοξάζων γ' ἁμῇ, 3.1-3), is revisited to fully expose Odysseus's unscrupulousness: "For are you accusing me from precise knowledge or from opinion?

---

[36] Active during the period 450-20 BCE.

[37] Odysseus took the arms of Achilles from Ajax, son of Telamon, and caused him to commit suicide; see Gantz, *Early Greek Myth*, 629-34. He also urged the Greeks to stone Ajax, son of Oileus, on account of his rape of Kassandra while she was Athena's suppliant (Gantz, *Early Greek Myth*, 695-7), and physically abused Thersites, the anti-hero of the *Iliad*, who exposed Agamemnon's greed (*Iliad*, 2.211-69).

[38] According to the *Cypria* reported by Pausanias (10.31.1-2), Odysseus caused Palamedes to drown with Diomedes's help; cf. Gantz, *Early Greek Myth*, 604-7, West, *The Epic Cycle*, 123-6.

[39] Smyth, *Greek Grammar*, §340, 1245-9.

[πότερα γάρ μου κατηγορεῖς εἰδὼς ἀκριβῶς ἢ δοξάζων;]" (22.6-7). A series of conditions ensues (22.8-15), targeting the plaintiff's lack of evidence. With a simple condition, Palamedes establishes the fact that, if the accusation is based on knowledge, Odysseus must have seen the undertaking or participated in it; if he has seen it, then he can describe it in detail; if he has participated in it, then he is liable to the same charges as Palamedes; if he has received information from somebody who took part in the deed, then that person, whoever he is, has to reveal himself and give testimony. Concluding with a sneer at Odysseus's character, namely that for him it was possible to find not only witnesses, but also false ones (23.6-8),[40] Gorgias proceeds to argue that the case for the prosecution was constructed from opinion.

Addressing Odysseus with the phrase, "most audacious of all people [πάντων ἀνθρώπων τολμηρώτατε]" (24.2-3),[41] Palamedes employs the superlative of the adjective τολμηρός, "audacious," a *hapax* in Gorgias, to further discredit the capital charge against him as one based entirely on opinion (24.2-5). Furthermore, he uses simple conditions to point out the dead end to which Odysseus has led his own case: that, through his alleged treason, Palamedes combines in his persona the diametrical opposite (*enantiōtata,* 25.2) qualities of *sophía,*[42] sound judgement, and *manía,* madness. By demonstrating that he could not be both prudent and insane, the defendant aims to bring forth the disposition of the case through additional simple and mixed conditions. Consequently, Palamedes summarizes: "If, on the one hand, I am prudent (σοφός, 26.7) then, on the other, I have not made a mistake [οὐχ ἥμαρτον, 26.6-7]; if, however, I have made a mistake, then I am not σοφός (26.7-8)." By exposing the self-contradictory nature of Odysseus's accusations, he also reveals his falsehood: "in either case, you would be a liar [ἂν

40 Spatharas, "Patterns," 397-8.

41 I find McComiskey's translation "most reckless of all humans" most accurate ("Holistic Reading," 19); cf. also Montiglio, *From Villain to Hero,* 42-43.

42 I translate *sophia* as "sound judgement" to render the notion of skills required to make prudent choices in everyday life; see also *LSJ* s.v. On the argument from antinomy, see Spatharas, "Patterns," 401-2.

εἴης ψευδής]" (26.8-9). This summary takes us back to the origin of the antagonism between the two men, Odysseus's use of *manía* in his attempt at draft evasion. Because of Palamedes's *élenchos,* this *manía* did not work then, and, hopefully, thanks to Palamedes's renewed *élenchos,* Odysseus's accusation of *manía* against him will be overthrown just as easily.

Nevertheless, as he makes clear, Palamedes does not wish to rake up the past, even though he could accuse Odysseus of many and serious crimes, both old and new (πολλὰ καὶ μεγάλα καὶ παλαιὰ καὶ νέα, 27.1-2); instead, he wishes to be acquitted on the merit of his own good deeds, and not of Odysseus's bad ones (27.1-5).[43] With a future more vivid condition,[44] he kindly requests the court's tolerance for singing his own praises, also appealing to their first-hand knowledge of his character:

> Therefore, I ask you [δέομαι οὖν ὑμῶν], if I remind you [ἂν ὑμᾶς ὑπομνήσω] of just a few of the noble things that I have done, that not one of you begrudge [μηδένα φθονῆσαι] what I say, but that you consider it necessary [ἀλλ' ἀναγκαῖον ἡγήσασθαι] for someone accused of terrible and untrue things to also speak a little of his true and good actions to you who know them; indeed, this gives me the greatest pleasure (28.5-9).

With a potential optative, Palamedes declares that no one could ever bring before the court a true accusation of wickedness against him (29.3-5), also equating Odysseus's accusatory *logos,* with its shocking lack of evidence,[45] to "an unchecked vitriolic attack *ad hominem* [λοιδορίαν οὐκ ἔχουσαν **ἔλεγχον]"** (29.6-7).[46] It is not a coincidence, of course, that the term *élenchos* is employed in connection to the

[43] McComiskey, "Holistic Reading," 19; see also Lampe, "*Logos* of Ethics," 119; Dimos G. Spatharas, "Self-Praise and Envy: From Rhetoric to the Athenian Courts," *Arethusa* 44.2 (2011): 199-219, especially 203, 210.

[44] Carried out with ἄν with the subjunctive and an expression equivalent to the future indicative, the present indicative of the verb δέομαι with the infinitive; see also Smyth, *Greek Grammar,* §2326.

[45] "No proof whatsoever," οὐδεμίαν ἀπόδειξιν, 29.6.

[46] See also Spatharas, "Patterns," 400n17.

prosecution's *loidoría* (shameless blame that can seem to be bordering on verbal abuse). Well attested in classical authors and especially orators,[47] the two terms often occur together in order to differentiate between *loidoría* and *aitía* (mere accusation or invective without proof), on the one hand, and *elenchos* (scrutiny or proof), on the other. In his 355 BCE forensic speech *Against Androtion,* Demosthenes articulates this differentiation most aptly:

> But I think you [addressing the judges] should first of all consider carefully in your own minds that blame [*loidoría*] and accusation [*aitía*] are very far removed from proof [*élenchos*]. For, on the one hand, accusation [*aitía*] is when one merely makes a speech without providing the evidence necessary to support it [ὅταν τις ψιλῷ χρησάμενος λόγῳ μὴ παράσχηται πίστιν ὧν λέγει]; it is proof [*élenchos*], when one makes a statement and at the same time demonstrates the truth behind it [ὅταν ὧν ἂν εἴπῃ τις καὶ τἀληθὲς ὁμοῦ δείξῃ].[48]

Demosthenes's formulation of the gap between *loidoría* and *élenchos* applies particularly to Odysseus's case against Palamedes, given its lack of evidence and absence of witness testimonies. Palamedes's defense, however, is equally unable to provide either, even though, as he has emphasized, the burden of proof rests with his accuser (23). Therefore, it is of the utmost importance for him to not only expound on the integrity of his own character, but also underscore his contributions towards the betterment of life for humanity. Indeed, in addition to being free from fault [ἀναμάρτητος, 29.2, 30.2], Palamedes presents himself as "a great benefactor to the judges, to the Greeks, and to all people, not only the ones of the present, but also those of the future [μέγας εὐεργέτης ὑμῶν καὶ τῶν Ἑλλήνων καὶ τῶν ἁπάντων ἀνθρώπων, οὐκουν τῶν

[47] Based on a full-corpus, proximity lemma search at the *TLG*, out of the 12 attestations of the terms *loidoria* and *elenchos* in a 50-word context among classical authors, 10 are found in Demosthenes, one in Isaeus, and one here.

[48] Quoted from James H. Vince, *Demosthenes Orations, Vol. III.* Loeb Classical Library 299 (Cambridge, MA: Harvard University Press, 1964).

νῦν ὄντων ἀλλὰ καὶ τῶν μελλόντων]" (30.2-5), a self-portrait consistent with traditions that ranked Palamedes next to Prometheus.[49] Echoing Alcidamas's refutation, Palamedes's enumeration of his own benefactions to humanity aims at providing further (and compelling) evidence that, on account of his deep engagement with all things good, he also refrains from anything shameful or evil (31.3-4). Continuing his address to the judges, he appeals to the cultural value of reciprocity by means of a simple present condition, "I believe that, if I myself do not treat you unjustly, neither should I myself be treated unjustly by you [ἀξιῶ δὲ, εἰ μηδὲν αὐτὸς ὑμᾶς ἀδικῶ, μηδὲ αὐτὸς ὑφ' ὑμῶν ἀδικηθῆναι]" (31.5-6).

The defendant saves his most powerful conditional sentence for the end. With a present contrary-to-fact protasis and a future less-vivid-apodosis, Gorgias makes a broader statement about the inability of rhetoric to find the truth: "If it were possible for the truth about actions to become clear and obvious to an audience by means of speeches [εἰ μὲν οὖν ἦν διὰ τῶν λόγων τὴν ἀλήθειαν τῶν ἔργων καθαράν τε γενέσθαι τοῖς ἀκούουσι καὶ φανεράν], it would already be easy [for you] to pronounce a judgement based on what I have said [εὔπορος ἂν εἴη ἤδη κρίσις ἀπὸ τῶν εἰρημένων]" (35.1-3).[50] This mixed condition performs a twofold function. First, it

---

[49] On Prometheus and Palamedes as "first-discoverers" in Plato, see Philip S. Horky, *Plato and Pythagoreanism* (New York: Oxford University Press, 2013), 201-60, especially 211-21, 245. On Palamedes as a benefactor to humanity, see also Bassino, "Sophistic Hero," 43-50, Gantz, *Early Greek Myth*, 604; Knudsen, "Poetic Speakers," 39-40, and McComiskey, "Holistic Reading," 20-1.

[50] On this passage in the broader context of Gorgias's discourse on rhetoric's pursuit of the truth, and especially in *On Non-Existence*, see McComiskey, "Holistic Reading," 6-20; see also Jurgen Gatt, "Failing to Demonstrate Moral Self-Knowledge in Gorgias's *Palamedes*," in *Ageless Arete*, eds. Heather L. Reid and John Serrati (Siracusa: Parnassos Press, 2022), 152-3, Lampe, "*Logos* of Ethics," 119; Gerald J. Biesecker-Mast, "Forensic Rhetoric and the Constitution of the Subject: Innocence, Truth, and Wisdom in Gorgias's *Palamedes* and Plato's *Apology*," *Rhetoric Society Quarterly* 24.3-4 (1994): 148-66, especially 157; see also Segal, "Psychology of the *Logos*," 111-4.

disillusions the court about the ability of Palamedes's speech—or any speech for that matter—to find out the truth beyond any doubt, and second, it foreshadows Palamedes's warning to the judges about the consequences of an unjust verdict. Instead, Palamedes asks for some more time, and an examination of his case guided by the truth (35.5-6). Issued with an assertive future-more-vivid condition, this hypothesis brings us back to the beginning of the speech and Odysseus's potential characterization as *kákistos*: "If you kill me unjustly, it will become clear [φανερόν] to many; for I am innocent [ἁγνός], and your wickedness [κακότης] will be clear [φανερά] and well-known [γνώριμος] to all Greeks" (36.1-4). An additional future-more-vivid condition, carried out with the future indicative and a participial protasis, elaborates on the catastrophic consequences of such a mistrial [δικάσαντες ἀδίκως], reminding the judges that a wrongful conviction will constitute a moral failure on their part [ἁμαρτήσεσθε]; most importantly, this failure will be harmful to not only Palamedes and his parents, but also to the judges themselves, who will inevitably develop moral self-knowledge of their dreadful, godless, unjust, and lawless deed [ὑμῖν αὐτοῖς δεινὸν ἄθεον ἄδικον ἄνομον ἔργον συνεπιστήσεσθε πεποιηκότες] to have put to death, without having proven any obvious injustice or credible accusation [φανερὰν οὐδεμίαν ἀδικίαν οὐδὲ πιστὴν αἰτίαν ἀποδείξαντες], their fellow-Hellene and a great benefactor of Hellas (36.7-13).[51]

Palamedes's parting words to the judges constitute the essence of contrafactual elegance. Explaining why he will not summarize his argument, he pays a respectful compliment to the people who will decide his fate: "I have now said my part and I conclude. For it makes sense [λόγον ἔχει] to summarize a long argument to incompetent judges [φαύλους δικαστάς]; but it is not appropriate [οὐκ ἄξιον] to even think [ἀξιῶσαι] that the first Greeks among the first Greeks do not pay attention to or do not remember what has been said" (37.1-6). Effectively, Palamedes says, "if I were before incompetent judges [φαῦλοι δικασταί], I would have to summarize my argument; before you, however, who are the best of the best, there is absolutely no

[51] On moral self-knowledge in *Palamedes*, see Gatt, "Failure to Demonstrate," 146-54; on this passage see also Knudsen, "Poetic Speakers," 41-2.

need for me to do that." It is not a coincidence, I argue, that here we have the sole occurrence of the phrase φαῦλοι δικασταί (incompetent judges), in the extant Gorgianic corpus. Furthermore, it is not a coincidence that Palamedes's defense ends with a brilliantly compressed discourse on *axios* and its cognates, two of which are prominently featured in his closing statement. Well aware of any and all weak points in his speech, he considers it unworthy to even think that the best of the Greeks would not pay attention during court proceedings or would not remember what was said.

And yet they did not.[52] And Palamedes became an iconic victim of miscarriage of justice, a tradition meaningfully mentioned in Plato's *Apology of Socrates*; there, Socrates is looking forward to joining in the Underworld Palamedes and Ajax, the two famous victims of Odysseus's manipulative rhetoric:

> Indeed, I would find life there wonderful [θαυμαστή], every time I met Palamedes or Ajax, the son of Telamon, or anyone else of old who died as a result of unjust judgement [ὁπότε ἐντύχοιμι Παλαμήδει καὶ Αἴαντι τῷ Τελαμῶνος καὶ εἴ τις ἄλλος τῶν παλαιῶν διὰ κρίσιν ἄδικον τέθνηκεν], and compared my suffering to theirs [ἀντιπαραβάλλοντι τὰ ἐμαυτοῦ πάθη πρὸς τὰ ἐκείνων], it would not be unpleasant, I think. And the greatest pleasure would be to spend my time examining the people there as I do those here, and seeking to establish who of them is wise, and who thinks he is, but is not. (41a9-b7)

As James A. Coulter has shown,[53] Gorgias's *Palamedes* and Plato's *Apology of Socrates* are engaged in an all-encompassing dialogue

---

[52] Cf. Bassino, "Sophistic Hero," 50-51, Lampe, "*Logos* of Ethics," 117.

[53] James A. Coulter, "The Relation of the *Apology of Socrates* to Gorgias' *Defense of Palamedes* and Plato's Critique of Gorgianic Rhetoric," *Harvard Studies in Classical Philology* 68 (1964): 269-303. See also Guido Calogero, "Gorgias and the Socratic Principle *Nemo Sua Sponte Peccat*," *Journal of Hellenic Studies* 77.1 (1957): 12–17; Biesecker-Mast, "Forensic Rhetoric;" Giombini, *Gorgia epidittico*, 214-6; Claudia Mársico, "'Quiero morir muchas veces si esto es verdad' (Plat., *Ap.*, 41b). Sócrates,

manifested in both content and form.[54] Although the relationship between the two speeches is beyond the scope of this discussion, it is important to note that in both Palamedes constitutes a model of endurance in the face of judicial injustice. Interestingly,[55] the only other attestation of the verb ἀντιπαραβάλλω in Plato is in *Hippias Minor*, 369c7, where Hippias invites Socrates to debate the relative merits of their respective arguments on the subject of integrity of character between Achilles and Odysseus. Hippias claims that he will prove that Homer made Achilles better than Odysseus and free from falsehood, while he made Odysseus deceitful (δολερόν), extremely mendacious (πολλὰ ψευδόμενον), and inferior in character to Achilles (χείρω Ἀχιλλέως) (369 c3-5). Naturally, Hippias's characterization of Odysseus brings to mind Gorgias's own discourse on the great Ithacan as inherently (and traditionally depicted as) unscrupulous.

Xenophon's Socrates,[56] also sees himself in Palamedes, whose *kléos* he articulates through antagonism with Odysseus:[57]

> Moreover, I also [ἔτι] get comfort from the case of Palamedes, who died in circumstances similar to mine [ὁ παραπλησίως ἐμοὶ τελευτήσας]; for, to this day, he provides us with far finer themes for song [πολὺ καλλίους

Palamedes y los ejercicios retóricos en el horizonte del diálogo socrático," *Archai* 31 (2021): 1-19. On Odysseus as responsible for Palamedes's death in Plato, see Montiglio, *From Villain to Hero*, 51-55.

[54] For a comparative reading of the defenses of Socrates in Plato, Palamedes in Gorgias, and Hippolytus in Euripides, see Rafael Ferber, *Platonische Aufsätze*, 386 (Berlin: De Gruyter, 2020), 1-6; Alonso de Tordesillas, "Dispositivi dimostrativi utilizzati in tre modelli di difesa: Ippolito, Palamede e Socrate," in *Socratica III: Studies on Socrates, the Socratics, and the Ancient Socratic Literature*, eds. Alessandro Stavru and Fulvia De Luise (Sankt Augustin: Academia, 2013), 204-12.

[55] On the verb ἀντιπαραβάλλω in Plato's *Apology of Socrates*, see Tordesillas, "Dispositivi," 209, Coulter, "Relation of *Apology*," 297.

[56] On Palamedes in Xenophon see Francesco Mori, "Socrate, Palamede, é l' Empio Processo" *Maia* 70.2 (2018): 211-9, especially 214-17.

[57] See also Naoko Yamagata, "Use of Homeric References in Plato and Xenophon," *Classical Quarterly* 62.1 (2012): 130-44, especially 133-40.

> ὕμνους] than Odysseus, the man who unjustly put him to death [Ὀδυσσέως τοῦ ἀδίκως ἀποκτείναντος αὐτόν]. And I know that both time future and time past will bear witness for me too [καὶ ἐμοὶ], that I never wronged or corrupted anyone but rather benefited those who conversed with me by teaching them, without reward, every good thing that was within my power (*The Defense of Socrates*, 26).[58]

Here Xenophon underscores the literary posterity of Palamedes's validation by turning his sufferings into theme for song, and thereby counteracting his erasure from Homeric epic. Furthermore, in the *Memorabilia,* Xenophon has Socrates rank Palamedes next to Daedalus, the archetypal engineer and builder of the Labyrinth, portraying him as an equally legendary agent of wisdom: "Have you not heard of Palamedes's sufferings? For all the poets sing of him, how, on account of his wisdom, he was envied and caused to perish by Odysseus" (ὡς διὰ σοφίαν φθονηθεὶς ὑπὸ τοῦ Ὀδυσσέως ἀπόλλυται; 4.2.33.9). Finally, Xenophon mentions Palamedes's extraordinary wisdom also in the *Cynegeticus,* where, however, the hero's dire fate is blamed on evildoers (*kakoi*), and not on distinguished Greeks, like Odysseus and Diomedes, one of whom is almost *áristos* and the other equal to the noble ones; in this version, his death was also avenged more than any other mortal's—a reference to his father Nauplios's causing the shipwreck of the Greek fleet outside of Euboea (1.11.3-8).[59]

In conclusion, it can be said that Gorgias's Palamedes assimilates in his oratorical persona aspects of all of the above versions of the hero's profile, and especially his uncontestable moral and intellectual superiority over Odysseus. While the comparison between them is ongoing—as is their antagonism—Palamedes constantly rises above the envy, subterfuge, or wickedness to which Odysseus resorts in order to evade his opponent's *élenchos* or retaliate for it. Nevertheless, Palamedes finds in conditional sentences an efficient medium of exposing the vileness of Odysseus's discourse as well as the iniquity

---

[58] Quoted from: Edgar C. Marchant, *Xenophontis Opera Omnia*, Vol. 2, 2nd edition (Oxford: Clarendon Press, 1971).

[59] Apollodorus, *Library*, 6.8-11. Cf. Gantz, *Early Greek Myth*, 604-8, 695-7.

of his character. In his unrelenting refutation of Odysseus's malicious accusations, Palamedes enters a dialectic territory that forces him to establish the un-reality of his accuser's lies. For this purpose, his defense speech has to rely on contrary-to-fact conditions that search for the truth in both past and present yet fall short of fully revealing it, just as his defense speech presumably did in myth. After all, judges would be sure to issue fair verdicts, if speeches had mastered the art of finding out the truth.

Erminia Di Iulio[1]

Gorgias's Account(s) of "Seeing" in the *Palamedes*

In *The Rhetoric of Seeing in Attic Forensic Oratory*,[2] Peter O'Connell effectively puts emphasis on the pivotal role played by "sight" in the performance aspects of classical Athenian oratory. The book proceeds on the (embraceable) conviction that "ancient rhetorical theorists were aware that oratorical persuasion required more than just words."[3] O'Connell shows how the "civic gaze"—being "at the heart of Athenian citizenship"[4]—is also at the heart of Athenian courts, acknowledging that "within a single trial, therefore, jurors and litigants could experience the 'civic gaze' in a variety of overlapping ways centering on feelings of power and knowledge."[5]

Deciding whether such an approach is conclusive is not relevant for my purposes. What it is relevant is that, throughout the book, O'Connell also mentions, though briefly, Gorgias's *Defense of Palamedes*, which is not, of course, a forensic speech. He does so, however, because the *Defense of Palamedes* (hereinafter the *Palamedes*) clearly shares some common aspects with forensic speeches and because, as a matter of fact, the emphasis on "seeing" and "sight" in the *Palamedes* is nothing less than striking—indeed, its subtitle could perfectly be "Encomium of Vision."

It is exactly on the *Palamedes* that I wish to focus in this paper, proceeding on the conviction that its emphasis on "seeing" and "sight" is, on the one hand, a sign of a continuity with the past (the relevance of both "vision" and "sight" in the traditional or archaic account of knowledge and truth is well-known) and, on the other

---

[1] Erminia Di Iulio received her PhD in 2020 at Tor Vergata University (Rome, Italy). She works primarily on Gorgias and the epistemology of Early Greek Philosophy. She co-founded the open access journal *Synthesis: Journal for Philosophy*. She recently published *Gorgias's Thought: An Epistemological Reading* (Routledge, 2022).

[2] Peter A. O'Connell, *The Rhetoric of Seeing in Attic Forensic Oratory* (Austin: University of Texas Press, 2017).

[3] O'Connell, *Rhetoric of Seeing*, 2.

[4] O'Connell, *Rhetoric of Seeing*, 9.

[5] O'Connell, *Rhetoric of Seeing*, 12.

hand, a sign of a continuity with the present and future (i.e., precisely forensic oratory). Indeed, such a twofold continuity is one of the (many) elements that make the *Palamedes* exceptionally interesting.

Accordingly, in what follows I aim to address and exploit Gorgias's account of "seeing" as it is displayed in the *Palamedes*. In order to do so, I shall embrace what we may define as a "lexicological" approach, where this label is meant to point out that the examination will proceed by focusing on the occurrences of the *verba videndi* in this text. Before addressing Gorgias's words, however, some preliminary remarks are in order.

First of all, it might be convenient to acknowledge something which is likely to strike the reader throughout the essay, namely, the fact that the *Palamedes* offers a very limited variety of terms related to the act of "seeing." Indeed, Gorgias mainly employs the verb *horaō* (and those verbal forms which are related to it, such as *eîdon, oîda,* and *synoida*): the only exception is in fact represented by the verb *skeptomai* occurring (just) twice (*Palamedes* 13; 20). In spite of this, his overall account of "seeing" is highly engaging.

Second, I should be explicit that, in my view, the main feature of Gorgias's account of "seeing" is that it is always epistemically connoted, in that the very act of "seeing" is always considered as the vehicle, means, or instrument of knowledge (or at least *information*) acquisition. As we shall see below, this consideration fits particularly the *Palamedes,* which is notably marked by a systematic use of the verbal forms *oîda* and *synoida* (both absent in the *Encomium of Helen* and in *On Not Being*).

Finally, and related to the second point: as I mentioned, O'Connell entitled his book *The Rhetoric of Seeing in Attic Forensic Oratory;* I further said that, in my view, the main feature of Gorgias's account of "seeing" is its *epistemological* connotation. This might be disorienting, for it might seem that rhetoric and epistemology are mutually exclusive, and that I am favoring the latter and rejecting the former. This is not precisely the case, though. The main point is that, following Edward Schiappa, I truly believe that it is not possible to approach Gorgias's texts with the dichotomy rhetoric/philosophy (epistemology) in mind; they should be read, rather, with a "predisciplinary approach." In Schiappa's words,

> the texts of 5th century Greek writers, especially those by the figures commonly referred to as the Older Sophists, ought to be approached with the awareness that certain 'disciplines' were not yet formalized either in theory or in practice. In particular, the dichotomy often used to distinguish between 'philosophical' and 'rhetorical' discourse is simply not evident in the texts of the 5th century that describe sophistic education [...]. Prior to the fourth century, one rarely finds a distinction between the art or skill of producing discourse that seeks 'truth' and the art or skill of producing discourse that seeks persuasion.[6]

This means that I assume both that it is perfectly legitimate to speak of "epistemological reading" and that such an approach is not to be understood as dismissing the rhetorical elements of Gorgias's texts. As a matter fact, the epistemological components and the rhetorical ones can be mutually enlightening.

This essay is structured as follows: in the first section, I shall take into consideration the occurrences of *eîdon* and *oîda*; in the second, I shall turn my attention to the verb *synoida*; in the third section, I will focus on the occurrences of the basic form of *horaō*; in the fourth section, I will examine the verb *skeptomai*; finally, in the fifth section, I will attempt to take stock, thus providing the main conclusions.

"If You Know, You Know *Because* You Saw": *Eîdon* and *Oîda*[7]

As is well known, the *Palamedes* revolves around the defense speech that Palamedes gave when falsely charged with treason by Odysseus. The defense is built upon two main lines of reasoning: on the one hand, Palamedes/Gorgias employs the so-called "argument

---

[6] Edward Schiappa, "Gorgias's Helen Revisited," *Quarterly Journal of Speech* 81.3 (1995): 310. Besides, one might argue that even rhetorical texts, strictly speaking, could (and perhaps should) be approached acknowledging their epistemological background.

[7] This section is largely based on what I have argued in Erminia Di Iulio, "Gorgia e la dimensione epistemica del vedere: le orazioni," in *Variazioni sul tema del vedere. Saggi sui verba videndi nella Grecità classica, ΔΗΛΩΜΑ. Studi di Lessicologia Antica*, ed. Francesco Aronadio (Napoli: Bibliopolis, 2021), 37-63.

from probability" (so familiar to forensic oratory), claiming that if he wanted to betray the Greeks, he would not have had the opportunity of doing it, and that if he had had the opportunity of betraying them, he would have not wished to do so (this argument takes up §§ 6-21). On the other hand, Palamedes speaks directly to Odysseus and to the jurors with the purpose of underscoring Odysseus's accusation, remarking that, because Odysseus's conviction that Palamedes is guilty stems from opinion, not from knowledge, it is not properly grounded. With these remarks in mind, we can now focus on the *Palamedes*.[8] In the fifth paragraph, Palamedes exclaims:

> *I know with the finest certainty* that the accuser accuses me *without possessing certain knowledge*; indeed, I know I have done nothing. *Nor do I know how someone could know that it actually is what did not happen*. If he [i.e., Odysseus] made the accusation believing that it is the case, I will show you, with a twofold argument, that he is not telling the truth. Indeed, neither would I have been able to do so, even if I wished to, nor I would have desired to accomplish such things even if I were able to do so.
>
> ὅτι μὲν οὖν οὐ *σαφῶς <εἰδὼς>* ὁ κατήγορος κατηγορεῖ μου, *σαφῶς οἶδα*· σύνοιδα γὰρ ἐμαυτῷ σαφῶς οὐδὲν τοιοῦτον πεποιηκώς· *οὐδὲ οἶδ'ὅπως ἂν εἰδείη τις ὂν τὸ μὴ γενόμενον*. Εἰ δὲ οἰόμενος οὕτω ταῦτα ἔχειν ἐποιεῖτο τὴν κατηγορίαν, οὐκ ἀληθῆ λέγειν διὰ δισσῶν ὑμῖν ἐπιδείξω τρόπων· οὔτε γὰρ βουληθεὶς ἐδυνάμην ἂν οὔτε δυνάμενος ἐβουλήθην ἔργοις ἐπιχειρεῖν τοιούτοις.[9] (emphasis mine)

This is a short yet crucial passage. Palamedes claims that he knows with the finest certainty (σαφῶς οἶδα) that Odysseus is accusing not

[8] Needless to say, in no way do I aim to provide an exhaustive analysis of this text. I will focus only on those elements relevant for my objective. Nonetheless, I proceed on the conviction that assuming such a specific perspective can shed light on Gorgias's philosophical account.

[9] Greek from Roberta Ioli (ed.), *Gorgia. Testimonianze e Frammenti* (Roma: Carocci, 2013). All translations, unless otherwise stated, are my own.

because he knows with certainty (οὐ σαφῶς εἰδὼς), but because he merely believes or guesses (οἰόμενος) that Palamedes betrayed Greece. If this is the case, Palamedes argues—that is, if Odysseus is accusing Palamedes because he guesses he did turn traitor—his accuser is not telling the truth (οὐκ ἀληθῆ λέγειν).

From the lexical point of view, many elements need to be emphasized: the expression *saphōs eidenai* recurs twice, clearly meaning "knowing certainly"; the verb *oîda* (in the present and optative form) recurs twice as well, with the meaning of "knowing"; the idiomatic expression *synoida emautō* (*saphōs*) (whose exact meaning and translation will be discussed below) recurs once. The use of the expression *saphōs eidenai*—and generally of *oîda* and *eidenai* in order to denote the "certain or infallible knowledge"—is a traditional element: the theme of *saphēneia* (clarity or evidence) clearly recalls the presocratic conception of knowledge as perceptual or, better, visual[10] (that is to say, a knowledge which is yet to become strictly propositional and conceptual in character).

Such a picture is fully consistent with other relevant passages from the *Palamedes*, namely §§3, 22, and 24. In §3, Palamedes wonders whether Odysseus is accusing σαφῶς ἐπιστάμενος (i.e., on the basis of a certain knowledge) or δοξάζειν (i.e., on the basis of opinion): the expressions σαφῶς ἐπιστάμενος in *Palamedes* 3 and σαφώς εἰδώς in §5 turn out to purportedly be synonymous in that they both denote, as we shall see, that kind of knowledge which is possessed by the eyewitness.

In *Palamedes* 22, Palamedes asks Odysseus:

> Do you accuse me because you *perfectly know* or because you have opinion? *If because you know, you know because you saw* or because you took part [in the event] or because you are informed by someone who, in turn, took part [in the event]. *If because you saw*, tell them the way, the place, the time, when, where and how you saw.

---

[10] In this regard, Mario Untersteiner (ed.), *I Sofisti. Testimonianze e Frammenti* (Milano, Bompiani, 2009) translations of σαφῶς as *chiaramente* (clearly) or *con chiarezza* (with clarity), are definitely on point.

> Πότερα γάρ μου κατηγορεῖς *εἰδὼς ἀκριβῶς* ἢ δοξάζων; *εἰ μὲν γὰρ εἰδώς, οἶσθα ἰδὼν* ἢ μετέχων ἤ του <μετέχοντος> πυθόμενος. *Εἰ μὲν οὖν ἰδών,* φράσον τούτοις <τὸν τρόπον>, τὸν τόπον, τὸν χρόνον, πότε, ποῦ, *πῶς* εἶδες· (emphasis mine)

This is a crucial passage for various reasons. Apart from restating the mutually exclusive opposition between knowledge and opinion, a specific account of "knowing" and "knowledge" is provided. Indeed, Palamedes claims "if you know, you know because you saw [εἰ μὲν γὰρ εἰδώς, οἶσθα ἰδὼν]" meaning both that the act of "seeing" grounds the state of "knowing" (suggesting that visual perception both causes and justifies knowledge which is, in turn, to be understood as "perceptual" in character) and that "knowing" in order to be reliable is to be understood as that possessed by the eyewitness. Besides, *eîdon* also occurs in the following sentence, when Palamedes urges Odysseus—assuming that he knows, because he saw—to testify "when," "where," and "how" he saw what he saw.

Finally, in *Palamedes* 24, Palamedes exclaims:

> As a matter of fact, it is evident that you do not possess knowledge about what you are accusing me of. What is left is that even not possessing knowledge, you have an opinion. You, the bravest man, relying upon opinion which is the less reliable thing, not knowing the truth—do you dare accuse a man of a crime which is punished with death? But this man, what do you know he did? Indeed, possessing opinion on everything is common to everyone, such that you are not wiser than the others. But it is necessary not to trust those who possess opinions, but those who possess knowledge nor evaluate opinion as more reliable than truth, but on the contrary, truth as more reliable than opinion.

> ὅτι μὲν οὖν οὐκ οἶσθα ἃ κατηγορεῖς, φανερόν· τὸ δὴ λοιπὸν <οὐκ> εἰδότα σε δοξάζειν. Εἶτα, ὦ πάντων ἀνθρώπων τολμηρότατε, δόξῃ πιστεύσας, ἀπιστοτάτῳ πράγματι, τὴν ἀλήθειαν οὐκ εἰδώς, τολμᾷς ἄνδρα περὶ θανάτου διώκειν; ᾧ τί τοιοῦτον ἔργον εἰργασμένῳ σύνοισθα; ἀλλὰ μὴν τό γε δοξάσαι κοινὸν ἅπασι περὶ

πάντων, καὶ οὐδὲν ἐν τούτῳ σὺ τῶν ἄλλων σοφώτερος. ἀλλ'οὔτε τοῖς δοξάζουσι δεῖ πιστεύειν ἀλλὰ τοῖς εἰδόσιν, οὔτε τὴν δόξαν τῆς ἀληθείας πιστοτέραν νομίζειν, ἀλλὰ τἀναντία τὴν ἀλήθειαν τῆς δόξης.

Once again, knowledge and opinion (and truth and opinion) are explicitly taken here as mutually exclusive: opinion consists in not knowing the truth (τὴν ἀλήθειαν οὐκ εἰδώς) and it is meant to occur only once knowledge is ruled out (τὸ δὴ λοιπὸν <οὐκ> εἰδότα σε δοξάζειν). Accordingly, it must be the case (δεῖ) that one relies upon or trusts (πιστεύειν) those who know (εἰδόσιν)—those who know, because they saw[11]—not those who, like Odysseus, merely believe or guess (δοξάζουσι). Consistently with *Palamedes* 22, knowledge is perceptually connoted, such that visual perception acts as its ground and justification: opinion must be rejected inasmuch as it is not reliable; it is not reliable because it is not grounded; but it is not grounded because it does not stem from perception or eyewitnessing. In short, opinion is wholly reduced to guesswork.

Besides, that εἰδόσιν here denotes "those who know, because they saw or because they were present when the relevant events took place" is confirmed by *Palamedes* 28, where Palamedes speaks to the jurors and says that he is going to recall some of his true merits (τι τῶν ἀληθῶν ἀγαθῶν)—true merits which, he remarks, the jurors already know (εἰδόσιν). In light of what has been said so far, we are in a position to understand the reason why Palamedes is so confident in claiming that the jurors do know that he is telling the truth: they themselves have been eyewitnesses of Palamedes's life, so that they cannot have doubt that he is recalling facts or events that actually occurred in the precise way he is saying—at this point it must be borne in mind that the jurors are Palamedes's companion, after all.

"Knowing": *Syn-oida*

Indeed, the idea that "knowing" is to be understood as (grounded in) "having seen" or "having been an eyewitness" is a

[11] In this regard, Untersteiner's translation of εἰδόσιν in this passage with "chi ha idee chiare"(those who have clear ideas) is inadequate, for it strongly dismisses the epistemological connotation of this occurrence.

crucial—and pervasive—one. In *Palamedes* 15, Palamedes claims: "I will provide as a reliable testimony that I am telling the truth my life so far; of this testimony you are eyewitnesses: you live with me and thus you know that [ὡς δ'ἀληθῆ λέγω, μάρτυρα πιστὸν παρέξομαι τὸν παροιχόμενον βίον· τῷ δὲ μάρτυρι μάρτυρες ὑμεῖς ἦτε· σύνεστε γάρ μοι, διὸ σύνιστε ταῦτα]." This passage gives a nod to something that, as Peter O'Connell rightly remarks, "extends throughout the entire tradition of forensic oratory," that is, "the strong rhetorical connection between presence, witness, and truth. [Indeed,] things that are supported by the testimony of witnesses who were present are equated with things that are true, and they are said to be the best basis for making just decisions."[12] The expression ὡς οὖν ἀληθῆ λέγω, μάρτυρας τούτων παρέξομαι ("I will provide testimony that I am telling the truth") is in fact a common place in forensic oratory, and there are many similar examples in speeches by other orators.[13] Palamedes's case, however, is slightly different, for the eyewitnesses he intends to call are the jurors themselves.

In this regard, the expression *σύν-εστε* γάρ μοι, διὸ *σύν-ιστε* ταῦτα ("you live with me and thus you know that") is quite significant, in that it is not merely restating the link, which has been so strongly emphasized thus far, between "seeing" and "knowing." More precisely, such an expression stresses the link between "living together" and "knowing together" or, more intelligibly, the link between "sharing lives" and "sharing knowledge." By means of the verb *syn-oida*—meaning here both, and I would say simultaneously, "sharing pieces of knowledge" and "being eyewitnesses"—Palamedes/Gorgias puts emphasis on the "shareability" of experiences which leads to a peculiar sort of knowledge: namely, that knowledge which is shared, if not produced, by a community. That is to say, the jurors are not properly "eyewitnesses" of something Palamedes did (i.e., people who happened to be present to the relevant events); more exactly, they are actually (and deeply) involved in Palamedes's life, they have been an active part of it (as the connection between σύνεστε and σύνιστε clearly shows).

---

[12] O'Connell, *Rhetoric of Seeing*, 88.

[13] O'Connell, *Rhetoric of Seeing*, 209n26.

Accordingly, it seems that we may conclude that the sort of knowledge which is referred to in *Palamedes* 15 is the most valuable and certain because its object is something that the knowing subject has personally experienced and contributed to accomplish—it is no accident that *syn-oida* can also mean "being accomplice." Such a picture is restated in §11, where Palamedes hypothetically assumes that he did betray the Greeks and that he did so for money. Still, he goes on, he could not have done all of this alone:

> [...] certainly it is not something which can be accomplished alone. But with others? Who? Obviously with accomplices. Free men or slaves? As far as free men, I live with you. Who, among you, knows? Speak!
>
> ἀλλ' οὐχ ἑνὸς ἡ πρᾶξις. ἀλλὰ μεθ ἑτέρων; τίνων; δηλονότι τῶν συνόντων. πότερον ἐλευθέρων ἢ δού-λων; ἐλευθέροις μὲν γὰρ ὑμῖν σύνειμι. τίς οὖν ὑμῶν ξύνοιδε; λεγέτω!

Once again, the link between *syneimi* (meaning "being together" and "living together") and *syn-oida* is highly remarkable. As I mentioned, *syn-oida* can mean "being accomplices." The line of reasoning is plain: if Palamedes had betrayed the Greeks, he would have done this thanks to the help of some accomplices; but, since Palamedes and the jurors shared their lives, the accomplices should be sought among the jurors themselves. If so, they would know the truth, inasmuch as they would have been personally involved in the crime.[14] In order to express this sort of knowledge, Palamedes/ Gorgias employs *syn-oida* once again.

All things considered, *syn-oida* seems to denote that sort of knowledge possessed by someone who has personally experienced something, that stemming from one's own experience:[15] I know that you had coffee this morning because I made it for you and you actually drank it in front of me. This is not the whole story, though.

---

[14] Cf. Antiphon 1.9; 5.53. Michael Gagarin (ed.) *Antiphon: The Speeches* (Cambridge: Cambridge University Press, 1997).

[15] Cf. Plato, *Theaetetus*, 206a. Franco Trabattoni (ed.), *Platone. Teeteto*, trans. Andrea Capra (Torino: Einaudi, 2018).

As we briefly saw in the previous section, *syn-oida* occurs in *Palamedes* 5, where Palamedes actually claims:

> I know with the finest certainty that the accuser accuses me without possessing certain knowledge; indeed, *I am well aware of having done nothing*. Nor do I know how someone could know that it actually is what did not happen. If he [i.e., Odysseus] made the accusation believing that it is the case, I will show you, with a twofold argument, that he is not telling the truth. Indeed, neither would I have been able to do so, even if I wished to, nor I would have desired to accomplish such things even if I were able to do so.
>
> ὅτι μὲν οὖν οὐ σαφῶς <εἰδὼς> ὁ κατήγορος κατηγορεῖ μου, σαφῶς οἶδα· *σύνοιδα γὰρ ἐμαυτῷ σαφῶς οὐδὲν τοιοῦτον πεποιηκώς*· οὐδὲ οἶδ'ὅπως ἂν εἰδείη τις ὂν τὸ μὴ γενόμενον. Εἰ δὲ οἰόμενος οὕτω ταῦτα ἔχειν ἐποιεῖτο τὴν κατηγορίαν, οὐκ ἀληθῆ λέγειν διὰ δισσῶν ὑμῖν ἐπιδείξω τρόπων· οὔτε γὰρ βουληθεὶς ἐδυνάμην ἂν οὔτε δυνάμενος ἐβουλήθην ἔργοις ἐπιχειρεῖν τοιούτοις. (emphasis mine)

For present purposes, the relevant expression clearly is σύνοιδα γὰρ ἐμαυτῷ σαφῶς οὐδὲν τοιοῦτον πεποιηκώς (I am well aware of having done nothing). Indeed, this is a formulaic expression, where *syn-oida* is linked to *emautō*. Because of the link between *syn* and *emautō*, the meaning of the verb shifts from "knowing with others" to "knowing with(in) oneself" or, more intelligibly, to "being aware of"[16] or "knowing in one's conscience,"[17] this latter occurring regularly in forensic oratory where it, as Michael Gagarin notes, "is frequently followed by expressions of wrongdoing (e.g., that I have done something wrong); it thus comes to mean 'I have a guilty conscience' even without further supplement."[18]

---

16 Cf. Aldo Brancacci, "Coscienza e reminiscenza. Dall'*Apologia* al *Menone*," ed. Maurizio Migliori et al., *Interiorità e anima. La psyche in Platone* (Milano: Vita e pensiero, 2007), 1–9.

17 Cf. Plato, *Republic*, 331a.

18 Antiphon 5.53, 5.93; 6.1; 6.5. Gagarin, *Antiphon*, 219.

In *Palamedes* 5, by means of this expression, Palamedes/Gorgias, on the one hand, puts emphasis on the fact that the "knowing" denoted by the expression *syn-oida emautō* is the most certainty one can possess[19]—given that it is directed toward an internal mental state (Palamedes is claiming that he knows that "he did nothing wrong": this is a mental state, after all); on the other hand, he seems to acknowledge the impossibility of successfully sharing his own "awareness" with the jurors, thus alluding to the "solipsistic" ending of the *Palamedes*.

The emphasis on the "awareness-motif," but not on that of "privacy," connotes the last occurrence of *syn-oida* in *Palamedes* 24:

> As a matter of fact, it is evident that you do not possess knowledge about what you are accusing me of. What is left is that even not possessing knowledge, you have an opinion. You, the bravest man, relying upon opinion which is the less reliable thing, not knowing the truth—do you dare accuse a man of a crime which is punished with death? But this man, what do you know he did? Indeed, possessing opinion on everything is common to everyone, such that you are not wiser than the others. But it is necessary not to trust those who possess opinions, but those who possess knowledge nor evaluate opinion as more reliable than truth, but on the contrary, truth as more reliable than opinion.
>
> ὅτι μὲν οὖν οὐκ οἶσθα ἃ κατηγορεῖς, φανερόν· τὸ δὴ λοιπὸν <οὐκ> εἰδότα σε δοξάζειν. Εἶτα, ὦ πάντων ἀνθρώπων τολμηρότατε, δόξῃ πιστεύσας, ἀπιστοτάτῳ πράγματι, τὴν ἀλήθειαν οὐκ εἰδώς, τολμᾷς ἄνδρα περὶ θανάτου διώκειν; ᾧ τί τοιοῦτον ἔργον εἰργασμένῳ σύνοισθα; ἀλλὰ μὴν τό γε δοξάσαι κοινὸν ἅπασι περὶ πάντων, καὶ οὐδὲν ἐν τούτῳ σὺ τῶν ἄλλων σοφώτερος. ἀλλ'οὔτε τοῖς δοξάζουσι δεῖ πιστεύειν ἀλλὰ τοῖς εἰδόσιν, οὔτε τὴν δόξαν τῆς ἀληθείας πιστοτέραν νομίζειν, ἀλλὰ τἀναντία τὴν ἀλήθειαν τῆς δόξης.

[19] Cf. Plato, *Phaedrus*, 235c. R. Velardi (ed.), *Platone, Fedro* (Milano: Bur, 2006).

Here, as we have seen, Palamedes exposes that Odysseus's accusation springs from "opinion" not "knowledge," and asks: "But this man [i.e., Palamedes himself], what do you know [σύνοισθα] he did?" This is of a particular interest, because Palamedes is not simply asking what the man did, but rather what Odysseus *knows* he did: surely, on the one hand, Palamedes aims to emphasize again that Odysseus does not possess (certain) knowledge, but, on the other, he might also be suggesting that, because Odysseus is one of his companions, if he really were in the position to know that Palamedes did betray the Greeks, this would mean that he, Odysseus, was one of his accomplices (that is, he would be guilty too).

To sum up, it seems that two shades of "knowing" are coexisting within the semantic field of *syn-oida*, the meaning of which actually varies in accordance with the varying of the subject associated with the verb *oîda* thanks to the preposition *syn*. That is to say, if by means of the preposition *syn* the knowing subject and his community are joined together, the verb points to the meaning of "knowing together"/ "sharing knowledge" and, by extension, to the meaning of "being implicated into the same deed." Instead, if the preposition is, so to speak, connecting the knowing subject with themselves, the verb points to the inner dimension of the self (the conscience), thus assuming the meaning of "being fully aware of one's mental states" and, by extension, that meaning alluding to the private dimension of one's mental states. In any case, and this is the common element, *syn-oida* points to that sort of knowledge that has its source in the subject's own experience.[20]

For the sake of clarity, we might perhaps say that both *synoida* and *oîda* denote that sort of "knowing" that leads to possess "first-hand knowledge"; but, while the latter presumes a kind of "third-person point of view" (in that the eyewitness is, by definition,

---

[20] It might be of interest that *syn-oida* in its double meaning is employed synonymously to *syn-epistamai* in *Palamedes* 21 and 36. In 21, Palamedes claims that, had he been guilty, he could have not hoped to be welcomed by his accomplices, due to the fact that they would have *known* he was not worthy of trust. In 36, Palamedes speaks to the jurors and claims that if they condemned him to death, they would *know in their heart* that they would be making a terrible mistake.

someone who is *not* implicated in what they saw), the former presumes a "first-person point of view" (in that it points to that knowledge possessed by someone who *is* implicated in the facts).

"Seeing" and "Being Seen": *Horaō*

As far as *horaō* is concerned, we need to observe that it occurs just twice in the *Palamedes*—moreover, in a passage that goes easily unnoticed, but is quite interesting. In *Palamedes* 12, Palamedes argues that he could have never let someone into the Greek camp:

> It would of course have been *visible* to all. For life is under the open sky (this is an army we are talking about) in a military camp, and everyone *sees* everything and every-one *is seen* by everyone else. Therefore, for me to do all these things was altogether and in all ways impossible.[21]
>
> ἅπασιν ἄρα *φανερὰ* γένοιτ ἄν. ὑπαίθριος γὰρ ὁ βίος· στρατόπεδον γάρ ἐστιν ἐν ὅπλοις, ἐν ᾧ πάντες πάντας *ὁρῶσι* καὶ πάντες ὑπὸ πάντων *ὁρῶνται*. πάντως ἄρα καὶ πάντῃ ταῦτα πράττειν ἀδύνατον ἦν μοι. (Emphasis mine)

Thus, because "everyone sees everything and everyone is seen by everyone else," the fact, had it happened, would have been "visible" or "evident" to everyone—this being the case, Palamedes is implying, it is clear as well that nothing happened.

The link between *horaō*—the subjective act of "seeing"—and *phanera*—the objective property of being visible and therefore graspable—is quite remarkable. On the one hand, the objective side of reality is thought of as something which is, we might say, *available* to the observer; on the other hand, the predisposition to observe is what makes room for the very possibility of such an availableness. Indeed, the main point is that the objective "evidence" or "manifestation" needs to be recognized as such by someone who is ready to grasp it: there is nothing to see if nobody is here to see it. In this regard, O'Connell interestingly notes that

> this reciprocal use of 'seeing' (*horao/eidon* or *opsis*) and 'being visible' (*phaneros/phainomai*) is common in Greek

[21] O'Connell, *The Rhetoric of Seeing*, 96.

> literature. It is most familiar in descriptions of epiphanies, where the seeing and reciprocal visibility are often followed by a verb of recognition (*gignosko*, less often *noeo*; e.g., *Iliad* 1. 194-200; *Odyssey* 16.155-163 […]), but it appears in a wide variety of situations that refer to seeing, including Xenophon, *Agesilaus* 7.2 […]; Aristotle, *History of Animals* 8.48631a15-20 […]; Theophrastus, *History of Plants* 7.4.3; Autolycus, *Risings and Settings* 2.1 […].[22]

Accordingly, O'Connell rightly proposes to understand *phaneros* as "visible because seen by witnesses"—I would just add the specification "potential witnesses."

To sum up, *horaō* seems to denote the "predisposition to observe or notice," in the sense that its object is precisely "something that does not go unnoticed." In doing so, *horaō* does not straightforwardly mean "knowing"; still, it constitutes its prerequisite, since that which is not seen (that which goes unnoticed) cannot be known either.

"There is Nothing to See": *Skeptomai*

The time has come to address the verb *skeptomai* that, as I mentioned at the beginning, occurs twice in the *Palamedes*. In both cases (*Palamedes* 13 and 20), Palamedes urges the jurors to take into consideration, thus carefully examining, his arguments: in 13, the expression is σκέψασθε κοινῇ καὶ τόδε; in *Palamedes* 20, the expression is σκέψασθε καὶ τόδε. In *Palamedes* 13, right after having argued that he could not have let the accomplices into the Greek camp without being noticed, Palamedes concludes that, had he had the opportunity to betray, still, he would have not wished to do so. Indeed, he rhetorically asks, what reasons could induce an honorable man to betray his own country? In *Palamedes* 20, he enumerates the overwhelmingly unpleasant consequences he should have been forced to face, had he actually betrayed.

In short, *Palamedes* 13 deals with the reasons behind the (hypothetical) betrayal, whereas *Palamedes* 20 deals with its costs. This is not a minor point, for it marks the first relevant element, that is, the fact that—while the other occurrences I took into consideration

---

[22] O'Connell, *The Rhetoric of Seeing*, 212.

thus far have a correlative which is both objective and objectual—the things the jurors are urged to reflect upon are not an observable event, let alone a real one. Indeed, the betrayal is not mentioned directly, but indirectly, by means of its hypothetical causes and its unpleasant results (as we have seen). The second relevant point is that the cognitive activity denoted by the verb *skeptomai* is performed by the jurors, who still need to make a judgment (indeed, both Odysseus and Palamedes did make a judgment, even though the former stems from opinion, whereas the latter stems from knowledge): as such, they are pressed to examine and evaluate Palamedes's arguments.

To be very clear, then, the juror's cognitive state is neither true nor false (at least, not yet); or, to put it otherwise, it is both epistemologically and ontologically un-committing. Further, and consequently, it is entirely figurative. As O'Connell effectively puts it, "Since 'look into' (*skopeo/skeptomai*) frequently occurs in forensic oratory to call the jurors' attention to an important point, its connotation of mental consideration is often stronger than its connotation of physical sight."[23]

Generally speaking, however, it is highly likely that the employment of a verb whose original connotation is so strongly related to "physical sight" is not accidental. O'Connell himself successfully shows that

> part of the challenge of making a good forensic speech [...] is encouraging the jury to associate themselves with witnesses *so that they visualize the speaker's version of events and conclude that his arguments rest on visual evidence*. One way the speakers do this is by using a vocabulary of demonstration and visibility to describe their speaking and the jurors' hearing.[24]

In all evidence, such a remark does not seem to perfectly fit the *Palamedes*, given that it revolves around something that has not happened. As I mentioned earlier, Gorgias's use is entirely

[23] O'Connell, *The Rhetoric of Seeing*, 106.

[24] O'Connell, *The Rhetoric of Seeing*, 107 (emphasis mine).

figurative. Consistent with this, *skeptomai* in the *Palamedes* is usually translated as "examining" or "taking into consideration"—this is how Untersteiner, Giombini, Ioli, and Bonazzi, among others, understand it.[25] These translations are aimed at emphasizing that the meaning of this verb is related, broadly speaking, to the semantic field of "investigation" and to that of "evaluation."

Still, it might be striking that a verb whose original meaning is "to see" or "to look" is used to refer to something that cannot be seen. True, this sort of "mismatch" between the verb and its object is easily explained once we realize that both the meaning of "examining" and that of "considering" are consolidated and non-technical—that is, they represent the usual meaning the verb expresses regardless of the specific context. Still, it is fascinating (although entirely conjectural) to put forth the hypothesis that, by employing a *verbum videndi*, Gorgias is exactly emphasizing that there is nothing to be seen (and to see), inasmuch as nothing has happened. Once again, it is to be stressed that the jurors are urged to pay attention to the hypothetical reasons behind the hypothetical betrayal and its unpleasant consequences (had it happened): that is, the betrayal is taken into account only indirectly.[26]

All in all, leaving conjectures aside, it seems that Gorgias's use of *skeptomai* is consistent with O'Connell's description of its meaning,

---

25 Untersteiner, *Sofisti*; Ioli, *Gorgia*; Stefania Giombini, *Gorgia Epidittico* (Perugia: Aguaplano, 2012); Mauro Bonazzi (ed.), *I Sofisti* (Milano: Bur, 2007).

26 Something along these lines goes for the occurrence of ἐπιδείκνυμι in *Palamedes* 5: Εἰ δὲ οἰόμενος οὕτω ταῦτα ἔχειν ἐποιεῖτο τὴν κατηγορίαν, οὐκ ἀληθῆ λέγειν διὰ δισσῶν ὑμῖν ἐπιδείξω τρόπων· οὔτε γὰρ βουληθεὶς ἐδυνάμην ἂν οὔτε δυνάμενος ἐβουλήθην ἔργοις ἐπιχειρεῖν τοιούτοις. "If he [i.e., Odysseus] made the accusation believing that it is the case, I will show you, with a twofold argument, that he is not telling the truth. Indeed, neither would I have been able to do so, even if I wished to, nor I would have desired to accomplish such things even if I were able to do so." Once again, O'Connell emphasizes the visual connotation of ἐπιδείκνυμι which is normally translated with "demonstrating," but whose original meaning is "showing," "making evident."

that is, "calling the jurors' attention to an important point." By opening the sentence with this verb in the imperative form, Palamedes puts emphasis on what he is going to say; urging listeners (and readers) to pay particular attention to some very specific (as it is lexically marked in both occurrences by *tode*), yet significant point—a point that plays a pivotal role in the present investigation.

Conclusion

Let us take stock of the uses of verbs for "seeing" in the text:

1. *Oîda*, often in association to *saphōs*, is used both to denote that certain knowledge possessed by the eyewitness and to mark the distance between "knowledge" and "opinion" (or between "knowing" and "guessing").
2. *Eîdon* stands for the cognitive act of "seeing" as "acquiring a perceptual content that is fully informative and therefore epistemically justifying": the paradigmatic expression is οἶσθα ἰδών (you know, because you saw) in *Palamedes* 22.
3. Generally speaking, *syn-oida* points to that knowledge proceeding from the subject's own experience either because the cognitive act of knowing is directed toward one's own mental content (the paradigmatic expression is *synoida emautō*) or because it is directed toward something that has been done or produced by the subject and their community (whether narrow or large). This second nuance grounds the extended meaning of "being accomplices" or "being implicated in (something)."
4. As for *horaō*, I said above that it seems to denote the "predisposition to observe or to notice," for its object is "something that does not go unnoticed." In doing so, on the one hand, it points to the traditional framework according to which what is real/true is first and foremost suitable to be seen or noticed; on the other hand, it alludes to the necessity of eyewitnesses in order for something to be considered real/true (and therefore relevant) in courtrooms.
5. *Skeptomai* denotes that sort of "seeing" that has lost his physical connotation. Accordingly, its object is not observable; indeed, it is

what in principle cannot be observed (for it did not happen). As such, the verb denotes a fully mental observation: that is, the act of "gazing at" something that is particularly significant in the development of the argument; some specific element that can turn out to be conclusive in view of final judgment.

I declared in the opening lines that, due to the emphasis on "seeing" and "sight," had the *Palamedes* a subtitle, it could be "Encomium of Vision." I further argued that Gorgias's account of "seeing" is not only "generically" interesting, but rather "epistemically" interesting. Indeed, as we have seen, the verbs related to the act of "seeing" are employed by Gorgias to denote a large variety of cognitive—and epistemologically connoted—activities; moreover, other verbs of knowledge are notably (almost) absent. I then concluded that assuming a "predisciplinary approach"—that is, one that does not understand the dichotomy philosophy/rhetoric as exclusive—can actually improve our comprehension of Gorgias's texts.

Broadly speaking, the overall purpose of this analysis was to bring to the fore the specific character of the *Palamedes* in order to shed new light on Gorgias's thought as a whole. More specifically, I attempted to emphasize what might be defined as the "in-between" character of Gorgias's epistemology. As we have seen, Gorgias's *lexicon*, on the one hand, is fully consistent with—and, to some extent, anticipates—that of forensic oratory and, on the other hand, echoes resoundingly that of early Greek epistemology. Besides, this scenario fits the picture that I sketched in the opening lines, where I made explicit that the upcoming analysis would have relied upon the conviction that Gorgias's account of "seeing" and "sight" is the sign of a continuity with the past (the relevance of both "vision" and "sight" in the traditional or archaic account of knowledge and truth is well-known) as well as the sign of a continuity with the present and the future (i.e., precisely forensic oratory). I would say that this is everything but a minor point—indeed, such an "in-between" character is precisely the reason why we should call for a better evaluation, other than comprehension, of Gorgias's thought. Accordingly, the present essay aims to be a first step towards both.

Enrico Piergiacomi[1]

Gorgias's Laughter, or: Laughing Against Philosophy?[2]

Comedy as Refutation in Gorgias

One of Gorgias's instructions to his pupils is to employ the art of antilogical contradiction to win a debate. If the rival delivers a serious speech, it should be countered with a ridiculous answer; by contrast, if he gives a ridiculous speech, it should be countered with a serious response. This instruction is preserved in three sources. The first one comes from book III of Aristotle's *Rhetoric*, which places Gorgias's claim within a more general reflection on humor:

> As for laughter, since it seems to have some use in debate and Gorgias rightly said [*orthos legon*] that one should spoil [*diaphtheirein*] the opponents' seriousness with laughter and their laughter with seriousness, the number of forms of laughter have been stated in the *Poetics*, of which some are appropriate for a gentleman to use and some not. Each speaker will take up what suits him. Irony is more gentlemanly than buffoonery: for the ironist makes a laugh for his own amusement, the buffoon for the amusement of others.[3]

---

[1] Enrico Piergiacomi was Francesco De Dombrowski Fellow at Villa I Tatti | The Harvard University Center for Italian Renaissance Studies (Florence) and is Visiting Researcher at the Center for Religious Studies of the Bruno Kessler Foundation (Trento) in Italy.

[2] I thank my wife Maria Pavlova for revising the English of this paper as well as Fulvia de Luise, Massimo Pulpito, Phillip Mitsis, and Stefania Giombini who discussed the ideas expressed here. I also thank Heather Reid and Shane Ewegen for including this essay in the proceedings, and the latter also for editing the previous version of the text.

[3] Aristotle, *Rhetoric* III 1419b3-9 (s= B12 DK, D18 LM). Translation from George A. Kennedy, ed., *Aristotle: On Rhetoric. A Theory of Civic Discourse* (Oxford: Oxford University Press, 2007), 248. "DK" refers to Chapter 82 of Hermann Diels, Walter Kranz, eds., *Die Fragmente der Vorsokratiker*, 3 vol. (Berlin: Wiedemann, 1956), "LM" to Chapter 32 of André Laks, Glenn Most (eds.), *Early Greek Philosophy, Volume VIII* (Cambridge, MA: Harvard University Press, 2016).

The second and third sources are the comments on 473e2 made by Olympiodorus in his *Commentary on Plato's "Gorgias"* and by an anonymous scholiast of the same Platonic dialogue. In the passage in question, Polus—Gorgias's pupil—ridicules Socrates's claim that committing an injustice is worse than suffering it (461b3-481b5). Both commentators note that this is precisely Gorgias's instruction to destroy a serious thesis through laughter:

> 'What's this, Polus? You're laughing?': Polus laughed at this point. So Socrates asks, 'Is laughing an alternative form of refuting and are you refuting through laughter?' Note that there is a saying of Gorgias's, giving the instruction: 'If your opponent speaks seriously, laugh, and you will defeat him [*ekkroueis auton*]. If he laughs when you are speaking seriously, exert yourself in order that his laughter should not be noticed.' So it was as a student of Gorgias that Polus laughed.[4]

> This is Gorgias's teaching: to solve [*ekluein*] the opponents' concerns by laughing and rejecting ridiculous things with serious things.[5]

It is not fully clear which of these three sources preserves Gorgias's original instruction. While we can probably disregard the scholium, considering that its author does not display any profound knowledge of the sophist's work, it is difficult to decide in favor of Aristotle or Olympiodorus. Both seem to know Gorgias well. Aristotle often refers to his ideas and instructions.[6] Olympiodorus mentions Gorgias's treatise *On Not Being, or On Nature*, calling it a

---

[4] *Commentary on Plato's "Gorgias"* 20.5 (om. DK and LM), translation from Robin Jackson, Kimon Lycos, Harold Tarrant, eds., *Olympiodorus: Commentary on Plato's* Gorgias (Leiden: Brill, 1998). The text corresponds to source T7 of Robert L. Fowler, ed., "Polos of Akragas: Testimonia," *Mnemosyne* 50.1 (1997): 27-34.

[5] Maria Carbonara Naddei, *Gli scoli greci al* Gorgia *di Platone* (Pàtron: Bologna, 1976), 78.

[6] Cf. the overview by Renato Laurenti, "Le citazioni di Gorgia in Aristotele," in *Gorgia e la sofistica*, eds. Luciano Montoneri, Francesco Romano (Catania: Università di Catania, 1985), 357-88.

"not unadorned treatise,"[7] which means that he could have read it. However, it is probable that Aristotle should be preferred for the following three reasons. First, Aristotle maintains that Gorgias's remarks on the use of laughter in a rhetorical debate are correct (*orthos legon*), which suggests that he could be directly quoting his words. By contrast, Olympiodorus and the anonymous scholium both state that there is a saying attributed to the sophist that can be used to describe Polus's behavior. Second, Aristotle uses the verb *diaphtheirein* to refer to the act of destroying the opponent, which is a term that we find in §17 of *Palamedes*, where it is said that the traitor of one's homeland destroys (*diaphtheirei*) the crowd.[8] Neither Olympiodorus's *ekkroueis* nor the scholium's *ekluein* feature in Gorgias's extant works. Finally, one cannot exclude the possibility that Olympiodorus's version could be an explanation of the second half of the instruction that Aristotle leaves unexplained, namely how one is supposed to react to an opponent who laughs at us. The answer is that one must pretend to take no notice of the opponent's laughter. If so, it follows that Olympiodorus's source is Aristotle and that Aristotle's shorter version is more historically reliable.

The three accounts also differ in their contextualization of Gorgias's instruction. Aristotle seems to say that the sophist's advice pertains to a rhetorical debate. After all, Gorgias's instruction is found in the *Rhetoric*. Olympiodorus's and the anonymous scholiast's comments on Polus's laughter at Socrates suggest instead that Plato knew that Gorgias might have thought that this strategy could be employed in a philosophical debate.[9] Laughing at an opponent's seriousness means to undermine his serious thesis, which in this case is the claim that justice is better than injustice. This might mean that Gorgias's instruction also implicitly refers to the

---

[7] *Commentary on Plato's "Gorgias,"* paragraph 9: *sungramma ouk akompson* (= R23 LM, om. DK). Further arguments in Roberta Ioli, ed., *Gorgia: Testimonianze e frammenti* (Roma: Carocci, 2018), 156.

[8] On the term, cf. Ioli, *Testimonianze e frammenti*, 265.

[9] This point is also noticed by Stefania Giombini, *Gorgia epidittico* (Perugia: Aguaplano, 2018), 143; Ioli, *Testimonianze e frammenti*, 265; and Robert D. Metcalf, *Philosophy as* Agôn*: A Study of Plato's* Gorgias *and Related Texts* (Evanston: Northwestern University Press, 2018), 94 and 100-1.

audience. If one demonstrates that the opponent's serious thesis is actually ridiculous, then those who listen will not accept it and favor the one that counters it—again, in Polus's case, that injustice must be obviously preferred to justice.

The question of whether the instruction of fragment B12 can be interpreted as a philosophical weapon—and not only a rhetorical one—has not attracted scholarly attention. The most complete account provided by Consigny only uses the text for explaining Gorgias's style and polemic humor.[10] In what follows, I propose that Olympiodorus and the scholium could be trusted as sources that show that the instruction could have also been used for rebutting philosophy. It can be maintained that Gorgias did not give his instruction in a specific context. Whether one debates against a serious rhetorician or a serious philosopher, one will win if one uses laughter as one's weapon.

Evidence on Gorgias's Use of Laughter

Before moving to the more specific thesis that Gorgias might have used laughter more generally in a philosophical debate, it is necessary to establish whether one can trust Aristotle and Olympiodorus when they say the sophist taught that one should undermine one's opponent's reasoning by laughing at it. There is evidence in favor of this. It could be noted first of all that some sources report that Gorgias praised his capacity to improvise a speech at an opportune moment and that he considered this aspect so important that he even wrote about this subject.[11] It is possible that

---

[10] Scott Consigny, *Gorgias: Sophist and Artist* (Columbia: University of South Carolina, 2001), 75, 166-76, 192-6. Cf. also Marie-Pierre Noël, "L'enfance de l'art. Plaisir et jeu chez Gorgias," *Bulletin de l'Association Guillaume Budé* 1 (1994): 74-5.

[11] Dionysius of Halicarnassus, *On Literary Composition* 12 (= B13 DK, D12 LM), with (for example) Renzo Velardi, *Gorgia. Retorica e filosofia* (Urbino: Argalìa, 1971), 202; Marie-Pierre Noël, "*Kairos* sophistique et mises en forme du *logos* chez Gorgias," *Revue de philologie, de littérature et d'histoire anciennes* 72.2 (1998): 233-45; John Poulakos, "*Kairos* in Gorgias's Rhetorical Compositions," in *Rhetoric and Kairos: Essays in History, Theory, and Praxis*, eds. P. Sipiora, J.S. Baumlin (Albany: State

his instruction to use laughter against a serious opponent, and the reverse, is also a form of *kairos*. One can take the opportunity of a serious speech for improvising a mocking answer, or a mocking speech for improvising a serious reply.

On the other hand, other sources confirm that Gorgias used laughter to rebut some serious claims of rival sophists. According to Plato,[12] Gorgias claimed that he only taught how to deliver clever speeches, and ridiculed those who promised to teach virtue.[13] These sources include Protagoras[14] and Prodicus, the latter of whom was the author of the tale of Heracles's having to choose between Virtue and Vice.[15] Prodicus was also derided by Gorgias for having repeated the same speeches many times,[16] i.e., for being unable to catch the *kairos* and deliver new speeches.

Another piece of evidence consists in a fragment of a speech delivered in front of the citizens of Larissa. The source is Aristotle,[17] who reports the following. The Lariseans were proud of their noble origins, implying that this superiority was rooted in their innate nature. Gorgias showed the absurdity of this belief by claiming that

---

University of New York Press, 2002): 89-96; Mario Untersteiner, *I sofisti*, presentazione di Fernanda Decleva Caizzi (Milano: Mondadori, 2008), 178-82, 293-6; Ioli, *Testimonianze e frammenti*, 208-9 and 264-7.

[12] *Meno* 95c1-4 = A 21, D47 LM.

[13] This seems to contradict Plato's claim that the sophist wanted to teach about justice and a moral life (*Gorgias* 460a3-4). I agree with Maurizio Migliori, *La filosofia di Gorgia* (Milano: CELUC, 1973), 125-31, and Ioli, *Testimonianze e frammenti*, 87, that Gorgias laughs at the *promise* that one will learn virtue. I add the further proof that he praised tragedy, which fulfills its *promise* to deceive audiences (cf. *uposchomenos* in Plutarch, *On the Glory of Athens* 348B11-C8 = B 23 DK, D35 LM).

[14] 80 A 5 DK, 31 P13a LM (= Plato, *Protagoras* 348e4-349a4) and Vincenzo di Benedetto, "Il *Peri tou me ontos* di Gorgia e la polemica con Protagora," 306-7, who adds *Protagoras* 318a6-9 and 319a6-7.

[15] Xenophon, *Memorabilia* II 1.21-34 = 84 B 2 DK, 34 D21 LM.

[16] Philostratus, *Lives of the Sophists*, I proem = A 24 DK, D11b LM. The text is absent from all the collections, including Robert Mayhew, ed., *Prodicus the Sophist* (Oxford: Oxford University Press, 2011). Prodicus replied to Gorgias (cf. Plato, *Phaedrus* 267a6-b5 = 84 A 20 DK, 34 D11a LM).

[17] *Politics* II 1275b26-30 = B19 DK, D53 LM.

this "nobility" was a rhetorical construction, or a product of the city's own constitution, using the following ridiculous analogy to prove this. Just as there are mortar-makers who make mortars, there are also "Larisean-makers" (*larisopoious*) who are producers (*demiourgoi*) of the "Lariseans," namely the civic magistrates.[18] Now, Aristotle adds that this speech was delivered partly in an ironic manner (*eironeuomenos*). And we have seen at the beginning, from the context of the quotation of fragment B12 DK, that irony is one of the forms of humor that intends to destroy a serious opponent. It could be then supposed that Gorgias's speech against the Lariseans is an application of this strategy. The sophist undermines the serious claim that the Lariseans have a noble *nature* with a pun that shows instead that nobility is a *cultural* construction.

Humor may also be present in all of Gorgias's fragments that are characterized by an excessively tragic, pompous, and poetic tone. Most of them are found in Aristotle's discussion of frigidity in Chapter 3 of book III of the *Rhetoric* (1405b35-1406b14), namely of the style that is perceived as obscure and ridiculous due to its extravagance or inappropriateness (cf. 1406a32-35, esp. *geloion* in l. 32). He lists three compounds ("beggar-mused flatterers," "forsworn," "right-solemnly sworn") and two metaphors ("pale and bloodless doings," "you have sown shamefully and have reaped badly"). He also recounts the following anecdote. Gorgias exclaimed, in a tragic manner, "Shame on you, Philomela!" to a swallow that let fall its droppings on him, pretending that the bird was the maiden Philomela who—according to the myth—had been transformed into this animal. Since defecating on a man is shameful for a young girl, the swallow deserves the scolding.[19] Two more fragments are quoted

---

[18] The best explanation of the pun is by Alonso Tordesillas, "Aristotele, Gorgia e i mortai di Larissa," in *Aristotele e la storia*, eds. C. Rossitto, A. Coppola, F. Biasutti (Padova: CLEUP, 2013), 139-147, who builds a convincing parallel between the *demiourgoi* of B19 DK and Gorgias's definition of rhetoric as a producer of persuasion (*peithous demiourgos*), attributed to him by Plato (*Gorgias* 453a2, 454e9-455a1).

[19] These texts correspond to fragments A23 and B15-16 DK, D43-44 and R10a-c LM. I am using Kennedy's translation: *On Rhetoric*, 202-4. On

by Athanasius of Alexandria and the pseudo-Longinus as examples of frigid and ridiculous expressions: "Xerxes, the Zeus of the Persians" and "vulture, living tombs."[20]

Now, there are two ways of interpreting the ridiculous frigidity of Gorgias's tragic expressions. On the one hand, it could be supposed that their ridiculousness is unintentional. This is surely the interpretation given by Athanasius and the pseudo-Longinus. On the other hand, it is possible to read this ridiculousness as intentional, which has led scholars like Rosenmeyer and Consigny to suppose that Gorgias produced a parody of tragedy.[21] This also seems to be Aristotle's exegesis. In the above-mentioned chapter of the *Rhetoric*, he says that frigidity is intentional in the verses of iambic poets and comic playwrights (1406b3-7), after which he quotes some fragments of Gorgias and tells the anecdote of Gorgias rebuking the swallow/Philomela. The juxtaposition seems to suggest that the sophist wrote these tragic lines with a comic spirit. Moreover, a few pages later (*Rhetoric* III 1408b10-20) Aristotle affirms that Gorgias pronounced these pompous poetic expressions not passionately (i.e., truly) like Isocrates (*Panegyricus* 96, 186), but ironically (*met' eironeias*) like in Plato's *Phaedrus*.[22] Now, I suggest that these fragments are also

---

the anecdote of Gorgias rebuking the swallow/Philomela, cf. Thomas Rosenmeyer, "Gorgias, Aeschylus, and *Apate*," *The American Journal of Philology* 76.3 (1955): 226 and 249-50.

[20] Cf. *peri geloiode* in Athanius of Alexandria, *Commentary on Hermogenes' "On Legal Issues"* 14.180.16-19, and *gelatai* in pseudo-Longinus, *On Sublimity* 2.3 = B5a DK, D30 LM.

[21] Rosenmeyer, "Gorgias, Aeschylus, and *Apate*," 225-7, Consigny, *Sophist and Artist*, 168 and 181-4. Ioli, *Testimonianze e frammenti*, 272, supposes a parody of parasites and of Orphic poems. See also Jonas Schollmeyer, *Gorgias's* Lobrede auf Helena (Berlin: De Gruyter, 2021), 34-6, who supposes that Gorgias drew from line 1021 of Aristophanes's *Frogs* the (parodic?) judgment that Aeschylus's *Seven against Thebes* is "full of Ares" (B 24 DK, D36 LM = Plutarch, *Table Talks* VII 715D11-E3).

[22] The source is omitted in Diels-Kranz and Laks-Most, but included in Thomas Buchheim, ed., *Gorgias von Leontinoi: Reden, Fragmente und Testimonien* (München: Meiner, 1989), 134 and 204-5, who suggests that Aristotle has also in mind Plato, *Phaedrus* 238c9-d3, 241e1-7.

evidence of Gorgias's use of laughter for destroying a serious opponent, in this case the seriousness of tragedy.

This seems to contradict Gorgias's famous praise of tragedy, defined as "a deception in which the one who deceives is more just than the one who does not deceive, and the one who is deceived is more intelligent than the one who is not deceived."[23] Some scholars were led by this fragment to suppose that tragic poetry corresponds to the persuasion of the deceptive *logos* of the *Encomium of Helen* that shapes or changes our opinions, since *logos* produces the same cathartic effect of tragic fear/piety and the same deceptions of opinion (*doxes apatemata*) that are created by poetical magic.[24] Others go even further and claim that the sophist considered life itself to be a tragedy, referring to the third thesis of *On Not Being*. Since this argument shows that there is no correspondence between language and reality,[25] Gorgias may have used it for concluding that the deceptive *logos* shapes our reality by determining or changing our opinions, just like tragic poetry creates a fictional reality on stage.[26] However, this interpretation is not without alternatives. One could also propose that tragic poetry may provide just an example of the persuasion of the deceptive *logos* of the *Helen*. After all, Gorgias says

---

[23] *On the Glory of Athens* 348B11-C8 (= B 23 DK, D35 LM), trans. Laks Most.

[24] Compare *Encomium of Helen* 8-11 with the famous definition of tragedy in Aristotle, *Poetics* 1449b22-28, and cf. Charles Segal, "Gorgias and the Psychology of the Logos," *Harvard Studies in Classical Philology* 66 (1962): 122-32; Willem J. Verdenius, "Gorgias's Doctrine of Deception," in *The Sophists and Their Legacy*, ed. G.B. Kerferd (Wiesbaden: Steiner, 1981), 116-28; Kurt Sier, "Gorgias über die Fiktionalität der Tragödie," in *Dramatische Wäldchen*, eds. E. Stärk, G. Vogt-Spira (Zürich: Olms, 2000), 586-613; Roberta Ioli, *Il felice inganno. Poesia, finzione e verità nel mondo antico* (Milano-Udine: Mimesis, 2018), 137-52.

[25] Anonymous, *On Melissus, Xenophanes, Gorgias* 6.21-25; Sextus Empiricus, *Against the Mathematicians* VII 83-86 = B 3 DK, D26 LM.

[26] Cf. especially Velardi, *Gorgia*, 148-52, 180-1, 210-1; Untersteiner, *I sofisti*, 159-84, 215-40, 279-86; Thérèse Pentzopoulou-Valalas, "Gorgias: philosophe du tragique de la condition humaine," in *Plato, Poet and Philosopher*, eds. E. Moutsopoulos, M. Protopapas-Marneli (Athen: Academy of Athens, 2013), 181-91; Milena Bontempi, *La fiducia secondo gli antichi* (Napoli: Editoriale Scientifica, 2013), 98-110.

in §13 that in order to learn how a speech can easily create new opinions or change old ones, we must also consider the speeches of scholars of heaven, the contentions of public debates, and the contests of philosophers. In this sense, Gorgias's praise is more a praise of deception than a praise of tragedy. Now, if we abandon the identification of *logos* with tragic poetry,[27] nothing precludes us from supposing that tragic language could be parodied and that opinions represented on stage could be reshaped just as any other opinion. After all, this is what happens in the *Helen* itself, which wants to modify the popular opinion (i.e., deception), based on the fictions of poets (including the tragic ones), that Helen was responsible for her choice to follow Paris to Troy, while in reality she was prevented by a superior force (love, divine necessity, etc.) from exercising her free will (§2). If these observations are plausible, it could be added that fragment B12 suggests that one can win a debate against the solemnity of tragedy through laughter, or challenge deceptive tragic speeches by employing the deception of *logos*.

This claim could be connected to one last piece of evidence: the conclusion of the *Helen,* which claims that the whole speech is, for the sophist, an amusement or *paignion* (§21). The term has puzzled scholars, since it seems to downplay the speech that describes the power of *logos* and shows the innocence of Helen to an innocuous *divertissement*. In order to solve the difficulty and defend the seriousness of the *Helen*, it has been suggested that *paignion* means "educative game" and that, therefore, speech is pleasurable and playful in form but serious in its ideas (i.e., the problem of free will) and in its ends (e.g., to train to reason carefully, or to deliver persuasive orations),[28] or that the word is a metaphorical reference to

---

[27] Further arguments in Stephen Halliwell, *Between Ecstasy and Truth: Interpretations of Greek Poetics from Homer to Longinus* (Oxford: Oxford University Press, 2011), 275-77.

[28] Cf., e.g., Giombini, *Gorgia epidittico*, 142-4; Roberto Velardi, "Il λογισμός di Gorgia," in Id., *Retorica, filosofia, letteratura. Saggi di storia della retorica greca su Gorgia, Platone e Anassimene di Lampsaco* (Napoli: Istituto Universitario Orientale, 2001), 37; Vessela Valiavitcharska, "Correct Logos and Truth in Gorgias's Encomium of Helen," *Rhetorica* 24/2 (2006): 147-61, esp. 157-8.

the power of fancy or imagination,[29] or that the sophist is recognizing with an ironic smile how strong the power of his seduction is.[30] Noël puts forward the interesting hypothesis that Gorgias wants to create an enigma and, therefore, she presents his writing as both indebted to previous poetry and a new kind of prose.[31] Some suppose, finally, that Gorgias intends to produce an honest self-parody, namely, to confess that even his writing is full of limits and artificial conventions.[32] However, I tend to be more convinced by those scholars who suppose that the *paignion* qualifies the *Helen* as a speech that is designed to ridicule and comically abuse the solemn poets who accused Helen of having willingly followed Paris.[33] The refutation of the charge of ill-will against Helen is qualified as a "child's game," or an opinion that was easy to argue and impose on the audience. This seems perfectly reconcilable with the contents of fragment B12, which may be implicitly at work in the *Helen*. If one wishes to convince the tragedians that Helen is to blame, one can just claim one's speech is a *paignion*, thus suggesting that the whole poetic tradition leveled ridiculous charges at this woman.

Laughing Against Philosophy (and Eleatism)?

I believe that the evidence collected and analyzed in the previous section has demonstrated the plausibility of the first thesis of my essay, namely, that Gorgias made recourse to laughter in order to undo his serious opponents. I can now move to the second part of my argument: that the instruction of fragment B12 could have also been used against philosophers.

---

29 Sier, "Gorgias über die Fiktionalität der Tragödie," 588-9; Bontempi, *La fiducia secondo gli antichi*, 107.

30 James I. Porter, "The Seductions of Gorgias," *Classical Antiquity* 12/2 (1993): 267-99; Stephen Makin, "Amusing Gorgias: Why Does the *Encomium of Helen* End as It Does?," *Ancient Philosophy* 33 (2013): 291-305; Halliwell, *Between Ecstasy and Truth*, 269-70.

31 Noël, "L'enfance de l'art," especially 85-93.

32 Consigny, *Sophist and Artist*, 176.

33 Giuseppe Mazzara, *Gorgia. La retorica del verosimile* (Sankt Augustin: Academia, 1999), 188-9; Consigny, *Sophist and Artist*, 174, 194-7, esp. 196; Schollmeyer, *Gorgias's Lobrede auf Helena*, 30-7 and 316-7.

In a very generic way, this argument rests on the fact that the above-mentioned references to the debates of the philosophers (*Encomium of Helen* 13) and the *Peri tou mē Ontos* (*On Not Being*) clearly point to Gorgias's interest in philosophy. One could also mention the participation of the sophist in the dialogue with Socrates in Plato's *Gorgias* and the maxim of the *Gnomologium Vaticanum* that compares those who neglect philosophy to the suitors of Penelope.[34] However, what is missing from this evidence is an explicit link with Gorgias's instruction to use laughter in a philosophical debate. In Plato's *Gorgias*, the sophist always remains serious when reacting to Socrates's arguments, contrary to his pupil Polus who cannot help laughing with contempt.

It would also be tempting to further support this argument by using Athenaeus of Naucratis and Philostratus as witnesses. The former says that Gorgias compared Plato's *Gorgias* to an iambic (i.e., comic) text and quotes Hermippus of Smyrna, who says in his biography *On Gorgias* that when Plato tried to shame Gorgias for having received from the Athenians a golden statue in his honor, the sophist replied by ridiculously comparing the philosopher to a "new Archilochus."[35] The latter tells an anecdote that also gives evidence of the use of seriousness against a scornful philosopher. When Chaerephon—Socrates's pupil—made fun of the sophist's seriousness (*ten spouden tou Gorgiou diamasomenos*) by asking him "why beans puff up the belly but not fire," he refused to answer the question and instead made the harsh reply that "earth grows fennel stalks to be used against people like you."[36] Unfortunately, it is clear

[34] *Gnomologium Vaticanum* 743n166 = B 29 DK, P22 LM. But this maxim is doubtful, due to the fact that a similar thought is also attributed to Aristippus by Diogenes Laertius, *Lives of the Philosophers* II 79, found in Gabriele Giannantoni, ed., *Socratis et Socraticorum reliquiae* (Napoli: Bibliopolis, 1990), source IV A 107.

[35] Athenaeus of Naucratis, *The Sophists at Dinner* XI 113 = 15a DK, 32 P24 LM, F41; Jan Bollansée, "Hermippos of Smyrna (1026)," in *Die Fragmente der Griechischen Historiker*, ed. G Schepens (Leiden: Brill, 1999).

[36] Philostratus, *Lives of the Sophists* I proem (= A 24 DK, P21 LM), trans. by Laks-Most, *Early Greek Philosophy VIII*, 135. The source is omitted from Giannantoni, *Socratis et Socraticorum Reliquiae*.

that the two sources are too fictitious to be reliable. The most that can be said about Athenaeus's source is that the witness notes correctly that Plato's *Gorgias* was indeed a parody of the sophist's activity.[37] Further doubt on Philostratus can also be shed by pointing out that Chaerephon is presented by Plato as a friend of Gorgias.[38] It is evident that a *philos* could not have ridiculed the sophist as harshly as happens in the anecdote.

Is it inevitable, then, to conclude that only Olympiodorus represents the source that attests that the instruction of B12 was applied in a philosophical polemic? My final hypothesis is that the answer should be negative, for I suppose that an implicit sign may be found in Gorgias's *On Not Being*, which almost all scholars consider to be a treatise aimed at refuting the ontology of Parmenides.[39] Far less agreement exists with regard to the three arguments that nothing exists, nothing can be known, and nothing is communicable. Scholars debate on whether Gorgias's *On Not Being* is a serious philosophical work that proposes a theory of language

---

[37] I agree with Brad Levett, "Platonic Parody in the *Gorgias*," *Phoenix* 59.3/4 (2005): 210-227. On Athenaeus's reference to the golden statue and the "new Archilochus," cf. Alberta Lorenzoni, "Platone 'novello Archiloco' e l' 'aureo' Gorgia (Athen. XI 505de; Plat. *Phaedr.* 235d-236b), *Eikasmos* 6 (1995): 109-20.

[38] *Gorgias* 447b2: *philos gar moi Gorgias*. Noël, "*Kairos* sophistique," 237-38, and Ioli, *Testimonianze e frammenti*, 90, read the anecdote as an example of Gorgias's *kairos*.

[39] Cf., for example, Olof Gigon, "Gorgias 'Über das Nichtsein'," *Hermes* 71/2 (1936): 186-213; Hans-Joachim Newiger,*Untersuchungen zu Gorgias's Schrift* Über das Nichtseiende (Berlin-New York: De Gruyter, 1973); Guido Calogero, *Studi sull'eleatismo* (Firenze: La NuovaItalia, 1977), 189-268; Velardi, *Gorgia*, 186-96; Patricia Curd, "Gorgias and the Eleatics," in *La costruzione del discorso filosofico nell'età dei Presocratici*, ed. Maria Michela Sassi (Pisa: Scuola Normale Superiore di Pisa, 2006), 183-200; Mazzara, *La retorica*, 33-118. Others think that the enemy is Protagoras (di Benedetto, "Il Περὶ τοῦ μὴ ὄντος di Gorgia," 287-307), or Melissus (cf. Ioli, *Testimonianze e frammenti*, 154), or philosophy in general—cf. Adolfo Levi, *Studi su Gorgia* (Gubbio: Oderisi, 1941), 22-24, Untersteiner, *I sofisti*, 230-1.

and reality[40] or a rhetorical speech that does not really defend the anti-Eleatic conclusions which are drawn from it.[41] In the present essay, I do not intend to dwell on the question of its content, but rather I would like to suppose that the sophist may have rebutted Parmenides through a sort of "philosophical rhetoric." The expression suggests that Gorgias builds counterarguments against Eleatism in the language of the philosophers, i.e., a dialectic language, yet his rebuttal of Eleatism is consistent with the rhetorical strategy presented in fragment B12. Parmenides delivers a serious speech that the sophist wants to undermine through laughter, or with a reasoning that is intentionally ridiculous, for it arrives to the impossible theses that nothing exists, nothing can be known, and nothing can be communicated.

That said, we must acknowledge that the summaries of *On Not Being* provided by the anonymous pamphlet *On Melissus, Xenophanes, Gorgias* and by Sextus Empiricus do not feature words or expressions that could be explicitly connected to the language of humor. At the same time, it has been noted that the title and the style of the treatise might deliberately want to parody Parmenides.[42] I would add here that one could interpret as parodic also some passages of Sextus's summary of *On Not Being* that attribute to Gorgias the idea that, if we bring Eleatism under rational scrutiny, then Eleatic reasoning is revealed to be *atopos* or absurd, i.e., ridiculous. It is true that the *atopia* could refer to a logical or epistemological absurdity.[43] And it might be true that the use of *atopos* could be a choice of Sextus rather than of Gorgias.[44] However, what is logically or epistemologically absurd may be ridiculous. And even if *atopos* is a word chosen by Sextus, it could well be a translation of a term used by Gorgias.

---

[40] Cf. the scholars quoted in notes 22, 24, and 39 as well as George B. Kerferd, "Gorgias on Nature or That Which is Not," *Phronesis* 1.1 (1955): 3-25, and Mario Bonazzi, *I sofisti* (Roma: Carocci, 2010), 39-52.

[41] Consigny, *Sophist and Artist*, 60-92, 189; Giombini, *Gorgia epidittico*, 47-62.

[42] Consigny, *Sophist and Artist*, 173-4; Makin, "Amusing Gorgias," 292.

[43] Gigon, "Über das Nichtsein," 207-8; Mazzara, *La retorica*, 18, 20-1, 46.

[44] Carl Joachim Classen, "L'esposizione dei sofisti e della sofistica in Sesto Empirico," *Elenchos* 13.1-2 (1992), 75.

To further support my claim, it is also useful to note that some sources attest that philosophers were derided for their *atopia*. More precisely, it is possible to find a connection between *atopos* and *geloios*. These sources include Protagoras's and Meletus's laughter against the absurd views of Socrates;[45] Aristotle's eleventh (comic) objection in book III of the treatise *On Heavens* (307a19-24) to the four elements defended in Plato's *Timaeus* (54b6-d3, 56c8-e1)[46]; Epicrates's satire of the *atopia* of the ancient Platonists;[47] Arcesilaus's and Cato's mockery of the Stoic paradoxes;[48] and Plotinus's ludicrous judgment about those who negate providence (*Enneads* II 9.16). Proclus's *Commentary on Plato's "Parmenides"* also shows that the Peripatetics derided the ontology of Parmenides as *atopos*[49] and that already Zeno of Elea noticed that Eleatism was rejected with laughter by some unnamed adversaries:

> You have mentioned something that happened accidentally. The truth is that the book comes to the defense of Parmenides's argument against those who try to make fun [*komodein*] of it by claiming that, if it is one, many and laughable [*polla kai geloia*] self-contradictions result from that argument.[50]

---

[45] Plato, *Apology of Socrates* 26d1-e4, and *Protagoras* 361a3-b3.

[46] The parodic intent is noted by Simplicius, *Commentary on Aristotle's "On Heaven,"* 664.26-27.

[47] Athenaeus of Naucratis, *The Sophists at Dinner* I 54 = fragment 10 of Rudolph Kassel, Colin Austin, eds., *Poetae comici graeci. Vol. 5* (Berlin-New York: De Gruyter, 1986), 153-63.

[48] For the former, cf. Plutarch, *Against the Stoics on Common Notions* 1078C5-D7 = F73 of Simone Vezzoli, ed., *Arcesilao di Pitane: l'origine del Platonismo neoaccademico* (Brepols: Turnhout, 2016). For the latter, see Plutarch, *Comparison between Demetrius and Cicero* 1.5.

[49] Cf. 716.25-717.13. It is possible that the first Peripatetic who did so was Aristotle himself in book I of the *Physics*. Cf. the convincing arguments of Diana Quarantotto, "Aristotle's Way Away from Parmenides' Way: A Case of Scientific Controversy and Ancient Humour," *Elenchos* 37.1-2 (2016): 207-228.

[50] Plato, *Parmenides* 128c5-d2 = 29 A 12 DK, 20 R2 LM, trans. Laks-Most, *Early Greek Philosophy*, vol. 5, 193-5, slightly modified.

With due caution, it is not implausible to suppose that one of these laughing enemies of Eleatism includes Gorgias. He may then be included in this crowd of ridiculers of philosophical absurdities.

To return to Sextus's version, it should be noted that it is normally considered as less reliable than the version given by pseudo-Aristotle. Sextus might aim at transforming the Gorgianic theses into a skeptical discourse about the criterion.[51] Migliori also tries to explain the differences between the two texts by supposing that the latter is actually the source of the former.[52] However, Rodriguez and Giombini have argued that Sextus may be more reliable than it sounds.[53] My personal proof of this is that the word *atopos* could be more consistent with Gorgias's possible intent to ridicule Parmenides according to the principle of fragment B12. Sextus may eventually distort the arguments of the sophist, not his comic spirit.

It remains to analyze the arguments of *On Not Being* which are absurd, and hence ridiculous *per se*. According to the first one (VII 67),[54] if we claim that non-being is, then at the same time we would say: (1) non-being is, since it *is* what is not; (2) non-being is not, for it is thought of as not being. But defending simultaneously (1) and (2) is absurd, therefore what is not is not.[55] At first sight, Gorgias

---

[51] Classen, "L'esposizione dei sofisti e della sofistica in Sesto Empirico," 72-8; Roberta Ioli, "Gorgia scettico? Una riflessione sulla presenza del sofista nelle opere di Sesto Empirico," *Rheinisches Museum für Philologie* 152.3/4 (2009): 331-57; Roberta Ioli, ed., *Gorgia di Leontini: Su ciò che non è* (Olms: Zürich-New York, 2010), 36-50 and 167-71.

[52] Migliori, La filosofia di Gorgia, 61-2.

[53] Cf. Evan Rodriguez, "Untying the Gorgianic 'Not': argumentative structure in *On Not-Being*," *The Classical Quarterly* 69.1 (2019): 87-106; Stefania Giombini, "Why Sextus? The *Pros logikous* as Reliable Source for Gorgias's *Peri tou me ontos*," *Studia Philosophica Wratislaviensia* 14.1 (2019): 83-96.

[54] This and subsequent quotations are taken from *Against the Mathematicians*.

[55] The argument is considered Gorgianic by Kerferd, "Gorgias on the Nature or That Which is Not," 14-5, Giuseppe Mazzara, *Gorgia ontologo e metafisico* (Palermo: Ila Palma, 1982), 25-37, and Bonazzi, *I sofisti*, 43. For

apparently reiterates Parmenides's rejection of non-being, or what is not, since it cannot be known or expressed.[56] In reality, the sophist may be arguing that his adversary admits (1), when he says that what is not *is* what is not (v. 3 of B2: *ouk estin… esti me einai*), and also (2), when he affirms that one cannot think that what is not is not (vv. 13-14 of B7/8: *oude noeton / estin opos ouk esti*). So, Parmenides is confuted because his serious rejection of non-being turns out to consist in the ridiculous claim that non-being is and is not at the same time.

Another passage seems to address the Parmenidean arguments that being is one, since it is indivisible and continuous (B7/8.9-11, 27-30, 47-54). Gorgias argues (VII 70) that it is absurd to think that what *is* is enclosed within itself. This seems to be a translation of Parmenides's idea that the continuity of being implies that it is homogeneous in its boundaries (v. 54: *oi gar pantothen ison, omos en peirasi kurei*), which is refuted by adding that in a being of this sort the container (*to en oi*) or the place that contains (*topos*) and the content (*to en autoi*) or the body that is contained (*soma*) will be identical.[57] But this will mean that what *is* actually consists in two beings, another ridiculous absurdity: what is one is also multiple.

In the third passage (VII 73), Gorgias states that it is absurd to conceive a continuous being that is also indivisible. It is worth quoting his argument in full:

> And in a different way: if it is, it is either one or multiple. But it is neither one nor many, as will be proven; so what is is not. For if it is one, it is either a quantity, or continuous, or a magnitude, or a body. But whichever of these it is, it is not one: if it is constituted as a quantity, it will be divided; if it is continuous, it will be cut; in the same way, if it is thought as a magnitude, it will not be indivisible; and if it

the differences with the pseudo-Aristotle, cf. Newiger, *Untersuchungen*, 29-39, and Calogero, *Studi sull'Eleatismo*, 194-202.

[56] 28 B 2, 6, 7/8 DK (= 19 D6-8 LM). Here and in what follows, I use the numeration of Giovanni Cerri, ed., *Parmenide: Poema sulla natura* (Milano: Rizzoli, 1992).

[57] The proof that Gorgias might have reasoned in this way is provided by Ioli, "Gorgia scettico?," 334-5.

> turns out to be a body, it will be triple, for it will have length, breadth, and depth. But it is absurd [*atopon de*] to say that what is is not any of these: so what is is not one.[58]

The interesting part of this argumentation is that Gorgias does not directly ridicule Parmenides. Its conclusion shows that what the sophist finds absurd/ridiculous is that being cannot be conceived as continuous. In this respect, Parmenides is right.[59] The problem is that his adversary is doomed to suffer defeat in a different way in the previous absurdity of VII 70, namely, to qualify being as one and multiple at the same time: for what is continuous could be divided into many parts. So even if Parmenides is not ridiculed for admitting to the existence of a non-continuous being, he nonetheless becomes ridiculous for implicitly admitting that a single being is many.

The final argument that qualifies the Parmenidean ontology as absurd is repeated twice in a long passage of the second thesis of *On Not Being*, according to which what *is* is unknowable, and so cannot be rationally grasped or thought (VII 78-82). This rebuts Parmenides's doctrine that thinking and being are the same (B3, B7/8.39-41), as well as the claim that one should not trust sight and hearing in a rational enquiry (B7/8.1-6). Gorgias reads the first doctrine (§78) as the idea that thoughts (*ta phronoumena*) are things that are (*ta onta*). Such a reasoning implies (§79) that things that are not (*ta me onta*) will not be thought (*ou phronethesetai*).[60] Gorgias interprets the second doctrine as the claim that we should not doubt our thoughts, only because they grasp things that are not grasped by sight and hearing. He may affirm that Parmenides is saying that we

---

[58] Trans. Laks-Most, *Early Greek Philosophy*, vol. 8, 235.

[59] VII 73, on which see Adolfo Levi, *Studi su Gorgia*, 19. Gorgias's argument actually here takes as its target a being which may be one also because it is conceived as quantity, magnitude, and body. Here I ignore these qualifications, since they seem not to be among the properties of Parmenides's being. For more details, cf. Gigon, "Über das Nichtsein," 198-9, Newiger, *Untersuchungen*, 71-3, and Ioli, *Su ciò che non è*, 157n19.

[60] On the historicity of this argument, cf. Victor Caston, "Gorgias on Thought and Its Objects," in *Presocratic Philosophy Essays in Honor of Alexander Mourelatos*, eds. Victor Caston, Daniel W. Graham (London-New York: Routledge, 2002), 222-4.

cannot reject the rational properties of being (uniqueness, indivisibility, continuity, etc.) just because we see and hear many divisible and non-continuous entities (§81). Now, Gorgias finds absurd or ridiculous these conclusions because they fall against two plain counterfactuals:

> And that is why, in general, if it happens to what is to be thought of, it will happen to what is not to not be thought of. But this is absurd [*atopon d' esti touto*]. For Scylla, Chimera, and many things that are not are thought of. (VII 80)
>
> So that if someone has the thought that chariots are racing in the sea, even if he does not see them, he must have the conviction that chariots really are racing in the sea. But this is absurd [*atopon de touto*]. (VII 82)[61]

Both absurdities could be interpreted as the accusation that Parmenides is contradicting what will be described as the principle of the *adaequatio rei et intellectus*.[62] Scylla, Chimeras, and chariots that can cross the sea do not exist, nor are perceived through sight and hearing, yet the intellect is able to think of them. One could even add that Gorgias knows that Parmenides must recognize this last point. After all, he opened his poem about being by imagining chariots that fly to a realm where a goddess reveals the true ontological wisdom.[63] Therefore, Parmenides's identification of being and thought is ridiculous for the following reason: it admits that non-existent things are not thought and that anything that is thought but escapes sensation must exist, with the result that he cannot distinguish

---

[61] Trans. Laks-Most, *Early Greek Philosophy*, 237-239.

[62] Mazzara, *La retorica*, 42-49, e *Ontologo e metafisico*, 107-11. The historical reliability of the argument that creates a conflict between senses and thought is corroborated by its reception in lines 1-26 of Aristophanes's *Thesmophoriazusae*. Cf. Steve Hays, "On the Skeptical Influence of Gorgias's *On Non-Being*," *Journal of the History of Philosophy* 28/3 (1990): 335-7.

[63] B1 (= D4 LM). Untersteiner, *I sofisti*, 231, and Caston, "Gorgias on Thought and Its Objects," 224, think instead of a polemic reference to the creations of poets.

between fictional entities and real ones.[64] According to Gorgias, this rejection of Eleatic ontology will strengthen the perspective that what is cannot be thought of and apprehended.

However, as I said at the beginning of this section, this essay will not examine the theoretical implications that can be drawn from the sophist's laughter at Parmenides. For now, suffice it to say that, if we accept the supposition that the sophist defended a "philosophical rhetoric," it could be argued that laughter may display a philosophical spirit. In other words, Gorgias laughs at the seriousness of Parmenides in order to remove the rationality or "aura" from his arguments and to reveal how absurd the philosophy that he defends really is.

Appendix. Alcidamas's and Agathon's *Paidia*

We saw at the beginning of this essay that Gorgias's instruction to ridicule a serious adversary was surely put into practice by his pupil Polus. What can be said about the two other pupils of the sophist, i.e., the rhetorician Alcidamas of Elea and the tragedian Agathon? Both conclude one of their writings with the word *paidia* and scholars agree that this is the equivalent of Gorgias's conclusive use of *paignion*. The former does so in the work *On Those Who Write Written Speeches, or On Sophists*,[65] the latter in the praise of Eros that Plato attributes him in the *Symposium*.[66] Nobody, however, has

---

[64] I agree with Untersteiner, *I sofisti*, 234.

[65] §34. Translation from Juan Luis López Cruces, Javier Campos Daroca, Miguel Ángel Márquez Guerrero, eds., *Alcidamante de Elea: Testimonios y fragmentos* (Madrid, Editorial Gredos, 2005), 76-92. From now on, I refer to the work just with the title *On Sophists*. For the parallel between Alcidamas's *paidia* and Gorgias's *paignion*, cf. O'Sullivan, *Alcidamas, Aristophanes and the Beginnings of Greek Stylistic Theory* (Stuttgart: Franz Steiner Verlag, 1992), 31, 64, 84-5, Noël, "L'enfance de l'art," 73-4, Ruth Mariß, ed., *Alkidamas: Überdiejenigen, die schriftliche Redenschreiben, oder über die Sophisten* (Münster: Aschendorf, 2002), 311-2, and Cruces-Daroca-Guerrero, *Testimonios y fragmentos*, 92n145.

[66] Cf. 197e6-8 and Robert G. Bury, *The* Symposium *of Plato* (Cambridge: Heffer and Sons, 1909), 84; Pierre Léveque, *Agathon* (Paris: Les belles lettres, 1955), 123n4; Kenneth Dover, *Plato's* Symposium (Cambridge:

investigated whether this parallelism is indeed an application of the Gorgianic instruction of fragment B12. I think that the answer can be affirmative.

Alcidamas's *On Sophists* laughs twice (§11, 21) at the authors of written speeches, including poets and philosophers,[67] who are also described as people who claim to possess a solemn wisdom[68] and be able to educate others (§15). In the section where he explains why he continues to write instead of making only oral and improvised speeches, he declares that writing could be a pleasurable or amusing way to earn fame among the Greeks (§§29-33, especially 33). The reference to the *paidia* in the conclusion of the *On Sophists* might then hint at the fact that his text intends to destroy the seriousness of speech-writers (i.e., to apply the instruction of Gorgias's fragment B12)[69] and to gain the pleasure of amusement. This last notion could also find a parallel at the end of his work on Homer, if we accept that Alcidamas declares here to have written on Homer's birth and poetry for entertainment (*paidias charin*). Even this activity is then presented as a means for gaining pleasure and earning fame.[70] According to this

---

Cambridge University Press, 1980), 123; Noël, "L'enfance de l'art," 72-3; Esteban Bieda, "Gorgias en el *Banquete* de Platón. Ecos del *Encomio de Helena* en el discurso de Agatón," *Elenchos* 31.2 (2010): 223, 227, 240.

[67] Cf. *poietas* in §2 and *poietes logon* in §34. Although I am aware that these words refer generically to the creators of written speeches (O'Sullivan, *Alcidamas, Aristophanes and the Beginnings*, 52-3; and John V. Muir, ed., *Alcidamas: The Works and Fragments* (London: Bristol Classical Press, 2002), 42-3), I believe that poets can be included among speech-writers, for the writings of the latter are said to be more similar to those of authors of poems (§12). Philosophers are mentioned in §15. On Alchidamas's conception of philosophy, cf. Mariß, *Alkidamas*, 95-9.

[68] Cf. §1 (sophian semunontai), §30 (te dunamei sumnunomenois), and Mariß, Alkidamas, 89-90.

[69] *Contra* Yosef Z. Liebersohn, "Alcidamas' *On the Sophists*: a Reappraisal," *Eranos* 97 (1999), 115, who says that laughing against speech-writers is a common rhetorical device.

[70] I refer to ll. 19-20 of the Michigan Papyrus 2754 (= fragment 6 of Cruces-Daroca-Guerrero, *Testimonios y fragmentos*), which could also be read as *paideias charin*. In defense of *paidias charin*, cf. O'Sullivan, *Alcidamas,*

interpretation, one can suppose that the fragment of a lost work that says "bringing no such plaything to his poetry" (i.e., another reference to the writing of a *paignion*)[71] has a negative connotation. Since Alcidamas considers the *paidia* as a means for crushing his serious opponents and earning fame in a pleasurable manner, he might affirm that a poet who does not write for amusement is one of the many bad speech-writers.

As regards Agathon's praise of Eros in Plato's *Symposium* (194e4-197e5), one could perhaps find an application of Gorgias's fragment B12, if we suppose that his speech is considered a playful way to deride the serious claims in the speech that was previously delivered by Phaedrus (178a6-180b7).[72] After all, the conclusion of lines 197e6-8 shows that the tragedian wants to address him in his *paidia*. It could then be supposed, for example, that Agathon laughs at Phaedrus's claim that Eros is the oldest of the mortals (178a9-c2) with a funny description of this god's delicate youth,[73] or at his idea that love bestows gifts especially on the beloved (178c2-d1 and 180a7-b2), which is ridiculed by affirming that the lover wants the goods

---

Aristophanes and the Beginnings, 63-5. *Contra* Liebersohn, "Alcidamas' *On the Sophists*," 123-5, who affirms that the playfulness is for Alcidamas a way to educate or instruct a more intelligent kind of reader, and Muir, *Alcidamas*, 92, who affirms that *paidia* means that "Homer is now becoming light entertainment."

[71] Guido Avezzù, ed., *Alcidamante: Orazioni e frammenti* (Roma: L'Erma di Bretschneider, 1982), 93. The text corresponds to fragment 19 of Cruces-Daroca-Guerrero, *Testimonios y fragmentos*: *ouden toiouton athurma te poiesei prosferon*. The source is Aristotle, *Rhetoric* III 1406b13-14—the same text that gives evidence about Gorgias's possible use of frigidity as a form of a parody of tragedy (*supra*, §2). We have no evidence that this practice was recovered by Alcidamas.

[72] To my knowledge, nobody has put forward this claim before. For the presence of Gorgias in Agathon's speech, cf. Bury, *The* Symposium *of Plato*, xxxv-vi, and Bieda, "Gorgias en el *Banquete* de Platón," 213-41. On the more general influence of the teachings of the sophist on tragedy, cf. Léveque, *Agathon*, 119-37.

[73] 194a8-196a1. On the comic element of this passage, cf., e.g., Dover, *Plato's* Symposium, 124-5. For humorous elements of Agathon's praise, cf. Valiavitcharska, "Correct *Logos* and Truth," 154.

deriving from beauty firstly for himself or herself and only secondarily in favor of his or her beloved (197b7-c3).

This is a brief overview of the reception of Gorgias's instruction in the works of his early pupils. The topic could be extended to consider the later tradition, in particular Plato, who also qualifies writing in general as a *paidia* and makes recourse to playfulness in his serious research (cf., e.g., *Phaedrus* 276b1-e3, *Philebus* 30e6-7). This, however, falls outside the scope of the present investigation.

Edward Schiappa[1]

Plato or Gorgias?: Considering the Origins of the Word *Rhētorikē* in the *Gorgias*[2]

I published an article in 1990 asking the question "Did Plato Coin *Rhētorikē*?" that I answered by advancing two claims.[3] The first is that Plato's *Gorgias* (*ca.* 387 BCE) contains the earliest surviving instance of the word in Greek literature. The second is that Plato is the likeliest suspect for having coined the word, given his documented penchant for coining words about verbal arts, including *dialektikē, eristikē,* and *antilogikē.* A third claim, developed in subsequent projects, is that the dating of the word's origin *matters* for reasons I shall revisit anon. There have been critiques of these claims, of course, but my sense is that they largely have stood the test of time and that most scholars are now cautious about using the term *rhētorikē* when interpreting theoretical texts that antedate Plato's dialogue, *Gorgias*.

Maria Tanja Luzzatto (hereafter L) challenged my claims in a lengthy essay in 2020.[4] To simplify a long and detailed essay is not easy, so I stress what I find most salient to L's essay, which may not be the same as other readers. Nonetheless, in my opinion, L's essay advances one major argument and a series of auxiliary points. Her primary thesis is that Plato's dialogue is a faithful representation of the historical Gorgias: "when Socrates/Plato takes issue with opinions voiced by celebrated sophists we may reasonably surmise that he refers to their authenticated beliefs, since fake copies could be easily detected and would never deceive contemporary readers."[5]

---

[1] John E. Burchard Professor of Humanities, Massachusetts Institute of Technology, USA.

[2] My thanks to John T. Kirby and Thomas Schirren for helpful feedback to this paper and to Maria Tanja Luzzatto for her thoughtful engagement of my work.

[3] Edward Schiappa, "Did Plato Coin *Rhētorikē*?" *American Journal of Philology* 111.4 (1990): 457-70.

[4] Maria Tanja Luzzatto, "Did Gorgias Coin *Rhētorikē*? A Rereading of Plato's *Gorgias*," *Lexis* 38.1 (2020): 183-224.

[5] Luzzatto, "Did Gorgias?" 190.

Based on this assumption of historical fidelity, L infers that the portrayed-Gorgias's use of the term *rhētorikē* therefore cannot be anachronistic (as I have argued), so it is plausible for L to pose the titular question "Did Gorgias Coin *Rhētorikē*?"

A good deal of L's essay is made up of a number of arguments that respond to various points I have made in support of the general thesis that *rhētorikē* does not appear to be a term in use prior to Plato. I characterize these points as subsidiary and do not have the space to reply to them here. For example: I suggest that the absence of the word *rhētorikē* in Aristophanes's texts, especially *Clouds*, is noteworthy and indirectly supports my argument about the 4th century BCE appearance of the word *rhētorikē.* L disagrees. Though we shall continue to disagree, I consider such arguments ancillary because even if L is correct that my account of Aristophanes is deficient in some manner, her critique does not provide evidence for her claim that Gorgias coined *rhētorikē.*

Accordingly, I focus in this paper on L's primary thesis concerning Plato's *Gorgias*. First, I present arguments for Plato being the likely suspect for coining the word *rhētorikē*; some but not all of these arguments I have presented before. Second, I argue that Plato's dialogue is an unreliable historical guide, both in general and in particular with regard to the word *rhētorikē*. Evidence for L's primary thesis, in other words, is insufficient to establish that Gorgias coined the term *rhētorikē* or used it in the 5th century. Third, I suggest that even if L is correct, the hermeneutic implications of what I have called "the origins of *rhētorikē* thesis" is intact and that the word's popularization by Plato and Aristotle led to important changes in theorizing and teaching what we now call the Art of Rhetoric.

Plato and *Rhētorikē:* A Brief Review of the Case

I begin this section by reminding readers that I am far from the first to observe that the earliest appearance of the word *rhētorikē* is in Plato.[6] If I may quote a footnote of mine:

---

[6] I have argued that Alcidamas's recorded use of *rhētorikē* in *On Sophists* comes well after Plato's *Gorgias*. L disagrees (219-220) but does not engage the specific textual evidence I provide pointing to a later date.

> Over fifty years ago Werner Pilz noted in passing that "*rhētorikē* findet sich nicht vor Plato" *(Der Rhetor* 15n1). Similarly, Wilhelm Kroll noted: "Das Wort *rhētorikē* begegnet zuerst bei Platon" ("Rhetorik," *RE* supp. 7 [1940]: 1039). The same point is made by Josef Martin, *Antike Rhetorik,* 2; LSJ, s.v. "*rhētoreia*"; J.W.H. Atkins, "Rhetoric, Greek," *The Oxford Classical Dictionary* (Oxford: Clarendon Press, 1949), 766; H. Hommel (and Konrat Ziegler), "Rhetorik,'" *Der Kleine Pauly* (München: A. Druckenmüller, 1972), 4: 1396.[7]

What this simple philological datum means is that the word does not appear in a number of 5th and even 4th century BCE texts where we might expect it to be used, including all of the surviving texts and fragments of the so-called Older Sophists, 5th century drama and comedy, including Aristophanes and Euripides (both of whom were familiar with the Sophists), the historians Herodotus and Thucydides, and the orators of the era. The word also is not found in the texts of Isocrates, Plato's contemporary and rival educator.

The text known as *Dissoi Logoi* or *Dialexeis* is generally dated as from 400 BCE, and section 8 is especially relevant as it addresses the characteristics of a person who wishes to give sound advice to the city: "The man acquainted with the skills [*technē*] involved in argument [*logon*] will also know how to speak correctly [*orthos legein*] on every topic." To speak well, a person must know the laws and the "truth of things" of which they would speak. If there was a late 5th century sophistic passage in which one would expect to find the word *rhētorikē*, this surely is one.[8]

We have two texts (*Helen* and *Palamedes*) and two reconstructions of a third (*On Not Being*) by Gorgias, and nowhere can the word *rhētorikē* be found, despite the fact that Gorgias was not

---

See Edward Schiappa, *The Beginnings of Rhetorical Theory in Classical Greece* (New Haven: Yale University Press, 1999), 19-21.

[7] Edward Schiappa, *Protagoras and Logos: A Study in Greek Philosophy and Rhetoric*, 2nd ed. (Columbia: U. of South Carolina Press, 2003), 59n5. Originally published in 1991.

[8] Schiappa, *Protagoras*, 42.

shy about his innovations in the use of written prose. Unlike Plato, Gorgias *never* uses a word that ends with *-ikē* (as in "art of") in his surviving texts at all. His *Helen*, creative in a number of respects, including the fact it may have self-consciously inaugurated the genre of prose *encomia*, features the first recorded explicit definition of a word, uses the unusual word *logismos* (reasoning) to describe its method, and offers a secular theoretical account of the workings of *logos*.[9]

In sum, philologists have not identified a precedent for the use of *rhētorikē* prior to Plato's *Gorgias*. Not only did Plato have opportunity, he also had a clear literary *modus operandi* that makes him a likely suspect. The available philological evidence suggests that Plato may have coined many dozens or even hundreds of words with *-ikē* or *-ikos* endings to advance his philosophical account of the relationship between knowledge and skill. Ammann finds more than 180 words ending with - *ikē* in Plato, used as an attribute adjective of *technē* or as a substantive with the article in the feminine (*hē rhētorikē*).[10] Plato was particularly inventive with *-ikē* words for the verbal arts in his dialogues, including eristic (*eristikē*), dialectic (*dialektikē*), and antilogic (*antilogikē*).[11]

I know of no scholar who has questioned the claim that Plato coined the important word *dialektikē.* At no point does Plato portray

---

[9] Schiappa, *Beginnings*, Chapter 7.

[10] Ammann. Adolf Nadir, *-ΙΚΟΣ bei Platon: Ableitung und Bedeutung mit Materialsammlung* (Fribourg: Paulusdruckerei, 1953), 227, reckons that of the 390 *-ikos* terms he finds in Plato, slightly more than 70% cannot be attested prior. According to Pierre Chantraine, *Études sur le vocabulaire grec* (Paris: Librairie C. Klincksieck, 1956), 98, of the 350+ different *-ikos* words in Plato, more than 250 are not found in earlier texts. G.B. Kerferd and Kenneth Dover point out that Amman does not provide evidence for his claim that the practice of creating *-ikos* terms originates with the Sophists. Dover asks: "May not Plato's -ικος have been autochthonous?" K.J. Dover, *The Classical Review* 5.2 (1955): 207. See also G.B. Kerferd, *Journal of Hellenic Studies* 75 (1955): 167.

[11] See *LSJ*, s.v. *antilogeō, dialekteon,* and *eristes.* Also, a search through the *TLG* for *antilogik-, eristik-,* and *dialektik-* confirm that Plato's use of the *-ike* forms is the earliest we have.

Socrates as treating the term as novel, though it is not difficult to track how Plato appropriates a sophistic conception of discussion, *dialegesthai,* eventually naming the proper art of philosophical dialogue "dialectic."[12] Thus, Plato is quite willing to put a vitally important word into Socrates's mouth that is almost certainly anachronistic. Parallel behavior can be found with regard to the words for eristic (*eristikē*) and antilogic (*antilogikē*). If Plato did not hesitate to put such words in Socrates's and others' mouths, there is no reason to doubt his willingness to put one in Gorgias's.

One of the most influential legacies of Plato's *Gorgias* is its philosophical worldbuilding. As many scholars have noted, the vocabulary describing those we now easily identify as sophists and philosophers in the late 5th and early 4th centuries BCE lacked what can be described as denotative conformity.[13] There was disagreement about who should "count" as a sophist or philosopher, and on what the emerging discipline of the philosopher (*philosophos*) should focus.[14] In that historical context, Plato's *Gorgias* made what Debra Nails describes as a perfect "'college brochure,' contrasting Socratic

---

[12] David M. Timmerman and Edward Schiappa, *Classical Greek Rhetorical Theory and the Disciplining of Discourse* (Cambridge: Cambridge University Press, 2010), 17-41. On the origins of dialectic see Richard Robinson, *Plato's Earlier Dialectic* (Ithica: Cornell University Press, 1941), especially 92-95.

[13] *Denotative conformity* refers to the degree to which a given community of language users agree to refer or denote a given phenomenon with a common term. Sometimes the lack of agreement reflects a lack of a shared definition, while other times there may be disagreement about which definition best fits a phenomenon. See Edward Schiappa, *Defining Reality: Definitions and the Politics of Meaning* (Carbondale: Southern Illinois University Press, 2003).

[14] Most recently see Christopher Moore, *Calling Philosophers Names: On the Origin of a Discipline* (Princeton: Princeton University Press, 2020) and Trinidad Silva, "Naming the Wise: the *Sophos*, the *Philosophos* and the *Sophistēs* in Plato" (Ph.D. Dissertation, University College London, 2017). When conducting my research in the 1990s, I was influenced significantly by Alexander Nehamas, "Eristic, Antilogic, Sophistic, Dialectic: Plato's Demarcation of Philosophy from Sophistry," *History of Philosophy Quarterly* 7 (1990): 3-16.

oral methods with three successively less reputable characters."[15] Thus, his early dialogues are particularly valuable indicators of how Plato saw his educational goals and practices as different from his competitors, including Isocrates. Indeed, R.L. Howland argues that "as far as the *Gorgias* is concerned it would probably be generally admitted that the attack on rhetoric is intended to refer to Isocrates as the most influential contemporary teacher of it."[16] D.S. Hutchinson agrees and describes Plato's "polemic against his main competitors in the higher education market," Isocrates being "foremost" among them.[17] Hutchinson identifies three specific pedagogical elements expressed in Isocrates's *Against the Sophists*—one's practical abilities are endowed by nature, trained by experienced, and improved through education—that are critiqued in Plato's *Gorgias* for being empirical knacks rather than theoretically based.[18]

In *Gorgias*, the depiction of legitimate and illegitimate arts in 464b-465b proved influential (especially for his student, Aristotle[19]) and it was also highly creative. The important role of introducing new *-ikos* and *-ikē* terms as part of Plato's philosophical worldbuilding in later dialogues, primarily *Sophist* and *Statesman*, has been well documented,[20] but their importance in *Gorgias*, especially for tracking the origins of *rhētorikē*, bears emphasis. Of the eight key terms in his paired set of analogies, the earliest citation of six of the words in *LSJ* is from Plato (underlined below):

---

[15] Debra Nails, *Agora, Academy, and the Conduct of Philosophy* (Dordrecht: Springer, 1995), 214.

[16] R.L. Howland, "The Attack on Isocrates in the *Phaedrus*," *Classical Quarterly* 31.3 (1937): 151-59.

[17] D.S. Hutchinson, "Doctrines of the Mean and the Debate Concerning Skills in 4th c. Medicine, Rhetoric, and Ethics," *Apeiron* 21.2 (1988): 27.

[18] Hutchinson, "Doctrines," 29-30. See also W. H. Thompson, *The Phaedrus of Plato* (London: Whttaker and Co., 1868), xvi, 174.

[19] Aristotle, of course, continues the practice of what I call philosophical world-building throughout his writings, often coining new words and new distinctions. With regard to *-ikos* and *-ikē* terms specifically, Chantraine, *Études*, 141, notes that it is not by chance that we have listed in Aristotle six or seven hundred adjectives ending in *-ikos*.

[20] See Chantraine's discussion of *Sophist* and *Statesman* in *Études*, 138-41.

Body (*sōma*)
Cosmetics (*kommōtikē*) : Gymnastics (*gymnastikē*) : :
Cookery (*opsopoiētikē*) : Medicine (*iatrikē*)

Politics (*politikē*)
Sophistic (*sophistikē*) : Legislation (*nomothetikē*) : :
Rhetoric (*rhētorikē*) : Justice (*dikaiosynē*)

In sum, given that Plato had both motive and opportunity, and a well-documented practice of coining terms similar to *rhētorikē* in the process of his philosophical world-building, I remain convinced, after 30+ years of debate, discussion, and reflection, that Plato remains our likeliest suspect as the originator of the word *rhētorikē*. I turn now to the question of whether Plato's dialogue provides compelling evidence otherwise.

The Testimony of Plato's *Gorgias*

At the heart of L's thesis is the belief that Plato's *Gorgias* is reliable testimony that the historical Gorgias identified his teaching as *rhētorikē*.[21] This belief, in turn, relies on the assumption that Plato would not put words into a character's mouth that the historical figure would not have used. She states, "Plato could not have used Gorgias or Protagoras or Hippias as fictional spokesmen of unlikely statements they had never made without immediately bringing discredit on his own replies to them."[22]

I believe the assumption that Plato would not take liberties with his representation of the historical Gorgias is false. I cannot here provide systematic evidence of Plato's historical distortions, but fortunately other scholars have done so already. Sir Kenneth Dover states, "Plato writes not as a scholar" but "from first to last as an

---

[21] L is certainly not the only scholar to treat the account of Gorgias in Plato's dialogue as generally faithful. For a review, see Maureen Taylor and Edward Schiappa, "How Accurate is Plato's Portrayal of Gorgias of Leontini?" in *Rhetoric in the Vortex of Cultural Studies*, ed. Arthur Walzer (Minneapolis: Rhetoric Society of America, 1993), 23-31.

[22] Luzzatto, "Did Gorgias?" 190. L states that the whole enquiry of the dialogue takes its "cue from Gorgias's claim on *Rhētorikē* in the opening pages" (187) but in fact it is Socrates who introduces the word with the curious phrase "what is called rhetoric."

advocate." "It would be wrong to imagine," Dover suggests, that Plato "necessarily observes the standards of veracity which we demand of a historian."[23]

Similarly, Ruby Blondell's insightful book, *The Play of Character in Plato's Dialogues*, notes that Plato and other writers of the Socratic dialogues "were not bound by canons of historical accuracy." Quoting Arnaldo Momigliano, Blondell says "As a genre, the Socratic discourses occupied a 'zone between truth and fiction . . . between fact and imagination'."[24] Charles Kahn lays out a compelling case for recognizing "how misleading the Socratic literature can be for anyone who approaches it in search of historical information." With respect to Plato's *Gorgias*, in particular, Kahn argues that "the dialogue is full of historical references that cannot be combined in a coherent date."[25] Kahn's conclusion is echoed by Reginald Allen, who describes *Gorgias* as so "riddled with anachronism" that "tense distinctions lose all meaning."[26]

Irwin identifies some of the historical inconsistencies in *Gorgias*:

- Death of Pericles presented as recent (429)
- Gorgias's visit (427)
- Prediction about Alcibiades (pre-415)
- Archelaus coming to power (413)
- Reference to Euripides's *Antiope* (408)
- Reference to the trial of the general after Arginusae (405).[27]

---

23 Kenneth Dover, *Plato: Symposium* (Cambridge: Cambridge University Press, 1980), viii, 9.

24 Ruby Blondell, *The Play of Character in Plato's Dialogues* (Cambridge: Cambridge University Press, 2002), 32.

25 Charles H Kahn, "On the Relative Date of the *Gorgias* and the *Protagoras*," *Oxford Studies in Ancient Philosophy* 6 (1988): 100-101.

26 R.E. Allen, *The Dialogues of Plato, vol. 1* (New Haven: Yale University Press, 1984), 189.

27 Terence Irwin (trans.), *Plato:* Gorgias (Oxford: Clarendon Press, 1979), 109. See also E.R. Dodds. *Plato:* Gorgias (Oxford: Clarendon Press, 1959), 17-18; A.E. Taylor, *Plato: The Man and his work*, 6th ed. (London: Methuen, 1949), 104-5.

In other words, the event depicted in Plato's *Gorgias* simply could not have happened, so the text itself stands as a caution against taking it literally as a historically accurate depiction.

Two other textual clues support the hypothesis that the portrayal of Gorgias using the word *rhētorikē* was anachronistic. First, as many commentators have noted, Socrates makes the uncharacteristic and implausible claim that he alone practices the true political art—*politikē technē*—and hence is Athens's only true statesman (521d6-8).[28] Given that *politikē technē* is Plato's locution being put in Socrates's mouth, it increases the plausibility that Plato would put words in Gorgias's mouth that he would never have said (more on this momentarily). Second, the first time the word *rhētorikē* appears in the dialogue, it is introduced by Socrates with a noteworthy turn of phrase: *ten kaloumenēn rhētorikēn,* "what is called rhetoric." Socrates could have said "what you call rhetoric" or simply "rhetoric" had the term been Gorgianic. Prefacing the word with "what is called" or "so-called" signals to the reader that the term is novel, at the very least.[29]

Several scholars have argued that the phrase *ten kaloumenēn rhētorikēn* proves, as L believes, that the word *rhētorikē* was already in use since no one in the dialogue objects to Socrates's use of it.[30] In fact, the first journal editor who considered "Did Plato Coin *Rhētorikē*?" rejected it solely based on that phrase in the *Gorgias*. In a sense, then, the present paper functions as an additional reply to those scholars as well. Once we set aside, or at least question, the assumption that Plato is providing accurate linguistic history in a dialogue full of neologisms and anachronisms, I think the phrase actually makes more sense as a signal that something is afoot.

---

[28] For a helpful discussion of the passage that reviews earlier literature and tries to describe the sense of true political art that Plato meant to convey, see J. Clerk Shaw, "Socrates and the True Political Craft," *Classical Philology* 106 (2011): 187-207.

[29] For additional arguments see Schiappa, *Beginnings*, 17-20. L rightly criticizes me for suggesting the translation "what is being called rhetoric." We agree that the introduction of the word *rhētorikē* can be described as "self-conscious" (218-219), we just disagree on why.

[30] Summarized in Schiappa, *Beginnings*, 17-18.

To understand how the text of Plato's *Gorgias* would have been understood in its original historical context, scholars have pointed to what Arlene Saxonhouse calls the "unspoken theme" of war.[31] As Robin Reames notes, "A devastating defeat at Sicily, Alcibiades's treachery, the fall of Athenian democracy, and the installation of the tyrants in Athens would necessarily be evoked by any reference to Sicily, the very thing that is foregrounded in the Gorgias dialogue."[32] That context makes it clear to contemporary readers what Plato sees at stake; namely, a choice between his vision of a life of *philosophia* and the life of the *rhētōr*—the word closest to politician at the time.[33] Recognition of this larger context reinforces interpretations that see the persuasive function of Plato's *Gorgias* as pitting Plato's educational mission against his main rival, Isocrates:

> The *Gorgias* documents Plato's growing disillusionment with public life, and its writing was, in Guthrie's words, a result of an 'emotional crisis' experienced by Plato after Socrates's death. The *Gorgias* was not written as a philosophical treatise on rhetoric but as a broader attack on the life of fourth-century politicians. The issue is made explicit by Socrates: 'Our argument now concerns ... the way one ought to live: whether it is the life to which you summon me, doing such manly things as speaking in public, practicing rhetoric, engaging in politics as you do now; or whether it is this life of mine in *philosophia*' (500cl-8). As I have said, the term *rhētōr* in the fourth century designated a specific class of individuals who spoke often in court or the assembly. Plato opposed education aimed at producing such orators because he did not trust the training

---

[31] Arlene W. Saxonhouse, "An Unspoken Theme in Plato's *Gorgias*: War," *Interpretation* 11.2 (1983): 139-169.

[32] Robin Reames, *Seeming and Being in Plato's Rhetorical Theory* (Chicago: University of Chicago Press, 2018), 43.

[33] Schiappa, *Protagoras and Logos*, 44-45: "By the time *rhētorikē* was coined, *rhētôr* had an established, specific meaning: a politician who put forth motions in court or the assembly. Accordingly, *rhetor-ike* meant 'art of the rhetor'."

> to produce proper statesmen. Hence, whether he originated the term or not, *rhētorikē* was a useful label for Plato to use to distinguish Isocrates's (and others') training from his own.[34]

Such an interpretation of Plato's *Gorgias* situates it as what Hutchinson and Johnson call an "apotreptic protreptic" reply to Isocrates's *Against the Sophists*—generally read as an introduction and invitation to his school. An apotreptic protreptic contains both a critique of *philosophia* and a call to a better version.[35] Both Isocrates and Plato contrast what each sees as an inferior approach to *philosophia* with their preferred version. Plato's coinage of *rhētorikē* was an ingenious way to critique the pedagogical mission of Isocrates's school without legitimating or even acknowledging Isocrates's use of the word *philosophia*.

The last point I wish to make concerning the unreliability of Plato's *Gorgias* is that once we move beyond the text of the *Gorgias*, the representation of Gorgias's thought (as best we can reconstruct it) does not square with Gorgias's own texts. The description of *logos* one finds in the *Helen* is quite different from that found in Plato's dialogue. Socrates asks Gorgias, "Of what objects does *rhētorikē* provide knowledge? [*peri ti tōnoantōn estin epistēmē*]." Gorgias answers "*peri logous*" (449d9-el). The dialogue then addresses the question, "With what sorts of *logoi* is rhetoric concerned?" Gorgias makes the unlikely concession that not all kinds of *logoi* fall under *rhētorikē,* only some. Eventually Gorgias is forced by Socrates to limit the scope of rhetoric to the law courts and the assembly—quite different than the broad scope of *logos* described in Gorgias's *Helen*.[36] And, as mentioned earlier, the surviving texts of Gorgias never once include a word ending with *-ikē,* as in "art or skill of."

---

[34] Schiappa, *Protagoras and Logos*, 46.

[35] D.S. Hutchinson and Monte Ransom Johnson, "Protreptic and Apotreptic: Aristotle's Dialogue *Protrepticus,*" in *When Wisdom Calls: Philosophical Protreptic in Antiquity*, eds. Olga Alieva, Annesmaré Kotzé, and Sophie Van der Meeren (Turnhout, Belgium: Brepols, 2018), 111-54.

[36] Schiappa, *Beginnings*, 72-73.

Bruce McComiskey argues that a close comparison of Plato's dialogue with Gorgias's own texts suggests the account has been filtered through Plato's own philosophical categories and is not a faithful account of Gorgias's thinking. He contends: "Socrates must coax Gorgias into accepting three respective binary oppositions: (1) knowledge *[epistēmē* or *mathēsis]* versus opinion *[doxa* or *pistis],* (2) instruction *[didachē]* versus persuasion *[peithō],* and (3) language *[logos]* versus content *[pragma]* in the definition of a *technē*."[37] McComiskey notes that although Plato's Gorgias "readily assents to any claim Socrates cares to make, a closer look at the extant Gorgianic texts reveals the absurdity in the assertion that Gorgias the sophist would have uttered agreement with any of Socrates's claims about rhetoric or any of the binary oppositions that Socrates sets up to make those claims."[38] Though there are details in McComiskey's account with which I do not agree, the basic point he makes strikes me as correct: The philosophical world-building put forth by Plato and into which the art of rhetoric is placed cannot be squared with Gorgias's own words about *logos*.

To be sure, we are dealing with matters of probability and not certainty. Nonetheless, putting together the available clues gives us considerable justification *not* to take Plato's portrayal of Gorgias as historically faithful, both in general and in particular with respect to the origins of the word *rhētorikē*. To sum up, those clues include 1) Plato's distinctively original language, especially his creation of new terms to designate arts and verbal arts in particular; 2) the infamous phrase with which he introduces the term: *tēn kaloumenēn rhētorikēn*, signals something is afoot; 3) the various blatant anachronisms of the dialogue overall; and 4) documentable distortions of Gorgias's thought as found in his own writings. For these reasons, I concur with Blondell's conclusion that "We cannot count on Plato to give a historically useful snapshot of Gorgias's own [language] usage."[39]

---

[37] Bruce McComiskey, *Gorgias and the New Sophistic Rhetoric* (Carbondale: Southern Illinois University Press, 2002), 21.

[38] McComiskey, *Gorgias and the New Sophistic Rhetoric*, 21.

[39] Ruby Blondell, email exchange with the author, October 4, 2021.

Dating the word *Rhētorikē:* What Does it Matter?

I hope that the previous two sections make the case that Plato remains the likeliest suspect for coining the word *rhētorikē.* In this final section, I contend that even if L is correct, the hermeneutic implications of what I have called the origins of *rhētorikē* thesis is intact and that the word's popularization by Plato and Aristotle led to important changes in theorizing and teaching what we now call the Art of Rhetoric.

A later dating of the origins of the word *rhētorikē* led myself and others to conduct research that can be described as deconstructive and constructive. By "deconstructive" I refer to research efforts that challenge or undercut the traditional account of rhetorical history, and by "constructive" I refer to research that proffers new historical claims or interpretations. For obvious reasons, I can only briefly summarize such scholarship here. In *The Beginnings of Rhetorical Theory in Classical Greece,* I identified 17 points that characterized what I believed the scholarly literature took as the "standard account" of early Greek rhetorical theory and that I felt were belied by the evidence. These include:

1. The Art of Rhetoric originates with Corax of Sicily around 467 BCE.
2. Corax was probably the teacher of Tisias, a fellow Sicilian.
3. Corax and/or Tisias authored the first *technē,* or book designated as an Art of Rhetoric.
4. Corax/Tisias may have been the first to define rhetoric, specifically as the "artificer of persuasion."
5. An important contribution of Corax/Tisias's handbook was the identification of the parts of forensic speeches.
6. Corax/Tisias's primary theoretical contribution was their identification of the "argument from probability."
7. By the end of the 5th century BCE, written technical handbooks were commonly available to which people could turn to learn rhetoric.

8. Most early teaching of the Art of Rhetoric, including that of Corax/Tisias, concentrated on forensic rhetoric.
9. At least some of the handbooks included discussion of style.
10. No 5th century BCE rhetorical handbook exists now because Aristotle's writings made them obsolete.
11. Though specific doctrines may have varied, there was a commonly identified group of individuals in the 5th century known as the Sophists: Protagoras, Gorgias, Hippias, Prodicus, Thrasymachus, Critias, and Antiphon.
12. The most important shared characteristic of the Sophists was that they all taught the Art of Rhetoric.
13. The rhetorical teaching of the Sophists was amoral.
14. The Sophists were relativists who eschewed any positive notion of "truth" in favor of subjectivism.
15. The Sophists were more concerned with teaching political success than pursuing "truth," *per se*.
16. Plato's philosophical rhetorical theory was formulated primarily in response to 5th century rhetorical theory.
17. Plato's philosophical rhetorical theory can be distinguished from Sophistic rhetorical theory by its commitment to truth—even when truth conflicts with political success.

In *Beginnings* I provided my case for rejecting or revising each of these 17 points. To this list I would add two other "deconstructive" elements: First, contrary to some historical accounts, a standard division of speeches into *prooemium, prosthesis, diegesis, pistis,* and *epilogos* cannot be documented prior to the 4th century, nor can such terms be documented as terms of art in the 5th century applied to speeches or prose discourse. Poetic and epic compositional habits described as "ring composition" are likely better explanations for recurring prose patterns.[40] Second, George A. Kennedy's categories

---

[40] Timmerman and Schiappa, *Classical Greek Rhetorical Theory,* 137-170. The relevant chapter was written with Wilfred E. Major.

of technical, sophistic, and philosophical rhetoric are problematic as descriptors of 5th century texts relevant to the history of rhetorical theory.[41]

Obviously, time and space do not permit me to revisit all of these points, but to me what is even more important than precisely *who* coined the word *rhētorikē* is approximately *when,* since a later dating led me to question the standard account. To the best of my knowledge, few of the deconstructive elements I have identified here have been contested in the literature.

Moreover, I have spent a good deal of time putting forth constructive claims, mostly about Protagoras, Gorgias, and Isocrates. Constructive claims about Protagoras, all found in *Protagoras and Logos,* include:

1. The historical significance of Protagoras's (hereafter P) fragments is clearest when read as advancements of Heraclitean insights and responses to Eleatic philosophy.

2. P's "there are two *logoi* about every thing" fragment is not simply a claim that we can argue about anything, but an extension of Heraclitean philosophy that represents an advancement from compositional analysis toward what we would now call attributional analysis.

3. P's "weaker/stronger" *logoi* fragment is not an amoral description of rhetoric but as advocating the strengthening of a preferred but temporarily weaker *logos* to challenge a less preferable but temporarily stronger *logos* of the same experience.

4. P's Human-Measure fragment is best appreciated historically as a humanist response to Parmenides's monism and implies an early expression of what we now call a frame of reference and "objective relativism."

5. P's "impossible to contradict" fragment can be understood as anticipating Aristotle's law of noncontradiction, and resonates with P's other fragments about objects' qualities and frames of reference.

---

[41] Schiappa, *Beginnings,* 30-82.

6. P's particular uses of the Greek verb "to be" (*einai*) is highly unusual for his time as the word was a key object of analysis by writers we now call philosophers. His use of the term, especially in the Human-Measure fragment and a passage "concerning the gods," was distinctive and provocative.

7. P's "concerning the gods" fragment is an early expression of secular humanism that may have opened a lost treatise about humans, perhaps as described by Plato in P's "Great Speech" in the dialogue *Protagoras*.

8. P may have advanced an analogy that became common in classical Greece between speech and medicine: *Logos* is to the mind/soul as medicine is to the body.

9. As others have noted, P provided the first theoretical rationale for participatory democracy, describing *logos* as the best means by which the polis deliberates and makes decisions.

10. Protagoras was not refuted and rejected by Plato and Aristotle as much as his ideas were assimilated into their thinking about what we now call epistemology and metaphysics.

I do not claim originality with respect to all of these claims, but my point is that setting aside the word *rhētorikē* back in 1987-89 while working on my dissertation enabled me to "see" Protagoras's contributions more clearly, without the traditional philosophy versus rhetoric lens. More to the point for this paper, the same can be said about my efforts to come to grips with the fascinating and challenging texts of Gorgias (hereafter G), developed in my book *The Beginnings of Rhetorical Theory in Ancient Greece*. For example:

1. G's distinctive style played an important transitional role in promoting and advancing performance-prose composition in early Greek literature. Descriptions of his prose as "poetic" refer to his word choice rather than his prose meter or rhythm.

2. G's *Helen* may have inaugurated the prose genre of the encomium. G advanced 5th century "rationalism" by enacting innovations in prose composition; identifying *Helen* as "epideictic" or a veiled defense of Rhetoric is problematic; and

Helen's most significant theoretical contribution was to provide a secular account of the workings of *logos*—an account that functioned as an exemplar for later theorists.

3. G's *On Not Being* (*ONB*) has been misunderstood at times by trying to classify it as Rhetoric *or* Philosophy. *ONB* was a response to Eleatic tracts about "Being" by Parmenides, Melissus, and Zeno that functioned both as entertainment and what we would now call serious philosophy.[42]

4. A formalization of G's *ONB* suggests that if viewed in isolation, G's argument is unpersuasive and invalid, but if the intertextual linkages with Parmenides are considered, G's argument gains both rhetorical and philosophical strength.

In the 1990s I also revisited relevant 4th century BCE texts, starting with those of Isocrates. As a result, I joined the growing club of scholars interested in revisiting Isocrates and engaging his texts without forcing him into the rather hackneyed play of Rhetoric versus Philosophy. Isocrates never used the word *rhētorikē* in his writings, instead describing his education as *philosophia* and *logōn paideia*. Isocrates can be read as a forerunner to contemporary pragmatism, both in his emphasis on practical philosophy and connecting pedagogy with civism.[43] Isocratean *philosophia* can be understood as the cultivation of practical wisdom through the production of ethical civic discourse.[44]

The so-called *Rhetoric to Alexander* does not use the word *rhētorikē*, thus providing an interesting text of the 4th century outside of the Platonic/Aristotelian tradition. Arguably the text has affinities with what George Kennedy described as philosophical, sophistic, *and* technical traditions, as well as being an early treatise on argumentation.[45]

---

[42] On the philosophical importance of Gorgias's writings, see now Erminia Di Iulio, *Gorgias's Thought: An Epistemological Reading* (London: Routledge, forthcoming 2023).

[43] Schiappa, *Beginnings*, 162-184.

[44] Timmerman and Schiappa, *Classical Greek Rhetorical Theory*, 43-66.

[45] Timmerman and Schiappa, *Classical Greek Rhetorical Theory*, 115-136.

I also found that by attending to the specific vocabulary of the time, interesting and unexpected results emerged. For example, unlike such terms as *rhētorikē* and *dialektikē,* the Greek words for oratory (*rhētoreia*) and "to orate" (*rhētoreuein*) are rarely used even in the 4th century and were put to very little conceptual use.[46]

One of my favorite projects was a reexamination of the word that led to "dialectic." As mentioned previously, *dialegesthai* (holding dialogue) can be appreciated as a sophistic term of art. Plato's coining of *dialektikē* was part of an on-going effort in his work to "discipline" *dialegesthai* into his philosophical theory and pedagogy.[47]

The catalyst for all of this work was the conviction that scholars for too long relied on the trustworthiness of Plato's and Aristotle's accounts of their predecessors. In the history of philosophy, that trust has been abandoned in favor of efforts to recover the *ipsissima verba* of those predecessors and limiting use of Plato and Aristotle to points of reception by which one might triangulate the meaning of, say, Parmenides's or Heraclitus's fragments. My modest contribution has been to try to extend that process to such figures as Protagoras, Gorgias, and Isocrates, and of course I have hardly been alone in that effort. One of the most remarkable advancements has been Michael Gagarin's provocatively titled essay, "Did the Sophists Aim to Persuade?" in which he argues that the long-held belief that the primary activity of the Sophists was to teach rhetoric *qua* persuasion is mistaken.[48]

Thus, I end this paper by noting that even if L is correct that Gorgias coined the word *rhētorikē,* there is still much to be learned by assuming his use was not influential until reported in Plato's *Gorgias*. We don't need the word *rhētorikē* to understand the texts that precede the dialogue, and frankly they make more sense without it.

---

46 Schiappa, *Beginnings,* 155-161.

47 Timmerman and Schiappa, *Classical Greek Rhetorical Theory,* 17-41.

48 Michael Gagarin, "Did the Sophists Aim to Persuade?" *Rhetorica* 19.3 (2001): 275-291.

Yosef Z. Liebersohn[1]

Gorgias in Plato's *Gorgias, Hē Kaloumenē Rhētorikē*, and the Birth of Rhetoric[2]

According to a longstanding scholarly view, rhetoric was invented in Sicily circa 467 BCE. At that time, so the thinking has run, tyranny was out, democracy was in, and people began to show up at courts and public gatherings. The first work on such presentations, *Art of Rhetoric*, has been ascribed by tradition to two somewhat enigmatic figures, Corax and Tisias, who, according to this narrative, together developed a theory of persuasive speaking.[3] In 1990, Edward Schiappa challenged this view,[4] which he later referred to as "the Standard Account of Rhetoric's Beginnings."[5] According to Schiappa and others,[6] rhetoric as a full-fledged art dates to no earlier than the beginning of the 4th century BCE. Schiappa points to the

---

[1] Yosef Z. (Yossie) Liebersohn is an associate professor at Bar-Ilan University (Israel) who specializes in Classical and Hellenistic philosophy. He is the author of *The Dispute Concerning Rhetoric in Hellenistic Thought* (Vandenhoek and Ruprecht, 2010) and *Who is Afraid of the Rhētōr: An Analysis and Exegesis of Socrates and Gorgias' Conversation in Plato's Gorgias* (Gorgias Press, 2014). In addition, he has published widely on Plato's *Crito* and *Gorgias*, Aristotle's *Rhetorica*, Seneca, Epicurus, and the Stoics.

[2] An earlier version of this essay was presented at Fonte Aretusa's conference on Gorgias and Plato's *Gorgias* in 2021. I am indebted to the conference organizer, Heather Reid, as well as my co-panelists, Shane Ewegen and Sonja Tanner, for their comments and questions during the conference. I am also indebted to Ryan Drake and Jill Gordon, for their thoughts on a subsequent version of this essay.

[3] See also George A. Kennedy, *Classical Rhetoric and its Christian and Secular Tradition from Ancient to Modern Times* (Cambridge: Cambridge University Press, 1980), 18-19. For more references, see Edward Schiappa, *The Beginnings of Rhetorical Theory in Classical Greece* (New Haven: Yale University Press, 1999), 4.

[4] Edward Schiappa, "Did Plato Coin *Rhētorikē*?," *American Journal of Philology* 111 (1990): 457-70.

[5] Schiappa, *The Beginnings*, 3, passim.

[6] E.g., Thomas Cole, *The Origins of Rhetoric in Ancient Greece* (Baltimore: Johns Hopkins University Press, 1991).

absence of the term *rhētorikē* in 5th century BCE texts, and claims that the notions of "technical rhetoric," "sophistic rhetoric," or "philosophical rhetoric" require reconsideration. He traces the birth of rhetoric to none other than Plato and Aristotle,[7] arguing that in their struggle against the sophists, these authors actually conceptualized the sophists' praxis, thus inventing *rhētorikē*.

Yet, Schiappa does not entirely reject the existence of rhetorical theory in the 5th century BCE. He argues, rather, that the Platonic use of the term *rhētorikē* was a gamechanger in the field. His analysis pivots on the term "discipline," by which he refers mainly to two characteristics. The first concerns conceptualization, the second, the presentation of philosophy as the adversary of rhetoric. In his view, 5th-century BCE texts are "predisciplinary," since the distinction between philosophy and rhetoric had not yet been established.

While principally accepting Schiappa's view, I will seek to strengthen his argument as well so as to expand it in two distinct ways. First, I wish to argue that rhetoric as it is presented in Plato's *Gorgias* not only does not contradict Schiappa and those who follow him, but that it can even support them. Second, I argue that while rhetoric might achieve a high level of conceptualization and even reach the status of a discipline, it cannot properly be considered an art, since awareness of a unique *materia* of its own remains absent. Schiappa concentrates on the pair "rhetoric/philosophy," and rightly so. Only when philosophy is taken as an opponent of rhetoric by specifying their different aims (seeking truth as opposed to seeking success) can rhetoric be deemed a discipline. Yet, rhetoric has another counterpart: politics. I claim that rhetoric had to be severed from its historical root of politics in order to become a discipline in its full meaning. As presented in the conversation between Socrates and Gorgias in Plato's *Gorgias*, rhetoric is thus not yet disconnected from politics.

---

[7] Schiappa's thesis has gained support over the years and today seems to have become scholarly consensus. See Edward Schiappa, "Twenty-Five Years after "Did Plato Coin *Rhētorikē*?": An Episodic Memoir," in *Rhetoric Review* 35.1 (2016): 1-9. My paper is therefore not limited to Schiappa's thesis alone, but targets a much wider audience.

In what follows, I shall focus on Gorgias as he is represented in Plato's *Gorgias*, and especially on the word *rhētorikē* as it appears in his conversation with Socrates. I detect a correlation—probably intended by Plato—between the status of rhetoric in the time depicted in the *Gorgias* (somewhere between 429 and 405 BCE)[8] and the way in which the term *rhētorikē* appears in the conversation. I will show that the articulation of this term by those who practice this occupation is optional, and that the absence of a formal-technical term to define this art reflects its attachment to the field of politics. The teachers of this period considered themselves to be engaged in politics, and the term *rhētorikē* did not yet denote for them a fully independent field. Notably, it was their own teaching of the subject that would catalyze a new field.

Rhētorikē in Context

In considering the term *rhētorikē*, it is important to take into account both its immediate and its wider contexts. The scholarly literature has largely dealt with the former, namely, the participle *kaloumenē*, which qualifies the word *rhētorikē* on its first appearance within the *Gorgias*.[9] On Polus's speech at 448c4-d3, Socrates comments: "For I see plainly, from what he has said, that Polus has had more practice in *kaloumenē rhētorikē* than in *dialegesthai* [δῆλος γάρ μοι Πῶλος καὶ ἐξ ὧν εἴρηκεν ὅτι τὴν καλουμένην ῥητορικὴν μᾶλλον μεμελέτηκεν ἢ διαλέγεσθαι]." Scholars debate whether *kaloumenē rhētorikē* means "what is known as" or, as Schiappa argues,

---

[8] The *Gorgias* is well known for its inconsistencies with regard to the dramatic date. The earliest indication is 429 BCE where Pericles's death is described as a recent event. The latest date is a reference to the trial of the generals after the battle of Arginusae in 405 BCE. See Alfred. E. Taylor, *Plato: The Man and his Work* (London: Methuen, 1926), 104-105; see also Eric R. Dodds, *Plato: Gorgias* (Oxford: Clarendon Press, 1959), 17-18. See also n34 below.

[9] As was noted long ago this appearance of *rhētorikē* in Plato's *Gorgias* is our earliest extant use of this term in Greek literature as well. See Werner Pilz, *Der Rhetor im Attischen Staat* (Weida: Thomas and Hubert, 1936), 15n1; see also J. W. H. Atkins, "Rhetoric, Greek," *The Oxford Classical Dictionary* (Oxford: Clarendon Press, 1949), 766; see also Josef Martin, *Antike Rhetorik: Technik und Methode* (Munchen: Beck, 1974), 2.

"what we are now calling."[10] But there is also the wider context, which takes us back to the very beginning of the conversation.

The *Gorgias* is subtitled "On Rhetoric." Although Plato was probably not responsible for this description,[11] no one doubts that rhetoric is the main topic in the *Gorgias,* at least in the first conversation between Socrates and Gorgias.[12] But rhetoric can be discussed from many different angles, and it is important to be exact. Two facts demonstrate that teaching is the axis around which rhetoric is discussed in the *Gorgias*. First, the dialogue is divided into three conversations of three characters who have something in common: their group comprises a teacher (Gorgias)[13] and his two pupils (Polus and Callicles). Second, Socrates refutes Gorgias by using the device of the "bad pupil," who subverts what he has learned from his teacher.[14] Equipped with this orientation, we now

---

[10] See Schiappa, *The Beginnings*, 468-9. As I shall show below, one can argue for Schiappa's case even in maintaining the traditional rendering of "what is known as."

[11] It is probably Alexandrine. See Dodds, *Plato: Gorgias,* 1 and n1.

[12] I shall leave aside the issue of whether Plato is justified in considering Gorgias to be engaged with rhetoric. Nowadays, scholars seek to differentiate between the sophist and the rhetor (Schiappa, *The Beginnings,* 48-65), but see 465c1-5: "as self-adornment is to gymnastic, so is sophistry [*sophistikē*] to legislation [*nomothetikē*]; and as cookery is to medicine, so is rhetoric [*rhētorikē*] to justice [*dikaiosunē*]. But although, as I say, there is this natural distinction between them, they are so nearly related that sophists and orators are jumbled up as having the same field and dealing with the same subjects."

[13] Gorgias is explicitly referred to as a teacher at 459e3: σὺ ὁ τῆς ῥητορικῆς διδάσκαλος (you as the teacher of rhetoric). However, the term "sophist," which usually is attributed to Gorgias, is not attributed to Gorgias in the *Gorgias* at all.

[14] To this, one can add Gorgias's long speech at 456a7-457c3, where he tries to defend himself and remove any responsibility for the misbehavior of his bad student. Why Socrates does not accept this defense and makes Gorgias responsible for this student (and does it in a manipulative way) is an interesting question that is beyond the scope of this paper. See Yosef Z. Liebersohn, "Polus the Unsung Hero: On the

approach the dialogue and Socrates's object of interest. Referring to Callicles's suggestion to come to his house, where Gorgias will give Socrates and Chaerephon (Socrates's friend/pupil) a "performance" to make up for the one they missed by arriving too late (447b7-8), Socrates says:

> Thank you, Callicles: But would he consent to discuss with us? For I want to find out from the man what is the *dunamis* of his art, and what it is that he professes and teaches. As for the rest of his performance [*epideixis*], he must give it us, as you suggest, on another occasion.
>
> Εὖ λέγεις, ὦ Καλλίκλεις. ἀλλ' ἆρα ἐθελήσειεν ἂν ἡμῖν διαλεχθῆναι; βούλομαι γὰρ πυθέσθαι παρ' αὐτοῦ τίς ἡ δύναμις τῆς τέχνης τοῦ ἀνδρός, καὶ τί ἐστιν ὃ ἐπαγγέλλεταί τε καὶ διδάσκει· τὴν δὲ ἄλλην ἐπίδειξιν εἰς αὖθις, ὥσπερ σὺ λέγεις, ποιησάσθω. (447b9-c4)

Here it is important to pay heed to both content and form, and especially to the connection between them. The structure is a doubt cast by Socrates, and the reason (*gar*) for the doubt. As to the content, Socrates doubts if Gorgias will be willing (and one might doubt also if he is able) to *dialegesthai*, and the reason for this doubt is Socrates's wish "to find out from the man what is the *dunamis* of his art." This means that there is something in Socrates's wish that cannot be handled by an *epideixis* (i.e., a speech) but only by *dialegesthai* (i.e., a conversation in the maieutic method).[15] This "something," I suggest, has to do with the tension in which rhetoric stands at the time it is depicted in the *Gorgias*, and which is reflected in Socrates's words cited above: "what is the *dunamis* of his art, and what it is that he

---

Significance of Polus and Socrates's Conversation with Polus in Plato's *Gorgias*," *For a Skeptical Peripatetic: Festschrift in Honor of John Glucker*, eds. Y. Liebersohn, I. Ludlam and A. Edelheit (Sankt Augustin: Academia, 2017), 64-77.

[15] Gorgias and Callicles are not necessarily aware of this difference. In his answer at 447c5-8, Callicles refers only to the *epideixis*, and further on, Gorgias seems to see the difference between the two as between *makrologia* and *brachulogia* alone (449b9-c6).

professes and teaches." Socrates formulates his quest in a subtle manner, indicating a tension between what the teacher professes and what he actually teaches. Here is my translation: "what is the *dunamis* of his art, and what it is that he professes and [sc. what it is that he] teaches." Socrates's question has two parts, the second of which should be subdivided. The first part consists of the words "what is the *dunamis* of his art," while the second part, "what it is that he professes and [sc. what it is that he] teaches," indicates how one might answer the first. The tension between "what it is that he professes" and "[what it is that he] teaches" is reflected in the use of the word *dunamis*.

The Greek term *dunamis* can have different meanings. In the current context, it seems to refer to "strength" in the sense of power which at first can be concealed, and only later unfolds its influence.[16] The answer to our *dunamis* question lies, then, in the second part of the question. But, as this second part itself is made up of two parts, it appears that the answer lies in the *tension* between these two parts. In order to decipher the *dunamis* of his art, one needs to note two aspects of the teacher's activity, namely, "what it is that he professes" as opposed to "and [sc. what it is that he] teaches." In other words, if we consider what the teacher professes on the one hand, and what he truly teaches on the other, we will be left with the "*dunamis* of his art." Already here we assume a tension (or gap) between the teacher's declarations (i.e., his consciousness) and his behavior (i.e., his praxis). The teacher might think of himself as teaching one thing, while in fact he is teaching something else entirely. We are not necessarily dealing with a charlatan, however. It is possible that the teacher is unaware of the strength of his art. Socrates will later reveal to the reader, but first and foremost to Gorgias himself, the *dunamis* of his art. This tension between the teacher's perception of his subject

---

[16] At 455d6-7, Gorgias strives to show Socrates all the power (i.e., the real power) of his art. The implication is that the true power of his art is often hidden and must be revealed: "Well, I will try, Socrates, to reveal (*apokalupsai*) to you clearly the whole power [*dunamin*] of rhetoric." The use of the word *dunamis* together with the verb *apokaluptō* (i.e., to disclose) is striking.

and his actual subject helps to account for the odd way in which the dialogue continues after Socrates poses his question to Callicles. At the same time, this continued conversation can serve to strengthen such tension.

In asking Callicles about the *dunamis* of Gorgias's *technē*, we detect a strategy which can be described as follows. First, Socrates tries to speak with Gorgias's pupil, Callicles, about the *dunamis* of Gorgias's teaching (447b9-c8). Second, Chaerephon (Socrates's friend and pupil) tries to make Gorgias refer to himself as *rhētōr* (447c9-448a5). Third, Polus (Gorgias's pupil) is asked to call Gorgias *rhētōr* (448a6-c9). Finally, Gorgias is encouraged to call himself *rhētōr* (448d1-449a6). We will examine these attempts below, but even now we can see that once the question about the *dunamis* of Gorgias's art is not answered (Callicles suggests that Socrates ask Gorgias directly), the alternatives are Gorgias hearing his pupil calling him *rhētōr* or Gorgias referring to himself as *rhētōr*.[17] How the conversion of the original question concerning the *dunamis* of Gorgias's art into the new question "who he is" (i.e., how Gorgias is to be called) helps Socrates is an intriguing topic that I shall leave aside.[18] As I am interested here in the term *rhētorikē*, the following should suffice. Socrates's fourth attempt, namely, encouraging Gorgias to call himself *rhētōr*, yields the term *rhētorikē*. Moreover, while Socrates's attempts to either make Gorgias refer to himself as *rhētōr* or make his pupil refer to him as *rhētōr* fail, Gorgias is shown to refer to his art as *rhētorikē*—though with a reservation. Let us look closely at the text.

Callicles suggests that Socrates turn directly to Gorgias (447c5-8), and Socrates seems to agree: "What a good idea [ἦ καλῶς λέγεις]." Then comes a strange shift: "Ask him, Chaerephon [ὦ Χαιρεφῶν, ἐροῦ αὐτόν]." Instead of Socrates posing the question to

[17] In other words, Gorgias, who is called *rhētōr* (either by himself or by his pupils), seems to replace the "finding out the *dunamis* of his art." Socrates seems to believe that by having Gorgias called *rhētōr* he achieves what he would have achieved by asking Callicles about the *dunamis* of his teacher's art.

[18] I have dedicated an entire book to this question: Yosef Z. Liebersohn, *Who is Afraid of the Rhētōr: An Analysis and Exegesis of Socrates-Gorgias' Conversation in Plato's Gorgias* (Gorgias Press, 2014).

Gorgias, as one would expect based on the former's response, Socrates instructs Chaerephon to ask Gorgias. Leaving this shift aside for a moment, one wonders *what* Chaerephon is to ask Gorgias. Socrates does not explain, and, indeed, this is exactly what Chaerephon now asks Socrates: "What am I to ask?" In light of the aforementioned tension in Socrates's question at 447b9-c4, we perhaps can understand Chaerephon's confusion. As Socrates's question consists of two parts, the second of which is subdivided, it is not clear what he wants Chaerephon to ask Gorgias. Yet, the real surprise is still ahead. To Chaerephon's question, Socrates does not refer either to the "what it is that he professes" or to the "what it is that he teaches" but, in an additional shift, tells Chaerephon to ask Gorgias "who he is [Ὅστις ἐστίν]." To the incomprehension of Chaerephon as to the meaning of this question, Socrates explains that it refers to Gorgias's title as one who has a certain *technē*. As the one who is busy with shoemaking is called a shoemaker, Gorgias, who occupies himself with a specific activity, must have a name that indicates this activity. How can we explain these shifts?

As I see it, changing the question from what is the *dunamis* of Gorgias's *technē* to "who he is" is directly related to changing the one who is about to answer, from Callicles to Gorgias. Initially, Socrates intended to ask the pupil (Callicles) about the *dunamis* of Gorgias's teaching, since it is only the pupil who really knows what his teacher teaches.[19] But as Callicles does not take up the challenge and instead suggests that Socrates ask Gorgias himself, the question itself has to be modified. If Gorgias is now the interlocutor, the question about the *dunamis* is no longer relevant, since Gorgias cannot reliably answer such a question. But then, why tell Chaerephon to ask Gorgias? Why not ask him himself? By instructing Chaerephon to

[19] Note that Gorgias is entirely peripheral to the opening of the dialogue. He is present, but it is Socrates and Callicles who are dominant. Moreover, it is possible that Socrates and Chaerephon came on purpose immediately after Gorgias has finished his performance (*epideixis*). Dramatically, of course, Chaerephon is the one who caused this delay, but it is Plato who arranges the scene such that the identification of the *dunamis* of Gorgias's art is disconnected from Gorgias himself. It is therefore unnecessary to come for his *epideixis*.

ask Gorgias, I suggest, Socrates draws Polus (Gorgias's pupil) into the conversation. Again, we detect the Socratic strategy, namely, it is the pupil, be it Callicles or Polus, who will reveal what Gorgias actually teaches. Polus can only be brought into the conversation by assigning the question "who is he?" to Chaerephon. Socrates knows that Polus's concern for his teacher's dignity will prevent him from allowing Gorgias to answer the question. Thus, when Chaerephon, who is given an example by Socrates from the field of shoemaking (447d3-5), turns to Gorgias and even obtains Gorgias's consent to answer him (447d6-448a5), we find Polus breaking into the conversation as the proposed interlocutor (448a6). As long as Socrates is asking the question, Gorgias might answer, but if Chaerephon is the one who asks, it should be Polus who answers.

Now, in the third attempt, Polus, who inherits the "Who is he?" question, is being asked by Chaerephon: "Now, since Gorgias has knowledge of some art, what would we correctly call him then?" (448c2-3). Polus, who has been provided examples from medicine and painting, should have answered simply "a *rhētōr*." This is based on the assumption that Gorgias's art is *rhētorikē*, and, as one who is occupied with *iatrikē* (medical art) is referred to as an *iatros* (doctor), one who is occupied with *rhētorikē* should be referred to as a *rhētōr*.[20] Polus, as we could have guessed, does not answer "a *rhētōr*," but he also does not suggest any other term used to refer to artists, even though he agrees that Gorgias practices a kind of art. Instead, Polus delivers a fine speech in praise of Gorgias's art and of Gorgias as an artist. Possibly, he feels that his teacher has been insulted by Chaerephon's comparison of Gorgias's art to inferior arts such as shoemaking and painting.[21] Nonetheless, *within* this speech Polus

---

[20] I skip here the alternative title for the artist, ending with *-ikos* (*rhētorikos, iatrikos*). This option appears quite late in the *Gorgias* (455b4) and has its own reason, which I here leave aside. See Liebersohn, *Who is Afraid*, 52 and n6. On the ending *-ikos* in Plato, see Adolf Ammann, *Ikos bei Platon: Ableitung und Bedeutung mit Matterialsammlung* (Freiburg: Paulusverlag, 1953).

[21] Indeed, Polus's speech is an *encomium* directed at Chaerephon's *psogos* and it is even hinted at by Socrates in his answer at 448e2-4. See especially the verb *engkōmiazeis* and the participle *psegontos*.

could—and, arguably, *should*—have brought up either the term *rhētōr* or the term *rhētorikē*. However, he does not, although he refers to both periphrastically. Thus, Socrates fails in his third attempt, namely, getting Polus to refer to Gorgias as a *rhētōr*.

Since Polus does not refer to Gorgias as a *rhētōr*,[22] Socrates's next move is to attempt to get Gorgias to refer to himself as such. It is now that Socrates turns directly to Gorgias, and it is here that we encounter what I alluded to above as the wider context of the place of *rhētorikē* in the *Gorgias*. Inserting the term *rhētorikē* is part of Socrates's strategy to make Gorgias refer to himself as a *rhētōr*.

The Insertion of *Rhētorikē*

Socrates now turns to Gorgias and complains that Polus did not fulfill his promise to Chaerephon. Moreover, to the teacher's confusion, he goes on to explain that Polus did not provide an answer to the question that was posed to him (448d1-5). When Gorgias suggests that Socrates turn to Polus directly with his question, Socrates says that he prefers Gorgias to answer instead (448d6-8), offering the following explanation: "For I see plainly, from what he has said, that Polus has had more practice in *kaloumenē rhētorikē* than in *dialegesthai*" (448d8-10).

Syntactically, this additional clause explains why Socrates prefers to speak with Gorgias. Dramatically, however, the clause might have an additional motivation, since Gorgias, who has promised to answer any question raised by anyone, anytime (447c5-8), might have responded in any case.[23] Indeed, why not seize another opportunity to impress Socrates?

---

[22] In fact, the original plan was for Callicles to refer to Gorgias as a *rhētōr*, but the principle is the same—a pupil referring to his teacher as a *rhētōr*. In addition, we recall that instructing Chaerephon to ask Gorgias "who is he?" at 447d1 was aimed at bringing Polus into the conversation. It is rather the pupil who is to refer to his teacher as a *rhētōr*. Unlike Polus, Chaerephon is not Gorgias's pupil.

[23] This is explicitly what he does after his *epideixis,* as Callicles says at 447c5-8, and both Chaerephon and Callicles promise Socrates a private *epideixis* by Gorgias at their place (447b2-3 and 447b7-9, respectively).

In order to understand why Socrates uses the term *rhētorikē* at this precise time, we need to look carefully at his question at 449a1-4 and Gorgias's response at 449a5. After Socrates explains to Gorgias that Polus is proficient in rhetoric but not in *dialegesthai*, Polus interrupts, inquiring what it is about his speech that did not serve as a sufficient answer to Chaerephon's question (448e1). Socrates furnishes this information (448e2-449a2) and concludes with a direct appeal to Gorgias to provide an answer nearly repeating the question which was posed to Polus one line earlier (449a2-4). Notably, the question posed to Polus is clear, and the question posed to Gorgias is not (below, I explain how the latter can be understood in two different ways). This lack of clarity with what concerns the question posed to Gorgias is apparent not only to the reader but also to Gorgias himself.[24] Moreover, the insertion of *rhētorikē* earlier (448d9) is connected to this intricate question, as we shall now see.

Socrates's question to Gorgias contains an ambiguity that gets lost in translation. The Loeb translation will be used as a starting point for our discussion, but we will see that the translator had to choose one of the two readings that Gorgias himself is supposed to choose. Later, we will see the different possibilities for understanding the question, all of which are contained within its Greek phrasing.

Socrates asks Gorgias, "Gorgias, do tell us yourself in what art it is you are skilled, and hence, what we ought to call you [ὦ Γοργία, αὐτὸς ἡμῖν εἰπὲ τίνα σε χρὴ καλεῖν ὡς τίνος ἐπιστήμονα τέχνης]" (449a2-4). Gorgias's terse response is difficult to parse: "Rhetoric, Socrates [τῆς ῥητορικῆς, ὦ Σώκρατες]" (449a5).[25] This question and its answer can be translated in two distinct ways, depending upon how one interprets the second part of the question, and especially the exact meaning of the particle *hōs*. Let me explain.

Socrates's question consists of two clauses but not necessarily two questions. The first possibility is to see here one question alone, "How should one refer to you [τίνα σε χρὴ καλεῖν]?," where the

---

[24] And, we can assume, it was carefully designed by Socrates.

[25] It is worth noticing the genitive case in Gorgias's response, which relates to the genitive of the second part of Socrates's question.

second clause is nothing but an accepted observation, namely, "being expert in a certain art" [ὡς τίνος ἐπιστήμονα τέχνης]. In that case, we should translate the question thusly: "Being expert in a certain art, how should one refer to you?" However, that would render Gorgias's answer, "Rhetoric, Socrates," unintelligible. The second possibility is that "how should one refer to you [τίνα σε χρὴ καλεῖν]" is the main question, and that ὡς τίνος ἐπιστήμονα τέχνης is meant as something between a supposition and a hypothesis which Gorgias is asked to confirm. This option yields two possible queries:

1) How should one refer to you; being expert in what art?
2) How should one refer to you, being expert in a particular art?[26]

Gorgias's answer makes perfect sense if it is answering question #1. In that case, Socrates has changed his question and Gorgias provides an answer to the new one. If question #2 is at issue, Gorgias's answer is a kind of outburst. In that case, Gorgias would be answering the second part of the question with "rhetoric, Socrates." The sophistic formulation of the Socratic question gives Gorgias an equal choice of answering the question, "how should one refer to you?" or "being expert in what art?" In other words, Gorgias has to choose between mentioning *rhētōr* and mentioning *rhētorikē*. Gorgias's choice of "being expert in what art" tells Socrates (and the reader) something about the teacher's world. Gorgias, for whatever reason, cannot call himself a *rhētōr* and therefore chooses the term *rhētorikē*. Now we understand why Socrates inserted the sentence using the term *rhētorikē* at 448d8-10: he wished to offer Gorgias an alternative later.

To sum up the inquiry thus far. Socrates sought to make Polus refer to his teacher, Gorgias, as a *rhētōr*. This attempt failed, and Socrates then tried to make Gorgias refer to himself as a *rhētōr*.

---

[26] In Greek, this second possibility would require τινος to be enclitic, but Plato wrote without accents. Indeed, the decision of ὡς τίνος (where τίνος is accented) rather than ὥς τινος (where ὥς is accented), probably made in the Hellenistic period, is already a choice concerning the exact meaning of Socrates's question. Socrates of the conversation (and Plato who shaped his character thusly) had a privilege that we lack today.

Taking into account that doing so might be difficult for Gorgias, Socrates formulated his question in such a way that Gorgias had an "out." Thus, Gorgias could choose between referring to himself as a *rhētōr* and calling his art *rhētorikē*. He chose the second option.

Socrates will continue with his efforts, now with Gorgias calling his pupils *rhētores*, but since my aim here is limited to identifying the exact status of rhetoric as an art in the consciousness of those who taught it, I will end the philological analysis of the text at this point. We still do not know why Socrates is obsessed with Gorgias being referred to—either by his pupil or by himself—as a *rhētōr*, but we now know a few important things about these term *rhētorikē* and what its unique appearance in the *Gorgias* teaches us about the status of rhetoric as seen through the text and by its author:

1. Plato's *Gorgias* deals with rhetoric, especially in its first part (i.e., the conversation with Gorgias). However, unlike other Platonic dialogues that deal with terms such as "courage," "justice," or even virtue itself, we nowhere find in the *Gorgias* the typical Socratic question, which in our context should have been "what is rhetoric?" Socrates's first question about rhetoric asks rather about its *dunamis*.

2. Even in asking about the *dunamis* of rhetoric, the term *rhētorikē* is absent. It is only referred to in the phrase "the *technē* of his art."

3. It is only after Polus's speech that *rhētorikē* appears in the dialogue, and there it is done *en passant*.[27] The reader is left with the impression that everyone is familiar with this term (and so the words *kaloumenē rhētorikē* can remain understood as "what we call *rhētorikē*"). Gorgias does not ask what the word *rhētorikē* means, and Socrates does not preface its use with any information. The same is true of Polus: he breaks into the conversation, disagreeing with Socrates (448e1), but does not inquire about *rhētorikē*. If this term had been unfamiliar to either

[27] *Pace* George A. Kennedy, *A New History of Classical Rhetoric* (Princeton, NJ: Princeton University Press), 7n3: "the dramatic date of the dialogue is in the late 5th century, and both Gorgias and Polus are represented there as accepting the term without objection."

> Gorgias or Polus,[28] they would likely have asked. Importantly, however, this does not mean that *rhētorikē* was for Gorgias and his students a well-defined term, as it is nowadays. Had *rhētorikē* been the accepted term to denote Gorgias's occupation and teaching, it should have appeared before its first use by Socrates. It was rather Polus who had to mention it in his famous speech at 448c4-9. Polus could have used this term there and, indeed, should have used it, if it had the meaning and status it has nowadays.

Everyone, it seems, knows that Gorgias and his pupils are occupied with a *technē*, albeit a *technē* without a definite name. Today, we readily refer to Gorgias's *technē* as "rhetoric," but care should be taken to avoid imposing modern notions on an ancient text. While Gorgias refers to his *technē* as *rhētorikē*, he does so only after Socrates has named it thus.

At the time depicted in our conversation, I argue, rhetoric had not yet been defined as a self-standing *technē*; the absence of a decisive denomination emphasizes this status. Perhaps Gorgias and his students did not bother to give their occupation a specific name. Many possibilities were available, including "the art which deals with what is just and unjust," "the finest art of all," and eventually *rhētorikē*.[29] This flexible nomenclature reflects the status of the art itself. I claim that the way in which *rhētorikē* appears in our conversation attests to the particular place it had both in reality and in the consciousness of those who were versed in it (i.e., Gorgias and

---

[28] It is worth noting that even Schiappa (*The Beginnings*, 19) concedes that the term *rhētorikē* could have been used before Plato. Thus, Plato can be taken as a reliable source for the use of the term *rhētorikē* even in the 5th century BCE, though not in the same meaning it had in the 4th century BCE. See also below.

[29] One of the options we saw earlier of translating the second part of Socrates's question at 449a3-4—"Being expert in a certain art, what should one call you?"—might strengthen my case. Socrates is not evading the name *rhētorikē*, but rather refers exactly to Gorgias's way of thinking. He has a *technē* whose name is not yet fixed.

his pupils). By having Socrates introduce *rhētorikē* as he does, Plato subtly situated the term as a reference to a yet dependent discipline.

I opened this paper with Schiappa's well-known thesis that dates rhetoric to the 4th century BCE and even later. The textual analysis presented here supports this view but, as noted, aspires to expand it as well. For Schiappa, Plato simply erred by attributing the art of rhetoric to the historical Gorgias. In detecting the exact location and context of the term *rhētorikē* as we did here, I suggest modifying this view slightly, and advocating for Plato. Three reasons can be brought to bear for such a revision:

1) First, Gorgias of the *Gorgias* should not be identified with the historic Gorgias. Plato's dialogues are philosophical dramas. The actors in these dialogues—though based on actual people, most of whom are known to us from other sources—are fictitious in that the dramatist molds them according to his own aims. Plato tends to leave facts as facts, but shapes codes of behavior, arguments, and the like in accordance with the message he wishes to convey in each dialogue.[30] Gorgias is indeed a well-known historic figure whom we know also from other sources. He will never appear in Plato, for example, as poor, or from a place other than Sicily, but his exact views concerning his occupation with its terminologies and the like are left in the hands of the playwright. The reader is left to glean information about prevailing views, linguistic usages, and the like from his or her analysis of the interaction between the characters, especially the ways in which Socrates addresses his interlocutors.[31] Plato had no intention of presenting the historical Gorgias, and thus

[30] More on the dramatic method in analyzing Plato's dialogues with references to scholarly literature can be found in Yosef Z. Liebersohn, "Rhetoric: Art and Pseudo-Art in Plato's *Gorgias*," *Arethusa* 38 (2005): 306-9.

[31] See also Michael C. Stokes, *Dialectic in Action: An Examination of Plato's* Crito (Swansea: Classical Press of Wales, 2005), 31, who comments on the *Crito*. His words are relevant to any other dialogue: "one ought in the first instance to interpret the characters of a given dialogue out of that dialogue."

the mismatch between the character in the dialogue and the historical Gorgias should not bother us too much. In the *Gorgias,* Plato critiqued 5th century BCE teachers who occupied themselves with *logoi* and taught their students mainly to compose speeches on civic affairs. These teachers are represented by the character Gorgias, whose historical equivalent was no doubt also a teacher. Moreover, as I will argue below, his attack was more focused on the future of the activity than on its then current condition.

2) If, regarding the historical Gorgias, Plato is not—and need not be—accurate, regarding the teaching of "rhetoric" and the status of "rhetoric" in the second half of the 5th century BCE, Plato should be considered a highly reliable source. He provides a sophisticated presentation of the state of this art, which is in fact an "art in formation." As we have shown, Plato does not make ready use of the term *rhētorikē* to describe the Gorgias's activity. He carefully positions *rhētorikē* as an optional term. Moreover, he makes it clear that it is not a term that Gorgias or his students[32] would necessarily have chosen to describe their work.

3) Finally, considering the structure of the dialogue as a whole and the way in which Gorgias's personality is presented in the dialogue, we have good reasons to assume that Plato deliberately situated the scene of the dialogue in an intermediate stage regarding rhetoric. As we have already noted, the dialogue is made up of three interconnected conversations, with the interlocutors consisting of a teacher and his two pupils. Notably—although this is rather overlooked in the scholarship—Gorgias is shown to be present in the conversations with his pupils Polus and Callicles. Gorgias's appearances in the two other conversations—in that of Polus's at 463a5, and in that of Callicles's at 497b4-5, 8-10, 506a8-b3—seem marginal and may be Plato's way of conveying to the reader that the *Gorgias* consists of

---

[32] Here, with regard to the status of rhetoric in the 5th century BCE, there is a parallel between Gorgias the Platonic character and the teachers of that time, including the historical Gorgias. See next section.

one single conversation, namely, that between Socrates and Gorgias. Since Gorgias is not fully aware of what he is teaching, however, he has to learn this from his pupils. In other words, Socrates speaks with Gorgias through his conversations with his pupils. Gorgias, who hears Polus speak with admiration of Archelaus, king of Macedonia who harmed his own family (471a4-d2),[33] and hears Callicles's speech at 482c4-486d1, including his statement "but nature, in my opinion, herself proclaims the fact that it is right for the better to have advantage of the worse, and the abler of the feebler" (483c8-d2), ought to consider why Polus and Callicles wish to be his students. We hence find a generation gap built into the structure of the dialogue. When it comes to the art of rhetoric, Gorgias the teacher is far from his students Polus and Callicles. Thus, within the *Gorgias*, what we learn about rhetoric by the conversations with Polus and Callicles should not be attributed to Gorgias their teacher.[34]

---

[33] Later on, Polus reveals to Socrates, and especially to Gorgias, the purpose of rhetoric as he sees it. He expresses surprise at Socrates's behavior: "As if you, Socrates, would not accept the liberty of doing what seems [sc. best] to you to do in your city rather than not, and would not envy a man whom you observed to have put someone to death as he thought fit, or deprived him of his property or sent him to prison!" (468e6–9). This is the aim of Polus, and to achieve it he has become the student of Gorgias and of his art, rhetoric.

[34] Perhaps—and this is only a wild suggestion—the probably-deliberate chronological inconsistencies found in the *Gorgias,* which are well-noted in scholarly literature (see Charles H. Kahn, "On the Relative Date of the *Gorgias* and the *Protagoras*," in *Oxford Studies in Ancient Philosophy* 6 (1988): 101) have to do with this gap between the teacher and his pupils. Plato, indeed, did not fix the dramatic date of the *Gorgias* in a specific time, but by checking the exact references to historical events in the dialogue we discover that the earlier event hinted at is 429 BCE (Pericles's death) and the latest is 405 BCE (the trial of the generals after the battle of Arginusae). It may be the case that Plato had to extend the dialogue's dramatic time over more than two decades to reflect the gap between the teacher and his students.

When we examine Gorgias's personality in the *Gorgias*, the results are similar. Gorgias is a good man who believes he is benefiting society and even promoting justice. He is a teacher who deals with *logoi*, namely, the composition of speeches. He is depicted as someone who loves to help others from other fields as well—including his own brother, a physician. In the famous speech at 456a7-457c3, he emphasizes the duty of his pupils to use what he teaches only for the good (456e2-457b5). Socrates, for his part, is represented as respecting Gorgias, reserving his critique of rhetoric as an art (462b8-9), and his feeling that rhetoric is disguised flattery (465b1-c3) for the conversation with Polus.

Gorgias, as he is depicted in the *Gorgias* by Plato, represents the typical teacher of *logoi* in the second half of the 5th century BCE. He is a good man, a teacher who is busy with speeches (not necessarily with rhetoric), who is not fully aware of what he teaches. This is not so far from Schiappa's view of the historical Gorgias. Thus, I suggest that we can hold the view that rhetoric is a product of the 4th century BCE without labelling Plato's dialogue as anachronistic.[35]

Rhetoric vs. Politics

Thus far we have shown how Plato in the *Gorgias* was careful not to ascribe to his Gorgias the consciousness of one who deals with rhetoric in the full sense of this word, namely, as a discipline. According to Schiappa and those following his views, rhetoric was "founded" only when what was still only a "practice of oratory" became a "specific domain of theorizing."[36] Schiappa identifies the

---

Thus Dodds, *Plato: Gorgias*, 17, who inferred from these inconsistencies that for Plato the dialogue is taking place "in no particular year," might be right but should also be slightly revised: "in no particular year between 429-405 BCE."

[35] "The more likely scenario is that Plato's attribution was simply anachronistic" (Schiappa, *The Beginnings*, 18).

[36] "First, a distinction needs to be made between the use of the word *rhetoric* to denote the practice of oratory and the use of the word to denote a specific domain of theorizing. The first sense, rhetoric as persuasive speaking or oratory (what Kennedy calls "traditional rhetoric"), obviously occurred long before Plato, but is distinct from the second

emergence of rhetoric, with its distinction from philosophy, by defining a different aim for each, seeking success as against seeking truth:

> prior to the coining of *rhētorikē,* the verbal arts were understood as less differentiated and more holistic in scope than they were in the fourth century; the teaching and training associated with *logos* do not draw a sharp line between the goals of seeking success and seeking truth as is the case once Rhetoric and Philosophy were defined as distinct disciplines.[37]

Herein lies the second argument of this paper. Rhetoric as an independent art requires not merely distinction from philosophy: there is also the matter of politics. For Gorgias and teachers like him during the 5th, and perhaps even the early fourth centuries, politics was the general context in which their occupation was practiced. Those teachers dealt broadly with *logos* without differentiating between what would later become rhetoric and philosophy.[38] But this very preoccupation with *logos* is concerned mainly with *ta politika,* namely, civic affairs. Even the term *rhētōr* in the 5th century BCE—and this word plays a crucial part in Plato's *Gorgias*—designates a specific group of people, namely, the more-or-less professional politicians who spoke in the courts or in the assembly.[39]

---

sense, the history of rhetorical theory. What this book addresses is the emerging status of rhetoric *as a distinct subject or discipline*—the status of rhetorical theory qua rhetorical theory in Greece [...] [T]his book is concerned with the status of conceptual or metarhetoric that attempts to theorize about oratory [....] [S]elf-conscious artistry of persuasive efforts prior to Plato" (Schiappa, *The Beginnings,* 21-22; my emphasis).

[37] Schiappa, *The Beginnings,* 23.

[38] "Rhetoric—though it would later become a distinct subject—was still a largely undifferentiated part of skill in *logos*" (Schiappa, *The Beginnings,* 72).

[39] Based on Schiappa, *The Beginnings,* 169. See also Dodds, *Plato: Gorgias,* 194 note on the word ῥήτορα (449a6); Kennedy, *A New History,* 3–5. See also Isocrates, *Antidosis* 256: "while we call eloquent [i.e., rhetoricians]

The political (i.e., civic affairs) context of Gorgias's occupation can be seen in the *Gorgias* as well. Asked by Socrates "what subject is it, of all in the world, that is dealt with by these speeches employed by rhetoric," Gorgias answers: "The greatest of human affairs, Socrates, and the best [τὰ μέγιστα τῶν ἀνθρωπείων πραγμάτων, ὦ Σώκρατες, καὶ ἄριστα]" (451d7-8), which evidently refers to politics, as Irwin has shown.[40] Moreover, Gorgias's examples of the *dunamis* of his art are mainly taken from the political arena, such as his example from the speaker who can beat the professional physician—or any other professional—by his speech before the assembly and be elected as a physician (456b6-c6). And finally, Socrates describes rhetoric in the *Gorgias* as "a semblance of a branch of politics [πολιτικῆς μορίου εἴδωλον]" (463d1-2).

Nonetheless, we ought to be cautious about defining the subject matter of rhetoric as "political affairs." Political affairs are not yet rhetoric's *materia* in the sense that rhetoric has selected it from among other *materiae*. In fact, the sphere of political affairs constitutes a kind of "built-in" *materia*,[41] dependent only on the context in which rhetoric has appeared. When Gorgias is asked about rhetoric—"with what particular thing is its skill concerned?"—his answer is *peri logous* (concerning speeches; 449d9-449e1), since neither he nor any other teacher in the 5th century BCE can say more. It takes Socrates more than seven Stephanus pages to elicit from Gorgias what these *logoi* are about, namely, *dikaia te kai adika* (justice and injustice; 454b7).

It is only when rhetoric detaches itself from its root, *politikē*, that it will begin to engage with everything. Notably, however, we find

---

those who are able to speak before a crowd [καὶ ῥητορικοὺς μὲν καλοῦμεν τοὺς ἐν πλήθει λέγειν δυναμένους]." For further references of *rhētōr* in the sense of politican see Schiappa, "Did Plato Coin *Rhētorikē*," 457n2.

[40] Terrence Irvin, *Plato: Gorgias* (Oxford, Clarendon Press, 1979), 115. See also Arist. *Pol.* 1253a31.

[41] On the close interaction between rhetoric and politics—even as late as Aristotle's time—see *Rhet.* 1356a25-26 where Aristotle conceives of rhetoric as "a certain offshoot [...] of the field concerning behavior which it is right to call politics [παραφυές τι ... τῆς περὶ τὰ ἤθη πραγματείας, ἣν δίκαιόν ἐστι προσαγορεύειν πολιτικήν]."

this trait of the speaking about everything in the very origins of rhetoric (in its pre-disciplinary stage in the 5th century BCE); its formal detachment from *politikē* will only bring out what has always been present.

In the *Gorgias*, rhetoric begins to split off from politics and perceive itself as an independent art. This is a liminal stage, and all liminal spaces are vague. Moreover, it is not only rhetoric that is at an intermediate stage: its practitioners, especially the teachers, are also at an intermediate point. They suffer from an interesting tension: while consciously they are doing one thing, in practice they are doing something else. Gorgias believes that he is helping others by dealing with the affairs of the polis (i.e., *politikē*); in reality, however, he is practicing, and ultimately creating, a new art, one that has little to do with assisting others.

I suggest that Socrates anticipated the future of rhetoric and the society in which it would thrive. Nonetheless, what Socrates saw remained unseen by those who engaged in this new art, as rhetoric and its practitioners were in the stage at which rhetoric had not yet revealed its *dunamis*. In Gorgias's consciousness, rhetoric engages with the "just and unjust" (454b7), and it is the best art of all (448c8-9). In practice, though, rhetoric does not deal with any specific sphere, and to say that it is the best art of all strains the limits of reason.

Conclusion

This essay has shown Plato in the *Gorgias* to be well-aware of the difference between rhetoric as perceived by teachers in the 5th century and the term as developed in the 4th century BCE. The *Gorgias* presents us with rhetoric in formation, with what concerns the very establishment of a new art. Rhetoric is in an intermediate stage. In the consciousness of those who teach it (represented by the Platonic character Gorgias), rhetoric is nothing but politics: the speaker is a politician who knows how to speak. Its sphere, if we are careful not to use the term *materia*, is the affairs of the polis, and its evaluation concerning its beneficence is wholly political. Yet, in practice, rhetoric is a formal art which can encompass even subjects about which the rhetorician has no real knowledge. The *Gorgias* was composed at a stage when Plato could foresee that what was in his day merely a practical occupation with perhaps a few general rules[42] was on the verge of becoming a full-fledged art. The process had been initiated but it was not yet completed. Rhetoric is thus not yet an art even in the first decades of the 4th century BCE. It is only when, first, the practice of oratory becomes a discipline denoting a specific domain of theorizing and, second, when this occupation is formally and consciously detached from politics, that rhetoric will have earned the status of an art.

---

[42] See, for example, the rules which are given in the *Phaedrus* 266d5ff.

Robert Metcalf[1]

Dunamis in *Agōn*: Gorgias of Leontinoi and Plato's *Gorgias*

An old story has it that Gorgias of Leontinoi actually read Plato's dialogue, *Gorgias*, and offered his own review of it: "It is said that after Gorgias himself had read the dialogue that bears his name, he said to his friends, 'How well Plato knows how to make fun of people [*iambizein*]!'" (82A15a). We can hope that this story is true—just because of how great a story it is—but even if it isn't true, it highlights the *comedic* character of Plato's portrait of Gorgias and others in dialogue with Socrates, and at the same time it underscores the difficulties surrounding the philosophical significance of what is comedic.[2] When Gorgias says that Plato knows well how to *iambizein* (to make fun of, lampoon, or mock) is he saying this to his associates *with laughter*? Does he perhaps admire Plato's ability to follow the Gorgianic recommendation, as found in Aristotle's *Rhetoric*, to destroy (*diaphtheirein*) an opponent's seriousness with laughter, and an opponent's laughter with seriousness (1419b3-5)? Or is he saying it more defensively, as if riffing on Socrates's response to Polus at one point in the dialogue: "What's this, Polus—you're laughing? Is laughter another form of *elenchos*—to laugh at it when something is said, instead of refuting it?" (473e). In other words, is Gorgias suggesting that Plato's dialogue did not treat him with the seriousness that his own theories deserve? It is not clear on the face of it how to read Gorgias's words in this story, and indeed this lack of clarity—or, to say it more positively, borrowing an expression from Nietzsche, this *pregnancy of meaning*—belongs more generally

---

[1] Robert Metcalf is Professor of Philosophy at the University of Colorado Denver, USA, author of *Philosophy as Agōn* (Northwestern University Press, 2018), and co-translator of Martin Heidegger's *Basic Concepts of Aristotelian Philosophy* (Indiana University Press, 2009).

[2] For philosophical studies of the comedic in Plato, see S. Montgomery Ewegen, *Plato's Cratylus: The Comedy of Language* (Bloomington: Indiana University Press, 2014), and Sonja Tanner, *Plato's Laughter: Socrates as Satyr and Comical Hero* (Albany: State University of New York Press, 2017), and their contributions to this volume.

to philosophical texts that are at once comedic and serious, where the comedic and the serious need not "destroy' one another exactly, but relate to one another in creative tension.[3] When, upon his entry as a speaker in the *Gorgias,* Callicles asks whether Socrates is serious (*spoudazei*) or just kidding around (*paizei*) (481b), he expresses precisely the puzzle that attaches to the dialogue throughout, as well as to Gorgias's words in the old story told about his reaction to the dialogue.[4]

In what follows, I argue that a close examination of Gorgias's writings, particularly the *Encomium of Helen,* alongside Plato's *Gorgias* shows us how seriously Plato took Gorgias's thinking, even in the midst of a dramatic portrayal that is thoroughly comedic, and further, that this serious encounter with Gorgias as a thinker is made possible by their shared appreciation of the agonistic foundation of philosophical thought.[5] Socrates is dramatized by Plato as practicing philosophy as a distinctive form of *agōn*—one that involves refutative argument (*elenchos*) with one's interlocutor, but also contestation (*diamachesthai*) of the Athenian *demos* as a whole. Furthermore, in the *Gorgias* we see Socrates at pains to distinguish this properly philosophical form of *agōn* from that practiced by Gorgias and his acolytes (cf. 505d-e, 526e), which Socrates condemns as shameful pandering (*kolakeia*) (465a). Thus, by focusing our

---

[3] I have addressed the creative tension between the comedic and the serious in Aristotle's defense of the principle of non-contradiction in *Metaphysics* Gamma, and its bearing on Socratic elenchos, in my essay "The True Character of Elenchos," *Internationales Jahrbuch für Hermeneutik,* V (2006): 201-223.

[4] John Beversluis, *Cross-Examining Socrates: A Defense of the Interlocutors in Plato's Early Dialogues* (Cambridge: Cambridge University Press, 2000), 43, argues that the "serious" cannot be divorced from what is "non-serious" about Plato's Socrates without "doing violence to both."

[5] See Edward Schiappa, *The Beginning of Rhetorical Theory in Classical Greece* (New Haven: Yale University Press, 1999), 10, for the argument that we should focus on Gorgias's *ipsissima verba* because Plato, like Aristotle, is not a reliable guide to Gorgias's thinking. What I wish to argue here is that a close study of Gorgias's writings shows how seriously Plato took Gorgias's theorizing.

attention on philosophical agonism in both Gorgias's writings and Plato's *Gorgias,* we may better understand how Plato has appropriated from Gorgias's thought the focal concepts of *dunamis* and *doxa,* and has dramatized them in the *Gorgias* in ways that are at once comedic and philosophically serious.

To begin, then, there is one text in particular in which Gorgias's thinking with respect to *agōn* is placed front and center:

> According to Gorgias of Leontini, 'A contest such as we have [*to agōnisma hēmōn*] requires two kinds of excellence, daring and wisdom [*dittōn aretōn deitai, tolmēs kai sophias*]—daring is needed to withstand danger, and wisdom to understand how to trip up the opponent. For surely *logos,* like the summons at the Olympic games, summons him who is willing [*kalei men ton boulomenon*], but crowns him who has ability [*stephanoi de ton dunamenon*]. (B8)[6]

In this text, Gorgias understands *logos* as an *agōn* comparable in instructive ways to the great *agōn* of the Olympian games, and, just as with athletic contests, the *agōn* of *logoi* crowns the one who shows forth ability or power: *dunamis*. Importantly, the ability or power at stake in the sort of *agōn* that Gorgias has in mind is one that comes to appear not by way of *logos* in what to us is the more familiar meaning—i.e., words or text—but *logos* in the sense of a rhetorical exhibition (*epideixis*) which is performed before an audience, attentive to the moment (*kairos*) and the opportunities for persuasion that are available in the moment.[7] *Logos* in this performative sense is a phenomenon which makes it difficult to distinguish between the persuasiveness of the speech-as-content and the persuasiveness of the speaker-as-performer. This distinctively rhetorical sense of *dunamis* in the *agōn* of *logoi* is reflected in Plato's *Gorgias,* since Gorgias claims, as part of his *epideixis,* to be able to answer whatever

[6] The source is Clement, *Miscellanies* I.51. In the very last line I have altered the translation from *The Older Sophists,* ed. Rosamond Kent Sprague (Indianapolis: Hackett, 1972).

[7] See Edward Schiappa, *The Beginning,* 100-102, for discussion of the performative character of Gorgias's sense of *logos,* in the context of which Schiappa describes Gorgias as a "prose rhapsode."

questions are asked of him (447c)—which is to say that Gorgias has trained himself to show forth an ability to persuade the audience before him, in the moment, where this ability is tested and/or contested by those gathered there. We should note the parallel between the daring (*tolmē*) and wisdom (*sophia*) highlighted in this passage and the character-traits that Socrates in Plato's *Gorgias* identifies as necessary in an interlocutor if their agreement (*homologia*) is to "get at the truth [ἕξει τῆς ἀληθείας]" (487e): namely, frankness (*parrēsia*) and knowledge (*epistēmē*) (487a).[8] In any case, Gorgias's remarks on the two kinds of excellence required of the speaker make it clear that in speaking of *logos* in Gorgias's sense, we are dealing not with a discursive "content" detachable from the speaker whose *dunamis* is at stake in the *agōn*, but rather with a performance before an audience wherein persuasion "happens"—sometimes in startling ways that suggest a "daimonic" power at work in *logos*.[9]

In Gorgias's *Encomium of Helen*, we find, once again, a treatment of *dunamis* with an eye to the *agōn* of *logoi*, and one that Plato clearly had in view when he wrote the *Gorgias*. To be sure, *dunamis* is the most prominent focal concept in Gorgias's text, as its overall structure makes evident: it is by theorizing the various *dunameis* that may have constrained and over-powered Helen that Gorgias

---

[8] The third character-trait identified by Plato's Socrates, "good will [εὔνοια],"is missing from Gorgias's account of *logos*, which suggests a key difference between Gorgianic rhetoric and Socratic *dialegesthai*. See William Desmond, *The Intimate Universal: The Hidden Porosity Among Religion, Art, Philosophy, and Politics* (New York: Columbia University Press, 2016), 380, for the argument that the *agōn* practiced by Plato's Socrates involves "a mingling of *polemos* and *philia*. If it were only the former, it would be less dialogue than destructive eris [….] In the *agon* of the dialogue, however implicit this is, we must be friends of truth, even if we are not always friends of one another." See also Andrew Fiala, "Philosophical Peace and Methodological Nonviolence," *The Acorn* 21.1-2 (2021): 21-49.

[9] Cf. *Gorgias* 456a, where Gorgias responds to Socrates's remark on the daimonic power of rhetoric by enthusing about how it "comprises in itself all powers [ἁπάσας τὰς δυνάμεις]."

absolves her of blame. In §20 of the speech, Gorgias writes that "whether she did what she did by love o'ermastered, or by *logos* persuaded, or by force ravished, or by divine constraint compelled," Helen is acquitted of any *aitia* in what happened.[10] Most important among the *dunameis* for Gorgias's purposes is that exercised by *logos*—for *logos*, according to §8 of the speech, "is a powerful lord [δυνάστης μέγας], who, with the finest and most invisible body, achieves the most divine works [θειότατα ἔργα ἀποτελεῖ]: it can stop fear and banish grief and create joy and nurture pity...."[11] Famously, Gorgias goes on to capture the power of *logos* by way of an analogy in §14: "The power of *logos* upon the structure of the soul [τοῦ λόγου δύναμις πρὸς τὴν τῆς ψυχῆς τάξιν] is the same as the structure [τάξις] of *pharmaka* upon the nature of bodies [πρὸς τὴν τῶν σωμάτων φύσιν]...."[12]

A number of scholars have drawn attention to the philosophical connections between Gorgias's *Encomium of Helen* and his speech in *On Not Being*, the latter text weaving together the comedic and the serious in arguing 1) that nothing is, 2) that even if something is, it is unknowable by human beings, and 3) that even if something is and is knowable, it cannot be expressed to others.[13] If, indeed, Gorgias's

---

[10] Gorgias, *Encomium of Helen* 20: Πῶς οὖν χρὴ δίκαιον ἡγήσασθαι τὸν τῆς· Ἑλένης μῶμον, ἥτις εἴτ ἐρασθεῖσα εἴτε λόγῳ πεισθεῖσα εἴτε βίᾳ ἁρπασθεῖσα εἴτε ὑπὸ θείας ἀνάγκης ἀναγκασθεῖσα ἔπραξεν ἃ ἔπραξε, πάντως διαφεύγει τὴν αἰτίαν;

[11] As Schiappa, *The Beginning*, 116 notes, "The amount of space he spends on each cause is noteworthy: Gods and chance are dealt with in one paragraph (6), as is force (7), while *logos* is addressed in seven (8-14) and passion in five (15-19). He then concludes by summarizing the causes and suggesting that he has accomplished his purpose."

[12] On the significance of embodiment and 'bodies' in Gorgias's *Encomium of Helen*, see Ryan Drake, "The Compulsion of Bodies: Infection and Possession in Gorgias's *Helen*," *Epoché* 25.2 (2021): 249-68.

[13] See Rachel Barney, "The Sophistic Movement," in *A Companion to Ancient Philosophy*, eds. M.L. Gill and P. Pelegrin (London: Wiley-Blackwell, 2009), 94, which captures the connection as follows: "The *ONB* shows what language cannot be: either a means of communicating the

On Not Being is meant to advance in all seriousness that *logos* is not a reflection or expression of "what is," then it would seem to follow that *logos* is autonomous, a *dunastēs megas* freed of any constraint upon it by an external "reality," as Rosenmeyer argues.[14] But this means that we should attend carefully to the mechanism by which *logos* exercises such power over those who are susceptible to it—and this is what Gorgias addresses in his account of *doxa* in the *Helen*.

For our purposes, the stretch of Gorgias's speech that is most illuminating is the analysis of *dunamis* by way of *doxa* (and *phainesthai*) in §13, where he writes the following:

> That persuasion, when added to *logos*, can impress the soul as it wishes, one should learn first from the *logoi* of the astronomers who, replacing one opinion with another, taking away one but creating another, make what is incredible and unclear seem apparent to the eyes of opinion; and second, compelling contests in *logoi* in which a single *logos* written with art but not spoken with truth may charm and persuade a large multitude; and third, the struggles of philosophical *logoi*, in which swiftness of thought is also shown making belief in an opinion easily changed.[15]

In this passage, Gorgias presents three different situations of *logos* where we can see the *dunamis* at work in *logos* impressing (*etupōsato*)

---

objective natures of things or of representing our ideas of them. The *Helen* expounds the alternative which remains, namely that language is simply a tool for manipulating behavior."

[14] Thomas G. Rosenmeyer, "Gorgias, Aeschylus, and Apate," *American Journal of Philology* 76 (1955): 225-60.

[15] *Encomium of Helen* 13: ὅτι δ ἡ πειθὼ προσοῦσα τῷ λόγῳ καὶ τὴν ψυχὴν ἐτυπώσατο ὅπως ἐβούλετο, χρὴ μαθεῖν πρῶτον μὲν τοὺς τῶν μετεωρολόγων λόγους, οἵτινες δόξαν ἀντὶ δόξης τὴν μὲν ἀφελόμενοι τὴν δ ἐνεργασάμενοι τὰ ἄπιστα καὶ ἄδηλα φαίνεσθαι τοῖς τῆς δόξης ὄμμασιν ἐποίησαν· δεύτερον δὲ τοὺς ἀναγκαίους διὰ λόγων ἀγῶνας, ἐν οἷς εἷς λόγος πολὺν ὄχλον ἔτερψε καὶ ἔπεισε τέχνῃ γραφείς, οὐκ ἀληθείᾳ λεχθείς· τρίτον φιλοσόφων λόγων ἁμίλλας, ἐν αἷς δείκνυται καὶ γνώμης τάχος καὶ . . . ὡς εὐμετάβολον ποιοῦσι τὴν τῆς δόξης πίστιν.

the soul "as it wishes": the *logoi* of astronomers, the compelling contests of *logoi* before a large multitude, and the "struggles" (*hamillas*) of philosophical *logoi*. Notice that the latter two situations are explicitly agonistic in format, and that the first situation described formulates what, presumably, Gorgias understands to be operative in all three situations—namely, the *phainomenal* character of *logos* in making something appear to the eyes of opinion (*phainesthai tois tēs doxēs ommasin*), such that one *doxa* is replaced with another.[16] The last part of the passage emphasizes the *changeability* of one's belief/conviction (*pistis*) in one's own opinion (*doxa*), "how things seem to one"—a changeability exploited by the swiftness of thought one might bring to bear on philosophical debate, or by the artfulness with which one composes a *logos* spoken before an audience, even if that *logos* abandons truth.

Here we should note two important details in this passage from §13 which bear on connections between Gorgias's theorizing of persuasion in the *Encomium of Helen* and Plato's dramatizing of persuasion (as well as failing-to-persuade) in the *Gorgias*. First, the fact that Gorgias has introduced *pistis* in relation to *doxa* as something altered through the operation of *logos*—rather than analyzing persuasion simply as the replacing of one *doxa* for another—allows for a complexity or nuance in his theory that has dramatic implications in Plato's dialogue, as we shall see. And second, the fact that the orator must make or create this *phainomenal* event to the eyes of *doxa* is something that we find underscored in sections 8-9 of the *Encomium of Helen*, where Gorgias writes that in order to show (*deixai*) that *logos* is a *dunastēs megas*, he "must offer proof to the opinions of my hearers [δεῖ δὲ καὶ δεῖξαι καὶ δόξαι τοῖς ἀκούουσιν]." This point illustrates the self-reflexivity of Gorgias's

[16] See Harold Barrett, *The Sophists: Rhetoric, Democracy, and Plato's Idea of Sophistry* (Novato, CA: Chandler and Sharp, 1987), 17, for the argument that, beyond the agonistic "content" in Gorgias's account here, the apagogic structure of Gorgias's *Helen* "insisted on a battle among ideas, on an agonistic clash promoting excitement [....] Gorgias structured an 'adversary' relation among ideas in testing arguments [...] [and] built in agitation and competition of reasons; form contributed to substance."

theory of *logos*, and the sort of self-reflexivity of *logos* that is mirrored throughout Plato's *Gorgias*. To be sure, Gorgias's acknowledged reliance on *doxa* has its downside, as he makes clear in §11: "On most subjects," he writes, "most men take opinion as counselor to their soul. But opinion, being slippery and insecure, casts those employing it into slippery and insecure successes." Self-reflexively, it follows that Gorgias's intended accomplishment in the speech, replacing one *doxa* for another in the effort to spare Helen "the injustice of blame [μώμου ἀδικίαν] and the ignorance of opinion [καὶ δόξης ἀμαθίαν]," may turn out to be a slippery and insecure *eutuchia*—perhaps no more than an amusement (παίγνιον), as he calls his account at the very end (§21).[17]

This account of power in the *Encomium of Helen* clearly lies in the background of Plato's *Gorgias* from the very outset, as Socrates announces his aim to discover "the power of the *technē* of the man [ἡ δύναμις τῆς τέχνης τοῦ ἀνδρός]" (447c, 450e, 451)—an aim which is realized when Gorgias asserts that rhetoric is

> the ability to persuade with speeches [τὸ πείθειν ἔγωγ᾽ οἷόν τ᾽ εἶναι τοῖς λόγοις] ... And I tell you that by virtue of this power [ἐν ταύτῃ τῇ δυνάμει] you will have the doctor as your slave, and the trainer as your slave; your money-getter will turn out to be making money not for himself, but for another—in fact, for you, who are able to speak and persuade the multitude [ἀλλὰ σοὶ τῷ δυναμένῳ λέγειν καὶ πείθειν τὰ πλήθη]. (452e)

Gorgias does not object when Socrates glosses the power at issue here as that of "making persuasion in the souls of those who hear it [πειθὼ τοῖς ἀκούουσιν ἐν τῇ ψυχῇ ποιεῖν]" (453a)—and it is this unidirectionality of rhetorical power as asserted by Plato's Gorgias which echoes Gorgias's lines in §12 of the *Encomium of Helen*: "For the *logos* which persuades the soul constrains the soul which it

[17] See W.J. Verdenius, "Gorgias' Doctrine of Deception," in *The Sophists and Their Legacy*, ed. G.B. Kerferd (London: Coronet Books, 1979), 116-128 for an analysis of Gorgias's *paignion* ending of the *Encomium of Helen* as paradoxically self-reflexive—a "Verfremdung" whereby the *logos* shows itself to be deceptive.

persuades, both to obey its utterances and to approve its doings."[18] Accordingly, what we find in Plato's *Gorgias* is a restatement of the theory of *dunamis* in *Encomium of Helen*—a theory according to which rhetoric is, as Ewegen puts it, "a technology of power."[19]

What unfolds dramatically in Socrates's questioning of Gorgias, in Plato's eponymous dialogue, is a radical inversion of the orator's account of rhetorical power: in place of *logos* as a *dunastēs megas,* compelling the souls of hearers and so "enslaving" the audience, we get a taxonomy of rhetoric as a form of *kolakeia,* subservient pandering to the audience in an effort to gratify its worst impulses (465a). The inversion effected here is no doubt serious, but also comedic—indeed, essential to the comedy is the performative character of the *logoi* in question: from Gorgias's attempted withdrawal from the *elenchos* (458b-d), to Polus's exasperated incredulity that Socrates would declare rhetoric to be *kolakeia* (461b-c), to his outright laughter at Socrates (473e), and then later to Callicles's sneering jokes aimed at Socrates's demagoguery (482c, 485a-e). The tension between the comedic and the serious is sustained throughout and amplified by the *agōn* of *logoi* in which they find themselves. As I have argued elsewhere at some length, the agonistic format of the exchanges between Socrates and his interlocutors is key to the way in which he carries out an *elenchos* of Gorgias, for it operates by way of "showing up" Gorgias as an interlocutor incapable of making good on his commitment to answer whatever he is asked and to stand his ground over against Socrates.[20] We can read Socrates's *elenchos* of Gorgias as using against Gorgias precisely the slipperiness and insecurity of *doxa* theorized in §11 of his *Encomium of Helen*. For, in Plato's dramatization of their exchange, Gorgias is clearly aware that his account of rhetoric as a dominating power relies on the *doxa,* the opinion, of the audience—

---

[18] Gorgias, *Encomium of Helen* 12 (in part): λόγος γὰρ ψυχὴν ὁ πείσας, ἣν ἔπεισεν; ἠνάγκασε καὶ πιθέσθαι τοῖς λεγομένοις καὶ συναινέσαι τοῖς ποιουμένοις.

[19] S. Montgomery Ewegen, *The Way of the Platonic Socrates* (Bloomington: Indiana University Press, 2020), 39.

[20] Robert Metcalf, *Philosophy as Agōn: A Study of Plato's Gorgias and Related Texts* (Evanston: Northwestern University Press, 2018).

i.e., how things seem/appear to them: the fact that Gorgias tried to exit the *agōn* at a key moment in Socrates's questioning of him, but is made to stay because, as he admits, it would be shameful for him to go back on his promise to answer any questions (458b-e), the fact that he ends up responding insincerely so as to spare himself the humiliation of being shown contradicting himself (461b-c)—all of this speaks to Gorgias's acute awareness of the slipperiness and insecurity of *doxa*. Throughout the exchanges between Gorgias and Socrates, the *doxa* at issue is not merely opinion-that-can-be-propositionalized; rather, it is *doxa* in the larger (and, dramatically, more interesting) sense involving Gorgias's reputation, his cachet—a *doxa* which requires, performatively, that Gorgias make good on his portrait of the rhetorically-skilled person being more persuasive than his opponent whenever he has to compete in *logos* (λόγῳ διαγωνίζεσθαι) in any gathering (456b-c), that he show himself "capable of speaking against everyone and about everything [δυνατὸς μὲν γὰρ πρὸς ἅπαντάς… καὶ περὶ παντὸς λέγειν] in such a way as to be more persuasive [ὥστε πιθανώτερος εἶναι]… about, in a word, whatever he wants [περὶ ὅτου ἂν βούληται]" (457a-b).[21] At the same time, it is this very slipperiness and insecurity of *doxa*—its liability to being shown up through *elenchos* and radically inverted—that makes for the dramatic comedy of the dialogue.

It is instructive that, following Gorgias's withdrawal from the *agōn* of *logoi* with Socrates, it is Gorgias's account of rhetoric's power along with his reputational standing that is at issue in the often-heated exchanges between Socrates, Polus, and Callicles. Socrates's portrait of rhetoric as shameful *kolakeia* rather pointedly gestures toward Gorgias the famed orator as a *kolax*.[22] Polus's furious response to Socrates shows the depth of his commitment to Gorgias the person and to Gorgianic rhetoric as a profession (461b ff.). Yet,

---

[21] At *Gorgias* 456c, Gorgias glosses the "use of rhetoric [τῇ ῥητορικῇ χρῆσθαι]" as a matter of engaging in *agōn* [ἀγωνίᾳ]—a point which Socrates will compel him to clarify, and which leads to the *elenchos* that follows.

[22] See E.R. Dodds, *Plato,* Gorgias (Oxford: Clarendon, 1959), 225, where it is noted that the Greek *kolax* finds its English equivalents in terms such as "lick-spittle," "bum-sucker," and the like.

Polus is incapable of understanding power except in the sense of someone being able to do whatever seems (*dokein*) good to him—a situation that Socrates makes fun of in the image he conjures up of a person armed with a knife in a crowded marketplace, who thinks himself possessing "tyrannical and astonishing power [δύναμίς τις καὶ τυραννὶς θαυμασία]" since he could murder anyone who it seems (δόξῃ) good to him to murder (469d). Socrates critiques Polus's conception of power, and self-reflexively critiques their proceeding by way of their opinion (*doxa*) on such matters, when he says to Polus: "But surely, that's not great power [τὸ μέγα δύνασθαι], merely doing what seems good to one [τὸ ποιεῖν ἃ δοκεῖ αὐτῷ]—or doesn't it seem so to you [ἢ δοκεῖ σοι;]?" (469d-e). Presumably, Callicles agrees with Polus that, no matter what arguments he presents, things seem to Socrates just as they seem to his interlocutors (471e)—for Callicles's question as to whether Socrates is serious (*spoudazei*) or is just kidding around (*paizei*) (481b) insinuates that there is a systematic insincerity on Socrates's part. He points out how ridiculous they would seem to be if in fact Socrates is right, for they would be doing the exact opposite of what they should (481c). In the exchange between Callicles and Socrates, there erupts a comedy of inversions: Socrates's agonistic prowess in carrying out an *elenchos* of Polus is likened to lisping child's play, something unmanly and worthy of a whipping (485a-e); Callicles's hypothesized Great Man, who shows forth the power of nature in trampling upon the *nomoi* of the weak (483c-484b), is likened to a catamite who enjoys being used and abused for another's pleasure (494b-e). How is this not a further illustration—both comedic and serious—of the slipperiness and insecurity of *doxa* recognized in Gorgias's *Encomium of Helen*? Callicles forcefully rejects Socrates's practice of *elenchos* in favor of *doxa* and the other good things that go with it (486c-d), and yet, after carrying out an *elenchos* of Callicles's conception of power, Socrates still gestures toward their reliance upon *doxa* when he says to Callicles: "I know well that should you agree with me in what my soul believes [εὖ οἶδ᾽ ὅτι, ἄν μοι σὺ ὁμολογήσῃς περὶ ὧν ἡ ἐμὴ ψυχὴ δοξάζει], then it is the very truth [ταῦτ᾽ ἤδη ἐστὶν αὐτὰ τἀληθῆ]" (486e).

The comedy of inversions dramatized in Plato's *Gorgias* is perhaps an especially vivid example of what Socrates said about elenctic contestation in general in the *Apology*. There, while denying that he was a teacher to anyone (*Apology*, 33a-b), Socrates nonetheless admitted that the young people of Athens would follow him around as he subjected others to *elenchos*, since, as he put it, it is "not unpleasant [οὐκ ἀηδές]" to watch someone being shown up in public (*Apology*, 33c). In the *Gorgias*, as elsewhere in Plato's dialogues, it is evident that that the "pleasure" involved in spectating upon *elenchos* is sometimes, at least, a pleasure tied to the underlying comedy. Yet, that *agōn* in its various forms should involve the showing-forth of *dunamis*, the power or ability of those engaged in the contest, as well as its seeming or appearing-to-the audience in this way, is something that should not surprise us—and indeed we find *dunamis* and *doxa* as structural components of philosophy as its own form of *agōn*. Philosophical agonism happens by way of a contestation in *logoi*, structured precisely in such a way that the ability or inability of the contestants comes to light (e.g., one's ability to give a compelling account, to defend oneself against objections, etc., or the inability of one's interlocutor to survive elenctic questioning).[23] And while the *Gorgias* shows the most sustained practice of and reflection upon philosophical agonism, this attention to the showing-forth of ability or inability at the heart of philosophy as *agōn* is a common theme in Plato's dialogues: from Socrates's observations on Euthyphro's inability to give an adequate account of piety in the *Euthyphro*, to the unforgettable portrait of the lawcourt-agonist at a loss in the so-called "Digression" of the *Theaetetus* (172d-177b), to the agonistic character of dialectic as theorized by Socrates in the *Republic* (534b-c). In each of these passages, we find the agonism in question operating by way of *doxa* not in the narrow

[23] See Heather L. Reid, *Athletics and Philosophy in the Ancient World: Contests of Virtue* (London and New York: Routledge Press, 2011), 4, for the argument that philosophy and Olympic-style athletic competitions share an orientation toward open and impartial testing, as opposed to dogmatic or "relativistic" standards; and further, that "Socratic *agōn* serves a personal examination function akin to the character-revealing or character-building aspects of athletic competition" (49).

sense of "opinion" but in the broader sense of *dokein/phainesthai* as a multi-faceted seeming or appearing—precisely because philosophy as *agōn* takes place within what we might call the *elenctic theater*, where the interlocutors come to be seen as capable or incapable by the audience and by themselves.

The Eleatic Stranger's account of *elenchos* as *katharsis* in Plato's *Sophist* offers a theoretical outline of the various elements of the *elenctic theater* dramatized in the dialogues: someone who "thinks he's saying something though he's saying nothing [διερωτῶσιν ὧν ἂν οἴηταί τίς τι πέρι λέγειν λέγων μηδέν]" is selected to undergo *elenchos*, and the cross-examination of him shows that his *logoi* contradict themselves (230b). Only by seeing this (ὁρῶντες) through *elenchos* are those who undergo it "set free from their inflated and rigid beliefs about themselves [περὶ αὑτοὺς μεγάλων καὶ σκληρῶν δοξῶν ἀπαλλάττονται]"; and, for the Eleatic Stranger, "no setting-free is more pleasant to hear or has a more lasting effect [τῶν πασῶν τε ἀπαλλαγῶν ἀκούειν τε ἡδίστην καὶ τῷ πάσχοντι βεβαιότατα γιγνομένην]" (230c). On this account, the soul will not benefit from learning until *elenchos*

> induces in the one undergoing it a state of shame [πρὶν ἂν ἐλέγχων τις τὸν ἐλεγχόμενον εἰς αἰσχύνην καταστήσας], removes the opinions that interferes with learning [τὰς τοῖς μαθήμασιν ἐμποδίους δόξας ἐξελών], and shows it forth purified, believing that it knows only those things that it does know, and nothing more [καθαρὸν ἀποφήνῃ καὶ ταῦτα ἡγούμενον ἅπερ οἶδεν εἰδέναι μόνα, πλείω δὲ μή]. (*Sophist* 230c-d)

Accordingly, shame is an essential component in any properly philosophical *agōn*, as attested to and reiterated across Plato's dialogues. Alcibiades's portrait of Socrates in the *Symposium*, as the one person able to make him feel shame (*Symposium*, 216b), to make him feel that his life was not worth living as it was (*Symposium*, 216a)—an effect brought about, he says, by listening to Socrates's *logoi* (*Symposium*, 215e)—points toward the centrality of shame within the philosophical practice of *agōn*. Even if I, the participant in *agōn*, do not appear to the audience to be inconsistent in the account

I am giving or incapable of defending the account against objections, I should appear so to myself, and the shame elicited by this appearing-incapable-to-myself is proper and possibly *kathartic*.[24] By the same token, my appearing-one-with-myself, in-harmony-with myself as I defend my account over objections in a well-structured philosophical *agōn*, brings to appearance a *dunamis* that cannot be overpowered or compelled simply by however many critics there might be out there—as if philosophical argument were decided by a popular vote (cf. *Gorgias* 472b-c).

In the theoretical outline of *elenchos* in Plato's *Sophist*, as in its dramatization in the *Gorgias*, we see a complexity in one's relatedness-to-one's-opinion-of-oneself—and it is precisely this complexity that Gorgias's distinction between *pistis* and *doxa* in the *Encomium of Helen* brings into focus. Thus, we can analyze the "inflated and rigid beliefs about themselves [περὶ αὑτοὺς μεγάλων καὶ σκληρῶν δοξῶν]" targeted by the practitioner of *elenchos* in Plato's *Sophist* as the sort of *pistis* vis-à-vis *doxa* that *logos*—in this case, Socratic *elenchos*—is capable of altering; on the other hand, one's confidence in one's *logos* having survived *elenchos*, one's sense of being in harmony with oneself and "being one" in Socrates's sense, no matter what one's opponents say (482a-c), is a phenomenon that we can analyze as the strengthening of *pistis* related to one's opinion (*doxa*) of oneself. To reiterate the point that I've been stressing throughout, *doxa* in the robust sense of a multi-faceted *dokein*/*phainesthai* plays a decisive role within philosophical agonism because what is being judged through *elenchos* is not just one's argument, but *oneself* as someone capable or incapable of defending that argument, articulating the argument in different words or generating revised arguments—and thus not merely saying the same thing the same way like a rhapsode reciting lines or an orator

[24] See Jill Gordon, *Turning Toward Philosophy: Literary Device and Dramatic Structure in Plato's Dialogues* (University Park: Pennsylvania State University Press, 1998), 129ff., for discussion of shame involving awareness of one's identity, and the possible transformation of one's identity in the face of Socratic questioning.

repeating stock-phrases.[25] Here we can appreciate the ironic distinction deployed by Socrates in the *Gorgias* between speaking toward the matter under discussion (*pros to pragma*) and speaking toward the person with whom he's engaged in *agōn* (*pros tina*) (457c-e). Socrates assures Gorgias that he's not after *him*, but that he's just focused on the matter at issue in their discussion (cf. 457e-458b). And yet, quite clearly, Socrates is also after Gorgias: the *elenchos* seeks to refute Gorgias's account of rhetoric as domination-of-the-audience and, at the same time, expose the Gorgianic orator as a *kolax* who panders to the audience.

As you can imagine, this reading of Plato's *Gorgias* is not without detractors. For example, Ewegen has challenged the ironic reading of Socrates deploying the distinction between speaking *pros to pragma*, and speaking *pros tina*, in his *elenchos* of Gorgias.[26] Whereas I find a great deal of ironic dissimulation in how Socrates presents himself to Gorgias and their audience in the dialogue, having as his agenda from the outset to deliver an account of rhetoric as flattery *precisely to expose Gorgias to the audience in the most unflattering way*, Ewegen has argued (against my reading) that Socrates is sincere in his self-presentation vis-à-vis Gorgias, and that his questioning of Gorgias should be read as an instance of philosophical "maieutics." In fact, Ewegen contends that Socrates surrenders his "will in the face of the *logos* so as to let truth come to pass," that Socrates's statements regarding rhetoric as *kolakeia* are, in his words, "more structurally akin to questions than they are to assertions," and so on.[27] While Ewegen is certainly insightful in emphasizing what he calls "self-erasure" in Socrates's philosophical activity, to my mind this erasure of one's self that is constantly underway in philosophical activity is neither incompatible with the agonistic character of *elenchos*, nor

[25] Compare *Protagoras* 328e-329b, where Socrates says, "[S]uppose you put a question to one of [the orators]—they are just like books [ὥσπερ βιβλία], incapable of either answering you or putting a question of their own"—at which point he likens these orators to "brazen vessels [that] ring a long time after they have been struck and prolong the note unless you put your hand on them."

[26] S. Montgomery Ewegen, *The Way of the Platonic Socrates*, 55n18.

[27] Ewegen, *The Way of the Platonic Socrates*, 40-42.

does it preclude Socrates being "after" Gorgias in his exchange with him, utilizing irony in order to accomplish this. In any case, the interpretive issues involved here are not limited to Plato's *Gorgias*, but apply to the question of irony across Plato's dialogues. While some interpreters are hesitant to see Socrates deploying irony if it involves dissembling (*eirōneia*) on his part, others—myself included—agree with Rossetti's analysis that "a tendency to concealment systematically marks Socrates's peculiar way of shaping dialogical interplay."[28]

What is worth pointing out in the present context is that there is an intriguing parallel between Socrates's use of irony in Plato's dialogues and the "performative" character of Gorgianic *logos* sketched out above. Schiappa has argued that *logos* in the performative sense theorized by Gorgias "gives control of the auditory experience more to the speaker."[29] Rossetti, offering almost a parallel analysis of Socrates's rhetoric, urges us to "focus on Socrates's peculiar way of shaping verbal interchanges":

> Replacing a speech with a talk or conversation, [Socrates] is able at once to bewilder his interlocutor by neutralizing the arguments of the latter and to convey the impression of opening new avenues for his thought and/or for his way of life [....] As a matter of fact, the character of these talks becomes part of the overall (macro-rhetorical) strategy [...] to lead the interlocutor into letting down his guard and to impose upon him a number of conversational obligations.[30]

---

[28] Livio Rossetti, "The Rhetoric of Socrates," *Philosophy and Rhetoric* 22(4): 233. On the complexity of irony, both Socratic and Platonic, and its structural significance for Plato's portrayal of Socrates, see Gordon, *Turning Toward Philosophy*, 118ff., and Charles Griswold, "Irony in the Platonic Dialogues," *Philosophy and Literature* 26 (2002): 84–106.

[29] Schiappa, *The Beginning*, 100.

[30] Rossetti, "The Rhetoric of Socrates," 227-228. Compare Xenophon's remarks on Socrates in *Memorabilia*: Critias and Alcibiades, two of the most ambitious men in Athens, were attracted to Socrates because they knew "that he could do as he wished in argument with anyone who

Similarly, Roochnik argues that Socrates's performance in dialogues like *Gorgias* can be analyzed in terms not far removed from those of Gorgianic rhetoric: "Socrates," he writes, "is himself manifestly rhetorical. He knows how to refute, how to embarrass, how to exhort others to philosophize. He is superbly responsive to the dramatic *kairos* in which he finds himself."[31] The use of irony on the part of Socrates, as well as on the part of Plato as author, complicates the distinction between the rhetorical and the philosophical, just as we have seen it bring together the comedic and the serious in creative tension.

Finally, the inescapable workings of irony, comedy, and agonistic struggle in Plato's *Gorgias* complicate any straightforward answer to the question, much debated in the scholarship, as to whether Socrates succeeds at what he aimed to accomplish with his interlocutors. The question is difficult in large part because we approach the dialogue with an orientation toward "success" or "failure" that presupposes an understanding of philosophy-versus-rhetoric which the dialogue itself calls into question.

The strange holding-together of the comedic and the serious in the agonistic drama of the dialogue, whatever we call it in terms of the philosophy/rhetoric divide, is a far cry from what Stanley Fish identified as the *desideratum* behind philosophical critiques of rhetoric: namely, "to establish a form of communication that escapes partiality and aids us in first determining and then affirming what is absolutely and objectively true, a form of communication that in its structure and operations is the very antithesis of rhetoric, of

---

conversed with him [τοῖς δὲ διαλεγομένοις αὐτῷ πᾶσι χρώμενον ἐν τοῖς λόγοις ὅπως βούλοιτο]" (I.2.14).

[31] David Roochnik, *Of Art and Wisdom: Plato's Understanding of* Technē (University Park: Pennsylvania State University Press, 1996), 233. See also David Roochnik, "Socrates' Rhetorical Attack on Rhetoric," in *The Third Way: New Directions in Platonic Studies*, ed. F. Gonzales (Lanham, MD: Rowman and Littlefield, 1995), 81–94, who notes this further similarity: "While Gorgias offers to field, and presumably answer, all questions, Socrates spends his days wandering the agora, asking all kinds of questions" (91).

passionate partisan discourse."[32] Has Socrates succeeded in *persuading* his interlocutors in the *Gorgias*? Certainly not by the terms set out in Gorgias's *Encomium of Helen*, since he has not (we suspect) effectively substituted one *doxa* for another in the souls of the interlocutors and their audience. At the same time, Socrates has succeeded in *unnerving* them—what else should we call his demonstrated ability to force Gorgias into withdrawing from the *agōn*, to provoke laughter and perplexed head-scratching from Polus, and to shock Callicles into an embittered silence by the dialogue's end? Socrates has, to use the theory from §13 in Gorgias's *Encomium of Helen*, in some way altered the *pistis*—the belief or confidence or conviction—with which they cling to the *doxa* at stake in their *agōn* with Socrates. And Plato's dramatizing this *unnerving* of a prominent orator along with his tag-team intellectual allies, even while they call Socrates "boorish" and "demagogic" and "nonsensical" and "violent"—well, it makes for some great comedy.

---

32 Stanley Fish, *Doing What Comes Naturally* (Durham and London: Duke University Press, 1989), 481.

Sonja Tanner[1]

Child's Play: The Power of Comedy in Gorgias of Leontinoi and Plato's *Gorgias*

A significant gap exists between the recent and ancient receptions of Plato's *Gorgias*. Contemporary scholars regularly remark on the bitterness and hostility of the dialogue, its mood is described as "dark gloom" and "somber darkness."[2] Fussi's title asks, "why is the *Gorgias* so bitter?"[3] Klosko calls the dialogue the "tragedy of philosophy."[4] While there are tragic elements in the dialogue, this reception does not match that from ancient sources. Athenaeus describes Gorgias's alleged response to it:

> It is reported that Gorgias, himself reading the dialogue named after him, remarked to his intimates, 'What nice satire Plato knows how to write! [ὡς καλῶς οἶδε Πλάτων ἰαμβίζειν].' And Hermippus in his work *On Gorgias* says, 'When Gorgias arrived in Athens after dedicating the gold statue of himself at Delphi, Plato, seeing him, said: "Here comes our noble and golden Gorgias!," to which Gorgias replied: "Noble indeed and new is this Archilochus that Athens has produced."'[5]

Kurke deems this anecdote a "chronological impossibility" and "doxographic fantasy […] for 'Gorgias' here characterizes Plato's

---

[1] Sonja Tanner is Professor of Philosophy and Director of Classics at the University of Colorado, Colorado Springs, USA. Her research interests focus on the intersections of philosophy and literature in Plato, and specifically the role of comedy in Plato's dialogues. She is the author of *In Praise of Plato's Poetic Imagination* (2010, Lexington), and *Plato's Laughter: Socrates as Satyr and Comical Hero* (2017, SUNY Press).

[2] James A. Arieti, *Interpreting Plato: The Dialogues as Drama* (Savage, MD: Rowman and Littlefield, 1991), 92n2 and 86, respectively.

[3] Alessandra Fussi, "Why Is the *Gorgias* So Bitter?" *Philosophy and Rhetoric* 33.1 (2000).

[4] George Klosko, "The Insufficiency of Reason in Plato's *Gorgias*," *Western Political Quarterly* 36.4 (1983): 593.

[5] Athenaeus, *The Deipnosophists,* trans. C.B. Gulick (Cambridge, MA: Harvard University Press, 1980), 11.505de.

genre as iambic blame poetry and identifies Plato himself with Archilochus, the preeminent archaic practitioner of this low form."[6] While generic identification may be too extreme—a function of Gorgias's own humor perhaps—the contrast in receptions raises the question as to whether the "low form" of comedy's presence may have been more apparent in antiquity. What might Gorgias and other ancient sources have seen in Plato's dialogue that scholars since have largely missed?

In what follows, I argue that Socrates plays the stock comic role of the elderly schoolboy in Plato's *Gorgias*, and that this implicates not only Callicles and other interlocutors, but perhaps also Gorgias himself (via the *Encomium of Helen*) in its comedy. Not only does recognizing the role and power of comedy change the tone of the dialogue, it underscores the dialogue as drama as well as shifting the focus inwards. Rather than merely turning laughter into a rhetorical jab against his agonistic opponents, Socrates turns laughter upon himself as a means of philosophical introspection and invites the dialogue's audience to do so as well. This result implies that the power of comedy includes opening up the possibility of a self-reflective laughter.

The *Gorgias*'s Theatricality

We tend to assume that the dialogues functioned in antiquity as they exist for us today, namely, as written texts to be read silently to oneself. Ancient receptions of them, as well as textual evidence, point in another direction. One clue as to why ancient sources read the *Gorgias* as more comical might lie here. As Nikos Charalabopoulos explains, ancient taxonomies of the dialogues divide them into trilogies in the 1st century CE by Aristophanes of Byzantium and tetralogies in the 2nd century CE by Thrasyllus, echoing the practice of dramatists.[7] A fragmentary passage in a 2nd century BCE papyrus found recently in Oxyrhynchos, Egypt, reads: "For the *Cratylus* used to be sung ([προ]ήιδετο) as a prelude, [bringing in] (his) teaching on

---

[6] Leslie Kurke, *Aesopic Conversations* (Princeton, NJ: Princeton University Press, 2011), 259.

[7] Nikos G. Charalabopoulos, *Platonic Drama and its Ancient Reception* (Cambridge: Cambridge University Press, 2012), 156-57.

correctness of names. Directly after this [dialogue] comes the *Theaetetus,* and following upon the *Theaetetus*, the *Sophist* and *Statesman.*"[8] A third-century papyrus also found in Oxyrhynchos contains fragments from the *Protagoras,* which include dots and strokes above the words suggesting ekphonetic notation, similar to the musical notation later used for the singing of Gospels in church.[9] In *Sympotic Questions,* furthermore, Plutarch describes the ideal sympotic entertainment as productions of Platonic dialogues, writing that slaves (*paides*) recited the dialogues "by heart" and modulated their voices (*phōnēs plasma*) and postures (*schēma*) according to the words, adding that "men of rigorous education and culture loved these productions immensely."[10] Athenaeus's *Deipnosophists* (376c-383f) offers similar testimony on the dialogues' performances as dinner theater.[11] While it is not my intention here to *prove* that Platonic dialogues were usually recited or performed, it is enough to recognize this as a reasonable possibility, and to read the *Gorgias* with this possibility in mind.

Textual evidence supports a dramatic reading of the dialogues. The *Gorgias* begins with a scene shift from the marketplace to Callicles's home. There are several references to what Tarrant calls a "stage-crowd" in *Gorgias* as if to a chorus (458b-c, 473c, 506a).[12] Interlocutors refer to an audience, delineating the "actors" from those listening, a move typical of theatrical performance. Gorgias says to Socrates: "we should keep in mind *the people who are present here* [...] before you came, I gave *them* a long presentation" (458 b-c, emphasis mine).[13] Chaerephon employs such deictic language characteristic of theater, saying "you yourselves hear the commotion *these men* are making" (458c). Gorgias does too, saying "if it suits *these people...*" (458e). The dialogue makes references to dramatic costume,

---

[8] Quoted from Sedley's translation in Charalabopoulos, *Platonic Drama,* 193.

[9] Charalabopoulos, *Platonic Drama,* 156-57.

[10] Plutarch. *Moralia, Volume IX,* trans. E.L. Minar (Cambridge, MA: Harvard University Press, 1961), 711bc.

[11] Discussed by Charalabopoulos, *Platonic Drama,* 215-23.

[12] D. Tarrant, "Plato as Dramatist," *Journal of Hellenic Studies* 75 (1955): 86.

[13] Plato, *Gorgias,* trans. Donald J. Zeyl in *Complete Works,* ed. John M. Cooper (Indianapolis: Hackett, 1997), 791-869.

such as padding or stays (*schēmasin*) and make-up (*chrōmasin*) (465b4).[14] Socrates uses musical and theatrical examples (501d-502c), saying "I think it's better to have my lyre or a chorus that I might lead out of tune and dissonant, and have the vast majority of men disagree with me and contradict me, than to be out of harmony with myself, to contradict myself, though I'm only one person" (482b-c). Such examples support Arieti's conclusion that "the *Gorgias* is a play in three acts and a prologue and epilogue."[15] Recognizing the dialogue's drama and theatricality impacts how we read it.

What sort of drama do we find in the *Gorgias*? Nightingale writes that "the coupling of the low and the high, the clownish and the serious, produces a vigorous hybrid; a text that constitutes itself by appropriating and defamiliarizing both tragedy and comedy."[16] While the dialogue is multigeneric, its heavy comic influence tends to be ignored, as though comedy is incompatible with serious philosophy. Further, dramatic pieces that are self-aware, address or refer to their audiences, or openly mention dramatic accoutrements and the trappings of theater (thus breaching the fourth wall) are metatheatrical comedy.[17] Socrates claims that performances that aim solely at giving audiences pleasure constitute flattery (501d1-502d8). These include dithyrambic choruses, aulos- and kithara-playing, and tragedy. What is striking is what is left out: "in the present passage comedy is left unmentioned. Presumably Plato thought that it *did* perform a useful social service by calling attention to abuses, and in

---

[14] E.R. Dodds, *Plato's Gorgias* (Oxford: Oxford University Press, 1959), 230.

[15] Arieti, *Interpreting Plato*, 81.

[16] Andrea Nightingale, "Plato's *Gorgias* and Euripides' *Antiope*: A Study in Generic Transformation," in *Classical Antiquity* 11.1 (1992): 141.

[17] Niall Slater, *The Theatre of the Mind* (Princeton: Princeton University Press, 1985), 14 describes metatheatre as self-conscious theatre that "demonstrates an awareness of its own theatricality." Charalabopoulos, *Platonic Drama*, 152 allows for the inclusion of the Platonic dialogue, defining it as "the evocation of theatrical discourse in the framework of dialogic text and its impact on/significance for the generic identity of the dialogue." On metatheatricality in Plato, see Sonja Tanner, "Trading Places and Parasites: The Metatheatrical Comedy of Plato's *Protagoras*," *Epoché* 25.2 (2021): 293-307

particular by mocking the sovereign *demos* itself."[18] Of what might comedy be capable? What is its *dunamis*?

Gorgias himself locates the *dunamis* of rhetoric in its effect upon the hearers. In the *Encomium of Helen*, Gorgias suggests as much in describing how *logos* is received. The power of *logos* for Gorgias is addressed as such:

> The effect of speech upon the structure of soul is as the structure of drugs over the nature of bodies; for just as different drugs dispel different secretions from the body, and some bring an end to disease, and others to life, so also in the case of speeches, some distress, others delight, some cause fear, others embolden their hearers, and some drug and bewitch the soul with a kind of evil persuasion.[19]

The *dunamis* of the *logos* acts like a drug (*pharmakon*) on the psyche (*Helen* 14). If Gorgias is successfully availing himself of the power of *logos* through his encomium, his listeners are entranced. Gorgias elaborates that "the power [δύναμις] of the incantation [ἐπῳδῆς] enchants and persuades and moves it by sorcery [γοητείᾳ]" (*Helen* 10). It is not only the effect of *logos*, but specifically its effect upon the *emotions* that drives its *dunamis*: "Through its compelling power over the emotions the *logos* becomes a δυνάστης μέγας (8) which accomplishes 'divine deeds' (θειότατα ἔργα) in arousing pity and fear, pleasure and pain."[20] If we have misread the tone of the *Gorgias*,

---

[18] Dodds, *Plato's Gorgias*, 322.

[19] Gorgias, *Encomium of Helen*, 14: Τὸν αὐτὸν δὲ λόγον ἔχει ἥ τε τοῦ λόγου δύναμις πρὸς τὴν τῆς ψυχῆς τάξιν ἥ τε τῶν φαρμάκων τάξις πρὸς τὴν τῶν σωμάτον φύσιν.

[20] Charles P. Segal, "Gorgias and the Psychology of the Logos," *Harvard Studies in Classical Philology* 66 (1962): 120. Assuming Gorgias has a consistent understanding of *logos* and its *dunamis*, what is in the *Helen* is inconsistent with what is attributed to him elsewhere. Plato's Protarchus says, "On many occasions, Socrates, I have heard Gorgias insist that the art of persuasion is superior to all others because it enslaves all the rest, with their own consent, *not by force*, and is therefore by far the best of all the arts" (*Philebus* 58a-b; my emphasis).

this becomes exacerbated. That we *have* misread it as merely a bitter, acrimonious, and hostile dialogue is supported by its many uses of comic language, examples, and tropes.

Socrates's Use of Comic Language and Examples

The *Gorgias* uses overtly comic language. At 499b9, Callicles says to Socrates, "even if a person grants some point to you in jest, you gladly fasten on it, the way boys do," to which Socrates replies: "Oh [ἰοὺ ἰοὺ], Callicles! What a rascal you are. You treat me like a child" (499b9). The exclamation ἰοὺ ἰοὺ is one of surprise, or as Dodds points out, "pained astonishment," but the expression has distinct roots in comedy, recognized in Aristophanes as a comical cliché.[21] The chorus in Aristophanes's *Clouds* describes a personification of Comedy who modestly avoids using comic clichés: "see how modest she [Comedy] is […] who […] has come, having stitched to her no leathern phallus hanging down […] nor does the old man who speaks the verses beat the person near him with his staff […] nor does she shout ἰοὺ ἰού."[22]

In addition to its being the opening cry of the comedy, ἰοὺ is repeated four more times in the *Clouds* and in other comic plays.[23] That these were already cliché in Aristophanes's time renders them distinctly *passé* in Plato's, but this is not the dialogue's only use of comic and colloquial language. At 497b4, Socrates says "μηδαμῶς" (please don't!), a colloquialism frequent in Aristophanes.[24] Plato reproduces Gorgias's dialect at several points (452e and 456a-457c): according to the scholiast, Gorgias's words for handicraft (χειρούργημα, 450b) and for ratification (κύρωσις, 450b) are

---

Does persuasion control by force, as suggested in the *Helen*, or by consent, as implied in the *Philebus*?

[21] Dodds, *Plato's Gorgias*, 316.

[22] Aristophanes, *Clouds*, in *Complete Plays of Aristophanes*, ed. Moses Hadas (New York: Bantam, 1988), 518-562.

[23] These occur at lines 1, 518, 1170, 1321, 1476. In *Knights*, Cleon utters it after being struck by the sausage-seller: ἰοὺ ἰού, τύπτουσί μ᾽οἱ ξυνωμόται (Aristophanes, *Complete Plays of Aristophanes*, 451).

[24] Dodds, *Plato's Gorgias*, 313.

"Sicelisms," and thus add a mimetic touch to the dialogue.[25] At 490d10, Callicles asks ποίων ἱματίων: "What have overcoats to do with it?" Dodds writes that "picking up a word and flinging it back with a scornful ποῖος [of what kind] is a frequent repartee in Aristophanes and Plato."[26]

Threats of beating are another comic cliché mentioned by Aristophanes's chorus that recur in the *Gorgias*.[27] Flogging or beating (πληγήν, 480c, and also at 485c, 485d, 524c, 527d) are frequent, such as the "knock on the jaw" (ἐπὶ κόρρης τύπτοντα; 486c, 508d, and 527d) that is repeatedly threatened. At 486c2-3 Socrates warns of what is either comical or low to come with the term ἀγροικότερον (which means dwelling in the fields, common, or boorish). Dodds writes that "the 'coarse' expression is ἐπι κόρρης τύρροντα, 'giving him a crack on the jaw.' [...] Such a blow constituted a major assault (ὕβρις) in Attic law."[28] Recognizing such threats of beating as comic clichés instead of aggressive, physical threats dramatically changes the tone of the dialogue.

In the *Gorgias*, as in other dialogues, Socrates converses with the upper crust of Greek society, but he does not behave like it. Instead, he uses base examples to provoke his patrician interlocutors. Socrates compares what the rhetoricians think of as the "supreme art" of political activity—i.e., rhetoric—to cooking and other "low" activities.[29] He offers checkers as an example of a *technē* (450d). He speaks of itching and scratching (494c-d). At 516a, he mentions donkeys kicking, butting, and biting. Such examples are not without substance. As Dodds writes, "Callicles ridiculed the democratic politicians' futile attempt to tame the lion (483e); Socrates taxes them with precisely the opposite error—they have let the domestic herds

[25] Douglas M. MacDowell, and Gorgias, *Gorgias's Encomium of Helen* (Bristol: Bristol Classical Press, 1999), 258.

[26] The example he gives is *Clouds* 367, "ποῖος Ζεύς; οὐ μὴ ληρήσεις" (Dodds, *Plato's Gorgias*, 290).

[27] While it is often the *alazon*, or imposter, who is beaten, physical threats are not exclusive to imposters.

[28] Dodds, *Plato's Gorgias*, 278.

[29] Arieti, *Interpreting Plato*, 83-84.

run wild."[30] As we will see, these domestic herds include a range of animals from donkeys to stone-curlews, all to prod and provoke those with whom he is speaking. Socrates's choice in examples works in this sense, but also in another.

Socrates uses common examples to annoy his aristocratic interlocutors and his base, occupational examples successfully offend Callicles (491a and 517d-e).[31] Dodds claims that "Callicles objects to Socrates's cobblers and dry-cleaners, not because he denies that government is a τέχνη, but because he does not like to have the ἀμείνους compared to anything so low."[32] At 448b4-c1, Socrates gives the example of the shoemaker, which is substituted with more "polite professions" by Chaerephon.[33] Amongst Socrates's examples are birds that defecate and eat simultaneously (494b), compulsive scratchers (494c), and the *kinaidos* who not only plays the passive sexual role but also enjoys it (494e). Callicles cringes at this coarseness (494e) and complains about Socrates's talking of cobblers and fullers (491a) and to "things low and common" (φορτικὰ καὶ δημηγορικά; 482e). The passage from which several of these examples come offers insight into the larger strategy Socrates employs.

Using such common examples has a particularly acute effect when deployed against a serious answer. When Callicles ventures a definition of living pleasantly as "having as much as possible flow in," (494b) Socrates turns his serious attempt at definition into a vulgar comedy:

> Socrates: Isn't it necessary, then, that if there's a lot flowing in, there should also be a lot going out and that there should be big holes for what's passed out?
>
> Callicles: Certainly.
>
> Socrates: Now you're talking about the life of a stone-curlew instead of that of a corpse or a stone. Tell me, do you say that

[30] Dodds, *Plato's Gorgias*, 358.

[31] See Nightingale, "Plato's *Gorgias* and Euripides' *Antiope*," 140-41.

[32] Dodds, *Plato's Gorgias*, 290.

[33] Dodds, *Plato's Gorgias*, 191.

> there is such a thing as hunger, and eating when one is hungry?
>
> Callicles: Yes, there is.
>
> Socrates: And thirst, and drinking when one is thirsty?
>
> Callicles: Yes, and also having all other appetites and being able to fill them and enjoy it, and so live happily.
>
> Socrates: Very good, my good man! Do carry on the way you've begun, and take care not to be ashamed. And I evidently shouldn't shrink from being ashamed, either. Tell me now first whether a man who has an itch and scratches it and can scratch to his heart's content, scratch his whole life long, can also live happily.
>
> Callicles: What nonsense, Socrates. You're a regular crowd pleaser.
>
> Socrates: That's just how I shocked Polus and Gorgias and made them be ashamed. You certainly won't be shocked, however, or be ashamed, for you're a brave man. (494b-d)

Socrates masterfully twists a serious response into comedy, and he admits to having stunned Polus and Gorgias with the same tactic. He also flatters Callicles as being brave, goading him on. All of this comic material supports Gorgias's assessment of the eponymous dialogue, but he does not merely describe it as comic but as satirical.

Perhaps the most direct evidence for why Gorgias might have called the eponymous dialogue a lampoon lies in the parody of Gorgianic style in *Gorgias*. Levett argues that Socrates parodies Gorgias performatively "by means of his own rhetorical technique," polyptoton,[34] a rhetorical figure in which words of similar etymology are repeated. Polyptoton recurs at numerous points in the *Gorgias*: for example, at 487b4 (αὐτῶν αὐτὸς αὐτῷ ναντία…ἐναντίον, and at 448c7 (ἄλλοι ἄλλων ἄλλως). Such instances recall Gorgias's *Encomium* 11: ὅσοι δὲ ὅσους περὶ ὅσων.[35] In the *Phaedrus*, Socrates

---

[34] Brad Levett, "Parody in the 'Gorgias'," in *Phoenix* 59 ¾ (2005): 225.

[35] Dodds, *Plato's Gorgias*, 192.

names διπλασιολογία, or reduplicative speech, as a specialty of Polus's (*Phaedrus* 267b-c).[36] Accordingly, Socrates says to Polus: "Don't attack me, my peerless Polus, to address you in your own style" (467b-c). The style of the *Gorgias* is, Dodds claims, "Gorgian to the point of grotesqueness."[37] Plato also parodies Gorgias by introducing his reputed claim that he could answer anyone on anything, and yet Gorgias is quickly reduced to silence when he cannot answer Socrates's fairly simple question about his trade. The very fact that Polus and Callicles have the significant speaking roles that they do constitutes a joke on Gorgias. But Socrates's fun with Gorgias and friends does not end there.

Socrates the Opsimath

There is another answer to why Gorgias could have thought the *Gorgias* a lampoon. Socrates plays a comic role easily recognizable in antiquity but decidedly less so today: that of the opsimath, or late-learner. The late-learner is a comic figure described in Theophrastus's *Characters* 27, in Aristophanes's *Clouds,* and in Lucian's comic sketch *Hermotimus*.[38] The opsimath studies topics suitable for youth, but appears ridiculous in doing so at an advanced age among schoolboys of proper age. As Theophrastus characterizes him, the late-learner often forgets what he has learned, but is keen to show it off or compete in events for which he is no longer qualified. In the process, he makes a comic spectacle of himself. The late-learner thus exhibits a lack of self-knowledge.

Socrates plays this role in a number of dialogues.[39] In the *Euthydemus,* for example, Socrates indicates the role he is playing by

---

36 Dodds, *Plato's Gorgias*, 282.

37 Dodds, as quoted by Levett, "Parody in the 'Gorgias'," 219.

38 Harold Tarrant, "Plato, Prejudice, and the Mature-Age Student in Antiquity," in *Apeiron* 29.4 (1996): 106.

39 At the end of the *Laches,* for instance, the elderly Lysimachus and Socrates vouch to meet on the next day to return to school to learn some of the many things of which the dialogue has shown them to be ignorant. Lysimachus blames his old age and consequent forgetfulness for why he is unable to participate in the dialogue. This underlines the comedy

volunteering that he is currently studying music with Connus, who is referred to comically as an "old-man teacher" (*Euthydemus* 272c).[40] Tarrant claims that this term appears to be "a comic coinage, both because of its length and because it would fit comfortably into anapaestic or dactylic metre."[41] Socrates pulls his interlocutors into the role by indicating that Dionysodorus and Euthydemus had learned the sophistic art at a late age and not before (*Euthydemus* 303e). While Socrates may not be ashamed of playing such a role, Dionysodorus and Euthydemus certainly dislike the implications. Both the aged schoolboy and his teacher become comic fodder, as Aristophanes depicts Strepsiades and Socrates in the *Clouds*, where Socrates is the late-learner Strepsiades's teacher, who fittingly threatens his schoolboy with corporal punishment (*Clouds* 493-4).

Socrates plays the role of late-learner in the *Gorgias* as well. Perhaps in an attempt to thwart the tactic of taking seriously what was said in jest, Callicles tells Socrates that "if a person grants some point to you in jest, you gladly fasten on it, the way boys do [ὥσπερ τὰ μειράκια]" (499b6). Dodds explains that "adolescents are apt to take seriously what was meant only in play."[42] Callicles may imagine himself to have landed a blow on Socrates, who ought to be ashamed of the comparison to an elderly student and impressed by his mighty

---

of the dialogue's ending with two old men promising to become schoolboys. In the *Euthydemus*, the sophistic brothers mock Socrates for his age, and he responds by playing it up, characterizing himself as a schoolboy needing to be taught by Dionysodorus and Euthydemus, and offering to hand himself over to them for instruction (285c). See Sonja Tanner, *Plato's Laughter: Socrates as Satyr and Comical Hero* (Albany: SUNY Press, 2017).

[40] Athenaeus, *Deipnosophistae* 11, 114. See Tarrant, "Plato, Prejudice," 111. Athenaeus interprets the *Euthydemus* as a portrayal of Euthydemus and Dionysodorus as late-learners.

[41] Athenaeus, *Deipnosophistae,* 112. See R.S.W. Hawtrey's *Commentary on Plato's Euthydemus* (*Memoirs of the American Philosophical Society* 147, *Mnemosyne,* 1981), 46. Tarrant suggests the term likely to have come from Ameipsias's *Connus,* in which Socrates appears in his *tribon,* rather than the more sophisticated *himation.*

[42] Dodds, *Plato's Gorgias,* 316.

interlocutor. Quite to the contrary, Socrates embraces this role for himself with no apparent shame and makes explicit Callicles's machismo. Socrates asks Callicles if it is "*those* manly activities," (τὰ τοῦ ἀνδρὸς δὴ ταῦτα), and the life of a rhetor to which Callicles is urging him (500c4). Dodds describes this *tauta* as "contemptuous."[43] Why would this be an effective tactic against Callicles?

Callicles idealizes a sort of manliness that Socrates's role-playing dramatically undercuts. Dodds explains that "for the school to which Callicles belongs 'unmanliness' was (and is) the most damning reproach: they pride themselves on being 'real he-men' [ὡς ἀληθῶς ἄνδρες]."[44] Socrates takes this so far as to play not only an "unmanly" role; he plays that of a child. There are multiple mentions of children, including fearing beneficial (but painful) medical treatments like a child (479b), Socrates's remark to Polus regarding "treat[ing] people like children" (502e), and Polus's infantilizing retort to Socrates that "a child is often called as witness to the obvious" (470c).[45] Perhaps to emphasize this emasculation further, Socrates swears by Hera, a woman's oath, and elsewhere (449d5) swears "by the dog" (μὰ τὸν κύνα), an oath made by a slave in Aristophanes's *Wasps* (83).[46] Socrates is far from the Calliclean ideal of manliness.

Several translations bury this theme. At one point Socrates invokes the bogeywoman Mormo (Μορμολύττη ἄυ, 473d3), who was used by mothers and nurses to frighten naughty children.[47] Zeyl translates this as "you're *spooking* me, Polus, instead of refuting me"—thus, the mention of Mormo drops out of the translation.[48] Further, Socrates is accused of what Zeyl translates as "playing to the

---

[43] Dodds, Plato's Gorgias, 316.

[44] Dodds, *Plato's Gorgias,* Callicles refers to such lack of manliness or courage at 492b1 (διὰ τὴν αὑτῶν ἀνανδρίαν).

[45] Dodds refers us to *Lysis* 205c1, *Euthydemus* 301c1, and Aeschines's *Against Timarchus* 1163, regarding children being witnesses to what is obvious. Dodds, *Plato's Gorgias,* 241.

[46] Socrates repeats this oath to Hera at *Apology,* 24e, and *Theaetetus,* 154d.

[47] See Aristophanes, *Birds,* 1244.

[48] Find Donald Zeyl's translation of the *Gorgias* in Cooper, *Plato: Complete Works* (Indianapolis: Hackett, 1997).

crowd [νεανιεύεσθαι]" (482c4), but which literally means "to become a youth." Socrates lobs a similar accusation back at Callicles, suggesting he is ἀκκίζῃ, which Dodds translates as "playing the simpleton."[49] Dodds points out that "the verb is derived from *Akko,* the name of a proverbially stupid woman, and means to 'sham stupid,' then generally to dissemble or be coy" (497a7).[50] The gendered put-down, which Callicles would likely be sensitive to, drops out of the translation.

Callicles makes Socrates's role-playing explicit: "you show yourself to the world in the shape of a (school) boy [μειρακιώδει]" (485e-86a). The theme runs throughout their exchange. Callicles asks Socrates: "Aren't you ashamed, *at your age,* of trying to catch people's words?" (489b-c, my emphasis). His attempt at shaming Socrates backfires. The more that Socrates plays this role, and shamelessly at that, the more annoyed his interlocutors become. Callicles describes what Socrates does as "mischief" (κακουργέω, 483a). Socrates describes himself as being "lectured to" and a "worthless fellow" (488a-b). Perhaps to Callicles's increasing annoyance, Socrates embraces the jest, describing Callicles as "scolding" him (497b). Not only does Socrates openly accept the put-down, he takes it one step further.

Socrates turns this comic role against his interlocutors, for in playing the role of the aged schoolboy, he implies that his interlocutors, like Connus, are "old-man teachers." In just the sort of reversal one might expect from a comic hero, Socrates flips the script on Callicles, begging him to "go easier on me in your teaching, so that I won't quit your school" (489d). This holds particular weight for those who fancy themselves "*real* men," as Callicles has implied. Socrates has successfully countered Callicles's attack on philosophy as shameful for an opsimath (484c485e) by casting Callicles in the comic role of γεροντοδιδάσκαλος.[51] While comical in itself, this adds

---

[49] Dodds, *Plato's Gorgias,* 312.

[50] Dodds, *Plato's Gorgias,* 312.

[51] The *Gorgias* is not alone in making charges against the opsimath. The *Euthydemus* includes several attacks on late-learners by Dionysodorus

a further twist to Callicles's threat of beating (486c), for this threat now becomes twisted to support Callicles's comical role as an old-man-teacher. Socrates can use comedy in this way because it contributes to his claim at the end of the dialogue that "it's not *seeming* to be good but *being* good that a man should take care of more than anything" (527b). Playing comic roles operates within a realm of appearances, and not necessarily that of what truly is, but fighting the accuracy of such comic attribution is particularly difficult if one denies any distinction between appearances and reality. As long as Socrates makes Callicles and others who deny this distinction *appear* to be old-man-teachers, they have little to do in defense of themselves. Herein lies the power of comedy.

The *Dunamis* of Comedy

Comedy's *dunamis,* as it is employed in both Plato's *Gorgias* and in Gorgias's *Encomium of Helen,* exposes various levels of awareness in realms such as distinctions between appearances and reality, as well as in another sense. In this way, comedy can at times make a philosophical point more effectively than an argument can. Socratic child's play in the *Gorgias* directly implicates Callicles, but Gorgias himself may not escape the insult, for Socrates's schoolboy may reference Gorgias's *Encomium of Helen*. A similar reflection back upon Callicles and company pertains to Gorgias who, in the *Helen,* claims it as his own "plaything." As Pratt indicates, "*paignion* indicates something to be left behind when childhood ceases."[52] Gorgias would then seem to be eligible for the same insult Callicles thinks he is using against Socrates: that he is indulging in child's play at a ripe old age, and, like Socrates, Gorgias thus cuts a comical figure. If this is right, Socrates's comic role in Plato's *Gorgias* reaches past the dialogue to include Gorgias's writing. While Socrates may have felt

---

and Euthydemus. The *Laches* ends with Socrates's suggestion that he and the aged Lysimachus return to school to inquire further. Socrates, in the *Republic* (VII 537b ff), on the other hand, *recommends* learning for those over 55. For more on this comic trope and its occurrences in the dialogues, see Tanner, *Plato's Laughter.*

[52] Jonathan Pratt, "On the Threshold of Rhetoric," *Classical Antiquity* 34.1 (2015): 177.

no shame at being called an elderly schoolboy, Gorgias, in deeming the dialogue "satire," appears more sensitive to its bite. But such comedy does more than denigrate.

Gorgias's final description of his encomium as a *paignion* has prompted broad speculation as to its meaning. Poulakos argues that Gorgias's choice of Helen and the word *paignion* are designed so as to mask his work as harmless and avoid threatening the status quo.[53] Porter claims that the use of *paignion*, "the final word of the speech [...] is devastating [...] inasmuch as it scandalously empties out the contents of whatever comes before it. It has also achieved some of what it was intended to do: invite endless speculation."[54] Gomperz suggests that this use of *paignion* implies that Gorgias "held no theories at all" and that he was thus a "philosophical nihilist."[55] I wish to offer a more charitable alternative, one which might bring Gorgias slightly closer to Plato, even if Socrates uses this to take another crack at Gorgias in Plato's dialogue. I suggest that Gorgias might be offering an antidote to the bewitching spell of persuasion through his use of *paignion*.

Akin to metatheatricality, Gorgias's use of the *paignion* breaks with what has preceded it and has a peculiar effect upon the audience. Gorgias's *Helen* suggests that "the *dunamis* of the incantation [ἐπῳδῆς] enchants and persuades and moves it by sorcery [γοητείᾳ]."[56] Whatever enchantment Gorgias enacts through his encomium is broken upon the listener's arrival at the *paignion*. MacDowell notes on *paignion* that "one may imagine the twinkle in Gorgias's eyes as he reveals in the very last word that he regards the whole paradoxical composition as a game."[57] The term breaks the spell of what preceded it, prompting questions instead as to what Gorgias might mean by it. While this sort of rupture tends to occur

---

[53] John Poulakos, "Gorgias' *Encomium of Helen* and the Defense of Rhetoric," *Rhetorica: The History of Rhetoric* 1.2 (1983): 7. Poulakos indicates this as a sophistic practice in *Protagoras* 316c-317c.

[54] James I. Porter, "The Seductions of Gorgias," *Classical Antiquity* 12.2 (1993): 275.

[55] Gomperz as characterized by Segal, "Gorgias and the Psychology," 100.

[56] MacDowell and Gorgias, *Encomium of Helen* 10.

[57] MacDowell and Gorgias, *Encomium of Helen*, 40.

in comic parabases, Gorgias avails himself of a direct address here, for it is specifically "an amusement for myself [ἐμὸν δὲ παίγνιον]."[58] It is aimed at its audience.

The *dunamis* of comedy in the *Gorgias* does more than change the tone of the dialogue: it also affects its audience. Ancient sources focus appreciation of comic laughter on its reception and emotional impact. For Quintilian, laughter is irrational and emotional, and its reception is unpredictable, but it can remove hatred and anger in audiences. Pseudo-Longinus describes laughter as a *pathos*, and claims "its ability to persuade emanates from its power to affect the emotions of the listeners."[59] We might wonder who the "listeners" are in the case of Platonic dialogues, and how they ought to be affected by its comedy.

We get several hints at an unexpected answer in the *Gorgias*. At 455c-d, Socrates suggests to Gorgias: "Perhaps there's actually *someone inside* [τῶν ἔνδον ὄντων] who wants to become your pupil [....] Consider yourself being questioned by them as well." Dodds takes τῶν ἔνδον ὄντων here to refer to the people who have attended Gorgias's lecture. At 458b6, the same people are referred to as being τῶν παρόντων (the people *who are present here*).[60] But another possibility lies closer at hand. Socrates says to Polus that "I do know how to produce one witness to whatever I'm saying, and that's the man I'm having a discussion with" (474a-b). Further, at 480d, Socrates suggests that "he should be *his own* chief accuser." Might the one "inside" who could become a pupil be *within* Gorgias or Socrates himself? Does comedy create such an internal *elenchus*?[61] And if so, are we, the dialogue's listeners, being addressed here and

---

[58] MacDowell and Gorgias, *Encomium of Helen*, 26-27.

[59] Pseudo-Longinus (*Subl.* 38.5-6), as described by Dimos Spatharas, "Persuasive ΓΕΛΟΣ: Public Speaking and the Use of Laughter," *Mnemosyne* 59.3 (2006): 387.

[60] Dodds, *Plato's Gorgias*, 209.

[61] For more on the possibility of an internal *elenchus*, see Sonja Tanner, "The Mask of 'Socrates': Imaginary Ridicule, Metatheatricality, and Self-Knowledge in Plato's *Hippias Major*," in *Harkening Towards Thaleia*, Cambridge University Press, forthcoming.

asked to acknowledge our own, inner students? While this paper will not attempt an answer, a more modest possibility is at hand.

The *dunamis* of comedy can break the enchantment of rhetoric and provoke self-reflexivity.[62] One point Gorgias and Plato appear to share is their use of self-reflective *logos*. After dangling the possibility of limitless power to his audience in the *Helen*, Gorgias exposes this as a game. By directly addressing his audience, Gorgias breaks his rhetorical spell.[63] By playing the aged schoolboy, Socrates involves himself in the comedy and implicates his interlocutors as his old-man teachers. In doing so, Socrates may be presenting Gorgias himself as the object of ridicule inasmuch as he is the one playing with a *paignion*, like a child. Aristotle relays that Gorgias recommended countering an enemy's seriousness with laughter, and an enemy's laughter with seriousness.[64] In this instance, Socrates may have bested Gorgias at his own game and had the last laugh. Gorgias's *logos*—his *dunamis megas*—is humbled by, of all things, an old man acting like a child.

---

[62] This echoes Ewegen's notion of comedy as a radical and self-aware playfulness. S. Montgomery Ewegen, *Plato's* Cratylus: *The Comedy of Language* (Bloomington: Indiana University Press, 2014), 16.

[63] Nick Lowe, *Comedy* (Cambridge: Cambridge University Press, 2007), 27 finds a distinction here between comedy and tragedy, stating that "tragedy never openly breaches the 'fourth wall' dividing the world of the play from the world of its spectators." Instead, tragedy requires this illusion to remain unbroken.

[64] Aristotle, *Rhetoric* 1419b3-5.

S. Montgomery Ewegen[1]

The Comedy of Power in Plato's *Gorgias*

In *The Way of the Platonic Socrates*, I argue that Plato's *Gorgias* offers a radical rethinking and inversion of the traditional understanding of political power.[2] As I there attempt to show, the Socrates of the *Gorgias* develops a novel understanding of political power as a kind of *submissiveness* to the philosophical *logos*, a *receptivity* to the unfolding of truth in speech that stands in stark contrast to the domineering and masculinized view of power proffered by the rhetoricians (and embodied especially by Callicles). Such submissive receptivity as Socrates develops operates as a gesture of *deference* to the philosophical *logos*, a gesture that proves to be the very precondition for true political power properly understood, insofar as it allows the ruler to rule in accordance with the truth of things rather than merely in accordance with his potentially errant will.

Despite whatever virtues this analysis of the *Gorgias* may have, it suffers from an inexcusable failure: namely, the failure to account for the role that *comedy* plays in the text's rethinking of the nature of political power. This failure is especially unforgivable given how overtly and unmistakably *funny* the *Gorgias* is. Although not as outrageously funny as the *Euthydemus* (with its scenes of slapstick hilarity) or the *Cratylus* (with its protracted etymological farce), the *Gorgias* is nonetheless a strikingly comedic dialogue filled to the brim with jokes,[3] parody,[4] comic insults, and even vulgarity.[5] Despite the tendency of contemporary commentators to downplay or outright

---

[1] S. Montgomery Ewegen is associate professor of philosophy at Trinity College in Hartford, Connecticut, USA. He is author of *Plato's Cratylus: The Comedy of Language* (2014) and *The Way of the Platonic Socrates* (2020). He is also co-translator, with Julia Goesser Assaiante, of Martin Heidegger's *Heraclitus* (2018) and *Correspondence: 1919-1973* (2021), a collection of letters between Martin Heidegger and Karl Löwith.

[2] S. Montgomery Ewegen, *The Way of the Platonic Socrates* (Bloomington: Indiana University Press, 2020), Chapter 2.

[3] See, for example, 449d.

[4] See, for example, 466d.

[5] See, for example, 444e.

overlook such elements, there is some evidence suggesting that the comedic tenor of the text was more widely acknowledged in antiquity. As Athenaeus wrote in the 3rd century BCE, recounting a story about Gorgias,

> The story goes that when Gorgias himself read the dialogue named after him, he said to his friends, 'Plato is quite talented at writing satire [ἰαμβίζειν]!' Herrmippus says in his *On Gorgias*: 'When Gorgias visited Athens after dedicating the gold statue of himself at Delphi, and Plato saw him and said: "Our fine, gold Gorgias has arrived!," Gorgias responded: "And this is a fine new Archilochus[6] that Athens has produced!"'[7]

As Leslie Kurke observes, this account of Gorgias responding to Plato's depiction of him is almost certainly apocryphal; nonetheless, it points to an appreciation operative at the time of the "generically low, scurrilous elements in Plato's mimetic prose writing."[8] In other words, as early at 300 CE there was an awareness of the *lowly*, comedic aspects of the *Gorgias,* although this awareness has dissipated somewhat over the intervening centuries.

Crucially, the comedy of the *Gorgias* does not merely serve as dramatic ornamentation or literary embellishment, but also contributes directly to the philosophical accomplishments of the text. From the very beginning of the *Gorgias* until its end, comedy serves as a mechanism by which the traditional understanding of political power is philosophically assessed and ultimately overthrown. Phrased otherwise, the *Gorgias* stages a philosophical critique of the traditional understanding of power that is carried out in a largely comedic register, one that ultimately presents philosophy itself as comedic in certain ways.

---

[6] Archilochus is generally credited with having invented, or at least having made significant improvements upon, iambic meter.

[7] Athenaeus, *The Learned Banqueters,* ed. and trans. S. Douglas Olson (Cambridge, MA: Harvard University Press, 2009), 471-473.

[8] Leslie Kurke, *Aesopic Conversations: Popular Tradition, Cultural Dialogue, and the Invention of Greek Prose* (Princeton: Princeton University Press, 2011), 259.

The aim of the present paper is to correct my previous failures to account for the comedic character of the *Gorgias.* To that end, I will focus on three interrelated elements at play within the text—food, irony, and animals—showing how each contributes to the dialogue's overall comedic tenor. I will then turn to a consideration of the ways in which these comedic elements contribute to the philosophical assessment of political power that takes place within the dialogue. I will then conclude by offering a brief word regarding the comedy of the *Gorgias* more generally, especially as regards the conflict between the tragic and comedic views of political power presented in the text.

Food, Irony, Animals

The *Gorgias* begins with a jest—actually, it begins with two. Drawing on an old adage, Callicles begins the text with the following joke at Socrates's expense: "War and battle, Socrates—that's the way, they say, to participate in these" (447a). In other words, Callicles is ridiculing Socrates for being late and is suggesting, not so subtly, that he is a coward. Socrates's response is no less jocular: "Oh? Have we arrived, as the saying goes, too late for a feast?" (447a). With this, Socrates playfully misinterprets the meaning of Callicles's remark, drawing on the unsaid portion of the phrase (the entirety of which, as Dodds notes, was presumably something like the English adage "first at a feast, last at a fray").[9] Moreover, with this response Socrates reorients the discussion away from the polemical and toward the gastronomical, indicating that, for his part (and in clear opposition to Callicles) discourse is more akin to feasting than to fighting.

Additionally, Socrates's introduction of feasting at the outset of the text orients the text decisively toward a comedic register.[10] As John Wilkins has noted, "food and cooking are at the centre of the comic world."[11] Indeed, in nearly all of Aristophanes's plays, food plays a significant role, serving as one of the registers in which

[9] E.R. Dodds, *Plato's Gorgias: A Revised Text with Introduction and Commentary* (Oxford: Clarendon Press, 1959), 188.

[10] See Andrea Nightingale, *Genres in Dialogue: Plato and the Construct of Philosophy* (Cambridge: Cambridge University Press, 1995), 189.

[11] John Wilkins, *The Boastful Chef: The Discourse of Food in Ancient Greek Comedy* (Oxford: Oxford University Press, 2000), xxii.

comedy's emphasis on the *domestic* finds its expression.[12] As an expression and celebration of the domestic, the preparation and ingestion of food—along with its eventual expulsion—operates at the level of *lowness* on which Aristophanic comedy primarily depends.[13] Socrates's mention of food at the threshold of the text foreshadows the comedic lowness of the text to come, as well as the particular view of political power that Socrates will develop later on. (We will return to this view of political power below.)

Socrates employs various examples throughout the *Gorgias* that draw upon the gastronomical, so much so that Callicles eventually accuses him of a lack of urbanity.[14] Although each such example plays an important role within the unfolding of the dialogue—such as Socrates's expressly comedic use of food in his conversation with Callicles[15]—the most structurally significant instance occurs with Socrates's use of cookery (or opson-making: *opsopoiia*) as an analogy by which to better understand the nature of rhetoric, an analogy that only works because of the perceived lowness or vulgarity that belongs to cookery (462d). (Indeed, both it and rhetoric are explicitly said to be *agroikos*: boorish, rustic, or literally "of the countryside") (462e). Socrates's use of the analogy offends Polus precisely because it debases and degrades what Polus and his cohort consider to be "the greatest of human concerns, and the best" (451d). The use of a metaphorics of food, then, is one way in which the *Gorgias* operates at a low—which is to say, comedic—level. (In passing, we might also wonder if Socrates's emphasis on feasting at the outset of the text—that is, his stated eagerness for a feast of words—serves to align him with Heracles, that comic mainstay so often presented as being preoccupied with food.)[16]

---

[12] Wilkins, *Boastful Chef*, xvi.

[13] One can see such lowness emphasized in Aristophanes's *Wealth*, when Chremylus offers Cario various highbrow rewards (culture, honor, courage, etc.), only to have Cario reveal his true lowness by requesting bread, flat-cakes, dried figs, and lentil soup (*Wealth*, 189-193). (On the lowness of lentils in particular, see Wilkins, *Boastful Chef*, 13.)

[14] See 491a.

[15] See 490b-d; see also 518b.

[16] On the comparison of Socrates to Heracles, see *Phaedo* 89c.

The lowness of gastronomical matters is intimately connected with the second element of comedy at play within the *Gorgias*, namely, *irony.* Perhaps more than any other dialogue (with the possible exception of the *Cratylus*), the *Gorgias* presents Socrates engaging in ironic discourse—indeed, so much so that Callicles eventually calls him out on it (489e). To better understand the connection between irony and comedy, a turn to Leo Strauss's 1957 lectures on the *Gorgias* is instructive. Strauss there argues that irony—which he calls "the element of comedy"—consists of Socrates speaking with people who are "lower" than he is, i.e., people who are intellectually inferior.[17] Owing to their lowness, Socrates is obliged to meet them at their level—that is, he engages in forms of dissimulative discourse that conceal the higher wisdom of which he is capable. In this way, according to Strauss, Socratic irony operates as a "concealment of the higher"[18] by which he makes the intellectual inferiority of his interlocutors manifest to the readers, if not necessarily to themselves.[19] Irony is thus a vehicle by means of which the vertical gap separating the intellectually superior from the intellectually inferior is traversed.

As useful as Strauss's analysis is for grasping the essential connection between irony and comedy, it falls short on two major counts. First, the understanding of Socrates's irony as concealing his intellectual superiority is belied by the many passages across the corpus where Socrates insists upon his ignorance. Within the *Gorgias*, Socrates marks such ignorance at various points, such as when he tells Callicles that "I am not at all saying what I am saying as one who knows, but I am seeking in common with you" (506a), or when he,

---

[17] Leo Strauss, "Plato's *Gorgias*: A Course Offered in the Winter Quarter," 1957, ed. D. Stauffer (Estate of Leo Strauss, 2014), 14. Cf. Leo Strauss, *The City and Man* (Chicago: University of Chicago Press, 1964), 51.

[18] Leo Strauss, "Plato's *Republic*, 1957," ed. P. Ahrensdorf (Estate of Leo Strauss, 2014), 11.

[19] Sonja Tanner, *Plato's Laughter: Socrates as Satyr and Comical Hero* (New York: SUNY Press, 2017), xi-xii notes that irony tends to operate on an intellectual level (at one point referring to it as "laughter from above"), whereas laughter (and comedy more broadly) can operate on "a broader range of sources, including the physical."

in response to Callicles's surprise at something he had said, claims not to have been speaking at all, but rather merely allowing *philosophy itself* to speak (482a). Of course, one can take such statements as themselves demonstrative of a veiled superiority on Socrates's part; however, I submit that the sheer volume of such statements throughout the so-called Platonic corpus, as well as the extensive development of the theme of ignorance in multiple texts (such as the *Apology* and the *Symposium*), should compel one to take Socrates's insistence that he lacks knowledge as sincere. Moreover, as will be seen below, such ignorance—or, more precisely, such *knowledge* of one's ignorance—is an integral part of the view of political power that Socrates puts forth as a corrective to Callicles's.

Second, Strauss's understanding of irony as consisting of veiled superiority misses the full scope of its connection to comedy. Socrates uses irony to ridicule his interlocutors by bringing them before their own ignorance;[20] more specifically, he ridicules those who *pretend* to know, and who thereby attempt to veil their ignorance. Within the *Gorgias*, this is perhaps seen most brilliantly in Socrates's initial exchange with Gorgias, who over and over again demonstrates his inability to define his own art; it is also seen in Socrates's palpably comedic exchange with Polus. However, such irony, in addition to ridiculing his interlocutors, *also ridicules Socrates himself*—he who, *as a human being*, only has wisdom that is, as he says at *Apology* 26b, "worth little or nothing." In other words, Socratic irony is a mechanism by which the foolishness not just of particular human beings, but of human beings *as such*, is made manifest.

To be sure, by becoming aware of his ignorance, Socrates "ascends" beyond his interlocutors, and in this way could be said to be superior to them. However, the vertical distance that opens up between them is ultimately meaningless, given that human wisdom as a whole is worth little or nothing, and given that *all* humans (Socrates included) remain lowly and beneath the gods. (In this way, Plato's depiction of Socrates is not wildly different from Aristophanes's depiction in *Clouds*: Socrates is the fool who is

---

[20] See Bernard Freydberg, *Philosophy and Comedy: Aristophanes, Logos, and Eros* (Bloomington: Indiana University Press, 2008), 24.

"higher" than all of the other fools.) To the extent that Socratic irony draws attention to the essentially lowly nature of the human—that is, the manner in which the wisest human is he who, standing beneath the gods above, knows only that he knows nothing worthwhile—it remains an operation of comedy.[21]

This essential lowliness of the human condition is connected to the third aspect of comedy at play within the text, namely, the element of *animality*. Animals run rampant throughout the *Gorgias*. Most famously there is the plover (494b), adduced by Socrates as a comedic depiction of the life of pure pleasure, but there are also lions (483b), asses (516a), horses (416b), and cattle (484b); there is also the dog god to whom Socrates swears three times (461a, 466c, 482b), the highest frequency in any Platonic text. In addition, and much more significantly, there is the matter of the *dramatis personae*. As is frequently noted, Polus's name refers to a certain kind of colt (and, indeed, Socrates makes a joke to this effect) (463e).[22] It has also been observed that the name of Socrates's deme, *Alopoke*, mentioned by Callicles (495d), is a pun on the Greek word for "fox" (*alopex*). Moreover, as James Haden has noted, Socrates's mention of Callicles's deme, *Acharnai*, is also a pun, insofar as it sounds almost identical to the word *acharnas*, which refers to a certain kind of fish.[23] We can add to this the character Chaerephon, whom Aristophanes describes as looking like a bat.[24] Finally, there is Gorgias himself, whom Socrates elsewhere likens to a Gorgon, those serpentine and winged beasts.[25] Every character in the text, then, is paired with an

---

[21] I agree with Tanner's argument that it is a mistake to subsume comedy under the heading of irony (*Plato's Laughter*, 169n90). Indeed, I would suggest that one must go the other way, taking irony as one example of the sorts of comedy that one finds in the so-called Platonic texts.

[22] See, for example, Dodds, *Plato's Gorgias*, 226.

[23] James Haden, "Two Types of Power in Plato's *Gorgias*," *The Classical Journal* 87:4 (April 1992), 313-326. Haden also notes that such puns were characteristic of Old Comedy.

[24] *Birds*, 1564. Chaerephon was, as Deborah Nails, *The People of Plato: A Prosopography of Plato and Other Socratics* (Indianapolis: Hackett, 2002), 86 puts it, "a favorite of the comic poets for two decades."

[25] *Symposium*, 198c.

animal: Gorgias the winged serpent, Polus the colt, Callicles the fish, Chaerephon the bat, Socrates the fox.

As is well-attested, animals and animal similes figure prominently in Old Comedy.[26] Three of Aristophanes's plays—*Wasps*, *Birds*, and *Frogs*—were named after animals, and also had choruses consisting of the titular animals; additionally, the entirety of Aristophanes's corpus is replete with animal imagery. As Babette Pütz has argued, such animal imagery serves a largely derisive function within Aristophanes's work, providing comedy with "a special figurative language that is used to mock human characteristics."[27] (One thinks immediately of the chorus from the *Wasps*.) This figurative language has the effect of diminishing the stature of the characters by emphasizing their coarse and bestial aspects, thereby placing them on a level "somewhere between human and animal."[28] Phrased otherwise, such animal imagery serves as yet another comedic mechanism by means of which the lowly nature of the human being finds emphasis. By speaking of particular humans (or humanity more generally) in animalistic terms, Aristophanes emphasizes the baseness of the human, thereby underscoring its distance from the gods; and Plato, in subtly pairing each of his characters with an animal, draws upon this comedic practice.

One sees, then, that food, irony, and animality operate as three elements through which the comedy of the *Gorgias* is carried out, elements which work in tandem to underscore the essentially base and lowly character of the human being. Having now grasped the

---

[26] See Wilkins, *Boastful Chef*, 21: "Comedy regularly blurs the boundaries between animal, human, and god in its relentless pursuit of mocking bathos and its aggressive attack on established boundaries…." See also Roger Brock, who notes that "like the comic poets, Plato has a fondness for animal imagery." Roger Brock, "Plato and Comedy," in *'Owls to Athens': Essays on Classical Subjects Presented to Sir Kenneth Dover*, ed. E.M. Clark (Oxford: Clarendon Press, 1990), 45.

[27] Babette Pütz, "Good to Laugh With: Animals in Comedy," in *The Oxford Handbook of Animals in Classical Though and Life*, ed. by Gordon Campbell (Oxford: Oxford University Press, 2014), 197.

[28] Pütz, "Good to Laugh With," 198.

general parameters of these comedic elements, we now turn to a consideration of the ways in which they contribute to the philosophical critique of the traditional view of political power carried out by Socrates within the text.

The Comedy of Power

As James Haden has argued, the juxtaposition of fighting and feasting in the first lines of the *Gorgias* prefigures the inquiry into power carried out by the text as a whole. For Haden, Plato uses eating or ingestion as a metaphor for the sort of power practiced by the rhetoricians, namely, the power of "negat[ing] the independent selfhood of the other"[29] by dominating them by means of persuasive discourse.[30] *Contra* Haden, I would like to suggest that eating shows itself in the *Gorgias* as a metaphor not for the rhetorical understanding of power, but rather for the Socratic. Whereas, for the rhetoricians, power consists of the ability to persuade others by means of speech (452e), for Socrates it consists of an openness to philosophical dialogue, a receptivity to the unfolding of truth in *logos*. Such openness, manifest through the dialogue as a whole, is especially evident in Socrates's willingness to being refuted by Gorgias (457e), in his eagerness *to seek* along with Callicles (506a), and, most saliently, in his desire to continue investigating by means of dialogue even when Callicles will no longer participate in the discussion (505e). (This one-man dialogue is itself highly comedic, as is made clear by Socrates himself when he mentions the comic writer Epicharmus at its outset.) Throughout the text, Socrates is shown to be in a state of perpetual intellectual *hunger*, an insatiable desire for wisdom that is all the stronger owing to his awareness of his intellectual anemia. (In this register, it is worth noting Socrates's mention in the *Phaedrus* that he is *hungry* for speeches, just like an animal being seduced by food.)[31] Socrates's mention of feasting in his first words of the *Gorgias*, and his continual use of examples

---

[29] Haden, "Power in Plato's *Gorgias*," 319.

[30] Haden, "Power in Plato's *Gorgias*," 320.

[31] *Phaedrus* 230e. See also *Republic* 352b, and *Timaeus* 27b.

involving food, gesture toward the *limitless* character of Socratic inquiry and the *unquenchable* hunger he exhibits for knowledge.[32]

Such hunger for wisdom, insofar as it is grounded on *perpetual* hunger (i.e., Socratic ignorance), shows itself through the guise of Socratic irony. As argued above, in underscoring the essentially lowly and foolish character of the human condition, Socratic irony serves to illuminate the essential *powerlessness* of human wisdom when measured against the gods. By emphasizing his ignorance, Socrates demonstrates his unique wisdom: that is, he offers himself as a paradigm for how to properly relate to one's ignorance. Such a relation entails a gesture of deference to something *higher* than himself (i.e., the gods, the philosophical *logos*, etc.), and thus further marks the insignificance of the human condition. To proceed through life ironically, as Socrates does, is to live with the awareness that human life, and everything accomplished therein, is worth little or nothing when compared with that of the gods. Such an ironic comportment underscores the extreme limitedness of human affairs and the ways in which even the loftiest among them remain insignificant when measured against the divine. This essential lowliness of the human condition is perhaps best articulated by the Athenian in the *Laws* when he says that "by nature, god is worthy of a complete, blessed seriousness, but [...] what is human [...] has been devised as a certain plaything [*paignion*] of the god, and [...] this is really the best thing about it."[33] In other words, human life is something of a comedy.

However, within the *Gorgias*, it is precisely this position of comic lowliness that is ultimately shown to comprise political power properly understood. As I've argued elsewhere, the *Gorgias* carries out an overturning of the traditional understanding of political power as the willful dominating of others, showing it instead to

---

[32] In this sense, one could say that Socrates's comedic use of the plover (494b), which he adduces to describe Callicles, is no less appropriate to describe Socrates himself. The crucial difference is that Callicles is hungry for physical pleasure, while Socrates is hungry for intellectual inquiry.

[33] *Laws* 803c. See also 816e, where the same word (*paignion*) is used to refer specifically to comedic performances.

consist of a submissiveness to the power of the philosophical *logos*.[34] Such submissiveness is visible, for example, in Socrates's claim that it is better to be refuted than to refute (457e), and in his claim that he is not interested in defeating his interlocutors but rather in allowing the *logos* to unfold "for the sake of the *logos* [itself]" (453c). In other words, Socrates *defers* to the philosophical *logos*, allowing it to guide him, rather than trying to guide it willfully. Such deference reaches its apogee when Socrates tells Callicles that everything he has said up to that point was, strictly speaking, not said by himself at all, but rather by philosophy itself: "For she [...] speaks what you hear me saying now [...]; philosophy always says the same, and it is her speech that now fills you with wonder" (482a-b). This deference to the philosophical *logos* shows itself in the text to be nothing other than political power properly understood: for the true statesman is the one who *is ruled* by the *logos* rather than the one who (like Callicles) would exercise his will over others, and it is Socrates's posture of intellectual hunger (i.e., Socratic ignorance) that enables him to be ruled in this way.

Finally, as was shown above, the powerlessness of the human condition is further indicated through the use of animal imagery within the text.[35] Arlene Saxonhouse has convincingly argued that Plato's *Republic* employs animal imagery comedically in order to offer a criticism of the city in speech presented therein.[36] Regarding such imagery, she writes:

> Existing on a plane between the gods and animals, human beings frequently become in comedy creatures whose concerns illustrate their ties to the animal world. In tragedy, we try to become god-like and fail; in comedy, even as we succeed, we can appear to be only slightly above the animal

---

[34] Ewegen, *Way of the Platonic Socrates*, 52.

[35] On other uses of animal imagery in Plato, see Marina McCoy, "The City of Sows: Sexual Difference in the *Republic*," in *Plato's Animals: Gadflies, Horses, Swans, and Other Philosophical Beasts*, ed. J. Bell and M. Naas (Bloomington: Indiana University Press, 2015), 149-160.

[36] Arlene Saxonhouse, "Comedy in Callipolis: Animal Imagery in the *Republic*," *The American Political Science Review* 72:3 (1978): 888-901.

> world. Socrates's city [i.e., the city in speech] parallels comedy as it transforms the members of its guardian class from individuals with the potential for private virtue into the inhabitants of a barnyard.[37]

I suggest that the *Gorgias* accomplishes the same. By playfully providing us with a comedic menagerie of beasts engaging in a debate about proper human political matters, the *Gorgias* offers an assessment of the limitations of human political power and the sort of knowledge that would inform it.

This comedic critique of the human political enterprise, implied by the animal associations belonging to each character, plays out at the level of the conversation itself, and can be most clearly seen in Socrates's engagement with Callicles where he uses the image of the herdsman as an analogy for statesmanship. As Socrates suggests, a herdsman would be considered bad if the animals over whom he ruled turned out wilder than they had been before he ruled them (516a). His further suggestion is that Pericles, like a herdsman "of asses or oxen," ought to have made his human subjects less wild and more just. Moreover, it is said by Socrates, and agreed to by Callicles, that human beings are just "one of the animals" (516b). Statesmanship is thus more than an activity *analogous* to animal-rearing: it is just one other form of it![38] The statesman is the one who oversees the management and domestication of the human animal. Thus, it is not only Polus's coltish eagerness, or Callicles's bird-like insatiability, or Socrates's foxlike cleverness that is to be understood in animalistic terms: rather, it is the entirety of human beings in their political dealings. Suffice to say, such a scene serves to indicate the extent to which human political matters are characterized by a certain bestial lowliness, and that, no matter how important they may seem to us, they remain, at the end of the day, carried out by

---

[37] Saxonhouse, "Comedy in Callipolis," 888.

[38] To be sure, the comparison of the statesman to a herdsman was already well-established at Socrates's time; however, Socrates's derisive (i.e., comedic) use of the comparison is indicated in his introduction of "asses" into the animals being tamed. See Dodds, *Plato's Gorgias*, 358.

phaulos creatures who amount to little more than a gathering of beasts.

However, and crucially, it is precisely an awareness of this lowliness that allows one to open oneself to something higher: for only by embracing one's animality does one measure oneself against the gods, thereby correcting the all-too-human tendency to perceive oneself as a god.[39] Only by acknowledging one's finitude does one abandon the posture of willfulness and feigned wisdom that characterizes political power traditionally understood, a posture that prevents one from being open to the showing forth of truth in *logos*. Only one who remains cognizant of one's foolish, lowly, and animalistic nature—which is to say, one's *comedic* nature—opens oneself up for the unfolding of the truth in *logos*: and Socrates, as the paradigm of such openness, exemplifies this posture of animalistic folly, and thus of the *true* statesman. Socrates, as he who is most aware of his ignorance, is also he who is most aware of the comedy that is human life properly understood.[40]

Conclusions

Having now analyzed these three specific elements of comedy at play within the *Gorgias* and the manner in which they contribute to the philosophical critique of political power carried out within it, I conclude with a more generalized consideration of the comedic character of the text. In one of her characteristically exemplary works, Andrea Nightingale has shown that the *Gorgias* serves as a deliberate parody of Euripides's tragedy the *Antiope*.[41] As she argues, the *Gorgias* borrows certain structural and thematic elements from the *Antiope* and re-contextualizes them within a philosophical framework, thereby "transform[ing] a tragic drama into a quite different literary drama." This novel genre, which parodies both tragedy and comedy, moves beyond them into a "vigorous hybrid"

---

[39] See 491e ff., where Callicles extols the godlike power of rhetoric. See also 452e.

[40] On Socrates's view of himself as comedic, see, e.g., *Euthydemus* 287e. Cf. A. Michelini, "Socrates Plays the Buffoon: Cautionary *Protreptic* in the *Euthydemus*," *American Journal of Philology* 121 (2000): 514-517.

[41] Nightingale, *Genres in Dialogue*, 89.

that "constitutes itself by appropriating and defamiliarizing both tragedy and comedy."[42]

Although Nightingale's rich analysis offers crucial insight into the *Gorgias*, as well as into Plato's development of his own unique literary genre, I hope to have shown that the *Gorgias* remains essentially comedic in substance, despite its "defamiliarization" of the tragic and comedic genres. This has everything to do with the parodic character of the text.[43] Although Nightingale and others have argued that parody need not remain comedic in tone,[44] there is at least one essential sense in which the parody operative within the *Gorgias* does so: namely, the way in which it parodies the lives of inferior people, people who are *phaulos*, a parodic operation already observed by Aristotle in his *Poetics*.[45] Insofar as the *Gorgias* represents people who are inferior attempting something grand—namely, rhetoricians aspiring to political power, as well as human beings more generally attempting to attain true knowledge of the political good—it remains essentially comedic in this way.

Moreover, as Leo Strauss notes regarding the relationship between tragedy and comedy, "comedy parodies tragedy; tragedy does not parody comedy. Comedy builds on tragedy and presupposes it."[46] For Strauss, the parodic aspect of comedy is intimately connected to its ironizing element, i.e., the manner in which it conceals its grandeur precisely through its emphasis on the base and vulgar.[47] To this we could add that comedy is able to decontextualize and make use of tragic themes and elements in a manner that tragedy cannot do: for the presence of a repurposed tragic theme within a comedy in no way detracts from the comedy

---

[42] Andrea Nightingale, "Plato's *Gorgias* and Euripides's *Antiope*: A Study in Generic Transformation," *Classical Antiquity* 11:1 (April 1992): 141.

[43] Nightingale argues that parody "is the norm in the Platonic dialogues" (Nightingale, *Genres in Dialogue*, 194).

[44] Nightingale, *Genres in Dialogue*, 7.

[45] See Aristotle *Poetics*, 1448a13. On the role of parody in Aristophanes, see Heinz-Günther Nesselrath, "Parody and Later Greek Comedy," *Harvard Studies in Classical Philology* 95 (1993): 181-195, 185.

[46] Strauss, "Plato's *Gorgias*," 11.

[47] Strauss, "Plato's *Gorgias*," 11.

(and in fact accentuates it), whereas the presence of a comedic theme within a tragedy is fatal to the latter. Phrased otherwise, the moment a tragedy represents a comedic moment, it becomes a comedy: comedy thus supersedes and assimilates tragedy. So understood, the operation through which the *Gorgias* carries out its parodic imitation and evaluation of Euripides's *Antiope* could only be a comedic one; thus, Plato's literary form, as novel as it may be, bears structural and formal characteristics that align it more closely with Aristophanic comedy than with the tragedy that is so often mimicked and ridiculed within it.[48] In this way, one could understand Socrates's comment at the end of the *Symposium* that the same person must be able to write comedy and tragedy as suggesting that such a person must essentially tend more toward the comedic: that is, they must be able to make use of both comedic and tragic elements, as only the comic writer can do.[49]

There is also a more philosophical sense in which the *Gorgias* remains comedic: namely, the manner in which the text presents the comedic comportment toward political knowledge as preferable to its tragic alternative. Within the text, we are given a contrast between two ways of life: that most forcefully depicted by Callicles, the self-confident and tyrannical rhetorician, and that depicted by Socrates, the self-effacing philosopher who defers to the philosophical *logos*. As indicated at various points throughout the text, this contrast amounts to a conflict between tragedy and comedy—that is, between the tragic and comedic comportments toward political life—with the latter as the decisive victor. By way of conclusion, the parameters of this conflict will be briefly examined.

The proximity of philosophy to comedy is indicated by Callicles on a number of occasions, such as when he calls philosophers "laughably ridiculous" (484e) or calls Socrates a fool (489b) and

---

[48] Nightingale, *Genres in Dialogue*, 72, notes that Plato "is arguably more indebted to comedy than to any other literary genre." Although she is careful to track the comedic in the *Gorgias*, she nonetheless writes that "there is very little humor in the *Gorgias*" (187).

[49] One thinks again of Strauss, *The City and Man*, 62, who notes that Plato's texts as a whole tend toward the ridiculous and comical.

chastens him for his tendency to speak of lowly things (490c, 491a). Callicles's depiction of philosophy as comedic reaches its peak when he offers the following description of it:

> It falls to this man [i.e., the philosopher], even if he should have a very good nature, to become *unmanly* [ἀνάνδρῳ] and to flee the affairs of the polis and the marketplaces [...] and cower down and spend the rest of his life whispering in a corner with three or four young fellows, and never to utter a free and great and adequate remark. (485d; my emphasis)

In other words, philosophy is corrosive of a person's nature, effectively lowering that nature to the status of a fool or a slave—or, we might suppose, an *animal*.

By contrast, rhetoric is presented by Callicles, Gorgias, and Polus as being ampliative of one's nature, expanding it beyond the constraining measures of social convention. It is said variously by them to be the uncanny power to persuade all others and to make those others one's slaves (452e); a power to persuade anyone about anything one wills (457b); a tyrannical power to kill or excommunicate whomever one wants (466c, 469c); the power to thus act unjustly with impunity; the power to have limitless desires and the ability to fulfill them (491e, 494c). In other words, it is presented as a power beyond all other human powers, a kind of super-power that brings all other powers under itself (456a)—in a word, a *godlike* power.[50] The rhetorician—i.e., the tyrant—is he who acts as though he were a god, bound by no human social constraints whatsoever.

As Socrates is at pains to show through his conversations with all three rhetoricians, such an attitude remains tragic in certain essential ways. To begin with, such a power, while seemingly benefiting the one who wields it, in fact leads to their downfall: for, as Socrates argues, it is precisely the power to get away with injustice that has the most corrosive effect on the soul (479e). Moreover, such

---

[50] See Christina Tarnopolsky, *Prudes, Perverts, and Tyrants: Plato's* Gorgias *and the Politics of Shame* (Princeton, NJ: Princeton University Press, 2010), 112.

a power of limitless desire is, precisely owing to its limitlessness, insatiable; and the person with limitless desires is the person who will never be satisfied, and therefore never happy (493b). Finally, it is the implicit presumption of divinity operative in this view of power that perhaps most conspicuously marks the tragic character of the life of the rhetorician: for in feigning to be a god—i.e., in feigning to have true knowledge and power, like the gods—the rhetorician cuts himself off from the truth, and therefore from real power. Said otherwise, precisely because the rhetorician presumes to have true knowledge of the good (e.g., of human political life), he cuts himself off from the ability to inquire into the nature of that good, thereby closing himself off from exposure to the philosophical *logos*. In these ways, the life of the rhetorician—i.e., the tyrannical life—is both self-vitiating and self-defeating: it is, in a word, *tragic*.

By comparison, the life of the philosopher is the life that, precisely through emphasizing its lowness (i.e., its ignorance), opens itself to something higher and therefore to a genuine experience of the truth. One can see this by again looking to Callicles's description of philosophy. I have argued elsewhere that, given the critique of the traditional understanding of power carried out by Socrates's throughout the text as a whole, one can understand Callicles's remarks about philosophy as an unintentionally perfect depiction of the positive aspects of Socrates's philosophical practice. As I put it there,

> one could say that philosophy [...] leads one to drop the pretense and arrogant self-aggrandizement that so characterized Athenian masculinity and that characterizes Callicles's παρρησία. Further, philosophy leads one to retreat from political affairs and the business of the agora—a claim that Socrates himself makes in the *Theaetetus* when describing the philosopher (*Tht*. 173cff.), as well as in the *Apology* when describing his own practice (*Ap*. 36bff.). Moreover, philosophy leads one to whisper in a corner with a small group of people—rather than, for example, speaking abruptly and "frankly" within a crowded courtroom while under the pressure of the water clock. Finally, philosophy brings it about that its practitioner never utters "a free and

> great and adequate remark": that is, it brings it about that one, knowing oneself to be ignorant, never speaks one's own opinion as if it were adequate to the truth, as if it were sufficient, but instead withdraws one's own opinions in the face of a higher *logos*. So understood, one could say that Socrates's way of philosophy—a way that he has been depicting in both speech and deed throughout the *Gorgias*—agrees with Callicles's depiction of it; or, rather, it agrees with the words with which Callicles describes it, while those words must be understood in an entirely different sense based on the inverted understanding of power that the *logos* has brought about.[51]

In other words, these purportedly ridiculous characteristics of philosophy are actually what is most beneficial about it: namely, that by eschewing the epistemological presumptions characteristic of the rhetoricians and by instead adopting a posture of humility with respect to wisdom, philosophy opens itself to a genuine experience of the truth as it shows itself in *logos*.

Taking all of this in light of the preceding analysis, one could say that the depiction of Socrates as "ridiculous," intended by Callicles as an insult, in fact accurately captures the comedic comportment toward political knowledge that Socrates exemplifies. Precisely through knowing himself to be ignorant—knowing himself to be, therefore, more like a foolish beast than a god—Socrates adopts a position of humility that opens himself up to what is greater than himself: namely, the truth as it shows itself in *logos*. In this way, the comedic posture exemplified by Socrates demonstrates itself as being more capable of receiving the truth regarding what it means to rule a city well (i.e., truly) than the tragic posture exemplified by Callicles, who's pretense to wisdom is precisely what tragically cuts him off from it. The comedy of philosophy thus overcomes the tragedy of rhetoric and shows itself to be the truer and more legitimate form of statesmanship.

---

[51] Ewegen, *Way of the Platonic Socrates*, 49-50.

Coleen P. Zoller[1]

Taking Our Medicine: Justice and Reconciliation in Plato's *Gorgias*

Can Justice Be Restored in the Wake of Injustice?

For those like me who are interested in better understanding Plato's thinking related to peace, we must investigate his peace-seeking philosophical project more obliquely than we might expect. As Rick Benitez has noted,

> there is the fact that peace—on any specific conception of it—is not the subject of any dialogue of Plato's. Indices to Plato list 'peace' as the focus of only a few brief discussions within the *Laws* and the *Statesman.* Thus, when we seek to identify what Plato says about peace, we must have a qualified understanding of what we are doing [...] We should be prepared to extend our exploration into territory that Plato uses different words to describe.[2]

I concur with Benitez that better comprehension of Plato's thinking about peace forces us on a more circuitous route than we anticipate. The inquiry into peace will take us onto terrain such as thinking about the care of the soul, justice, and friendship.

Plato's ethical and political theories are a very important resource for philosophers and others interested in peace. One of the main considerations to which Plato draws our attention, especially in the *Republic,* is the matter of relationships and their harmony or disharmony. In the theory of justice Plato has Socrates defend in the *Republic,* harmony applies at two levels—first, among the individual soul's components, and second, among the collective community of

---

[1] Coleen P. Zoller is Professor and Chair of Philosophy at Susquehanna University in Selinsgrove, Pennsylvania, USA. She is the author of *Plato and the Body: Reconsidering Socratic Asceticism* (SUNY Press, 2018) and co-editor of *Athletics, Gymnastics, and Agon in Plato* (Parnassos Press, 2020). Her most recent article, "Plato and Equality for Women across Social Class," appeared in the *Journal of Ancient Philosophy*, 2021.

[2] Rick Benitez, "Plato's Conception of Peace: A Preliminary Exploration," *Theoria* 66; 2 (2019): 8-22, 9-10.

individuals and groups. *Relationships matter*— at the individual level among the different needs and talents of each aspect of the soul, and at the aggregate level among the members of the community. While not using words such as "peace" or "reconciliation," Plato's ethical and political theories build a world wherein we begin to make out the conditions for such desired outcomes as peace—whether peace occurs within oneself among the aspects of the soul (in the *Republic,* the aspects are rational, spirited, and appetitive) or with others in the community (in the *Republic,* the societal groups are philosopher-monarchs, auxiliary guardians, and craft workers).

Passages such as *Republic* 351d, 431e-432a, and 435b speak to relationships between virtue and justice and between justice and harmony, and they portray clearly the aspirations we should have to virtue, justice, and harmony within and among us. Plato has Socrates teach us that to know peace, we must know justice (*Rep.* 351d), and to know justice we must know virtue (*Rep.* 431e-432a, 435b). Or, to put that another way: No virtue, no justice; no justice, no peace. Plato's Socrates emphasizes the relationship between virtue and justice across dialogues, and in the *Republic* he links that sense of virtue as a prerequisite for justice to the relationship among the three aspects of the soul and the city. However, the *Republic* does not offer much by way of insight into *how* to restore justice when injustice does occur. When we think of how injustices cause the disharmonious conflicts that can block peace, it becomes crucial to ask what can and should happen in the wake of injustice. How unfortunate if the problem of injustice is compounded by the additional problem of unresolved conflict.

So, we must ask whether justice *can* be restored after injustice has occurred, and if so, *how* that happens? The issue of restoration for an unjust soul emerges in Plato's *Gorgias,* and this chapter will focus on the ideas of accountability and reconciliation in Plato's *Gorgias.* It will not surprise the scholars who identify conflict and war as the primary theme of the *Gorgias* that it is in this dialogue where we learn more about what should happen in the wake of injustice.[3] Plato utilizes analogical reasoning between the care of the body and the care of the soul in order to assert the idea of justice as the soul taking its medicine (*Grg*. 464c). This definition gives us a sketch of the process by which an injustice-doer will be returned to virtue.

For Plato, anyone who has committed injustice must submit to justice in order to return to the path of virtue through holding oneself accountable. The definition of justice as medicine emphasizes the prospect of an injustice-doer *being healed by justice*. In the *Gorgias*, Plato's Socrates emphasizes the psychic, political act of submitting to justice so that doers of injustice get the corrective treatment needed by their ailing souls. A natural question to ask about the healing process invoked by the *Gorgias*'s analogy scheme is whether Plato would hold up forgiveness or mercy as admirable. Yet, almost no one has asked whether Plato has reason to admire forgiveness or mercy.

Charles Griswold has asked why we do not find Plato admiring forgiveness in his corpus, and he swiftly rejects the idea that Plato could hold forgiveness in any positive regard.[4] On Griswold's pessimistic reading of Plato's philosophy, forgiveness is unnecessary and not worth admiring. Griswold chalks this up to what he describes as Plato's "perfectionism," contending that no imperfect individual or world can ever meet the standards Plato establishes. I argue extensively against that type of reading in *Plato and the Body: Reconsidering Socratic Asceticism* where I show the evidence for philosophers' engagement with this world and their work on human self-improvement rather than hubristic perfectionism.[5]

Nonetheless, though I do not share Griswold's point of view on Plato's overall philosophy being other-worldly and perfectionistic, I believe Griswold raises a good question about the absence of

---

[3] See Arlene W. Saxonhouse, "An Unspoken Theme in Plato's *Gorgias*: War," *Interpretation* 11.2 (1983): 139-169; Robin Reames, *Seeming and Being in Plato's Rhetorical Theory* (Chicago: University of Chicago Press, 2018), 43; and Ed Schiappa's chapter in this volume.

[4] Charles L. Griswold, "Plato and Forgiveness," *Ancient Philosophy* 27 (2007): 269-87.

[5] Coleen P. Zoller, *Plato and the Body: Reconsidering Socratic Asceticism* (Albany: State University of New York Press), 2018.

discussion of forgiveness in Plato's corpus. It should surprise anyone familiar with Plato that he does not have interlocutors get into serious philosophical conversation about forgiveness, given his extensive focus on internal strife, civic conflict, and war and his aspirational philosophy of virtue, justice, and harmony.[6] Forgiveness seems like a topic that might arise with frequency in conversations of virtue, justice, friendship, and harmony, especially in a culture as well acquainted with the idea of forgiveness as Griswold demonstrates the ancient Greeks were.[7]

It is true that, for Plato, forgiveness is not among the cardinal virtues alongside wisdom, courage, moderation, justice, and even piety. Yet, even if not among Plato's 'cardinal' virtues, we should ask whether a vision of the possibility for meriting something such as forgiveness may be imbued in Plato's thinking in the *Gorgias* about the importance of unjust souls submitting themselves to justice. Griswold contends that there is simply no such notion found in Plato's philosophy. By showing the prevalence among the Greeks of comments about forgiveness, he highlights how easily Plato could have discussed forgiveness and held it up as a positive virtue and yet did not. But it strikes me that Griswold moves quickly to his pessimistic conclusions, missing something important in Plato's thinking about the value of reconciliation within one's own soul as well as with others, even if it is only a mere sketch.

Ultimately, Griswold is correct that there is no explicit mention of forgiveness to be found in the *Gorgias* or elsewhere in Plato's writing. Yet, as we shall see in this chapter, with the definition of justice as psychic medicine in the *Gorgias,* Plato contemplates an act that has the potential to facilitate two distinct aspects in *the process of reconciliation*. To start with, taking one's psychic medicine involves a process of what I call "*self-reconciliation,*" returning one's soul to the state of being properly cared for—that is, virtue, the state from which doing injustice does not spring. Secondly, with the *Gorgias*'s definition of justice as psychic medicine, Plato hints that returning to virtue through the process of *self-reconciliation* is what will enable an

---

[6] See Benitez, "Plato's Conception of Peace," 11ff.

[7] Griswold, "Plato and Forgiveness," 271-5.

injustice-doer to *merit* something like forgiveness or mercy in the context of a process I call "*reconciliation with others*," namely, those who have been harmed by one's injustice. *Self-reconciliation* functions as the most basic aspect of the process of reconciliation because it appears that, for Plato, it serves as the starting point for the possibility of *reconciliation with others.*

One important factor in Griswold's critique of Plato with respect to the topic of forgiveness is his primarily Christian vision of forgiveness. The position that injustice-doers do not need to submit themselves to justice in order to deserve forgiveness diverges from the picture underlying Plato's moral and political philosophy. When Plato theorizes a return to virtue by submitting oneself to justice, he is calling for injustice-doers to reconcile first and foremost with themselves. Only a healed soul can achieve *self-reconciliation.* Secondly, Plato's concept that a lost soul may return to virtue through accountability helps us understand why someone who is not taking the Christian position developed a few centuries later may see fit to forgive an injustice-doer. Unlike in the Christian context, Plato consistently hints that the conditions for the possibility of something like forgiveness being proffered by one's victim(s) include giving oneself over to being justly held accountability.

In order to better understand what must occur in the wake of injustice, let us turn first to the *Gorgias*'s medicine-justice analogy. In the *Gorgias,* Plato has Socrates offer us a vision of earning our way back to the path of virtue by submitting to justice in order to heal one's diseased soul (464b-c). For now, keep in mind the *Republic*'s emphasis on justice as harmony—both within the soul and the community—as we explore Plato's notion of justice and healing in the *Gorgias.* After laying out the *Gorgias*'s position on justice and healing, I will draw connections with *Laws* 627d-628a and 862b-c, which cast some light on Plato's thinking about the process of *reconciliation with others.*

Justice and Healing in Plato's *Gorgias*

In the dialogue in which Plato has Socrates confront Gorgias of Leontinoi, the care of the soul is presented through a carefully-formulated set of analogies. Plato is well aware that his Socrates faces a serious challenge to persuade his interlocutors that taking good care of the soul matters and that one takes good care of the soul not by doing whatever one wants or by ruling over others. Plato is pioneering a theory of the soul and its proper care, and he has Socrates demonstrate how unfamiliar that new way of thinking about life is. The mission is not just to understand the distinction between oratory and philosophy but to see how essential philosophical activity is to taking good care of the soul.

In the *Gorgias,* Plato puts his Socrates up against the renowned rhetor from Sicily and empowers him with a very powerful rhetorical tool—namely, analogical reasoning—in order to give the mission a fighting chance. Plato uses analogical reasoning here because he relies upon the interlocutors and the audience of readers having great familiarity with the crafts that care for the body. He has Socrates utilize our familiarity with these in order to illuminate a new way of thinking about self-interest. Particularly, Socrates accentuates the importance of psychic health by piggybacking onto our sense of the importance of physical health. Psychic health is virtue, and we should aspire to that condition; and if one finds oneself veering off the path of wellness, then one needs the corrective treatment that Socrates calls "justice" at 464c.

In his conversation with Gorgias, Socrates attempts to illuminate the care of the soul, which here he describes as "politics." (*Grg*. 464b). Let us examine this analogical scheme built upon the parallel of body and soul. Plato writes:

> Come then, and I'll show you more clearly what I'm saying, if I can. I'm saying that of this pair of subjects there are two crafts. The one for the soul I call politics; the one for the body, though it is one, I can't give you a name for offhand, but while the care of the body is a single craft, I'm saying it has two parts: gymnastics and medicine. And in politics, the counterpart of gymnastics is legislation, and the part that corresponds to medicine is justice. Each member of these pairs has features in common with the other, medicine with gymnastics and justice with legislation, because they're concerned with the same thing. These, then, are the four parts, and they always provide care, in the one case for the

> body, in the other for the soul, with a view to what's best. (*Grg.* 464b-c)[8]

Plato uses this set of analogies with the care of the body to reveal his thinking about the care of the soul. In order to elucidate what this type of "politics" is, Plato has Socrates argue that just as gymnastics is the preventative care of the body, so is legislation the preventative care of the soul; and just as medicine is the corrective treatment for illness in the body, so is justice the corrective care of the soul (*Grg.* 464b-c). In this analogy, Socrates portrays "justice" as the medicine of the soul (*Grg.* 464c). What is justice? How could justice correct psychic illness? What can nourish and restore a soul that is ill?

Immediately following *Gorgias* 464b-c, Plato has Socrates assert that pastry baking is the knack that imitates medicine. His comments on pastry baking illuminate how Plato is using medicine here to illuminate justice. In setting the two *technai* that care for the body against their counterparts, which have a knack for imitating them, Plato sets medicine up as the genuine craft of correcting illness. When we consider pastry baking we may focus on our awareness of how the consumption of pleasurable but unhealthy pastries *causes* illness. Certainly, our familiarity with this information (what cognitive scientists call the "source analog") is part of why this analogy works well rhetorically to help us understand what Socrates is trying to say in the unfamiliar half of the analogy (what cognitive scientists call the "target analog").

However, we must observe that, in addition to our understanding of pastries as a source of illness, Plato also means here to invoke pastries as a false competitor to actual medicine, which promises to make one feel better but leaves one's illness unabated, and worsens the illness yet. We should treat pastries as both a source of illness as well as a palliative placebo that makes one's condition worse while alleging to make it better. In contrast, medicine is the genuine corrective, even if it does not taste good like eating pastry does. Medicine is authentic in its care for the body, even though it may not be palliative in the sense of feeling like relief.

---

[8] Plato, *Gorgias*, trans. Donald J. Zeyl, in *Complete Works*, edited by John M. Cooper, 791-869 (Indianapolis: Hackett Publishing, 1997).

Earlier on in the *Gorgias* Plato has Gorgias verbalize that a doctor could have to compete with and lose out to someone who lacks actual medical knowledge. He uses the example of an orator like himself who could triumph over the doctor because an audience of non-medical experts may not discern the difference in their status as experts (*Grg*. 456b-d). Here at 464d, Plato has Socrates imagine a similar competition but he replaces the orator with a pastry chef. Plato writes,

> Pastry baking has put on the mask of medicine, and pretends to know the foods that are best for the body, so that if a pastry baker and a doctor had to compete in front of children, or in front of men just as foolish as children, to determine which of the two, the doctor or the pastry baker, had expert knowledge of good food and bad, the doctor would die of starvation. (*Grg*. 464d)

By analogy, there is psychic pastry and psychic medicine. Some possible psychic equivalents to eating pastry rather than taking medicine include bad faith pretending ("This never happened—I have nothing to be ashamed of.") and blaming others ("Look what you made me do!"), which was a particularly common trope in the time of Gorgias and Plato, as Rossetti shows in his chapter. So, the doer of injustice seeking a return to virtue must not even nibble from the psychic pastry buffet. It is not the "good food" for the soul (*Grg*. 464d).

The contrast between the knack of pastry baking and the craft of medicine reminds us that patients with ill souls may prefer not to choke down their justice medicine. Why is atonement so hard for some children and adults alike to swallow? Given how universal Socrates think self-interest is, it may be difficult to apologize or make restitution if doers of injustice mistake atonement for something done only for victims rather than primarily for their own self-interest. In a different context—namely, when Socrates and Polus are thinking about distinctions such as "doing what one sees fit" and "doing what one wants"—Socrates makes clear that what will heal one's soul has instrumental value for the individual with a soul in need of healing. At *Gorgias* 467c, Plato has Socrates ask, "Do you think that people who take medicines prescribed by their doctors, for instance, want what they're doing, the act of taking the medicine, with all its discomfort, or do they want to be healthy, the thing for the sake of which they're taking it?" Plato has Socrates suggest an instrumental value to submitting to medicine, while asserting the inherent value of health. By analogy, the act of submitting oneself to justice is done first and foremost for oneself, for one's ailing soul, to function as a corrective for the original ill that had one in the position to commit injustice. In this way Plato portrays Socrates attempting to reshape the conversation about self-interest in terms of psychic health.

One of the key insights in the *Gorgias* is that those who commit injustice must be held accountable in order to restore health to their souls. At *Gorgias* 472e, Socrates introduces his position on the value of paying and receiving "what is due at the hands of both gods and men." Socrates then declares, "For I do believe that you and I and everybody else consider doing what's unjust worse than suffering it, and not paying what is due worse than paying it" (*Grg.* 474b). Socrates accentuates for Polus the indispensability of psychic health, and returning a corrupted soul to that state of virtue through paying what is due. Socrates mirrors the dichotomy between preventative care and corrective care in the politics analogy, and he gives us the idea that we should avoid committing injustice in order to care in a preventative way for the soul (*Grg.* 478c-d). That is then followed by the notion that paying what is due after injustice is how one cares for the soul correctively (*Grg.* 478e-479e). Socrates's final refutation of Polis demonstrates how essential accountability is to justice in Plato's ethical and political thinking. We must know how to take responsibility for our unjust actions if we are to return to psychic health, which is virtue.

The third passage of substance related to accountability in the *Gorgias* confirms in Socrates's discussion with Callicles that injustice-doers ought to submit themselves to accountability. In a robust passage Plato has Socrates say:

> Each of us must flee away from lack of discipline as quickly as his feet will carry him, and must above all make sure that he has no need of being disciplined, but *if he does have that*

> *need, either he himself or anyone in his house, either a private citizen or a whole city, he must pay his due and must be disciplined, if he's to be happy*. This is the target which I think one should look to in living, and in his actions he should direct all of his affairs and those of his city to the end that justice and self-control will be present in one who is to be blessed. He should not allow his appetites to be undisciplined or undertake to fill them up—that's interminably bad—and live the life of a marauder. Such a man could not be dear to another man or to a god, *for he cannot be a partner, and where there's no partnership there's no friendship*. Yes, Callicles, wise men claim that partnership and friendship, orderliness, self-control, and justice hold together heaven and earth, and gods and men, and that is why they call this universe a *world-order*, my friend, and not an undisciplined world-disorder [...] You've failed to notice that proportionate equality has great power among both gods and men, and you suppose that you ought to practice getting the greater share. That's because you neglect geometry. (*Grg*. 507d-508a; emphases added)

This fascinating speech by Socrates bears out the relational nature of justice. He once again highlights that what we do in the wake of committing injustice will have consequences for our relationships. Shame and accountability reveal a person's character, even when mistakes have revealed gaps in their psychic development.

The most important thing we can learn from the *Gorgias* about Plato's conception of the relationship between accountability and justice is that to return to a state of psychic health—that is, virtue—one must engage in the corrective treatment that Socrates calls justice at 464b-c. By defining justice in the *Gorgias* in terms of corrective healing, Plato's Socrates helps us imagine the role of accountability in the health of the soul. Injustice-doers who have "taken their medicine" are people who have held themselves accountable and have taken responsibility for their injustices. The justice-as-medicine notion implies that injustice-doers should strive after *self-reconciliation* and *reconciliation with others*, both of which are needed in the wake of injustice.

Here we can observe an important difference between the notion Plato is working out in the *Gorgias*—albeit without any explicit mention of the notion of forgiveness—and the Christian notion of forgiveness that develops a few hundred years after Plato's *Gorgias*. The understanding of forgiveness for which Jesus Christ advocates is predicated on the wrong-doer not needing to *earn* any mercy or forgiveness through submitting oneself to justice. If we put an act of Christian-style forgiveness up against the Platonic philosophical backdrop, even after a Christian extends mercy by "turning the other cheek" Plato's Socrates would still be concerned for the injustice-doer's soul festering in illness without the injustice-doer asking to be held accountable. This observation may tell us why Plato focuses more on the question of justice and healing than on the topic of forgiveness or mercy. Plato's philosophy warns against leaving the soul of an injustice-doer deteriorating in ill health.

In asserting this schema for self-care, Plato revises common sense notions of success as mere winning (for example, evading a charge when guilty). The sense of self-interest that emerges from Plato's *Gorgias* is not enjoying the power to do whatever one may see fit like Polus initially has in mind (*Grg*. 466b), the delights of a childish notion of freedom. Rather, self-interest requires a thoughtfulness to understand that in different circumstances one's judgement may call for feelings one typically avoids. For instance, Socrates says at the height of his refutation of Polus that

> we don't simply want to slaughter people, or exile them from their cities and confiscate their property as such; we want to do these things if they are beneficial, but if they're harmful we don't. For we want the things that are good, as you agree, and don't want those that are neither good nor bad, nor those that are bad. Right? (*Grg*. 468c)

Indeed, the self-interest for which Socrates advocates is predicated upon understanding what is good and seeking after it. As Saxonhouse writes of the *Gorgias*,

> The conception of power which Socrates proposes in this dialogue is not the power to fill another and satisfy her desires, not to make another serve one's own interests. It is

> a conception of power which can only be understood in terms of making one better, and making one better consists in making one aware of what one lacks—not the dockyards or imports or other such filth—but virtue.[9]

With Socratic self-interest, an injustice-doer seeks after goodness by going against the instinctual tendencies of most people to gloss over their injustice. Instead, injustice-doers embarking upon (or returning to) true self-interest should maturely submit themselves to justice, according to the Socrates of the *Gorgias* who aims to persuade us that genuine self-interest requires a willingness to admit wrongdoing whenever it occurs.

People work toward peace within the soul when they restore their unjust souls through corrective treatment. I concur with Nussbaum's depiction of the soul taking its medicine. Concerning the Hellenistic inheritors of this thinking about philosophy as medicine for the soul, she writes:

> Philosophy heals human diseases, diseases produced by false beliefs. Its arguments are to the soul as the doctor's remedies are to the body. They can heal, and they are to be evaluated in terms of their power to heal. As the medical art makes progress on behalf of the suffering body, so philosophy for the soul in distress [...] All accept the appropriateness of an analogy between philosophy and the art of medicine. And for all, the medical analogy is not simply a decorative metaphor: it is an important tool both of discovery and of justification [...].[10]

Socrates suggests that justice is the medicine needed by a soul that desires to overcome its vices. He emphasizes justice's power to heal. The act of submitting to accountability mitigates against future wrong doing by healing the illness in the soul.

Socrates's way of thinking about the care of the soul invites us to revise our notion of success to one that is more improvisational:

---

[9] Saxonhouse, "An Unspoken Theme," 165.

[10] Martha C. Nussbaum, *The Therapy of Desire: Theory and Practice in Hellenistic Ethics* (Princeton: Princeton University Press, 1993), 14.

instead of seeing the path to justice as only the road of perfect virtue, of never doing anything unjust, Socrates also considers the avenue of healing one's soul, of *self-reconciliation*. One who can submit oneself to justice can ultimately be successful in caring for the soul. So, yes, it is true that the *Gorgias* does not explore forgiveness or mercy. However, the self-care analogies demonstrate that there is a path that returns a wrong-doer to virtue. In surrendering oneself to justice, the wrong-doer begins the process of *self-reconciliation* within the soul, and that could be significant for the possibility for *reconciliation with others*.

Lessons on Reconciliation from the *Laws*

I want to suggest that we read Plato's position in the *Gorgias* concerning what ought to occur in the wake of injustice in connection with two passages in the *Laws*: 627d-628a and 862b-c, given their relevance to the matters of reconciliation. These passages in the *Laws* convey something about the conditions for *reconciliation with others*, and consulting them further illuminates the relationship between corrective justice and the overall reconciliation process.

In the first of these passages, the Athenian raises the issue of reconciliation. At 627d-628a the Athenian invites Clinias to think of a judge who must deal with a family of brothers in conflict caused by injustice. The *Laws* tells us that there is large cohort of brothers who have been unjust with a smaller number of other brothers who have been just. The Athenian conjures three possibilities: first, a judge who would kill the unjust brothers and have the just brothers run their own lives; second, a judge who would put the virtuous brothers in charge and allow the unjust brothers to live obediently under the rule of the just brothers, and third, a judge "who will take this single quarrelling family in hand and *reconcile* its members, without killing any of them; by laying down regulations to guide them in the future, he will be able to ensure that they remain on friendly terms with each other" (*Laws* 627e-628a).[11] The Athenian and Clinias agree the third is "incomparably better" (*Laws* 628a). And the Athenian calls this superior approach "the exact opposite of war" (*Laws* 628a). The Athenian then extends the topic beyond the unharmonious family to

---

[11] Plato, *Laws*, trans. Trevor J. Saunders, in *Complete Works*, 1318-1616.

the state level, imagining a parallel to the third 'family-court' judge who does not destroy the other in order that "peace would follow the civil war."

Instead, he imagines bringing peace through reconciliation, saying "alternatively, peace and friendship might be the result of reconciliation [φιλίας τε καὶ εἰρήνης ὑπὸ διαλλαγῶν γενομένης]" (*Laws* 628b). Interestingly, the Athenian immediately follows his preference for peace through reconciliation with an analogy to a doctor purging illness. Benitez notes that this fraternal strife passage "is designed to replace a desire for victory with a sympathetic will to reconciliation, depicted as true justice."[12] Benitez is correct, and paying attention to what positive conditions can follow from reconciliation, such as friendship and peace, gives us good incentive to pursue reconciliation in the wake of injustice.

The Athenian returns to the idea of reconciliation in the second of these passages from the *Laws*. There Plato has the Athenian call for reconciliation in order to make friends out of enemies in the wake of injustice. He writes:

> You see, my friends, in effect we should not simply call it 'just' when one man bestows some object on another, nor simply 'unjust' when correspondingly he takes it from him. The description 'just' is applicable only to the benefit conferred or injury inflicted by someone with a just character and outlook. This is the point the lawgiver has to watch; *he must keep his eyes on these two things, injustice and injury*. He must use the law to exact damages for damage done, as far as he can; he must restore losses, and if anyone has knocked something down, put it back upright again; in place of anything killed or wounded, he must substitute something in sound condition. *And when atonement has been made by compensation, he must try by his laws to make the criminal and the victim, in each separate case of injury, friends instead of enemies.* (*Laws* 862b-c; emphases mine)

[12] Benitez, "Plato's Conception of Peace," 18-19.

This passage conveys the urgent need for atonement in addition to giving us a sense of the relationship between reconciliation and the pursuit of justice and peace. This moment gives a window into the mature Plato's vision of what attempts at *reconciliation with others* will involve. To be clear: asking to be held accountable is not identical to asking for forgiveness or mercy, but the elder Plato reminds of the importance of *reconciliation with others* in the *Laws*, and there the Athenian understands submitting oneself to justice as a prerequisite for the process of attempting *reconciliation with others*. For Plato, *reconciliation with others* is not likely to occur if one has not undertaken *self-reconciliation*.

The account at *Laws* 862b-c focuses on the legislators' role in a reconciliation process involving a victim(s) of injustice and a perpetrator(s) of injustice, but we can see in these details a process that involves several aspects of reconciliation. A main emphasis here is the restoration of losses insofar as that is possible. Therefore, expressing a desire to improve the situation is one essential element in any reconciliation process. However, one cannot make something right again without taking responsibility in the first place for whatever injustice has occurred. Here I have described that first step in the reconciliation process as *self-reconciliation*. Having owned up to an injustice as the first step opens the door to engaging in honest conversation about the past and the injustice in question as a second step. After willingly participating in such honest conversation about the injustice, one has the best chance at understanding how to effectively make things better for the victim(s) of the injustice. So, we can think of expressing the desire to restore losses and set things back aright between the parties as another step in the process of *reconciliation with others*.

It seems to me implicit in these passages from the *Laws* that it takes more than mere restitution to make victims and perpetrators friends again. Yet, Plato does not make explicit that it is prudent for one looking to reconcile with one's victims to apologize, but he goes as far as to discuss the injustice-doer and those harmed being *friends* again rather than merely being reconciled. Plato's Socrates in the *Gorgias* and the Athenian in the *Laws* appear to intuit that the final crucial element with which the reconciliation process culminates is the injustice-doer apologizing. The injustice-doer who has completed the process of *self-reconciliation* is prepared to turn over a new leaf and behave more justly in the future. It seems a natural outcome of the *self-reconciliation* process to feel regret and a desire to express contrition. Perhaps alongside apologizing will be a request for mercy or forgiveness.

What could shift what Griswold calls the "moral relation between wrong-doer and wronged"? The wronged possesses a perception of being wronged by the wrong-doer both before and after the shift in the moral relation between them; what changes is the need for anger. Anger that can be foresworn is what changes the moral relation between wrong-doer and wronged. What has the power to soothe the anger of the wronged without instructing complicity or excuse? If we link these passages in the *Laws* to the *Gorgias* and its definition of justice as corrective treatment, we will have a better sense of what could possibly assuage victims harmed by injustice. The *Gorgias*'s notion of the soul taking its medicine in order to become healthier gives us insight into the process of *reconciliation with others* alluded to in the *Laws*, illuminating what could enable the wronged to feel differently about the wrong-doer.

The value of such actions as expressing remorse or extending forgiveness is that they give the victim and perpetrator the chance to let go of the past injustice and focus on better future possibilities. In the words of Griswold, "Indeed, part of what makes forgiveness so interesting is that it represents a change in the moral relation between wrong-doer and wronged that accepts the fact that wrong was indeed done, and done (in some sense) voluntarily."[13] The emphasis on reconciliation in these passages in the *Laws* should have us wondering why Plato would not seize the opportunity to have his interlocutors philosophically discuss forgiveness in a more extended fashion or explicitly hold repentance or forgiveness up as virtuous here or elsewhere in his dialogues.

Conclusion

Plato's Socrates uses the medical analogy in the *Gorgias* as a rhetorical mechanism in an attempt to persuade his interlocutors that

---

[13] Griswold, "Plato and Forgiveness," 275.

holding oneself accountable is healing and restorative, and lacking the capacity to take responsibility for one's actions leaves wounds to fester, which deteriorates and drains the soul further. In this essay, I have explored Plato's vision of the relationships among virtue, justice, and peace. In focusing particularly on how the *Gorgias*'s medical analogy helps us understand that set of relationships better, I have thought through how a sick soul "taking its medicine" initiates a process of healing and *self-reconciliation*. Asking to be held accountable facilitates both the potential *self-reconciliation* and *reconciliation with others,* whereas not submitting to justice appears to block the potential for *self-reconciliation* and *reconciliation with others*.

Marshaling evidence from *Gorgias* 464c, 474b, and 507d-508a, I have argued that, while forgiveness is not an *explicit* element in Plato's philosophy, injustice-doers who have held themselves accountable are healing souls, and those souls are the ones for whom mercy or forgiveness would not be amiss. In the *Gorgias*'s carefully formulated set of body-soul analogies, Plato initiates not a Greek concept of forgiveness but a sketch of what could make a doer of injustice earn the mercy or forgiveness that may be offered, or to use the language of the *Laws* 862c, to deserve *friendship* from those who have suffered from one's injustice. As noted already, Plato sees this restoration of friendship through the process of *reconciliation with others* as desirable by the time he is writing the *Laws*. We certainly can wish Plato had been more thorough and explicit in his writing about reconciliation, but it is not hard to see that, while admiration of forgiveness is not found in Plato's *Gorgias,* his sense of justice as psychic medicine is relevant to the process of fostering possible reconciliation with those harmed by one's injustice.

Plato's justice-*qua*-medicine project aligns with Benitez's sense of what we should expect to find in the Platonic corpus. Benitez contends that Plato's main focus in his comprehensive peace-seeking philosophical project is to identify and champion the "dispositions of peace," that is, the "states of character [...] that orient people towards peace,"[14] such as justice, moderation, simplicity, gentleness,

[14] Benitez, "Plato's Conception of Peace," 19.

and friendliness.[15] I agree with this as well, and it strikes me that being merciful or forgiving in certain circumstances could be understood as a "disposition of peace." So, we remain curious about what kept Plato from explicit, extended attention to peace. Yet, having explored the themes he does explicitly attend to, such as virtue, justice, and friendship after conflict, we can understand acts of submitting oneself to justice (*self-reconciliation*) and participating in the process of *reconciliation with others* as "dispositions of peace."

Although his thinking about morality and political life receives tremendous attention, we need greater insight into Plato's vision of the relationships among virtue, justice, and peace. Plato emphatically asserts that if we want to know harmony (including both inner peace *and* world peace), we must be just. And if we want to know justice, we must know virtue. Especially in the *Gorgias* and *Republic*, Plato has Socrates demonstrate that virtue is psychic health. And here the *Gorgias*'s body-soul care analogies demonstrate that psychic health requires seeking after healing and reconciliation in the wake of doing something unjust. Conversely, without accountability there can be no virtue or justice, and without justice there can be no peace. So, peace-seekers trying to understand the role of reconciliation in inner peace and world peace have a richer resource in Plato's *Gorgias* than may be widely realized.

---

[15] Benitez, "Plato's Conception of Peace," 20.

Made in the USA
Columbia, SC
06 January 2023

6b92afe7-a1eb-4706-b2d4-6c31002d466aR01